HUMAN SERVICES IN
CONTEMPORARY AMERICA

HUMAN SERVICES IN CONTEMPORARY AMERICA

EIGHTH EDITION

William R. Burger
Kingsborough Community College of the City University of New York

BROOKS/COLE
CENGAGE Learning

Australia • Brazil • Japan • Korea • Mexico • Singapore • Spain • United Kingdom • United States

BROOKS/COLE
CENGAGE Learning™

Human Services in Contemporary America, Eighth Edition
William R. Burger

Aquisitions Editor: Seth Dobrin

Assistant Editor: Nicolas Albert

Editorial Assistant: Rachel McDonald

Media Editor: Dennis Fitzgerald

Senior Marketing Manager: Trent Whatcott

Marketing Assistant: Darlene Macanan

Marketing Communications Manager: Tami Strang

Content Project Management: Pre-PressPMG

Creative Director: Rob Hugel

Art Director: Caryl Gorska

Print Buyer: Paula Vang

Rights Acquisitions Account Manager, Text: Roberta Broyer

Rights Acquisitions Account Manager, Image: Leitha Etheridge-Sims

Production Service: Pre-PressPMG

Photo Researcher: Pre-PressPMG

Cover Images:
Upper Left: Yellow Dog Productions/Getty Images
Upper Right: Brand X Pictures/Getty Images
Lower Left: Johannes Kroemer/Getty Images
Lower Right: Dave Nagel/Getty Images

Compositor: Pre-PressPMG

For product information and technology assistance, contact us at **Cengage Learning Customer Sales & Support, 1-800-354-9706.**

For permission to use material from this text or product, submit all requests online at **www.cengage.com/permissions.** Further permissions questions can be e-mailed to **permissionrequest@cengage.com.**

Library of Congress Control Number: 2009942950

ISBN-13: 978-0-8400-3207-2

ISBN-10: 0-8400-3207-2

Brooks/Cole
20 Davis Drive
Belmont, CA 94002-3098
USA

Cengage Learning is a leading provider of customized learning solutions with office locations around the globe, including Singapore, the United Kingdom, Australia, Mexico, Brazil, and Japan. Locate your local office at **www.cengage.com/global.**

Cengage Learning products are represented in Canada by Nelson Education, Ltd.

To learn more about Brooks/Cole, visit **www.cengage.com/brookscole.**

Purchase any of our products at your local college store or at our preferred online store **www.CengageBrain.com.**

Printed in the United States of America
3 4 5 6 7 14 13 12 11

About the Author

William R. Burger received his doctorate in social psychology, but his academic background also encompasses the fields of educational psychology and philosophy of education. While attending graduate school at Harvard University, he was awarded a research assistantship for his work in the area of community decision making.

Bill is the former director of the Mental Health and Human Services Program and is currently chairperson of the Department of Behavioral Sciences and Human Services at Kingsborough Community College of the City University of New York. He has served as a consultant to a variety of human services programs in New York and Massachusetts, has lectured at various colleges and universities, and has written a number of guest editorials for various newspapers.

Bill resides in New York and Massachusetts with his wife, two cats, and a dog.

CONTENTS

CHAPTER 5

The Human Services Worker   188

PREFACE

This text was written in the hope of enhancing the student's ability to help others with problems in their lives. The ability to help others in a professional context requires a base of knowledge along with a range of helping skills that can, to a large extent, be taught and learned. This text is intended to help the beginning student take the first steps toward acquiring the needed knowledge and skills.

The content provides a general introduction to the field of human services and is designed for introductory college courses in human services, mental health technology, social work, community mental health, and other human services programs. It is expected that most students who read this text are headed toward careers that involve direct contact with people. However, the book would also be useful to those considering administrative work in the human services.

Students in the human services typically begin their training with hopes of helping other people lead more fulfilling lives. Unfortunately, these hopes are sometimes dampened by the realities of the outside world. Although humanistic values do play an important role in present-day America, they must compete with other motives such as profit, power, and self-aggrandizement. In order to be effective, the human services worker must be able to face the harsh realities of our complex, imperfect society even while keeping the ideal society in mind and working toward it in a realistic way.

In the pages that follow, I have sought a balance between idealism and realism. I certainly do not intend to discourage idealism in students. However, experience has shown me that discouragement often attacks those who expect too much of clients, helping agencies, and themselves. This disillusionment can be avoided if the student knows what to expect.

This text offers a great deal of valuable information about human services, a field that has greatly increased in scope and complexity over recent decades. The material is presented in a provocative manner, raising issues not usually addressed in introductory texts. The impact of political, economic, and social pressures on human services is explored.

First the goals, functions, and organization of human services are examined in the context of contemporary social problems. Next the groups of people who receive help from human services are described. A historical survey of human services follows, providing a background against which current efforts can be viewed. The major theories that govern helping efforts are covered, along with techniques and methods. The student is also provided with practical information about career options in the human services field.

The final chapters are certainly unusual for an introductory text. I feel it is important for students to know something about how social policies are developed and about how human services workers might influence policies. These social policies, which determine who receives what kind of help, have a great impact on worker and client alike. It is undeniable that today's student is the policymaker of tomorrow.

In the chapter on prevention, I demonstrate a strong bias in favor of programs aimed at preventing problems and dysfunctions from developing in the first place. Frankly, I try to persuade students, instructors, and human services agencies that prevention programs should play a major role in the future of human services.

The text concludes with a sampling of current controversies affecting human services. This section is offered with the intent of fostering a realistic understanding of conflicts and issues that confront human services workers. In addition, I also discuss the issues of the various titles by which human services workers are identified.

The introductory course in human services is perhaps the most important a student will take. It is here that the student's attitudes and philosophy are developed. I believe that a humanistic perspective, combined with a realistic awareness of societal problems, provides the best foundation for creative and effective helping.

NEW TO THE EIGHTH EDITION

During the three years since the publication of the last edition of this text there has been historic change in this country. America became the first majority-white democracy in the world to elect an African American as its national leader. Barack Hussein Obama, the former democratic senator from Illinois, was elected the 44th President of the United States, sweeping away the last major racial barrier in American politics. It was a symbolic movement in the evolution of this nation's racial history: a breakthrough many believed was long overdue.

President Obama inherited a number of domestic and foreign policy debacles from the former two-term Republican president. President Obama is confronted with a nation well into a major recession, the likes of which have not been seen in seventy-five years. Our national unemployment rate is the highest in over a quarter of a century. The housing market has experienced a major decline, which in turn affects a significant number of businesses that rely on real estate development. A rise in home foreclosures is commonplace in many areas throughout the country. As a result of the sub-prime mortgage meltdown, major Wall Street firms declared bankruptcy and ailing bank and auto manufacturers asked for government bailouts.

The stock market has dropped to new lows, wreaking havoc to those with pensions and hopes for retirement. For most Americans working longer is no longer a choice but a necessity. Meanwhile, prices for essential items such as food, clothing, and energy continue to rise. On the foreign policy front, the United States is still heavily involved in military actions abroad, costing billions of taxpayer dollars that otherwise might be allocated to domestic priorities.

Events such as these often affect groups in need disproportionately. Consequently, the human services system must continue to adapt and change as necessary in order to be responsive to an ever changing cultural landscape. As I have stated before, to be effective on every level of our human services system, it is important for workers to understand the current social, economic, and political climate in which human services will operate. To this end, new material has been added to examine the various political and social changes emanating from the new Obama administration. There is new material on current controversies, substance abuse, and stress management. As the field of human services continues to evolve it is necessary to include new information on changes in licensure in various fields as well as examining emerging career paths.

In this edition, I have added two new additional features. The first is real life examples of the diversity of human services workers, written by the actual workers in the field. The second is a representative sample of actual jobs in the field from across the country along with salaries and job responsibilities. As before, many topics throughout the text have been expanded and/or updated to include the most current information.

This eighth edition was developed to provide the reader with a comprehensive framework of our contemporary human services system. Hopefully, having read this text you will be equipped with the essential information needed to be more effective in your chosen career path.

W.R.B.

ACKNOWLEDGMENTS

I wish to express my appreciation and gratitude to the various individuals who contributed to the preparation of this eighth edition. In particular I wish to acknowledge the scholarly contributions of Dr. Helaine Harris, Dr. Charles Guigno, and Professor Susan Ednie, all of whom are faculty within the Mental Health and Human Services Program, Kingsborough Community College of the City University of New York. I must also express my gratitude and many thanks to those individuals in the field who were kind enough to share their experiences in the "Real Life Human Services Work" sections of this edition.

I must also thank my friend and colleague Dr. Edward Martin for his invaluable technological assistance and his patience with this technologically challenged author. Special thanks goes to my wife, Mary Gifford, for her many hours entering my material onto our laptop. Also thanks to Ms. Sydell Basile for helping at the later stages of this manuscript to also enter material onto the disc.

Lastly, I would like to thank the Cengage Learning team and in particular, Ms. Rachel McDonald, editorial assistant, for her consistent attention to my various requests.

William R. Burger

HUMAN SERVICES IN CONTEMPORARY AMERICA

HUMAN SERVICES IN THE UNITED STATES TODAY

CHAPTER **I**

1

INTRODUCTION

Over the years, **human services** in the United States have evolved into a network of programs and agencies that provide an array of services to millions of Americans. The one feature shared by all of these services is that they are designed to meet human needs. Thus, this chapter begins with a consideration of the full range of human needs and the kinds of services that seek to meet them.

Some service agencies are devoted mainly to helping people meet basic survival needs such as food and shelter, whereas some are concerned with helping clients achieve more satisfying relationships or attain other kinds of personal fulfillment. **Primary social supports**, such as family and friends, also play a role in meeting human needs, and that role will be examined in this first chapter.

There is controversy about just what needs should be met by agencies supported by public or private funds. There is, in fact, a great deal of controversy about questions involving the scope and quality of human services. This chapter provides an overview of human services that addresses some of these questions.

Critics argue that human services are wasteful and inefficient, whereas supporters are convinced that more should be done to meet people's needs. Some social planners want to cut funds for services, but others demand increased funding. Because these conflicts are fought out primarily in the political arena, it is vital to grasp the liberal and conservative positions that underlie the countless debates about specific programs. Both positions are outlined here.

This chapter also includes a survey of some contemporary problems that may affect the ability of Americans to meet their own needs. For example, a victim of a natural disaster such as a hurricane or earthquake is very likely to need help from human services on an emergency basis. Social problems such as discrimination, poverty, and unemployment may also reduce a person's ability to be self-supporting. Victims of these problems may need help only temporarily or for an extended period.

So this chapter introduces some of the topics basic to a study of contemporary human services. At first glance, they may appear to be simple topics, but closer examination shows them to be very complex—so much so that the brief preliminary information given in this introductory chapter is elaborated on throughout the book.

HUMAN NEEDS: FOCUS OF HUMAN SERVICES

A number of schemes have been proposed for conceptualizing human needs. The one suggested by Maslow (1968) is useful for the present discussion. He conceived of needs as existing in a kind of pyramid, or hierarchy, as shown in Figure 1.1.

At the base of the pyramid are the basic **physiological needs** such as hunger, thirst, and the need for oxygen. These are matters of life and death. It is only when such survival needs are satisfied that the individual focuses on **safety needs**, which are met by a stable, predictable, and secure environment. Clearly, this type of environment requires decent housing in a safe neighborhood.

Once safety needs have been mostly satisfied, the need for belonging, or belongingness, and love begins to emerge, expressed by a desire for affectionate relations with others—one's family, lover, or some larger group. After the first three levels of needs—physiological, safety, and love/belonging—have been largely satisfied, **esteem needs** come to the fore, such as the need to be respected as a competent or even a superior person. Most of us desire the recognition and appreciation of others.

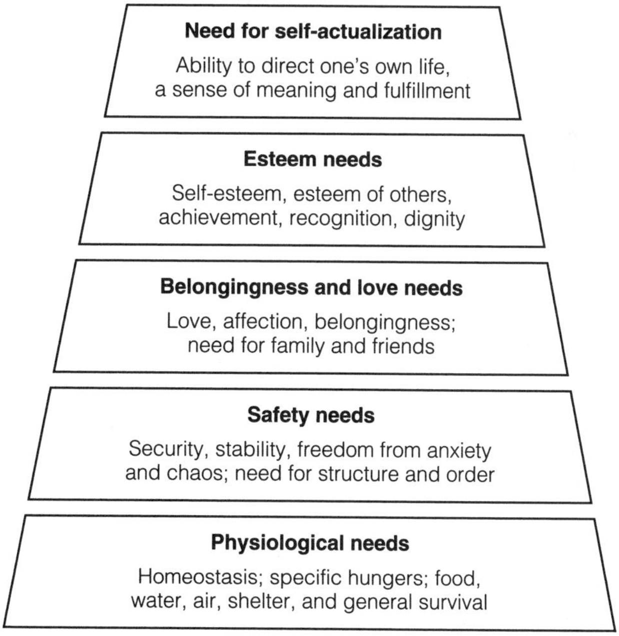

Need for self-actualization
Ability to direct one's own life,
a sense of meaning and fulfillment

Esteem needs
Self-esteem, esteem of others,
achievement, recognition, dignity

Belongingness and love needs
Love, affection, belongingness;
need for family and friends

Safety needs
Security, stability, freedom from anxiety
and chaos; need for structure and order

Physiological needs
Homeostasis; specific hungers; food,
water, air, shelter, and general survival

FIGURE 1.1 | MASLOW'S HIERARCHY OF NEEDS

The highest need, that for **self-actualization,** has to do with fulfilling one's innate tendencies and potentials. This need involves expressing one's inner nature and talents. For one person, the path to self-actualization might be artistic creativity; for another, it might be studying Eastern religions. This highest level of motivation generally becomes prominent in later life. Young adults are generally preoccupied with making a living and winning the love and approval of others. Maslow (1970) estimated that about 85% of average American adults have satisfied their physiological needs and that the percentage of adults with needs satisfied declines at each step up the hierarchy. At the top step, only 10% have attained satisfaction of self-actualization needs.

Maslow (1987) believed that needs arrange themselves in a hierarchy in terms of potency, that is, physiological needs are stronger than safety needs, which in turn are stronger than love needs, and so on. The higher the need, the less imperative its fulfillment is for sheer survival and the longer gratification can be postponed. Deprivation of higher needs does not produce the kind of desperate emergency reaction triggered by deprivation of lower needs. For example, needs for belonging are a luxury when food or safety is denied.

Maslow (1987) also pointed out that for higher needs to be satisfied, environmental conditions must be favorable. By this he meant that a person aspiring for gratification of higher needs must have a supportive family, a decent income, opportunities for a good education, and so on. People without these kinds of advantages face an uphill struggle to attain the higher levels of need satisfaction. In general, Maslow stated, counseling and psychotherapy are more appropriate and effective in helping people achieve higher needs than lower needs. At the lowest-need levels, psychotherapy is not much use at all. People who are struggling for basic survival are too worried and preoccupied to give much thought to higher needs. Social planners agree that society must offer tangible kinds of help like food and shelter and medical care to the truly disadvantaged.

Some human services devote themselves to safety needs. The criminal justice system, which includes law enforcement and corrections, is designed to meet safety needs. Citizens want to live in secure communities and go about their daily activities without fear of being threatened, robbed, or assaulted. To this end, the public spends millions for police, courts, and corrections. Chapter 2 discusses some reasons for the partial failure of the criminal justice system to create a safe environment.

One of the most consistent findings of social research is that the risk of physical or mental illness is greatest when the individual cannot find a place in the social order. Persons who have been deprived of meaningful social contact for any of a number of reasons are at relatively greater risk of developing tuberculosis, alcoholism, accident proneness, severe mental illness, and suicidal tendencies (Cassel, 1990). Accordingly, some human services are designed to help people feel that they belong and are valued members of a group. It is expected that such membership may help keep a person out of an institution and,

© Psychology Archives, University of Akron/Abraham Maslow Papers

Abraham Maslow

therefore, serve an important preventive purpose. For example, some agencies set up senior clubs for elderly people who would otherwise be living a lonely, isolated life. Another example is the establishment of psychiatric residences for former mental patients who have no family.

Some human services agencies are primarily concerned with meeting the higher needs for esteem and self-actualization. Others help meet these higher needs indirectly by fulfilling basic needs, thus allowing individuals to pursue higher needs on their own initiative. Education, particularly at the higher levels, is attuned to helping students attain fulfillment and satisfaction through pursuit of a career.

In general, human services workers encourage people to function at their highest possible level. More tangible kinds of help are provided in the form of scholarships and grants offered by a number of governmental and private agencies.

CRITICISMS OF MASLOW'S THEORY

The idea that our lower needs must be satisfied before moving to the next higher ones is contradicted by several kinds of evidence. In some societies, for example, people periodically go hungry but, at the same time, exhibit strong social ties and a strong sense of self. In fact, a certain degree of hardship in meeting basic needs can bring people together and give them a sense of purpose in working together to overcome adversity (Neher, 1991). Similarly, many couples in our own society report that a strong bond was formed during a period of early struggles that was weakened by later affluence. Contrary to Maslow's theory, these examples suggest that deprivation of basic physiological needs may sometimes facilitate satisfaction of higher needs, such as the need for intimacy. Aside from anecdotal evidence, there are a number of research studies that have attempted to test Maslow's concepts. The results, according to Neher's (1991) review, have been mixed: some support and others refute various hypotheses.

In general, the research conducted in work settings has not supported Maslow's theory. For example, Wahba and Bridwell (1976) asked workers to list their needs in order of importance and found that the rankings did not fit Maslow's hierarchy. Other investigators have suggested that more than one need may be operating at a time (Geen, Beatty, & Arkin, 1984). In other words, a person may be striving to fulfill simultaneously both basic and growth needs. Still other studies have suggested that moderate levels of deprivation stimulate creative potential, ward off boredom, and enhance a sense of competence (Neher, 1991). This idea runs counter to Maslow's notion that higher needs emerge only after fairly complete satisfaction of lower needs. It may be that some need deprivation is experienced as a challenge and, ultimately, is growth enhancing.

ROLE OF PRIMARY SOCIAL SUPPORTS IN MEETING NEEDS

Most people seek gratification of needs through a network of social relationships. For example, family, friends, and peer groups can meet needs for nurturance and intimacy. Religious and social groups help meet needs for belonging, esteem, and spiritual enrichment. A job satisfies crucial economic needs and also provides a setting for social interaction with coworkers. Additional support may come from informal social contacts, like bartenders and hairdressers, well known for listening sympathetically to the problems of their customers. This network of relationships, which makes up the primary **social support** system, is the traditional source of need satisfaction in our culture. One important feature of this support system is that usually some sense of mutual obligation underlies the transactions. In other words, a person is expected to give something, to meet certain needs of others, in exchange for what is received. Sometimes it is enough to simply let others know that one is ready to help if the need arises.

Too many people in this country are still sadly lacking in primary social supports. They may have no friends, no family, no job, and therefore no way to meet important needs. In some cases, a person may have family and friends who would be willing to help but who lack the means to do so. As detailed in Chapter 3, certain human services came into being to meet the needs of people who have nowhere to turn for help. Over the years, human services have expanded greatly and now go far beyond helping the poor, sick, and disabled. Gradually, they have taken over some of the functions of primary social supports. For example, the task of caring for poor elderly persons, once assumed by the family, is increasingly being accepted by government human services agencies.

SELF-HELP GROUPS

Self-help groups are basically mutual-help groups made up of people who have similar problems. They occupy a position somewhere between traditional social supports and formal agencies that provide services. The increasing popularity of these groups may be due partly to the decline of the extended family and other traditional sources of support in our society (Bloch, Croch, & Reibstein, 1982). Whatever the cause, these groups have grown from 300 in 1963 to 500,000 in 1992, with more than 15 million current members.

Riesman (2000) points out that "more Americans try to change their health behaviors through self-help groups than through all other forms of professional programs combined" (p. 47). What distinguishes these groups from formal service organizations is that they operate without professional leadership. Many professional therapists view self-help groups as useful adjuncts to treatment and urge clients to participate in them (Comer, 1996).

A wide variety of problems or disorders may be the focus of a self-help group. Alcoholism, drug abuse, compulsive gambling, bereavement, overeating, phobias, rape victimization, unemployment, and physical illnesses (for example, heart disease, diabetes, and cancer) are some examples of issues that may be addressed in support groups. Two advantages of self-help groups are that they are less expensive and, because they offer support from other people who share the same problem, less intimidating than professionally led groups. A number of self-help groups are mentioned or described in various sections of this book.

EFFECTS OF SOCIAL PROGRAMS ON PRIMARY SUPPORTS

During the 1960s, there was a vigorous expansion of social programs designed to eliminate poverty, remove slums, and improve the health and education of poor people. By the end of the decade, some social planners had come to realize that

(a) the programs were not always having the desired effect and (b) new problems were being created. For example, it appeared that welfare programs were having the unintended effect of breaking up families and sometimes leading to family nonformation. The programs were administered in such a way that a mother with limited income received not only cash but also a package of other benefits including medical insurance, food stamps, and rent subsidies. If a father was present, he was usually a low-paid worker at risk of being laid off. He could jeopardize the entire benefits package if he attempted to support the family alone. If he left, little effort was made by the welfare program to require him to support the family in any way. In fact, the family was more economically secure without him.

Clearly, the system provided little incentive for the family unit to stay together. The lesson to be drawn from this part of our national experience is that programs designed to help, however well intended, may have perverse or unexpected consequences. When these programs weaken the family and the neighborhood, there is good reason to be concerned. The strength of the primary supports of family and neighborhood is essential if individuals are to cope with a complex society. They are the basic linkages of one person to another. When the family is fragmented, what often follows is poor education, poor skills, and poor performance. This in turn causes the perpetuation of poverty, and the vicious cycle continues.

OVERVIEW OF HUMAN SERVICES

"What are human services, anyway?" is one of the questions students most frequently ask. It would be helpful to provide an "official" or generally accepted definition, but there is no such thing. Actually, ideas about human services have changed over the course of time. As discussed in Chapter 3, early approaches to human services were centered on the hazards of illness, disability, and economic dependence. Programs were designed to help people who were unable to take care of their own needs. It was recognized that people with little or no income in increasingly complex industrial societies were at risk of starvation or serious distress. This view, which equates human services with providing services only to the economically dependent, now seems rather narrow.

Another approach is to define human services in terms of the activities of modern society that enhance the well-being of its citizens. Hasenfeld (1983), for example, suggests that human services are designed to "protect or enhance the personal well-being of individuals" (p. 1). This is a broad definition that might include a wide spectrum of services, ranging from job creation to maintaining a clean, safe, and pleasant environment, all aimed at helping people achieve the highest possible level of self-sufficiency. Another more succinct definition of human services is offered by Alle-Corliss and Alle-Corliss (1998), who view human services as "encompassing professional services provided to those in need." Still another perspective is offered by Kanel (2008), who observes that "human services uses a multidisciplinary, holistic, and eclectic approach to helping people with various needs."

Experts do not agree on the range or type of helping activities that should be included in human services. A definition that falls between the very narrow and the very broad ones just discussed is preferable. Human services are organized activities that help people in the areas of health care; mental health, including care for persons with retardation; disability and physical handicap; social welfare; child care; criminal justice; housing; recreation; and education. Another type of service that might be included is income maintenance, a term that refers to programs like unemployment insurance and social security, which provide income to people who are unemployed or retired.

It should be noted that human services do not include the help given by family, friends, or other primary supports. To be considered human services, the help must be provided by some type of formal organization, be it a clinic, hospital, nursing home, agency, bureau, or other service institutions.

Obviously, human services have covered a lot of ground, having increased greatly in size and scope during recent decades in the United States. Currently included in **social welfare** are expenses for social security, welfare, veterans' programs, education, housing, and other public programs.

The federal government is the major provider of social welfare benefits. In fact, most of the huge federal **budget**, approximately 90%, goes for social programs of one kind or another. The Personal Responsibility and Work Opportunity Reconciliation Act of 1996—better known as The Welfare Reform Act of 1996—has had a significant impact on the cost of social welfare programs, the exact magnitude of which is still to be determined. By any standard, the human services industry is one of the largest industries in the United States. The Bureau of the Census lists many occupations that may be included under the heading of human services. The following chart highlights the projected percentage change between 1992 and 2005 of the fastest-growing occupations (*Statistical Abstracts of the United States*, U.S. Census Bureau, 1995):

Home health aides	139%
Human services workers	135%
Personal and home care aides	130%
Computer engineers and scientists	112%
Systems analysts	110%
Physical and corrective therapy aides	95%
Physical therapists	87%
Paralegals	84%
Occupational therapy assistants and aides	78%
Teachers of special ed	75%
Correction officers	70%
Child care	66%
Occupational therapists	60%
Respiratory therapists	48%
Psychologists	48%

HUMAN SERVICES WORKERS

The personnel at human services agencies can be divided into four general categories: (a) those who provide help to recipients, (b) supervisory personnel, (c) administrators who determine the policies of the agency, and (d) support personnel who do clerical, maintenance, and security work. In addition, some settings, such as hospitals and nursing homes, require kitchen, housekeeping, and other support workers. In smaller agencies, workers sometimes have to do work in several of these categories.

A great many job titles, positions, and professions are included under the general heading of human services worker. These range from positions that require relatively little formal training, such as mental hospital aide and teacher assistant, to those that require extensive formal training and education. Clinical and counseling psychologists, psychiatrists, social workers, and nurses are included in the latter category. Chapter 6 goes into detail about a wide range of career options in the field.

There is considerable variation in the extent to which different professionals identify themselves as human services workers. Social workers, for example, have generally been more accepting of the term than have psychologists or psychiatrists. The term *human services worker* is more than a way of identifying workers in a particular field; it carries with it a certain attitude or philosophy about the field. The underlying idea is that the separate disciplines should emphasize what they have in common—serving people's needs—rather than emphasize their differences.

Some activists would like to phase out specialty training in favor of generalist training in human services. However, there is considerable resistance to this idea from professionals who wish to preserve separate identities as psychologists, social workers, psychiatrists, and so on. Apologies are offered if all this sounds confusing; it is confusing because the field of human services is undergoing rapid change. It is not possible to know for certain how human services workers of the future will be trained or what their job titles will be.

KINDS OF HELP PROVIDED

Human services provide many kinds of aid and services. Perhaps the most basic kind of direct aid consists of tangible items such as food, clothing, shelter, tools, and other useful articles. Victims of natural disasters and homeless poor persons may be in dire need of this kind of help. The Salvation Army and the Red Cross are well known for providing hot meals and shelter to homeless people.

In most situations, cash transfers can readily be exchanged for needed goods and services. Social security, welfare, and unemployment insurance are among the most important benefits of this kind because millions depend on them for economic survival. These cash benefits can be used in any way the recipient sees fit. This freedom worries some politicians, who fear that the money will be used for nonessential or even destructive items. Consequently, some benefits are offered with strings attached—in other words, the benefits can be used only for some specified purpose. Food stamps, for example, are given to eligible poor persons but can be used only to buy food. Another example is a housing subsidy paid directly to the landlord for a welfare recipient's rent.

REAL LIFE HUMAN SERVICES WORK

Construct, Inc. is a community-based nonprofit organization serving the housing needs of south Berkshire county, MA. It was formed more than 40 years ago, just after the assassination of Martin Luther King, Jr., when a group of citizens gathered for conversations to address poverty issues in the 15 towns that comprise South Berkshire. In its early days, Construct built or rehabilitated 65 homes and sold them to low income first-time homebuyers. Since that time and until 1990, Construct also sponsored low-income housing projects. From its inception it has been the mission of Construct to provide affordable housing and housing/homeless supportive services to 15 towns in south Berkshire County.

I came to Construct, Inc. as a volunteer in 1989. I was in my third year of seminary and was very concerned about the lack of affordable housing in south Berkshire and the rising numbers of homeless, not only locally, but statewide and across the nation. Today, 20 years later, with the help of a strong and active Board of Directors, a small staff, and a fleet of volunteers from the community, Construct, Inc. has developed 53 units of affordable housing, 10 single rooms for homeless men and women, 7 supportive housing units, and manages another 10 units of affordable housing for the Community Development Corporation of South Berkshire. In addition, we have an adult homeless education program that serves an average of 35 adult learners each year and our homeless prevention program that serves an average of 500 households annually. We are largely supported by the very generous south Berkshire community, particularly by the interfaith community.

I came to this agency 20 years ago to find out about housing and homelessness and am still here. Another economic crisis (similar to the one in the 80's which gave rise to social concern about homelessness across America) has brought scores of new households to our door, seeking assistance with joblessness, foreclosure, or eviction. The agency is small enough that I am able to do much of the direct service work in addition to the administrative work. On a given day I may do a little of everything from bookkeeping, to grant writing, to staff supervision, to casework, plus unclog a toilet, or unload groceries from the Food Bank into the shelter pantry. I try to meet each person who is brought to our door, whether he is a chronically homeless man who has abused alcohol his whole life, a young teen addicted to heroin and carrying an "attitude," or a single mother with three children recently let got from a nursing position struggling to find new employment, where he or she is, in a spirit of compassion and nonjudgment, and we begin to build from there. Although I had clinical training when I was in seminary, over the years my best teachers have been the clients and residents themselves. I feel blessed by this job and the people I meet each day, and I hope that the work we do here together is a blessing in their lives as well.

Cara Davis, BA., M.DIV.

In addition to these forms of aid, some services are designed to increase clients' capacities to gain satisfaction of needs by their own efforts. The next few paragraphs give brief preliminary definitions of some of the major kinds of services offered by human services workers.

Primary prevention refers to services designed to prevent people from developing an illness or a psychological problem. These services are usually offered to healthy or relatively well-functioning individuals and often have an educational, or

Homeless shelter.

informative, component. A school program designed to inform teenagers of the hazards of alcohol abuse is an example of primary prevention.

Counseling helps people consider their choices and options in life. Counseling may focus on career choice, budgeting, legal matters, or marital problems. Career counseling, for example, may help a client select a suitable occupation, whereas marital counseling may focus on a decision about continuing a marriage. Some forms of counseling become involved in helping a client deal with personal problems and, therefore, overlap with psychotherapy.

Psychotherapy has the general goal of changing a client's behavior or emotional responses to improve psychological well-being. Typical goals are to reduce anxiety, to improve social relationships, and to control undesirable behavior patterns. Hence, such therapy carries an implication that the client suffers from some degree of psychological impairment.

Crisis intervention is a special form of help designed to meet the needs of a person faced with an unusually difficult life situation. The word *crisis* implies that the person's usual coping mechanisms may not be enough to handle the situation. There is a risk of severe emotional upset or even disorganization.

Situations that might trigger a crisis include loss of a loved one or being the victim of rape, assault, serious accident, or large-scale disaster. The helper provides support and suggests effective ways of coping with the crisis. The goal is not to change the person's personality but to restore the client to the precrisis level of functioning. Crisis intervention may be done in the context of face-to-face meetings or by means of a hotline. The latter is a telephone service that allows the caller to get in touch with a counselor at any time of the night or day. The most familiar hotlines are designed to help suicidal individuals. Hotline services are also available to battered women, to rape victims, and to people actively struggling with alcoholism or other chemical dependence. A closer examination of crisis intervention follows, in Chapter 5.

Rehabilitation is designed to help people with disabilities achieve the highest possible level of productive functioning. Some experts make a distinction between habilitative and rehabilitative programs: the former aim to help those who have never been productive, whereas the latter focus on restoring skills to those who were once capable. In either case, the emphasis tends to be on practical skills such as those involved in self-care and earning a living. The type of disability may be physical, emotional, or developmental.

Social support may be offered in various forms to those who can benefit from a strengthening of social ties. An example is a club for senior citizens that enables them to get together with peers once or twice a week. Other familiar examples are the athletic and social programs for teens provided by many Ys and community centers. In addition, many self-help programs such as Alcoholics Anonymous emphasize social support in their therapeutic approach.

Community organizing represents another indirect form of support for those in need. The general idea is that the human services worker works with community leaders to provide some program needed by an unserved population in the community. For example, the worker may help the community set up a training school for persons with delayed intellectual development.

Many human services agencies provide a mix of aid and services to clients. Both mental hospitals and prisons, for example, provide aid in the form of food and shelter and may also provide counseling, therapy, or rehabilitation.

The employment services of some states link direct cash benefits to job and career counseling. At the other end of the scale are smaller programs that offer only one service or a limited range of services to clients.

SPONSORS OF HUMAN SERVICES

Human services organizations may be sponsored, that is, organized and funded, by private citizens, by religious and other groups, or by government. Private agencies may be operated on either a profit-making or a nonprofit basis. Nursing homes, rehabilitation hospitals, and agencies providing home nursing care are often private profit-making corporations that are run in basically the same way as other businesses.

This means that management is under pressure by owners to keep costs down and to show a profit at the end of the year.

Many other private agencies are organized on a not-for-profit basis. Youth employment and child care agencies are sometimes nonprofit. The Red Cross and the Salvation Army are examples of large nationwide private human services agencies operated on a nonprofit basis. Typically, such agencies are controlled by a board of directors that lays down general policies and selects the administrative officers who are responsible for the day-to-day operation of the agency. These agencies raise money by appealing to the general public for donations. An important advantage of nonprofit status is that it exempts the agency from certain taxes, which, in effect, allows more of the income to be used for helping consumers of the service.

Religious and other groups also sponsor nonprofit helping agencies. The Federation of Jewish Philanthropies, Catholic Charities, and the Lutheran Brotherhood are supported by major organized religions. In addition, unions, fraternal organizations, and ethnic groups sponsor countless helping agencies all across the country. The necessary funds are raised by appealing to parishioners and members for donations. Increasingly, both private and religious agencies are making use of professional fund-raisers, who are paid on the basis of a percentage of the income they raise.

There has been an increase in voluntary giving in recent years due in part to the increase in natural disasters such as Hurricane Katrina in 2005. For example, Americans contributed $212 billion in 2001 in spite of the weakening economy and a shattering act of terrorism. According to the survey of the American Association of Fund-Raising Counsel Trust for Philanthropy, the biggest surprise was a sharp increase in giving to human services agencies, which received a bit under $21 billion. Individuals accounted for roughly 75% of the contributions (Strom, 2002).

Who receives this money? Religion gets the largest share, with the remaining funds divided by education, health, human services, the arts, and other causes. Not all of this private giving goes to help poor people. Much of the money goes to groups active in environmental issues, civil liberties, women's rights, pro- and antiabortion issues, museums, and symphony orchestras.

Although private and religious human services agencies are important, governments (local, state, and federal) have become the major providers of direct and indirect aid to those in need. The scope and purpose of huge federal programs such as social security will be discussed in the next chapter. State governments play a major role in education, administer unemployment insurance, and manage most of the nation's mental hospitals. Local governments are responsible for actual administration of welfare programs, and they also provide many other kinds of help, such as programs for seniors and teens.

STUDYING HUMAN SERVICES FIRSTHAND

One of the best ways to learn about human services is to identify and study the different agencies and facilities within your geographic area. This kind of study readily lends itself to a team approach because students can divide the work and share information with one another. The information can come from many sources, including literature available at agencies, on-site visits, and meetings with staff members.

Your class might list all of the human services agencies, programs, and facilities in your area and provide answers to the following questions:

- What are the stated goals of the agency?
- What needs does the agency attempt to meet?
- What population is served? Roughly how many people does the organization serve? Hundreds? Thousands?
- What does the service cost the consumers? What are the eligibility criteria?
- Where does the money come from? If several sources are involved, list them in order of contribution.
- How many and what kinds of human services workers are employed by the human services agency?

Individuals may also share their subjective impressions of the agencies they visited. Did they feel welcome? Did the service seem to be well organized? How were clients treated by staff?

HUMAN SERVICES WORKERS AND BUREAUCRACY

Students beginning their training in human services rarely express the ambition to become bureaucrats. Nevertheless, the great majority of them will eventually find themselves working in the type of organization called a bureau or a bureaucracy. The fact is that welfare agencies, hospitals, employment services, nursing homes, and psychiatric clinics are all examples of this kind of organization.

Bureaucracies, which may be small or large, public or private, are defined by certain formal arrangements including some form of central control and a clear division of labor among administrators, supervisors, workers, and clerical staff. The employees are usually arranged in a hierarchy from higher to lower, and exchanges between the lower and upper levels without "going through channels" are often discouraged (Macht & Ashford, 1990, p. 227). One of the frustrating features of the large bureaucracy is that it can make workers feel that their contributions are relatively insignificant. Each person may feel like a small cog in a big machine. Nevertheless, despite the shortcomings of these kinds of organizations, they have adapted and survived because no one has developed a more efficient means of providing services on a large scale.

According to a study by Macht and Ashford (1990), educators often fail to prepare students to become effective bureaucrats. When bureaucracy is discussed in class, it is often in terms of the potential conflict between agency goals on the one hand and client or worker goals on the other. Or the discussion may focus on the organization as a cause of low morale among workers. It is all too easy to lose sight of the fact that specialization of workers, clear lines of command, and other features of the bureaucracy enable it to deliver services on a large scale and in an efficient manner. Rather than focus on the negative aspects, it is more productive to help students develop the knowledge and skills to work effectively within the bureaucracy. To this end, the student should be acquainted with the patterns of organization in human services organizations.

In fact, a course in human services organizations might more appi taught at the undergraduate college level than at the graduate level. Sor pics explored in such a course would be the use of power, funding sour zation, and delivery of services. Particularly important would be a consideration of how to bring about constructive changes in a large organization.

THE TREND TOWARD PRIVATIZATION

The process of arranging for private companies to do certain jobs formerly done by government is called privatizing or **privatization**. Recent decades have seen an increase in the trend to privatize government services along with an increasing role for profit-making companies. The push to privatize is, in the opinion of one observer, a reaction against "the fact that much of government has become entangled in its own power, stifling creativity and productivity. Government agencies responsible for serving the people have become muscle bound, almost to the point of paralysis, when it comes to considering more effective performance" (Linowes, 1995, p. 86). Linowes adds that government agencies are trying to solve social problems with outmoded designs and solutions. Clearly, this investigator is giving voice to the dislike of government bureaucracies shared by many conservatives.

Opposition to the trend to privatize has come from government employees, including many human services workers. Perhaps the best-organized resistance has come from the nation's unions of public employees. Although industrial unions have declined in influence since the end of World War II, unions of government employees have increased in size and power. By the end of 1992, and for the first time in American history, more people were employed by governments than in manufacturing (Peterson, 1994, p. 190). Many government workers are organized into civil service employee unions. Like other special **interest groups**, these unions lobby state and local legislators, contribute to campaign funds, and may deliver a sizable block of votes in elections. The purpose of this lobbying is, of course, to secure the kinds of benefits unions have always sought for their members: decent pay, job security, and fringe benefits such as pensions and medical insurance. During recent years, an increasing number of taxpayers have begun to resent the favorable contracts won by these unions. By contracting with private companies to do certain jobs, it has been possible to cut costs while weakening the power of the unions. How are private companies able to achieve significant savings? They hire nonunion workers at salaries lower than those of union workers, and they typically provide limited (or no) fringe benefits.

This is of great importance to the reader for the obvious reason that government provides most human services. Here is a list of some of the services that have been privatized in some communities:

- Housekeeping, laundry, and food services for hospitals and prisons
- Transportation services to and from schools and other facilities
- Shelters and housing for the homeless
- Computer services for various human services agencies
- Jails for illegal immigrants
- Halfway houses and day hospitals for persons with mental illness

Halfway houses for released prisoners
- Recovery homes for alcoholics and drug addicts
- Fire protection

These examples show that parts of larger operations may be privatized by government. More ambitious efforts to privatize may involve entire programs and facilities. For example, Brown County, Wisconsin, has turned over its welfare program to an outside private organization, and Corrections Corporation of America has more than $100 million in contracts for prisons and detention centers in nine states (Linowes, 1995).

There are potential dangers involved in either government-run or privatized services. Programs run by government are at risk of becoming job programs for union employees and political appointees. The needs of the workers may take precedence over the needs of recipients. The danger of privatization, on the other hand, is that the profit motive may come to dominate all other considerations. For example, one firm providing halfway houses for prisoners was charged with hiring low-paid, untrained employees and with allowing living conditions in the facility to deteriorate markedly. Fire hazards such as exposed electrical wires went unrepaired, and vermin were permitted free run of the place (Sullivan & Purdy, 1995). There are even serious discussions today regarding the privatization of the social security system in spite of the possible problems and dangers to future recipients.

Suggestion for Class Report or Term Paper
Examine the effects of a specific program or service that has been privatized in your county or state. What was the effect on the government workers who previously provided the service? Describe the new workers in terms of salary and qualifications. Was there any change in the quality of the services provided? Interview some people who were directly affected by the change, and report their reactions.

SOURCES OF NEED SATISFACTION

The flowchart in Figure 1.2 illustrates the relationship among needs, primary sources of help, and human services.

A person in need often seeks help from primary sources such as family and friends before going to a human services agency. For example, a person with financial difficulties may seek help from the family before applying for welfare. Similarly, a person with emotional problems may seek advice from a priest, minister, or rabbi before going to a psychiatric clinic. It is often more comfortable to appeal to familiar persons than to an impersonal agency for help. The bureaucratic procedures of some agencies make people hesitate to go to them. Some agencies make clients wait for hours, require that complicated forms be filled out, and process the claims in a cold, perfunctory manner.

In some circumstances, however, a person may prefer to go to a human services agency rather than to a primary source. For example, a woman might want to conceal an unwanted pregnancy from family and friends. Or a person might feel too embarrassed about certain behaviors to even discuss them with friends or family. Child abusers, gamblers, and drug addicts may well fall into this category. In these

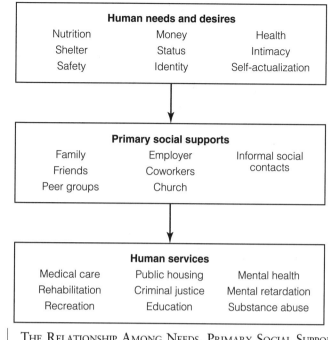

FIGURE 1.2 | THE RELATIONSHIP AMONG NEEDS, PRIMARY SOCIAL SUPPORTS, AND HUMAN SERVICES

cases, the human services agency offers the opportunity to deal with the problem in a confidential manner. And to those lacking primary social supports, the human services often represent the last defense against personal disaster.

FALLING THROUGH THE SAFETY NET

An unknown number of people need help from human services but don't get it. These are the people who fall through the safety net provided by basic services. Some needy people are not eligible for help based on the **criteria** of the agency in question. For example, a worker may not be eligible for unemployment benefits if he or she did not work for a specified number of months during the previous year. Other needy people may simply be unaware of existing programs. For example, some illegal immigrants do not know about programs designed to help them. Still other needy people may be fully aware of programs but are too proud to accept the help available.

What happens to those people who are not helped either by primary social supports or by human services? Many thousands of them end up in the streets. The story of America's homeless is told in detail in Chapter 2. Runaway children, long-term alcoholics, and former mental hospital inmates may be included in the ranks of "street people." During severe weather, some of them try to secure admission to jails or mental hospitals. Some depend on handouts from passersby, and many take meals provided by soup kitchens or shelters.

One of thousands of homeless people living in the streets of our cities.

There is continuing debate about what to do with these people, often with each agency or level of government trying to shift the responsibility to another. This controversy leads us to our next subject for consideration: the factors besides human needs that influence human services in the United States.

POLITICAL CONTROVERSY AND HUMAN SERVICES

The magnitude, scope, and purpose of human services are shaped only in part by people's needs. Other considerations are the resources available for helping and the attitudes of various groups toward human services. Unfortunately, there is no consensus on who should receive what kind of help. The ultraconservative view is that government support for human services should be cut to the barest minimum. Liberals see the need for increases in all human services. In our society, there is constant conflict between those who would cut and those who would increase expenditures for human services. This has resulted in an ebb and flow of government support for human services. One unfortunate consequence is that human services have not been allowed to develop in an orderly, rational manner. Services are initiated under one administration only to be limited or eliminated by the next administration.

Although the political forces underlying these conflicts are generally labeled liberal and conservative, people are not consistent within these frameworks. A particular individual may take a **liberal position** about one kind of service but a **conservative position** on another. Let's look more closely at these positions.

A CONSERVATIVE POINT OF VIEW

Conservatives wish to preserve traditional American values, including a strict adherence to the Constitution and respect for the rights and property of others. They profess a deep respect for the values of the American pioneer, with a strong emphasis on hard work, perseverance, and self-reliance. Jealous of their personal liberty, conservatives tend to distrust big government and wish to limit its role to the barest essentials. This resentment against interference extends into the economic sphere. Generally, conservatives favor a free market and maintain that free enterprise and the pursuit of private profit have made the United States the richest nation on earth.

However, the automatic, reflexive opposition to social programs that characterized many conservatives in the past is less prevalent today. Most conservatives currently recognize that there are some circumstances when people, through no fault of their own, require help from government. Few, if any, now favor elimination of the social security program, although some recommend a reorganization along the lines of a voluntary insurance program or some other form of privatization. Conservatives also accept the need for some form of welfare benefits for those who are unable to meet immediate needs. Nevertheless, they would like to see built into the system incentives for individuals to become self-supporting.

Conservatives also generally favor unemployment insurance, partly in recognition of the fact that workers are often caught up in economic problems beyond their individual control. It must also be recognized that all of these programs are beneficial to the economy because they help individuals maintain purchasing power. But conservatives are likely to oppose programs that go beyond meeting basic survival needs. They express concern that help from the government tends to weaken the initiative of the recipient, creating an attitude of passive dependence. They also believe that the federal government has assumed excessive control over our lives through its massive programs and that some power and control should be returned to the individual states.

A LIBERAL PERSPECTIVE

Liberals see themselves as champions of the disadvantaged. They are convinced that conservative rhetoric about liberty and self-reliance doesn't mean very much to a person who is hungry, broke, and unemployed.

The liberal tradition was carried on by the administrations of Harry Truman, John F. Kennedy, Lyndon Johnson, Jimmy Carter, Bill Clinton, and now Barack Obama. All perceived that government must take a leading role in working for the health, safety, and welfare of the people.

Cuomo (1994) has contrasted the liberal and conservative positions in the following way: Liberals accept the idea of collective responsibility, a sense that we are all in this together, whereas conservatives are more reluctant to get involved in sharing benefits or burdens. Cuomo argues that people don't have to love their needy neighbors, but they should at least consider their own self-interest in regard to the disadvantaged. "If we bring children into this world and let them go hungry and uneducated, if we are indifferent to the drugs and squalor that surround them ..., then all of us will share the outcome," he writes (p. 9), adding that we will all be obliged to spend more on jails and police while we live in fear.

ELECTION OF 2004: THE SECOND BUSH TERM AND THE CULTURE WARS

In order to more fully comprehend the issues facing the current Obama administration, one must take a brief look back at what was inherited from the former Bush administration.

After a close and bitter battle for the White House, George W. Bush was elected to a second term. The deficit was large, spending was at an all-time high, and we were a nation at war. Rather than addressing important domestic issues such as social policy achievement and health care progress, the Republicans, many complained, diverted attention to post-9/11 issues: safety from terrorism and fighting a war in Iraq.

The war in Iraq, which began in March 2003, had become increasingly unpopular by President Bush's second term. Initially, he requested that troops be sent to Iraq because it was suspected that Sadaam Hussein, the leader of Iraq, had weapons of mass destruction. After it was revealed that Iraq did not have these weapons, many people felt lied to, and the war became increasingly more unpopular. By the end of 2005, 1,260 troops had been killed (Associated Press, 2005).

In 2005 Bush received a confidence rating of only 35%, the lowest of any modern president. The growing disenchantment with the war in Iraq was one reason for Bush's decline in popularity. Furthermore, Bush would not present the American people with a clear timetable for ending the war. The war had already cost the United States billions of dollars, and more than $100 billion was requested at the end of 2005 (Associated Press, 2005).

During a particularly destructive hurricane season, which saw the unmatched devastation of hurricanes Katrina and Wilma, the gulf region of Louisiana and Mississippi suffered a terrible disaster. Most of New Orleans was decimated, due to the breaching of the levee system. The ineffective and untimely handling of Hurricane Katrina by the Federal Emergency Management Administration (FEMA) exposed how vulnerable the United States is to national disasters. Many felt that the devastation, which resulted in a great loss of lives and destruction of property, could have been prevented.

The Bush administration had been widely criticized for not being responsive to the needs of the poorest Americans. The U.S. Census Bureau revealed that the poverty rate rose 17% between the beginning of the Bush presidency and 2005. In addition, the U.S. infant mortality rate had risen for the first time since 1958 (CIA, 2005). Some blamed the lack of funds for human services on the war expenditures, while others blamed the tax cuts being given to the wealthiest Americans rather than to those from the lower or middle class. In 2005 a bankruptcy law was passed making it much more difficult for Americans to wipe out their debts. This law has the potential to keep many Americans from getting back on their feet following exorbitant hospital costs or credit card bills.

During this administration, the U.S. Supreme Court lost two of its justices. Sandra Day O'Connor resigned, and Chief Justice William Rehnquist died. President Bush appointed two conservative Republicans to the Court, John Roberts as chief justice and Samuel Alito to replace Justice O'Connor. Since the Supreme Court defines such important and timely issues as civil rights, the right to an abortion, individual privacy, the balance of the branches of government, and many other significant issues, these surely were critical appointments that will shape the face of the country for generations to come.

Election of 2008: The Obama Administration

When Obama first began his campaign for the Democratic Party nomination for president, most people believed that he was an "underdog" and a "long shot" to win the nomination. In hindsight, however, it is fairly easy to see how Obama won. His charisma, calm, reassuring personality, and message of change touched many Americans fed up with the seemingly endless war in Iraq and the policies of President Bush and his fellow Republicans. In addition, Obama ran a brilliant campaign using Internet-based social networking through Web sites such as MySpace, Twitter, and Facebook to create a grassroots, activist campaign.

This Internet-based social networking strategy allowed Obama to connect with and involve more people than ever before, particularly young people, most of whom had already used social networking technology and turned out to vote for Obama in record numbers. Internet-based social networking technology also provided the sense of accessibility and transparency that were key parts of Obama's campaign promises as this technology allowed supporters to get information on Obama's policy positions and campaign activities instantly. The Obama campaign also broke fund raising records by using the Internet to solicit small donations (called "microgiving") from millions of Americans. The technological sophistication of Obama's campaign also contrasted sharply with that of the Republicans who lagged far, far behind in the use of technology, and whose candidate, John McCain, admitted while interviewed on national television that he does not use a computer (Stein, 2008). Since being elected, Obama has continued using technology to reach out to Americans and to inform them of what is going on. His Web site (http://www.barackobama.com) invites all Americans to organize for policies that concern them, such as health care or the environment, and creates a simple online mechanism for doing this. Obama also instituted the first White House blog, an online "town hall" question-and-answer period during which citizens can ask the president questions, and the White House streams every Presidential event over its Web site.

Nagourney (2008) has described the election as a "national catharsis," during which people turned away from an increasingly unpopular president with unpopular foreign and domestic policies. Perhaps Obama's election was an international catharsis as well. People all over the world celebrated his election in a way that had never occurred when any previous U.S. president had been elected. As Bonner (2008) wrote in the *New York Times* on the day after the election, "Obama's campaign touched the nation and the world because we all want to believe that America is the land of extraordinary opportunity and possibility, where miracles happen."

Obama's campaign promises centered on five major areas of policy: 1) enhanced human services to improve quality of life and equality of opportunity, such as universal health care, tax credits for education, and help for America's cities; 2) elimination of wasteful government spending; 3) transparency in government (making governmental processes accessible for public review); 4) increased utilization of climate-friendly, "green" technologies and energy; and 5) increased use of diplomacy, as opposed to military action, in foreign policy, along with an end to the war in Iraq. During the campaign, however, major problems in the economy developed. By the time Obama was sworn into office, things had gotten so bad that Obama was faced with the worst challenges any president had faced in the last 75 years—wars in both Iraq and Afghanistan, high unemployment and severe economic recession along with huge problems in the financial, manufacturing, and housing sectors, and chronic health care, education, and environmental problems (Smith, 2009). As a result, Obama was forced to deal with urgent and immediate economic and military problems while at the same time trying to honor his campaign promises in other areas.

HUMAN SERVICES Despite the enormous challenges just described, Obama has managed to accomplish a considerable amount in his first few months in office. Because of the deep recession, Obama worked diligently to get the $787-billion American Recovery and Reinvestment Act (nicknamed "the stimulus package") passed by Congress. This law contained many provisions that honored Obama's campaign promise to enhance or maintain human services. It included tens of billions of dollars to ensure that there would be no cuts in **medicaid** and **food stamps**, and additional dollars for education, increased unemployment benefits, and TANF (public assistance) funding. The stimulus package also included tax cuts for people with low or moderate incomes, as well as a small one-time payment to all disabled veterans, and people receiving SSI (supplemental security income) and social security. Another important provision of the stimulus package that honors Obama's commitment to universal health care is the allotment of $25 billion to help unemployed people retain their health care benefits through their previous employer's health care plan. In addition to these provisions, the stimulus package also provides billions for improvement of highways and public transportation systems. Over 2,000 highway improvement programs have already been approved, providing well-paid jobs in all 50 states.

In addition to human services programs funded through the stimulus package, Obama has delivered on his promise to enhance human services in a number of other ways. Of all presidents, Obama is probably the one most concerned with our struggling inner cities. Early in his administration, he created a new national Office of Urban Policy to address these problems (Stein, 2009). Obama's Making Home Affordable program has helped financially strapped homeowners hold onto their homes by renegotiating the terms of their mortgages to make them more affordable and providing some cash assistance. Unfortunately, because the economy is so poor, reputable independent ratings companies have estimated that well over half of the homeowners assisted by this program will default on their mortgages again in six to twelve months because of job loss or credit card or other debt (Reckard, 2009). Obama also got a bill passed for a $2,500 tax credit to help individuals and families cover the cost of college tuition as well as an $8,000 tax credit for first-time home buyers. In addition, Obama has expanded national service opportunities more than any president since John F. Kennedy. The E.M. Kennedy Serve America Act provides small grants to be used for education for over 250,000 volunteers. It also encourages retirees to volunteer and provides them with a $1,000 education grant they can use for themselves or transfer to a child or grandchild (Toedtman, 2009). Finally, although the budget deficit may make it difficult for Obama to honor his promise of universal health care, he did conduct a day-long health care summit meeting at the White House in March of 2009, and he also created a fund to extend health care benefits to four million currently uncovered children in an un-orthodox way—by raising the federal tax on cigarettes a whopping 62 cents per pack. However, as critics have pointed out, this huge tax increase on cigarettes will prove a hardship for poor people who smoke (Woodward, 2009).

ELIMINATION OF WASTEFUL GOVERNMENT SPENDING   In his first few months, Obama has taken some significant steps to cut costs. During his first meeting with his new Cabinet, Obama ordered all department heads to eliminate waste and to cut their budgets by $100 million. He also got the departments of Defense and Veterans Affairs to coordinate with each other so that files of military personnel who are discharged will be automatically transferred to Veterans Affairs. This represents a huge gain in efficiency and a huge saving in administrative costs. Prior to Obama's presidency, the files of discharged military personnel had to be requested and delivered individually (Toedtman, 2009). In addition, the stimulus package included $19 billion to streamline and computerize the medical records of all Americans, a plan originally proposed by President Bush. Although this represents a huge initial investment, ultimately it will save money by reducing error, duplication of services, and time spent acquiring medical records. It will also make it substantially easier to gather **data** on which medical procedures are most effective, thus cutting costs by indicating which procedures are ineffective while also contributing to the overall health of the population.

TRANSPARENCY IN GOVERNMENT   As discussed above, Obama has utilized technology, both during his campaign and as President, to greatly increase the flow of information to the public as well as public access to Obama and his team. Honoring his promise for greater transparency, the administration has begun developing new Web sites where the public can follow the bidding process for federal contracts. This Web site will also include information on how much federal contractors spent on lobbying political officials and how well they did in completing previously awarded federal contracts.

CLIMATE AND ENERGY   The Obama administration has been instrumental in passing the first climate bill (The Waxman and Markey Cap and Trade bill) ever passed by a committee in Congress—a very significant achievement (Galbraith, 2009). In the cap-and-trade approach advocated by Obama, pollution sources are given a pollution allowance (a set amount of pollution they are allowed to create) for which they pay. If they develop or purchase new technologies that pollute less, they can profit by selling their excess pollution credits to other companies. The idea is to provide a financial incentive to pollute less (Tankersley, 2009). Obama hopes to use revenues from cap and trade to fund health care and provide energy tax credits to low- or moderate-income families. Waxman and Markey also includes green provisions for modernization of the electrical grid, production of electric vehicles, and increased energy efficiency in appliances and buildings (Broder, 2009). In addition, the stimulus package includes over $100 billion for other green efforts.

Some critics fear that Obama's aggressive climate and energy policies may slow economic and job growth because they impose higher energy costs on businesses that are already struggling to survive in difficult economic times (Walsh, 2009). A recent study of the results of the strict green laws implemented in Spain revealed that "going green" actually cost Spain thousands of jobs because many energy-intensive industries simply left Spain and relocated to other countries where cheaper energy was still available (Blankley, 2009). Other critics of Obama's green policies are concerned that increased energy costs will be passed on to the consumer and that this will disproportionately affect low-income people who pay a higher percentage of their of their income for gas, heat, and electricity (*Wall Street Journal*, 2009).

FOREIGN POLICY Since taking office, Obama has faced huge challenges in the area of foreign policy, including the two wars he inherited, ongoing tension in the Middle East, and the testing of a large nuclear weapon by North Korea in May 2009. A cornerstone of Obama's foreign policy has been reaching out to countries and groups who have been at odds with the United States. Early in his presidency, Obama took pains to try to connect with Muslims around the world by making an appearance in Turkey and giving a widely watched interview on Al Arabiya TV. He extended the hand of diplomacy to leaders in North Korea, Iran, Cuba, and Venezuela. North Korea and Iran reacted to these efforts with belligerence and defiance, but there have been gains—albeit small—with Cuba and Venezuela (Ward, 2009). Critics claim that Obama's diplomatic tactics may betray weakness (*Washington Times*, 2009) or inexperience (Ward, 2009).

However, even skeptics have given Obama high grades for his handling of the wars in Iraq and Afghanistan. Within a few days of taking office, Obama announced that he would end the war in Iraq within one year, and in the late spring of 2009, the military confirmed that it is on schedule for withdrawal by early 2010 (Adamy, 2009). Obama also acted decisively in Afghanistan, granting the long-standing request by U.S. military leaders of an additional 17,000 troops to prevent Taliban forces from regaining control of the Afghan government and to help Afghan security forces learn how to protect their own country. Obama also authorized economic aid to Afghanistan and neighboring Pakistan, and created a trilateral open dialog between himself and the leaders of Afghanistan and Pakistan to help root out terrorism (Obama, 2009, March 27, March 30).

OBAMA AND THE ECONOMY As stated above, Obama inherited the worst economic and financial crisis the country has faced since the Great Depression of the 1930s. In response, he has built upon some of Bush's bailout policies, but has also taken unprecedented steps with two troubled auto manufacturers—General Motors (GM) and Chrysler—and has embarked upon a bold spending plan that has taken the U.S. economy into uncharted economic waters.

Obama stated in his March 30, 2009 speech on GM and Chrysler that the federal government cannot stand by and let these two automotive giants fail. This stance has led to greater government involvement in private business than has ever happened before in the history of the United States. Obama's administration has provided tens of billions of dollars in TARP funds to keep GM and Chrysler running, engineered the firing and replacement of GM's CEO, and worked with executives from both companies on plans to make both companies financially stable. What is even more unprecedented in terms of government control of private business in this case, however, is the fact that under Obama's plan, 72% of GM will ultimately be owned by the U.S. government. Critics of such a high level of government involvement in private industry point to the fact that there has never been a single instance in history when government interference has improved a business or market. As Stansberry (2009, March) succinctly writes, the government's record in this area is "unblemished by success."

Obama has also embarked on a bold spending plan both to stimulate the economy and to deliver on his campaign promises. Taxes do not provide anywhere near sufficient resources to pay for Obama's plan, so he will be forced to borrow money, thereby increasing the budget deficit. To get an idea of the magnitude of this new debt, Obama plans to borrow more money in the next eight years than the amount borrowed by all previous U.S. presidents combined (Stansberry, 2009, April). The new debt alone will amount to an additional $74,000 for each family in America (Lambro, 2009). At least two questions arise in connection with this unprecedented borrowing and spending. First, are we unfairly burdening future generations with an enormous debt? Second, how will we pay it all back? These and other questions will need to be addressed as Obama continues his first term in office.

THE EBB AND FLOW OF SUPPORT FOR HUMAN SERVICES

Aside from threats to national security or catastrophes, a major factor that determines the degree of public support for human services is the state of the economy. In good times, tax revenues increase, and more money is generally made available for human services. During economic downturns, funding for services is likely to be reduced.

Changes in the public's attitude toward government also affect funding for services. In recent years, the public's confidence in government seems to have reached a low point. Some people feel that the less money sent to the government, the less government will have to waste.

Supporters of human services argue that it is futile to attempt to save money by cutting funds for human services programs. For example, if we pay less for child care services now, we will have to spend more later for supporting people in mental hospitals and correctional facilities. If we cut back on funds for **probation**, we reduce our chances of rehabilitating offenders. Overcrowding in our prisons coupled with a lack of therapeutic programs is responsible for the high rate of **recidivism**.

By shortchanging human services agencies, we prevent them from reducing the number of dependent and dysfunctional people.

Human services programs need sufficient funding and an orderly, predictable flow of funds from one year to the next to fulfill their missions. But the government, regardless of economic conditions, seems to provide for human services on a hand-to-mouth basis with the threat or actuality of significant cutbacks to individual program budgets always possible. These variations in funding are most often related to political and economic factors that have little to do with the needs of the agency or its clients. It is difficult to do an effective job, maintain employee morale, and keep the confidence of the clients under such unstable conditions. This is why human services workers are increasingly seeing the need to organize effective lobbying groups. They recognize that well-organized groups such as the gun lobby, the tobacco lobby, and other special-interest groups are often successful in securing favorable legislation. On a practical level, the political system works through the application of this kind of direct pressure. Unrepresented groups, no matter how worthy their cause, are likely to be overlooked. This issue is discussed in more detail in Chapter 7.

THE IMPACT OF CONTEMPORARY PROBLEMS ON NEEDS

Human services do not operate in a vacuum; they are shaped by social, environmental, political, and economic conditions that prevail in a given time and place. The purpose of this section is to pinpoint some problems that affect the ability of Americans to meet their own needs and, as a result, have an impact on human services.

NATURAL DISASTERS

Although **natural disasters** have occurred since antiquity, this topic is included in a discussion of contemporary problems because the rate of casualties from such events is increasing sharply and will continue to go up in the foreseeable future. A natural disaster can be defined as a phenomenon that may have devastating social consequences when the awesome forces of nature come into contact with people. On a worldwide basis, nearly a quarter of a million people die in natural disasters each year (Frazier, 1979). Earthquakes, floods, hurricanes, tornadoes, and volcanic eruptions are among the natural hazards with the greatest potential for destruction.

In the United States, several trends are serving to increase disaster tolls. One is the vulnerability brought about by increasing dependence on interlinked computer systems and surface electrical power lines. The New York City power blackout of 1977 was triggered by a lightning strike on electronic switching equipment. Another trend that increases the potential for disaster in this country is the shift in population. More and more people are moving into flood plains, seismic risk zones, and coastal areas exposed to hurricane winds, storms, and erosion. There is also an increased risk due to the spread of population to California, where landslides and earthquakes are serious hazards. More than half the U.S. population now lives in places highly susceptible to natural disasters (Frazier, 1979).

In the event of a disaster, people usually first seek help from family, friends, and neighbors. However, if conditions are severe, local service agencies are called on to help the sick and homeless. The police, fire department, church organizations, social welfare groups, and medical services may all play important roles, depending on the nature of the disaster. Restoring communication, effecting evacuations, rescuing survivors, and providing temporary shelter and emergency first aid are just some of the important jobs that may need to be done. Obviously, well-trained, well-organized service workers function more effectively than untrained ones. Many of these observations apply just as well to disasters for which humans are responsible, such as mine cave-ins or the collapse of buildings and other structures.

Hurricane Katrina, the third largest, most powerful storm of the 2005 hurricane season and the sixth strongest storm ever recorded in the Atlantic, breached the levee system that protected New Orleans from Lake Pontchartrain and the Mississippi River. Most of the city became flooded, and the damage to the coastal regions of Louisiana, Mississippi, and Alabama made Katrina the most destructive and costliest natural disaster in the history of the United States (Knabb, Rhome, & Brown, 2005). The official death toll was 1,322, although only 1,086 bodies were recovered. The estimated damage was from $70 billion

© Richard Carson/Reuters/Landov

Help in Houston following the Hurricane Katrina Disaster.

to $130 billion, and over 1 million people were displaced. Over 250,000 homes were rendered uninhabitable (Carney, Tumulty, & Thompson, 2005).

The mayor of New Orleans ordered the city evacuated on August 28, after Katrina was upgraded to a Category 5 storm. However, about 150,000 people were unable to leave because of the inaccessibility of buses, the short supply of rental cars, the halting of Amtrak and Greyhound service, and a short supply of fuel (Glaser & Grunwald, 2005). Many of these people were from the poorest neighborhoods of the city, where poor African Americans lived in segregated neighborhoods. These factors limited the most vulnerable of these residents from being able to flee the city in time. The New Orleans Superdome was available for people who were unable to leave. During the storm and after, over 60,000 people were housed in the Superdome, in deplorable and unsanitary conditions, which included lack of air conditioning, electricity, or running water. There was no help for these victims until the fifth day.

> These are the scenes of a dying city: an elderly woman dead in a wheelchair outside the convention center, a note on her lap bearing her name. A horrified family telling tales of pirates commandeering rescue boats at gunpoint. Corpses left rotting in broad daylight. Angry crowds chanting for the television cameras, "we're dying!" or simply "help!" (Dao, Treaster, & Barringer, 2005)

As plans were made for moving evacuees out of the Superdome to other shelters and temporary housing in other states, attention became focused on the victims of Katrina. The U.S. Census Bureau estimates the 2004 New Orleans population to be 20% white and 70% black. Within the city, the poorest tended to live in the lowest parts that were most likely to flood (Berube & Katz, 2005). Members of the Congressional Black Caucus, Black Leadership Forum, National Conference of State Legislators, National Urban League and the NAACP held a news conference criticizing the slow response to the evacuation and attributing it to the fact that those affected were the poorest in the region (NAACP, 2005). In addition, many citizens across the United States criticized the Bush administration's slow and poor response to the disaster. Some thought that racial bias played a role in the administration's indifference, while others believed that FEMA's response was inadequate across the board, even in the mostly white areas of Mississippi and suburban Louisiana.

Those who evacuated were dispersed to cities all across the United States. There were evacuees living in almost every state, and some were there for the long term. Many moved in with family; others were housed in hotel rooms and other temporary shelters, until they could find apartments of their own or return to New Orleans and the surrounding communities.

A Washington Post/Keiser/Harvard survey of evacuees (Morin & Rein, 2005) found that a large portion, about 50%, did not plan on returning to their communities. Forty-nine percent of evacuees in the Houston area said that they would not return to Louisiana.

The most vulnerable and destitute of Hurricane Katrina victims remained stuck in flophouse motels across the country. Even as the FEMA deadline approached for the evacuation from this temporary housing, local officials had realized that many of these victims had no place to go nor any chance of beginning their life anew in

Louisiana. Many victims were the homeless, elderly, disabled, or mentally ill. They were living in places like Houston, Texas, and Columbia, South Carolina. Local volunteer organizations delivered food, obtained furniture, provided medical services, and offered employment opportunities to those who had been displaced (Wilgoren, 2005).

The human services implications of this tragedy are great. Many agencies, including the Red Cross and many other relief agencies, had provided shelter, food, clothing, and counseling to victims of this crisis. Needing the most assistance were the economically marginalized, who could no longer count on family members for help but instead relied on local community agencies to help them resettle, gain employment, enroll children in schools, and avail themselves and their families of counseling. Of the 1 million displaced persons, 2,880 children had spent a significant amount of time separated from their families in Louisiana, Mississippi, and Alabama. Even those families that remained together had suffered the ordeal of being uprooted from their homes, schools, friends, and communities. Many had gone from shelter to shelter to shelter.

> Chelsea Jones, 13, has moved four times since Hurricane Katrina had destroyed her family's home in Gulfport, Mississippi. Initially, she and her family found refuge in a skating rink in Gulfport that was set up as a shelter for 119 people, though it lacked running water and air conditioning. If things were normal, Chelsea would be attending 7th grade and worrying about what to wear to school, instead of whether she has enough insulin for her diabetes (Glanton & Bowean, 2005).

However, very little will be normal for the children who have experienced this hurricane. Dr. Joseph Hagen, Jr., head of the task force on terrorism, said that even though the catastrophes of Hurricane Katrina resulted from an act of nature and not a deliberate act of terrorism, the children will have post-traumatic stress disorder, anxiety, and depression, and some will have suffered bereavement issues. Many have lost homes, pets, neighbors, and friends, and some have suffered the profound loss of parents. Many parents, so devastated themselves, may not be able to meet their children's emotional needs. The emotional problems of adults can make a child's fears much worse. Dr. Hagen emphasizes the role of communities, family doctors, pediatricians, schools, and the mental health resources of the communities in dealing with these needs (Hagen, 2005).

Experts predict that there can be a lifetime of crippling psychological problems that may result from the effects of displacement, loss, witnessing the deaths and suffering of others, and all of the psychological traumas that were experienced by survivors of the hurricane. It has been predicted that Katrina's impact on mental health is likely to last a long time. Thousands of patients have been reported as suffering from stress, **dissociative disorders**, depression, and other psychiatric conditions (Voelker, 2005).

THE NEEDS OF EMERGENCY SERVICES WORKERS   Although the victims of disaster are of immediate concern, the mental health needs of emergency workers must not be overlooked. In attempting to help victims under stressful and chaotic conditions, these workers may suffer extreme fatigue, stress reactions, and **burnout**. The National Institute of Mental Health (1985) has provided some suggestions that will help prevent and control stress among workers.

Preventive efforts might include predisaster training in the mental health aspects of the work. Workers can learn to recognize the stresses inherent in their work and to develop strategies for dealing with those stresses. For example, the workers can learn about resources, such as debriefing and counseling, available to them for dealing with stress. The workers should also receive training in their particular roles in the organization's overall plan and should participate in disaster drills.

During the disaster, workers should be provided with as much factual information as possible about what they will find at the scene, and they should be informed about the well-being of their family members. Workers should be checked by supervisors for signs of stress and perhaps rotated among assignments of varying difficulty. They should be required to take breaks, especially if their capacity to help is diminishing.

After the disaster, all who participated in the work should be debriefed. The debriefing may be one to one, or it may be conducted in a group meeting in which the emotional aspects of the experience are discussed. The leader should be skilled in group dynamics and be trained to handle strong emotions. The debriefing is usually held between 24 and 48 hours after the incident, allowing time to overcome the initial fatigue and numbness. Two to 4 hours should be allowed for the process, and both positive and negative emotional responses should be reviewed. Finally, the organization should have some means of monitoring the workers' recovery from traumatic events, and, if needed, workers should be referred for counseling.

TERRORISM

Since the horrible and momentous events of September 11, 2001, the lives of Americans have been significantly altered. The television and media coverage during the days, weeks, and months following the terrorist attack have made all of us suddenly aware of how vulnerable we are to further attacks. These were not the first acts of **terrorism** in the United States or the world; however, for the United States, these acts of terror came to symbolize a new era, one in which President Bush declared a worldwide "war on terrorism."

Terrorism is both a violent and political act. A symbolic target is selected to convey a political message to a group, usually a government, in an attempt to alter some form of government policy. The targeting of innocent people is central to the tactics of terrorism, setting it apart from other forms of warfare. The terrorists' goal is to disrupt the daily routines of people's lives and create psychological disequilibrium resulting in a heightened sense of vulnerability, insecurity, anxiety, and/or apprehension. In this goal, the terrorists unfortunately succeeded for the first time in the United States with the September 11 attacks and consequently increased the need for human services.

Additional stress is generated when warnings by the government of potential attacks are given without information on when, where, or what kinds of attacks are imminent. Further anxiety and a sense of helplessness occur due to lack of information on how to prepare for and deal with such events.

Medical disaster teams have been in place in large cities for some time, but the events of September 11 demonstrated the immediate and dramatic need to establish organized mental health disaster plans. According to Chip Felton, an associate commissioner at the New York State office of mental health, "the sheer scale of the event dwarfed most of our disaster mental health plans. In fact, the emotional force of the attacks was so strong that many officials suspected that even people used to coping on their own might seek professional help. Trauma experts warned that people with severe post-traumatic stress disorder might not come forward for months or years" (Goode & Eakin, 2002).

Specifically trained and coordinated mental health crisis teams worked alongside other medical teams to attend the physically injured as well as those in the immediate area who had witnessed the event. Even if one does not suffer a direct injury resulting from a disaster, actually witnessing a disaster can cause psychological trauma. Many viewers watching the news coverage of the September 11 attacks on television have reported symptoms of psychological trauma.

When the disaster teams arrive at the scene, the initial task is to assess the level of severity and the scope of need. All coordinated efforts focus on reducing an already chaotic situation. Mental health teams work directly with those most immediately affected, seeking to reduce their fears and anxiety, and facilitate emotional ventilation. The team members help to determine priorities for those who need immediate additional services. Within the next days and weeks following the disaster, team members meet with those affected individuals and possibly with their families to provide crisis counseling and whatever additional mental health and human services assistance that may be necessary.

The **incidence** of post-traumatic stress disorder (also known as crisis behaviors) is usually substantially higher for those individuals who had the greatest degree of exposure to the disaster. Human services workers providing crisis counseling in the periods after disaster, such as the one that occurred on September 11, work with individuals suffering from a wide range of problems. They may include severe depression, disorientation, hostility, phobias, hysteria, nervousness, sleeplessness, increased irritability, amnesia, or psychosomatic reactions and nightmares. More severe problems can include psychosis, characterized by an apparent personality change, highly unusual behavior, and irrational thinking. Human services crisis workers must be aware that emotional problems experienced by disaster victims may be severe. They must also recognize that such problems may not be readily apparent until months after the actual event.

Research in the field of crisis intervention and disaster response has indicated a pattern of post-disaster phases. These phases seem to indicate a sequence of reactions experienced by victims of disasters. Faberow (1977) surveyed a variety of the studies that are still relevant today. These phases are as follows:

Heroic phase	Individuals react to the immediate disaster through positive action, saving not only their own lives but the lives of others. A sense of shared experience, brotherhood, and feelings of altruism are present. This phase may last several weeks. Early crisis-behavior symptoms may develop.
Honeymoon phase	Focus is on rebuilding and regaining a sense of community and control. Expectations are high that organized help is forthcoming. Post-disaster behavioral symptoms are present. This phase may last up to six months.

Disillusionment phase	Individuals experience a loss of community and of a shared experience. Anger may develop from perceived delay or insufficient response to promised help. Emotional and/or behavioral problems may become apparent. This phase may last up to one year.
Reconstruction phase	Victims come to the realization that they alone must act to solve their own problems. Constructive efforts to resolve problems are initiated.

Solomon and Davidson (1997) estimated that about 5% of men and 10% to 12% of women in the United States will experience events in their lifetime resulting in post-traumatic stress disorder. One can only wonder if these percentages will rise in light of the escalating incidences of terrorism in the United States and the world. Since 2003, when the United States entered into the war with Iraq, there have been

Many soldiers have returned from the war with post-traumatic stress disorder.

more than 2,000 American fatalities reported at the time of this writing. As of 2009, the U.S. involvement in Iraq continues. It has long been a fact of war that one sees a dramatic increase in reported post-traumatic stress syndrome from those soldiers and civilians who have had prolonged exposure to the horrors of war. Military studies already indicate that nearly one in five soldiers returning from Iraq struggle with depression, anxiety, or post-traumatic stress disorder. Many veterans suspect that the numbers are much higher (Gettleman, 2006). If the problem is not treated in a timely manner, it can affect many aspects of the person's functioning for a long time, including personal relationships and success in the workplace, as well as creating problems such as drug and alcohol abuse.

The victims of war disasters and terrorism, however, are a small percentage of those who receive aid from human services. Most people who receive help are victims of longstanding social conditions such as poverty, discrimination, and technological change.

POVERTY

Poverty was the norm among the successive waves of immigrants to this country during the nineteenth century. Most immigrants regarded it as a temporary state that could be overcome by hard work and a bit of luck. During the 1800s, this optimism was justified by the dynamic growth of the nation and by the ample space for expansion westward. The enterprising individual had abundant opportunities, and the second generation was expected to surpass their immigrant parents in financial achievement.

In modern times, poverty sometimes tends to persist from one generation to the next. The poverty cycle is perpetuated by the fact that the disadvantages of poverty hinder the next generation's chances to succeed. Poor language skills and a lack of early environmental stimulation may make it difficult for children to take full advantage of educational resources. It becomes difficult for children to develop the skills and attitudes necessary to break out of the poverty cycle.

In past years, being poor did not necessarily mean one was at a greater risk of being homeless, but today, being poor is often one step away from not having a roof over one's head (Neukrug, 2008). Of all social problems, poverty is the one that has received the largest share of attention from social planners. Poverty is a critical problem because so many other problems are linked to it: juvenile delinquency, criminality, drug abuse, and mental illness are disproportionately represented in poor communities. Serious health problems and high rates of infant mortality are also found in poor neighborhoods. Disparities in health tend to fall along income lines everywhere: the poor generally get sicker and die sooner than the rich. But in the United States, the gap between the rich and the poor is far wider than in most other developed democracies, and it is getting wider (Gudraise, 2008). A current indication of hunger is participation in the Food Stamp Program. In May 2008, food stamp participation totaled about 28,400,000 persons, which represents an increase of more than 2 million people from the prior May figure (U.S. Census Bureau, 2008).

Affluent persons are often appalled by the conditions existing in poverty areas and sometimes blame the victims for choosing to live so badly. The poor, on the other hand, think of themselves as having few options and as being trapped by the culture of poverty.

Poverty is particularly a problem in the inner cities although clearly present in the more rural areas as well. Many of the big cities of this country contain decaying neighborhoods occupied mainly by poor households and devastated by arson, vandalism, high **crime** rates, and abandoned housing. Thus, urban areas tend to have a concentration of poor residents who have a great need for services and limited ability to pay for them. Controversy persists about what to do about this immense problem. Some social planners have thrown up their hands and suggested that it is futile to pour any more money into the inner cities. They fear that increased services would only attract more poor people to the cities. Others have proposed that city governments should do everything possible to encourage middle-class people to return to the big cities, thereby providing additional tax revenues, which could be used to benefit the poor population. By and large, however, the inner cities still constitute an enormous reservoir of unmet needs.

In addition to those social planners who have "thrown up their hands" at the plight of the poor in and out of the inner cities, some human services workers have also turned away from helping those living in poverty. Specht and Courtney (1994) comment on this phenomenon and add, "The poor have not gone away; there are more of them now than at any time in recent memory.... Certainly many professional social workers are still committed to the public social services, to helping poor people, and dealing with social problems..." (p. x).

PREJUDICE AND DISCRIMINATION

The problems of poverty, racism, and prejudice are so deeply intertwined in this country that it is difficult to talk about one without referring to the others. **Prejudice** is based on preconceived attitudes and feelings about certain races, religions, or ethnic groups and people of a certain gender. These attitudes reflect negative stereotypes that are often nothing more than simpleminded overgeneralizations about certain groups. Typically, such attitudes are not based on real experience with the group in question but are learned from prejudiced individuals.

Prejudicial attitudes not only attack the self-esteem of victims but are often the basis for **discrimination** in employment, housing, and education. Patterns of discrimination aim to keep certain minorities at the bottom of the economic ladder and in a specific neighborhood or **ghetto**. Although the United States has made progress in reducing discrimination in recent decades, the lingering effects of mistrust are still with us.

Discrimination against African Americans, Latinos, and women is discussed in the following sections. These groups are highlighted because of their large numbers and because of their great importance to human services. Many other groups have been discriminated against as well. Gays and lesbians, the victims of homophobia, continue to fight for equal rights in the workplace, recognition for their relationships, and protection from all forms of discrimination. Probably no other group has been treated with such consistent savagery as Native Americans. Brown's (1971) *Bury My Heart at Wounded Knee* provides a moving account of this shameful episode in American history. At times, Asian Americans have been victimized by the white majority. See the Additional Reading section at the end of the chapter for recommended books on this and related topics.

DISCRIMINATION AGAINST AFRICAN AMERICANS The African American people made slow but definite progress toward equality during the century following emancipation. This was followed by a period of accelerated progress beginning in the mid-1960s. The political initiatives of the 1960s and 1970s, described in Chapter 3, were successful in achieving a higher level of opportunity for African Americans. These positive trends continue to the present day. African Americans are gaining in political power, their income is on the rise, and more are now seeking higher education than ever before. As a result, a small but significant African-American middle class has been established. But it is also clear that much remains to be done. Many people in this ethnic group are still deeply rooted in poverty and deprivation. Per capita unemployment is significantly higher among African Americans than whites, and African-American teenagers have high rates of unemployment. A Census Bureau report confirmed that more African Americans are getting a piece of the American dream—finishing their educations and finding good jobs.

Among the social and ethnic groups, African-American households had the lowest median income in 2007 ($33,916), compared to the median of $54,920 for non-Hispanic, white households. Also, 24.5% of African Americans were living in poverty compared to 8.2% of non-Hispanic whites (*Federal Register*, 2009).

DISCRIMINATION AGAINST LATINOS Spanish-speaking Americans have also been victims of a pervasive pattern of discrimination that limits their opportunities for advancement. Virtually every indicator of well-being reflects the results of this discrimination: Their unemployment rates tend to be high, their health is not as good on average as that of whites, and their educational achievement scores tend to be low, partly because of the language barrier (Freeman, Jones, & Zucker, 1979).

Although Latinos are a smaller group than African Americans in the United States, it is difficult to determine their precise number. Included in their ranks are a large but unknown number of undocumented immigrants. Migrant workers are another group not usually included in census surveys.

In any case, Latinos cannot be considered a homogeneous group. Some can trace their ancestry back to the origins of this country and are well established in their communities. Many others are recent immigrants who came here looking for work. Those who came from Mexico tend to be concentrated in the Southwest, whereas Puerto Ricans tend to live along the East Coast. Many Cubans have settled in the greater Miami area. Other Spanish-speaking people have come here from Central and South America. The tendency of these various subgroups to retain their separate identities has frustrated efforts to join together to advance political and economic objectives. The recession of 2009 has hit Latino immigrants especially hard. They have suffered more job losses than most other workers, and their earnings remain lower than those of other groups. Among foreign-born Latinos, an estimated 47% are undocumented immigrants. Although some of these immigrants have been pushed by the economic slump to leave the United States, most have stayed and are struggling to hold on to jobs (Preston, 2009).

One group in urgent need of help is the migrant workers who follow the harvest from south to north along the Pacific Coast. The plight of these workers, who are mostly of Mexican origin, has been publicized in books, movies, and magazine articles. However, they have not benefited greatly from this media attention. They work for low pay and are often provided with filthy, substandard housing. The state laws regarding living conditions are sometimes ignored because of official indifference and corruption. Even today, they are very often exploited not only by the growers but also by recruiters who take a percentage of their wages. Perhaps the best hope of improving their living conditions comes from the increasing strength of agricultural unions.

Undocumented immigrants are another group in need of assistance. Although illegal workers come from Ireland, the Caribbean, Asia, and poor countries all over the globe, the great majority are Spanish speaking, with Mexicans making up the largest single subgroup. They may be employed in agriculture, the garment industry, factories, hotels, restaurants, gas stations, and many other settings. For the most part, they get the jobs that are dirty, demeaning, boring, offer little hope of advancement, and pay badly to boot (Crewdson, 1983). They typically lack union representation and do not usually receive sick leave, insurance benefits, or other fringe benefits. Their illegal status makes them easy prey for unscrupulous employers. These conditions still exist. To make matters worse, many American citizens resent their presence and blame them for taking away scarce jobs. Moreover, their position in this country has been made even more precarious by subsequent legislation.

The Immigration Reform and Control Act of 1986, the most important piece of legislation pertaining to immigration in decades, attempted to deal with the problem of illegal immigration by granting amnesty to undocumented aliens living continuously in the United States since January 1, 1982, and to agricultural workers if they worked here for at least three months between May 1985 and May 1986. The act also provides stiff penalties for employers who hire **undocumented workers**. In 1991 the federal government admitted that the 1986 law has not stopped the influx of illegal workers (Pear, 1991).

These workers are ineligible for welfare or other services sponsored by the government for the benefit of U.S. citizens, but they are periodically accused of taking advantage of these services anyway. The evidence reviewed by Crewdson (1983) suggests that they use social services far less than do American citizens. They tend to shy away from contact with authorities and sometimes even avoid services that are legally available to them. For example, they are sometimes reluctant to seek medical treatment except in emergency circumstances.

Unfortunately, the reluctance of many illegal immigrants to seek medical treatment poses a serious public health problem in southern California and other areas of high concentration of such immigrants, because they suffer higher rates of infectious disease than do American citizens. Obviously, these workers are not examined for communicable diseases before entering the country. They may seek help from agricultural unions, immigrant fraternal organizations, and church-sponsored helping agencies. For the most part, however, these private agencies do not have the resources to provide more than temporary emergency help for some of those who need it.

During the past decade, there were signs of increasingly negative attitudes toward the estimated 4 million illegal immigrants in this country (Verhovek, 1994).

This trend was most pronounced in states with large illegal populations, such as Florida and California. During 1994, Governor Lawton Chiles of Florida sued the federal government, asking for more than $1 billion in reimbursement for services it had been required to give illegal aliens. Governor Chiles, a Democrat, said the people of Florida were tired of spending huge amounts on services, education, medical care, and welfare for illegal aliens. In addition, there were the considerable additional expenses involved in jailing illegal aliens who committed crimes in the state. He argued that Florida was paying for the apparent inability of the U.S. government to protect its borders ("U.S. is sued over aliens," 1994).

California voters passed Proposition 187 during the election of 1994. This initiative, strongly backed by Governor Pete Wilson, would have cut off most government services to illegal aliens. Specifically, the measure would deny welfare, nonemergency medical treatment, and public schooling to this group.

There was no immediate impact from the law because federal and state judges blocked enforcement pending a review. Nevertheless, the passage of the measure illustrates the fact that Americans are becoming increasingly reluctant to provide services to these people. Although it is true that illegal immigrants contribute to the American economy, data provided by the Texas Office of Immigration suggest that on balance they cost more than they contribute in tax revenues. The greatest expense by far is associated with public schooling for the children of illegal immigrants.

The issue of illegal immigration raises important questions for class discussion:

- Should we as a nation put a stop to further illegal immigration? If so, how can we do this? If not, why not?
- Governor Pete Wilson favored a constitutional amendment that would deny citizenship to the children of illegal immigrants. What would be the consequences of such a step?

WOMEN'S ISSUES   We do not have definite knowledge of the status of women in prehistory (that is, before the development of written records). During the late 1800s, a number of authors advanced the idea that women tended to be dominant in some early societies; goddesses were worshipped, and women controlled religion, property, and marriage. These authors offered various explanations for the shift to male dominance that they supposed to have gradually taken place. Feminist authors attempted to bolster their current agendas by asserting that male dominance was culturally imposed and should be ended. Others argued that the evidence for matriarchies, or female-controlled societies, was not convincing and that males had always been dominant.

Feminist historians Anderson and Zinsser (1988) reviewed these writings and concluded that, simply, not very much is known about the relationships between men and women in early societies. There is no reason to believe that either male or female dominance was universal in prehistory. Nor can it be concluded that women's traditional role of giving birth and nurturing children was viewed as secondary or unimportant by members of early societies.

What is certain is that women were clearly subordinate by the time written records began to appear. How did this happen? Based on a survey of many early cultures, anthropologist Sanday (1981) concluded that as the number of early societies grew, they began to compete with one another for scarce resources. As war and forced migration became the means of survival, women began to assume a subordinate role to men. Physically stronger on the average, males were expected to be more active and aggressive than women. Weapons skills were taught to male children. Once warfare is present, a woman needs protection from other warriors, especially if she is pregnant or caring for an infant or young child. In warrior cultures, men came to be viewed as more valuable and important than women (Anderson & Zinsser, 1988).

Female subordination was enshrined in the earliest and most sacred writings of the Greek, Roman, Hebrew, Germanic, and Celtic cultures. This idea passed intact to the emerging European culture and was later embodied in Christian beliefs (Anderson & Zinsser, 1988). Women were generally excluded from important activities such as warfare, politics, philosophy, and even the study of sacred books. In the fourth century B.C., Aristotle proclaimed that the male is naturally superior to the female. (He also believed that women had fewer teeth than men.) In the first century A.D., Jewish men in their morning prayers thanked God for not having been made women.

Although there had always been women who believed in equal rights for women, it wasn't until the 1800s that they developed effective organizations to achieve this goal. In part, the move to organize was a reaction against changes in law, government, and the economy that were limiting women's options still further. Significant progress was made by women's movements in both Europe and the United States. Most women in affluent Western nations now enjoy full rights of citizenship, including the right to vote, have access to higher education, and enjoy significantly widened employment opportunities.

In past generations, women in this country were discouraged from entering certain jobs or careers. For example, mechanical work, physical sciences, administration, engineering, and police work have traditionally been considered male provinces. Females have been regarded as more suited to clerical and secretarial jobs as well as certain nurturing professions such as nursing and social work. During the past three decades, many occupations, professions, clubs, associations, and government positions—once reserved for men—were opened to women. Although it is true that one in five of all working women holds a secretarial or clerical job, it is also evident that women now make up a majority in a wide range of professions that were once male dominated (Roberts, 1995).

Although there has been an opening up in nontraditional areas, many women are still choosing nurturing professions. About 1 in 20 female workers is a schoolteacher, a proportion that hasn't changed much since 1940. Nursing continues to be a predominantly female profession, and the majority of psychologists are now women. Add to this the increasing role of women in other medical professions and their continued dominance in social work and it becomes obvious that women are the major providers of human services.

For a variety of reasons, women generally still earn less than men within a given job category. One reason is that women tend to have shorter job tenures than men because of their roles as mothers and homemakers. Women also tend to work more often at part-time jobs than men. The third reason is **sexism**, a pattern of discrimination against women. Some women activists have discerned a disturbing pattern: when women begin to dominate a field, the pay and prestige begin to go down (Roberts, 1995). There may be some truth to this idea, but there are also other reasons (detailed in Chapter 2) why salary levels have tended to stagnate in the human services field.

Perhaps even more significant than the movement of women into jobs once held by males is the great increase in the number of women who work outside the home. This has been called "one of the great transformations" in American society (Peterson, 1994, p. 140). Today, 60.2% of all American women aged 16 to 65 are in the labor force compared to 74.7% of the men (U.S. Bureau of Labor Statistics, 2001). Among younger workers, there are almost as many women in the workforce as men.

The women's movement, which did much to change attitudes about the role of women, is one factor that helped create this great change in American life. Although only a small percentage of women belong to activist groups such as the National Organization for Women (NOW), the basic concepts of the movement have become part of the thinking of many American men and women (Mehr, 1995, p. 281). The final victory of the movement was supposed to be passage of the Equal Rights Amendment to the Constitution, which would have made a person's sex an irrelevant distinction under the law. Although the amendment passed both houses of Congress in 1972, it failed to win ratification from the required three-quarters of state legislatures. A coalition of groups, composed overwhelmingly of women, fought against ratification. Apparently, the women's movement did not represent all women. Some continued to desire a traditional gender role of homemaker and mother (Finsterbusch & McKenna, 1994, p. 43). Therefore, there is some reason to believe that a significant number of women are not happy with the changes brought about, in part, by contemporary feminism.

A majority of women told Gallup in 1994 that the women's movement is hurting relations between the sexes. When asked whether the changes in women's lives have made life easier or harder than they were 20 years ago, 48% responded that life was now harder. Gallup polls also showed that large majorities believed that it is now harder for marriages to be successful, and a whopping 82% believed it is now harder for parents to raise children ("Has feminism made lives harder?" 1995). Another source of opposition directed at the feminist movement is based on the tendency of radical feminists to downgrade the traditional roles of women, viewing homemaking as mere drudgery.

QUESTIONS FOR CLASS DISCUSSION OR SPECIAL ASSIGNMENT

- What are the potential effects on human services of the changes in American society just discussed? Specifically, what sort of problems and challenges can be anticipated if a large majority of women continue to join the workforce?
- What might be the effect on children in a family in which both parents work?

Social Change

Americans are gradually changing their attitudes toward the poor and minority groups. Actually, this change is only one aspect of what amounts to a revolution in customs and attitudes that has taken place in the last few decades. One major trend has been a liberalization of attitudes toward sexual behavior. Homosexuals are pressing for social acceptance of their sexual orientation. Sex is more openly discussed than ever before, and premarital sexual relations are accepted by many teenagers. At the same time, women are challenging traditional roles, and there is much public discussion of alternative lifestyles. The rapid pace of social change, particularly during the late 1960s and early 1970s, has stimulated a conservative reaction that aims to preserve traditional social roles and customs. For example, members of the so-called Moral Majority championed a return to values based on fundamentalist religious beliefs.

Without taking sides in these controversies, it can be noted that the rapid pace of these developments has created a sense of insecurity in many individuals.

THE CHANGING AMERICAN FAMILY   Family therapists have observed an important change in the American family during the past several decades: The family is no longer organized primarily around child rearing (Carter & McGoldrick, 1989). The lower birthrate, longer life expectancy, and divorce and remarriage rates are some of the contributing factors. In the past, the lives of women were linked to their roles in child-rearing activities. Now, as previously noted, more women are entering the labor market and are developing personal goals and an identity apart from the home.

Women who choose primary career goals may find themselves wrestling with a severe conflict. For men, the goals of family and career are parallel, but for women, the goals are more likely to conflict (Carter & McGoldrick, 1989). This conflict is due to the perception that the primary responsibility for child care still rests with women. The traditional view that expects women to assume primary emotional responsibility for family relationships runs counter to the demands of a job or career. It is not surprising that more women than men seek counseling during the child-rearing years.

If it is true that child rearing no longer occupies center stage in family life, then what does? The new priority has been identified by some writers as individualism. This is the belief that people should seek their own happiness, develop their capacities to the fullest, and fulfill their own needs and desires.

In other words, the interests of the individual man and woman are taking precedence over the interests of the family. These personal goals are often centered around personal prestige, success, and the accumulation of material possessions. These values are by no means peculiar to the United States and may be found in many Western developed nations. In contrast, Eastern nations, such as India, are more likely to be organized around the family as the primary focus of daily life. An individual's identity is thus likely to be bound up with the family—usually the **extended family**.

Some social critics have expressed concern that children are becoming a liability to their parents. The millions of children not covered by health insurance are an example. Once cherished, children are now more likely to be merely tolerated by adults. In the worst cases, as described in the next chapter, children may be seriously abused or neglected. Social scientists have noted an emerging trend focused on the decade between the late teens and the late twenties. Some have characterized this period of time as a new addition to the developmental life cycle re "emerging adulthood." Studies indicate the average college student no years or more to graduate, often dropping in and out of school, relatic jobs and often times returning back home (Hulbert, 2005). This new transitional stage, if the trend continues, will clearly affect the expectations and structure of the American family.

Here is a brief listing of some of the changes in living arrangements and family structure that have taken place in recent years:

- Young women are more likely than their mothers were to live on their own rather than going right from school into marriage.
- An increasing percentage of the population of couples are living together, and sometimes having children, without marrying.
- An increasing percentage of women will never marry or have children.
- A little less than half of marriages end in divorce.
- Whether by choice or necessity, in present-day marriages both husband and wife are working.
- There has been a large increase in single-parent households in recent years.
- The number of homosexual people openly living together has also risen.

ECONOMIC AND POLITICAL FACTORS

Dramatic changes have taken place since the 1970s in the way income is distributed in the United States. In 1950, the very rich were a small number of elite professionals, bankers, and business leaders. Fewer than 1 million American families earned as much as $60,000. But by 1980, 2.7 million households counted incomes of more than $100,000, and by 1993, this fortunate group had doubled to 5.6 million households. At the same time, nearly 1 million households were enjoying incomes of over $200,000. "Nothing like this immense crowd of wealthy people has been seen in the history of the planet," commented a *New York Times* editorialist (Frum, 1995, p. A15). "This is the first time in history that we have had a mass upper class."

Unfortunately, most Americans today do not share in this great income surge. The proportion of American families earning less than $25,000, about 40%, has remained the same for 20 years (Frum, 1995). And the income of average families, adjusted for inflation, has remained about the same since the early 1970s.

Why were some able to do extremely well in the economic expansion of recent decades, whereas others are barely holding their own? It appears that highly educated, computer-literate workers, skilled in the art of manipulating information, are doing well in the current economy. However, people with limited education find themselves placed in jeopardy by far-reaching developments in the global economy (Peterson, 1994). Secretary of Labor Robert Reich, then in the Clinton administration, put it succinctly when he said, "If you are well prepared, technology is your friend; if you are not well prepared, technology is your enemy" (quoted in Simon, 1995, p. 959).

American workers are in essence competing against workers in other countries who are often paid less than them. Routine production work in manufacturing and in data processing can be—and is—done almost anywhere around the world. "So routine workers in advanced economies like the United States find themselves in competition with low-paid workers in Third World nations," explains Peterson (1994, p. 125). This competition is exerting downward pressure on the wages of unskilled workers. Along with these trends went a loss of power on the part of trade unions who formerly acted to protect the wages and working conditions of members. In a climate of global competition, an increase in pay for an American worker might place the company at a competitive disadvantage. In any case, the employer could hold out the threat of relocating overseas if wage demands were pressed.

Many skilled American workers can no longer find industrial employment at all and are seeking "traditional underclass jobs" as janitors, warehouse loaders, cleaners, and security guards. This trend exerts downward pressure on unskilled workers who face a tighter job market or are being pushed out into the cold. They may then join a large group of discouraged workers who no longer seek regular employment. The unemployed or marginally employed population is elaborated on in the next chapter. What do these trends mean for America's working poor? The fact is that millions of families hold two or three jobs but still can't afford the necessities of life. According to the U.S. Bureau of Labor Statistics, in 2001, there were over 7.5 million individuals holding more than one job.

Millions of people are just getting by, one crisis away from disaster. A crisis might be an illness to one person in the family, an unexpected loss or injury, or losing a job. The estimated 10 million working poor in the country are victims of global competition, as previously discussed. They are also being replaced by automated, programmed machines that require little human supervision. For example, robots are now doing welding and assembly jobs once done by human beings. Many of the working poor are now stuck in service jobs that take up so much time and energy that resuming education seems like an impossible dream. They are not eligible for government-sponsored training programs, do not receive free day care for their children, and often do not have medical insurance or retirement benefits. They constitute a large group, vulnerable to destitution, receiving little or no help from human services. It is becoming more difficult for them to move up the economic ladder and easier to slip into homelessness or welfare dependence.

The implications of these data are disturbing to human services workers. The trend is clearly in the direction of a two-tier society, with the very rich separated from the great mass of struggling poor people. The large number of very rich, coupled with the influence that their money assures, gives them increasing power in the political arena. The danger is that they may neglect the interests of their less affluent fellow citizens. We may slip into the situation that prevails in many poor developing countries: the poor simply do without the basic services that are considered essential in affluent nations.

PSYCHOLOGICAL STRESS

The large-scale problems just described have their final impact on individuals. In our complex, rapidly changing culture, it is probable that an individual will sometimes be frustrated in trying to meet the needs described at the beginning of this chapter. All kinds of obstacles, including prejudice, poverty, and other factors just reviewed, can stand in the way of fulfilling needs. Typically, disadvantaged people are preoccupied with basic survival needs, whereas the more affluent are concerned with higher needs relating to self-esteem and fulfillment of creative urges. To some extent, everyone experiences the pressure of these needs, and this is one important source of psychological stress.

Stress is sometimes defined as the strain imposed on an individual by threatening life events. However, it has been found that some desirable events, such as job promotion, may also impose strain on the individual. Bloom (1984) covers both possibilities by defining stressful life events as "those external events that make adaptive demands on a person" (p. 244). These events may be successfully handled or, in some instances, may lead to illness or psychological breakdown.

A team of researchers studied life events that occurred shortly before the onset of serious illness (Holmes & Rahe, 1967; Rahe, 1979; Rahe & Arthur, 1978). They developed a list of 43 life events and scaled them in terms of how much stress they evoke. Although the study took place years ago, the data are still relevant. The list is reprinted here as Table 1.1.

It is not particularly surprising that death of a spouse ranks as the most stressful kind of event. But it is surprising that joyful life events such as marriage or marital reconciliation prove to be more stressful than financial catastrophes such as bankruptcy or mortgage foreclosure. All of the events listed in Table 1.1 have one feature in common: They require a person to adjust to a change in his or her life situation.

It is not only major life events that have an effect on physical health but also the ordinary hassles of daily life. **Daily hassles** are those apparently minor events that can make you tense, frustrated, and irritable. Losing your wallet, getting involved in a minor car accident, and waiting in long lines are just a few of the bothersome situations that interrupt the smooth flow of daily events. When hassles take place frequently over an extended period, they can have a negative impact on health and well-being. In fact, one team of researchers reported that hassles far outweigh major life events in predicting psychological and somatic symptoms (Lazarus & Folkman, 1984, p. 312).

Some people are better able to tolerate stress than others. Stress tolerance is partly dependent on the amount of emotional support one receives from other people. This is why divorce or death of a loved one is particularly stressful; it leaves the victim to face the situation without familiar supports.

Certain personality traits also play a role in how a person handles stress. Kobasa (1979), for example, studied how a person can remain healthy in the face of great stress. She reported that those who do so have a clear sense of their values, goals, and capabilities; a strong tendency toward active involvement with the environment; and a belief in their capacity to control and transform life experiences. Longitudinal studies have consistently found correlations between a person's level of happiness and his or her longevity. The participants in these studies vary widely, including 180 nuns from the School Sisters of Notre Dame in Milwaukee, Wisconsin (Danner, Snowden, & Friesen, 2001), 2,282 senior citizen Mexican Americans in the Southwest (Ostir, Markides, Black, & Goodwin, 2002), and 255 medical students (Williams, Barefoot, & Shekelle, 1985).

TABLE I.I | SOCIAL READJUSTMENT RATING SCALE

Life Event	Stress Value
Death of spouse	100
Divorce	73
Marital separation	65
Jail term	63
Death of close family member	63
Personal injury or illness	53
Marriage	50
Fired at work	47
Marital reconciliation	45
Retirement	45
Change in health of family member	44
Pregnancy	40
Sex difficulties	39
Gain of a new family member	39
Business adjustment	39
Change in financial state	38
Death of a close friend	37
Change to a different line of work	36
Change in number of arguments with spouse	35
Mortgage or loan for major purchase (home, etc.)	31
Foreclosure of mortgage or loan	30
Change in responsibilities at work	29
Son or daughter leaving home	29
Trouble with in-laws	29
Outstanding personal achievement	28
Wife begins or stops work	26
Begin or end school	26
Change in living conditions	25
Revision of personal habits	24
Trouble with boss	23
Change in work hours or conditions	20
Change in residence	20
Change in school	20
Change in recreation	19

(*continued*)

TABLE 1.1 | CONTINUED

Life Event	Stress Value
Change in church activities	19
Change in social activities	18
Mortgage or loan for lesser purchase (car, TV, etc.)	17
Change in sleeping habits	16
Change in number of family get-togethers	15
Change in eating habits	15
Vacation	13
Christmas	12
Minor violations of the law	11

Source: Reprinted by permission of the publisher from "The Social Readjustment Rating Scale" by T. H. Holmes and R. H. Rahe, 1967, *Journal of Psychosomatic Research, 11,* 213–218. Copyright © 1967 by Elsevier Science.

Also referred to as "subjective well-being," happiness has been found to affect individuals' responses to life stress (Seligman, 2002) and is theorized to be composed of the following three variables: (a) a person's set range (about 50% of a person's level of happiness is thought to be influenced by the happiness levels of his or her parents); (b) the circumstances of one's life; and (c) the factors that are under one's voluntary control (such as a person's level of optimism and hope and the tendency to compartmentalize problems rather than to allow them to have wide-ranging effects).

DEVELOPMENTAL CRISES

Psychological stress is intensified at certain phases of a person's development or maturation. This kind of stress is the unavoidable consequence of moving from one phase of development to the next. The stages of development include the prenatal period, infancy, childhood, puberty, adolescence, young adulthood, middle age, old age, and death. During each transition from one stage to the next, a person is subjected to novel challenges and tasks that tend to increase anxiety. The changes might involve new responsibilities, bodily alterations, and new ways of relating to others. For example, the individual entering young adulthood has reached physical maturity and is expected to make serious plans for a career and to begin serious sexual relationships. The major thrust of a person's activities is toward the achievement of independent, self-supporting status. With support and nurturance from others, most are able to master the demands of the new phase successfully.

However, developmental stresses can overwhelm some individuals, particularly those whose needs for support and nurturance are not being met. There is a wide variation in how people react to developmental transitions. What is a crisis for one may be an interesting challenge for another. A crisis occurs when an individual feels overwhelmed by the demands of the next phase of development. If a person is completely unable to master the requirements of the next developmental stage, further growth is prevented. The consequences of this failure may range from temporary emotional disturbance to serious disorganization of personality.

During recent decades, there has been a marked change in attitudes of human services workers toward people in crisis. It is now accepted that people may become anxious or upset during transitions in development and that such reactions are not necessarily a sign of serious mental illness. Hoff (1978) points out that modern crisis **theory** has established a new approach to people with such problems. It is no longer assumed that they are completely irrational or that they cannot help themselves. Furthermore, it is becoming more accepted that it does not require a highly trained psychotherapist to help people get through a crisis. Counselors, police officers, nurses, laypersons with training in crisis intervention, and family members can be very helpful in getting someone through a difficult developmental phase. A more detailed discussion of crisis intervention follows in Chapter 5.

THE CRISIS IN HEALTH CARE

The health care system in the United States has become a major source of public concern in recent years. An editorial that appeared in the *American Journal of Public Health* charged that this country lacks a coherent national health policy and that the system has become indifferent to the real health needs of society (Sultz, 1991, p. 418). Sultz called for the creation of a network of health services that will care humanely for the poor, the sick, the elderly, and the most vulnerable Americans. We are falling far short of this goal. Although this country spends more on health on a per capita basis than does any other developed nation, millions of Americans do not have access to affordable health care. According to the Census Bureau, in 1999, there were 43.4 million people in the United States without health insurance (Kilborn, 1999). Herbert (1998) points out that among the 74 million children under the age of 18, over 20 million do not have access to adequate health care, and over 11 million are without insurance.

One of the major problems is that the costs of health care are running out of control. In 1999, the total National Health Expenditure, which includes building hospitals, clinics, and the cost of training medical personnel, was $1.2 trillion (U.S. Centers for Medicare and Medicaid Services, 2001). Why are costs so high? Here are some factors that play a role:

- The increasing costs of malpractice suits brought against providers are passed along to the consumer.
- The fear of malpractice leads to the practice of defensive medicine. To protect against being charged with malpractice, the doctor is likely to call for every test and diagnostic procedure that could possibly apply to a given case.
- Technological advances have led to the development of extremely costly medical equipment.
- Treatment is now available for some diseases (for example, kidney failure) that were formerly untreatable and, possibly, terminal.
- The administrative costs of processing millions of insurance claims are considerable.

- Owing in part to the fact that Americans are living longer, there is a large and growing population of people with chronic diseases.
- The costs of treating patients with acquired immune deficiency syndrome (AIDS) have added greatly to the strain on the system.

Another difficulty is that our system (if it can be called that) has become very complex and unwieldy. Many other developed nations provide medical care through a unified system of government-operated clinics and hospitals. In contrast, we provide health care via a bewildering mix of public and private facilities funded by a large number of private and government insurance programs. The government insurance programs, chiefly **medicare** for the elderly and medicaid for the poor, provide limited coverage to millions of Americans but do not cover the majority of working people. Many workers receive medical coverage instead as a fringe benefit of employment, usually through a private insurance company. The extent of coverage varies greatly, often with a single carrier offering a range of policies to choose from. Of course, the more limited the coverage, the more that must be paid out of pocket by the patient. The physician and patient are typically confronted with complex fee schedules detailing how much is to be paid for each medical procedure. Increasingly, insurance companies and HMOs are questioning doctors' judgments, particularly with regard to costly procedures. There is a chorus of complaints about the forms to be filled out and the difficulties involved in trying to deal with the impersonal bureaucracies that administer the programs.

Many people fall through the gaps in this network of coverage. When medical insurance is linked to employment, workers may lose it if they are laid off or fired from the job. Part-time workers, low-paid workers, and those employed by small firms are often without medical insurance at all. These people are in a serious dilemma; they can afford neither to buy their own insurance nor to pay for any extended medical treatment. Consequently, they put off doctor visits as long as possible and may end up in emergency rooms, being treated for a condition that has become serious or life-threatening through neglect. All too often, the emergency room is replacing the family doctor's office at a greatly increased expense. Furthermore, HMOs have increasingly dropped poor patients due to the lack of profit.

Another criticism of our health care delivery system is that it tends to emphasize treatment rather than prevention. Most health care providers define successful treatment as the elimination of disease. Physicians understandably give precedence to a patient with existing symptoms rather than to a healthy patient who wants a program of diet and exercise.

CANADIAN NATIONAL HEALTH PLAN: A MODEL FOR THE UNITED STATES?

The citizens of Canada are beneficiaries of one of the most comprehensive health insurance programs in the world. The plan uses provincial (provinces are like our states) tax money, supplemented by federal funds, to provide medical care to everyone at no charge. All medical care is free, including long-term home care and nursing home care in many provinces. There are no bills, and patients pay no money to doctors; the doctors bill the government. By and large, the doctors are satisfied with the system, although there have been battles with the government over fees. Doctors' charges for services are lower than in the United States, but so are administrative expenses and malpractice premiums (Rosenthal, 1991). Incredibly, the system provides health care to all at less cost than the U.S. system.

It sounds good, but, as in the U.S. health system, there are some disadvantages. The level of care is probably not as good for wealthy Canadians as that received by wealthy people in this country. There are sometimes waits for tests and treatment, and the system is slow to buy expensive new machines and procedures. Advanced diagnostic equipment is in short supply, and patients in both countries may have to travel in order to benefit from this equipment. Also, wealthy Canadians do not enjoy the same ready access to specialists as do wealthy Americans. The ratio of specialists to general practitioners is 1:1 in the United States compared to 1:4 in Canada.

The basic advantage of the Canadian system is that everyone is covered; the patient's financial status is never an issue. In the United States, there is a much greater variation in the level of care, depending on a person's income and resources. As we have seen, millions of people in the United States have no medical coverage at all, whereas the wealthy have available the latest in advanced medical technology.

THE EXAMPLE OF THE FEDERAL EMPLOYEE HEALTH SYSTEM   Another alternative is to model a nationwide health care system on the Federal Employees Health system, which covers nearly 10 million employees, retirees, and their dependents (Butler, 1993). Under this plan, the workers decide for themselves what services they want. Once a year, they receive information on a menu of perhaps two dozen insurance plans available to them where they live. The cost of premiums, the services covered, and the out-of-pocket expenses are all described in detail. The workers pay about one-third of the premium for whatever plan is selected, with the government paying the rest. The government has nothing to do with setting the prices or determining the benefits package.

One clear advantage is that costs are held down not by government regulation but by the competitive nature of this approach. Each insurer wants to attract clients to its program and tries to offer the most benefits for the least expense. The problem comes in with persons who have no employer to pick up the premium. In the case of a worker who was recently laid off, for example, the government would have to pay the entire tab. The costs would be considerable and would be added to the expenses already covered by medicaid and medicare.

MANAGED CARE

Managed care is an umbrella term for health care insurance systems that contract with a network of hospitals, clinics, and private providers (doctors, therapists, and so forth) who agree to accept set fees for each service or flat payments per patient. Managed care involves patient care that is not determined solely by the provider. It is estimated that managed-care organizations administer between 70% and 80% of the group health insurance coverage provided today in the United States.

The growth of managed care developed primarily from the government's response to the soaring costs of health care and the need for greater accountability to control these escalating costs. Over the past 10 years, the managed-care system has had a major impact on the delivery of human services. Reactions are varied. Some professional groups view managed care as a threat to their autonomy in setting their own fees and controlling their own course of treatment. They criticize the insurers for frequently providing only limited or assembly-line service and for intruding into the doctor-patient relationship. Other professional groups have found that managed care offers greater opportunities and a new and additional source of patient referrals.

To control and maintain cost, managed-care insurers often utilize the external review process. In this approach, before a major service can be provided or a professional reimbursed for a course of treatment, the managed-care organization must review the requested course of treatment. This often involves a peer review, provided by the insurer, of the proposed course of treatment to find the least expensive level of care that will satisfy the patient's needs. Those conducting external reviews often seek answers to the following questions:

- What is the problem?
- What is the proposed treatment?
- Why is the proposed treatment recommended?
- What evidence supports use of the proposed treatment?
- Is the recommended care cost effective?

If a visit to a provider is for minor or routine treatment, the provider or client need not initially contact the managed-care organization for approval as long as the treatment follows the preset managed-care guidelines. Additional features of the managed-care approach emphasize early detection and treatment, preauthorization for hospital admission, and continuous-care management. A vigilant and continuous management review helps the managed-care organization to insure that the treatment guidelines have been followed and to monitor the effectiveness and cost of service.

It must be remembered that most managed-care systems are profit-making organizations. The need to make a profit often creates conflicts and problems within the organizations and for the consumers. Loss of income, for example, has moved HMOs to drop poor and elderly members. Pear (1998) reports that potentially 300,000 beneficiaries could be dropped. The role of the case manager is examined more closely in Chapter 5. Several different kinds of managed care plans are available:

HMO: The health maintenance organization is the most highly structured, providing comprehensive health services for a fixed prepaid rate. Some HMOs have their own clinics, whereas others have a "panel" or network of independent doctors. Care is coordinated by a primary-care doctor or "gatekeeper." The main advantage is that costs are relatively low. The owners of small- or medium-sized businesses may find that this is the least expensive way of providing workers with medical coverage. The disadvantage is that patients are limited to the HMO's clinics and providers. If they go out of network, they must pay the costs out of pocket.

PPO: Preferred provider organizations are groups of doctors and hospitals that agree to provide health services at a fixed rate. The prospective patient is usually given a list of providers and may go directly to any of them. There is no gatekeeper or individual to coordinate care. Typically, the patient must pay a modest copayment fee for the service.

POS: Point-of-service plans also have networks of providers, but patients may seek treatment outside of the network if they are willing to pay a greater share of the cost. POS plans are becoming increasingly popular because patients need not forfeit their freedom to choose their doctors and hospitals. Some traditional HMOs, such as Kaiser Permanente, have started to offer a point-of-service option. Coverage for out-of-network benefits varies from plan to plan; for example, some pay 70% of what the HMO considers a "reasonable and customary" fee, which is generally less than the actual charge (Durkin, 1995).

The recent growth of managed-care plans is due to the fact that it was hoped they would provide a means of controlling the escalating costs of medical care. While rising costs have slowed down, other problems have been created. As previously stated, these plans are sometimes criticized for providing limited or assembly-line service and for intruding into the doctor-patient relationship. Furthermore, it is beginning to be recognized that many of the hoped-for goals of managed-care programs have not been reached. Kilborn (1998a) points out that they are entrenched in the economy and provide a different way to pay for care but not a better way to provide it. Many of the problems predicted by the opponents of managed care, such as denied, delayed, and inadequate medical care, have been realized. The rapid growth of managed-care programs has created such problems and is presently a major concern.

SUMMARY

The United States monitors its economic health by means of a sophisticated system of indicators that provide a basis for informed discussion about economic activity. In contrast, we do a relatively poor job of monitoring our social health. As Miringoff (1995) points out, social indicators appear less often and are assessed in isolation with no context or connection. Poverty, for example, is reported once a year and teenage suicide every two years. There are no national measures of homelessness and illiteracy. The Fordham Institute for Innovation in Social Policy has published an annual Index of Social Health for the United States. Although not as precise as our measures of economic health, it certainly represents a significant advance in social monitoring. The index consists of 16 social indicators, including infant mortality, child abuse, poverty, teenage suicide, drug abuse, unemployment, homicide rates, and others (Miringoff).

The results reveal a sharp decline in America's social health. The decline was due to increased numbers of children in poverty, increased child abuse and teenage suicide, lower average weekly wages, increased homicide rates, a widening gap between rich and poor, and other factors. It is clear that an increasing number of people need help from human services. It is therefore ironic, and troubling, that several trends are acting to reduce support for human services at this time. The huge deficits run up by the federal government were partly responsible for this predicament. The federal government spends more paying interest on the national debt than it does on all state and local governments combined. This payment does not build a single building, create a single job, or feed a single person (Cuomo, 1994, p. 5). The impact on human services is enormous because the debt severely limits our ability to fund services adequately and, at the same time, makes our social problems worse. Another trend is the belief on the part of some policymakers that human services programs are adding to our problems.

This may indeed be a time for honest self-examination by service providers. The criticisms of human services need to be taken seriously. Some agencies may in fact be bloated with political appointees and administrators who provide no useful services to anybody. Although we recognize the need for greater accountability and cost-effectiveness on the part of agencies, we are greatly concerned about the potential dangers of undisciplined cutting of essential services. As people fall through the safety net, they are more likely to become dysfunctional, unstable, and, possibly, violent. Human services are essential to a civil, well-ordered society. A failure to provide important services in a timely fashion is often counterproductive because more serious problems may be created. In the chapters that follow, many specific examples of this process are offered.

ADDITIONAL READING

Brody, R. (2005). *Effectively managing human service organizations* (3rd ed.). Los Angeles: CA: Sage.

Hacker, A. (1992). *Two nations: Black and white, separate, hostile, unequal.* New York: Scribner's.

Himmelfarb, G. (1995). *The de-moralization of society: From Victorian virtues to modern values.* New York: Knopf.

Kahn, W. J. (1999). *The a-b-cs of human experience: An integrated model.* Belmont, CA: Brooks/Cole, Wadsworth.

Katz, M. B. (2000). *The price of citizenship: Redefining the American welfare state.* New York: Henry Holt.

Lott, B. (1994). *Women's lives: Themes and variations in gender learning* (2nd ed.). Pacific Grove, CA: Brooks/Cole.

Luttwak, E. (1993). *The endangered American dream.* New York: Simon & Schuster.

Magnet, M. (1993). *The dream and the nightmare: The sixties' legacy to the underclass.* New York: Morrow.

Peterson, W. C. (1994). *Silent depression: The fate of the American dream.* New York: Norton.

Schaefer, R. T. (1995). *Race and ethnicity in the United States.* New York: Harper-Collins.

Unger, R., & Crawford, M. (1992). *Women and gender: A feminist psychology.* New York: McGraw-Hill.

Zastrow, C. (2000). *Social issues and solutions.* Belmont, CA: Wadsworth.

Zinn, H. (1999). *A people's history of the United States.* New York: Perennial Classics.

REFERENCES

Adamy, J. (2009, May 24). Mullen: U.S. is on schedule in Iraq. *The Wall Street Journal,* http://online.wsj.com

Alle-Corliss, L., & Alle-Corliss, R. (1998). *Human service agencies: An orientation to fieldwork.* Pacific Grove, CA: Brooks/Cole.

Anderson, B. S., & Zinsser, J. P. (1988). *A history of their own: Women in Europe from prehistory to the present* (Vol. 2). New York: Harper & Row.

Associated Press. (2005, December 27). Bush seeks to win more battles in 2006. *New York Times.*

Berube, A., & Katz, B. (2005). Katrina's window: Confronting poverty across America, http://www.brookings.edu/rios/data/sources/report

Blankley, T. (2009, May 27). Five million green jobs? *The Washington Times,* http://www.washingtontimes.com

Bloch, S., Croch, E., & Reibstein, J. (1982). Therapeutic factors in group psychotherapy: A review. *Archives of General Psychiatry, 27,* 216–224.

Bloom, B. L. (1984). *Community mental health: A general introduction* (2nd ed.). Pacific Grove, CA: Brooks/Cole.

Bonner, E. (2008, November 5). For many abroad, an ideal renewed. *The New York Times,* p. 1.

Broder, J. M. (2009, April 1). Democrats unveil climate bill. *The New York Times,* http://www.newyorktimes.com

Brown, D. (1971). *Bury my heart at Wounded Knee: An Indian history of the American West.* New York: Holt, Rinehart & Winston.

Carney, J., Tumulty, D., & Thompson, M. (2005, September 19). An American tragedy: 4 places where the system broke down. *Time.*

Carter, B., & McGoldrick, M. (1989). *The changing family life cycle: A framework for family therapy* (2nd ed.). Needham Heights, MA: Allyn & Bacon.

Cassel, J. (1990). The contribution of the social environment to host resistance. In M. R. Ornstein & C. Swencionis (Eds.), *The healing brain: A scientific reader* (pp. 31–42). New York: Guilford.

CIA. (2005, November 1). Infant mortality rate. *The World Factbook,* http:/www/ode1.gov/cia/publications/factbook/fields/2091.html

Comer, R. J. (1996). *Fundamentals of abnormal psychology.* New York: Freeman.

Crewdson, J. (1983). *The tarnished door: The new immigrants and the transformation of America.* New York: Times Books.

Cuomo, M. (1994). *The New York idea: An experiment in democracy.* New York: Crown.

Danner, D., Snowden, D., & Friesen, W. (2001). Positive emotions in early life and longevity: Findings from the nun study. *Journal of Personality and Social Psychology, 80,* 804–813.

Dao, J., Treaster, J., & Barringer, F. (2005, September 2). Storm and crisis: The evacuation; New Orleans is awaiting deliverance. *New York Times.*

Durkin, B. J. (1995, March 14). New choice on the road to managed care. *Standard Star,* Gannett Suburban Newspapers, pp. 1A, 2A.

Faberow, N. (1977). Mental health response in major disasters. *The Psychotherapy Bulletin, 10.*

Federal Register. (2009). Vol. 74, No. 14, January 23, pp. 4199–4207.

Finsterbusch, K., & McKenna, G. (1994). Is feminism a harmful ideology? In K. Finsterbusch & G. McKenna (Eds.), *Taking sides: Clashing views on controversial social issues* (8th ed., pp. 42–43). Guilford, CT: Dushkin.

Frazier, K. (1979). *The violent face of nature: Severe phenomena and natural disasters.* New York: Morrow.

Freeman, H. E., Jones, W. C., & Zucker, L. G. (1979). *Social problems: A policy perspective* (3rd ed.). Chicago: Rand McNally College Publishing.

Frum, D. (1995, August 14). Welcome, nouveaux riches. *New York Times,* p. 15.

Galbraith, K. (2009, May 22). The climate bill debate continues. *The New York Times,* http://greeninc.blogs.nytimes.com

Geen, R. G., Beatty, W., & Arkin, R. (1984). *Human motivation: Psychological, behavioral and social approaches.* Boston: Allyn & Bacon.

Gettleman, J. (2006, January 15). The stress of guarding the couch. *New York Times,* p. N25.

Glanton, D., & Bowean, L. (2005, September 25). After a hurricane, there's no such thing as normal. *Chicago Tribune*.

Glaser, S., & Grunwald, M. (2005, September 11). The steady build-up to a city's chaos. *Washington Post*.

Goode, E., & Eakin, E. (2002, September 11). Mental health: The profession tests its limits. *New York Times*, pp. A1, A16.

Gudraise, E. (2008). Unequal America. *Harvard Magazine*, July/August, 22–29.

Hagen, J. F., Jr. (2005). The Committee on Psychosocial Aspects of Child and Family Health and the Task Force on Terrorism: Psychosocial implications of disaster or terrorism on children: A guide for the pediatrician. *Pediatrics, 116,* 796.

Has feminism made lives harder? (1995, May/June). *The American Enterprise*, p. 19.

Hasenfeld, Y. (1983). *Human service organizations*. Upper Saddle River, NJ: Prentice Hall.

Herbert, B. (1998, August 31). Healthcare road trip. *New York Times*, p. A19.

Hoff, L. A. (1978). *People in crisis: Understanding and helping*. Menlo Park, CA: Addison-Wesley.

Holmes, T. H., & Rahe, R. H. (1967). The social readjustment rating scale. *Journal of Psychosomatic Research, 11,* 213–218.

Hulbert, Ann. (2005, October 9). Post teenage wasteland. *New York Times*.

Kanel, K. (2008). *An overview of the human services*. Boston: Lahaska.

Kilborn, P. T. (1998a, October 5). Reality of the HMO systems doesn't live up to the dream. *New York Times*, pp. A1, A16.

Kilborn, P. T. (1999). Uninsured in U.S. span many groups. *New York Times*, pp. A1, A17.

Knabb, R. D., Rhome, J. R., & Brown, D. P. (2005). Tropical cyclone report: Hurricane Katrina, 23–30 August 2005, National Hurricane Center, http://www.nhc.noaa,gov/pdf/tcr-AL122005_Katrina.pdf

Kobasa, S. C. (1979). Personality and resistance to illness. *American Journal of Community Psychology, 7,* 413–423.

Lambro, D. (2009, May 25). Obama's vast agenda spars bipartisan concern. *The Washington Times National Weekly*, pp. 6–7.

Lazarus, R. S., & Folkman, S. (1984). *Stress, appraisal and coping*. New York: Springer.

Linowes, D. (1995, November 15). The rationale for privatization. *Vital Speeches of the Day*, pp. 86–88.

Macht, M. W., & Ashford, J. B. (1990). *Introduction to social work and social welfare*. New York: Macmillan.

Maslow, A. H. (1968). *Toward a psychology of being* (2nd ed.). New York: Van Nostrand Reinhold.

Maslow, A. H. (1970). *Motivation and personality* (2nd ed.). New York: Harper & Row.

Maslow, A. H. (1987). *Motivation and personality* (3rd ed.). New York: Harper & Row.

Mehr, J. (1995). *Human services: Concepts and intervention strategies*. Boston: Allyn & Bacon.

Miringoff, M. L. (1995). Toward a national standard of social health. *American Journal of Orthopsychiatry, 65,* 462–467.

Morin, R., & Rein, L. (2005, September 16). Some of the uprooted won't go home again. *Washington Post*.

NAACP. (2005, September 16). Coalition of African American leaders call for a proactive and inclusive agenda: Hurricane relief efforts should also address poverty crisis in America, http://www.naacp.org.news/2005/2005–09–16.html

Nagourney, A. (2008, November 5). Democrats in congress strengthen grip. *The New York Times*, p. 1

National Institute of Mental Health. (1985). Disaster work and mental health: Prevention and control of stress among workers (DHHS Publications No. ADM 87-1422). Rockville, MD: Author.

Neher, A. (1991). Maslow's theory of motivation: A critique. *Journal of Humanistic Psychology, 31,* 89–112.

Neukrug, E. (2008). *Theory, practice and trends in human services.* Belmont, CA: Thompson Brooks/Cole.

Obama, B. (2009, March 27). Text: President Obama's remarks on new strategy for Afghanistan and Pakistan. *The New York Times,* http://www.nytimes.com

Obama, B. (2009, March 30). Transcript: Obama's announcement on the auto industry. *The New York Times.*

Ostir, G., Markides, K., Black, S., & Goodwin, J. (2002). Emotional well-being predicts subsequent functional independence and survival. *Journal of the American Geriatrics Society, 48,* 473–478.

Pear, R. (1991, August 7). U.S. intensifies campaign against employers of illegal aliens. *New York Times,* p. A10.

Pear, R. (1998, October 20). HMOs are retreating from Medicare, citing high costs. *New York Times,* p. A18.

Peterson, W. C. (1994). *Silent depression: The fate of the American dream.* New York: Norton.

Preston, J. (2009, March 22). *Remade in America.* New York Times, p. 2.

Rahe, R. H. (1979). Life change events and mental illness: An overview. *Journal of Human Stress, 5,* 2–10.

Rahe, R. H., & Arthur, R. J. (1978). Life change and illness studies: Past history and future directions. *Human Stress, 4,* 3–15.

Reckard, E. S. (2009, May 27). Many modified mortgages will default again, Fitch Ratings projects. *The Los Angeles Times,* http://www.latimes.com

Riesman, F. (2000, Summer). Self-help comes of age. *Social Policy,* p. 47.

Roberts, S. (1995, April 27). Women's work: What's new, what isn't? *New York Times,* p. B6.

Rosenthal, E. (1991, April 30). Canada's national health plan gives care to all, with limits. *New York Times,* pp. A1, A16.

Sanday, P. R. (1981). *Female power and male dominance: On the origins of sexual inequality.* Cambridge: Cambridge University Press.

Seligman, M. E. P. (2002). *Authentic happiness: Using the new positive psychology to realize your potential for lasting fulfillment.* New York: Free Press.

Simon, P. (1995, October 18). Throw out the pollsters: An interview with Paul Simon. *Christian Century,* pp. 958–960.

Smith, J. E. (2009, April 27). Changing the American mind. *International Herald Tribune,* p. 8.

Solomon, S. D., and Davidson, J. R. T. (1997). *Trauma: Prevalence, impairment, service use, and cost.* Journal of Clinical Psychology, *58.*

Specht, H., & Courtney, M. (1994). *Unfaithful angels.* New York: Free Press.

Stansberry, P. (2009, March). Obama's good intentions: How to profit from the ongoing debacle. *Porter Stansberry's Investment Advisory,* p. 1.

Stansberry, P. (2009, April). Your personal stimulus package. *Porter Stansberry's Investment Advisory,* p. 2.

Stein, J. (2008, July 7). What's John McCain's technology policy? *Mother Jones,* http://www.motherjones.com

Stein, S. (2009, April 29). Obama's first 100 days: 10 achievements you didn't know about. *The Huffington Post,* http://www.huffingtonpost.com

Strom, S. (2002, June 21). Charitable contributions in 2001 reached $212 billion. *New York Times,* p. A19.

Sullivan, J., & Purdy, M. (1995, July 23). Parlaying the detention business into profit. *New York Times,* pp. 1, 28.

Sultz, H. (1991). Health policy: If you don't know where you are going, any road will take you. *American Journal of Public Health, 81*, 418–420.

Tankersley, J. (2009, May 18). What is 'cap and trade'? *The Los Angeles Times*, http://www.latimes.com

Toedtman, J. (2009, April 29). What Obama's first 100 days have meant for 50 plus Americans. *AARP Bulletin Today*, http://bulletin.aarp.ogr

U.S. Census Bureau. (1995). Occupational outlook. *Statistical Abstract of the United States.* Washington, DC: U.S. Government Printing Office.

U.S. Bureau of Labor Statistics. (2001). Employed civilians by occupation, sex, race, Hispanic origin 1983 to 2000. In *Statistical Abstract of the United States.* Washington, DC: U.S. Government Printing Office.

U.S. Census Bureau. (2001). Educational attainment by race, Hispanic origin, and sex: 1960 to 2000. In *Statistical Abstract of the United States.* Washington, DC: U.S. Government Printing Office.

U.S. Census Bureau (2008). Retrieved April 19, 2009, from http://www.census.gov/hhes/www.poverty/povdef.html

U.S. Centers for Medicare and Medicaid Services. (2001). National health expenditures 1960 to 2000. In *Statistical Abstract of the United States.* Washington, DC: U.S. Government Printing Office.

U.S. is sued over aliens. (1994, April 12). *New York Times*, p. A13.

Verhovek, S. H. (1994, June 8). Stop benefits for aliens? It wouldn't be that easy. *New York Times*, pp. A1, B10.

Voelker, R. (2005). Katrina's impact on mental health likely to last years. *Journal of the American Medical Association, 294*, 1599–1600.

Wahba, M., & Bridwell, L. (1976). Maslow reconsidered: A review of research on the response hierarchy. *Organizational Behavior and Human Performance, 15*, 212–240.

Wall Street Journal. (2009, March 9). Who pays for cap and trade? http://online.wsj.com

Walsh, B. (2009, May 22). Greens celebrate cap and trade victory—cautiously. *Time*, http://www.time.com

Ward, J. (2009, June 1). Obama's diplomacy rebuffed by U.S. foes. *The Washington Times Weekly*, p. 3.

Washington Times. (2009, June 1). Editorial: North Korea tests Obama. p. 3.

Wilgoren, J. (2005, December 22). Destitute victims of hurricane remain stuck in hotels. *New York Times.*

Williams, R., Barefoot, J., & Shekelle, R. (1985). The health consequences of hostility. In M. Chesney & R. Rosenman (Eds.), *Anger and hostility in cardiovascular and behavioral disorders.* New York: McGraw-Hill.

Woodward, C. (2009, April 1). Promises, promises: Obama tax pledge up in smoke. http://www.breitbart.com

CHAPTER **2** | GROUPS IN NEED

CHAPTER CONTENTS

- Health Care for the Aged
- The Dementias
- Community Programs for Senior Citizens
- Nursing Homes
- Working with Senior Citizens

People with Disabilities

- Mainstreaming People with Disabilities
- Psychological Barriers against People with Disabilities
- The Rehabilitation Process

People with Mental Illness

- A Description of One Person's Experience with Mental Illness
- Prevalence of Mental Illness
- Trends in Mental Health Care
- Current Problems in Mental Health Care
- What Mental Health Services Are Needed?

Substance Abusers

- Alcoholics

Real Life Human Services Work

- Heroin Addicts
- Cocaine Abusers
- Methamphetamine Abuse
- Conflicting Approaches to the Drug Problem
- Interactions Between Legal and Therapeutic Approaches

Criminals

- Juvenile Offenders
- Adult Offenders

People with Mental Retardation

- Causes of Retardation
- Classifying People with Mental Retardation

The Homeless

- Why Are People Homeless?
- Attitudes Toward the Homeless
- Helping the Homeless

People Living with HIV/AIDS

- What Is AIDS?
- The AIDS Epidemic
- Who Are the Victims of AIDS?
- How Is the Disease Transmitted?

- Preventing the Spread of AIDS
- Care for People with AIDS
- AIDS and the Health Care System

Summary

Additional Reading

References

INTRODUCTION

This chapter is devoted to groups of people in need of help from human services. They are sometimes called target populations or consumers of human services. The poor, senior citizens, mental patients, abused children, and teenage runaways are examples of groups that have been targeted by specific programs and agencies. There is nothing permanent about target populations. Current public opinion, availability of funding, and political climate determine which groups may be relatively favored at a particular time. Populations that have always existed may suddenly be chosen for benefits. For example, victims of crime have only recently been targeted for benefits in a systematic way. The critical question of who determines which groups will receive aid is discussed in Chapter 7.

As there are literally hundreds of target groups of varying sizes, all of them cannot be covered here. Discussion is limited to some of the larger groups that are being helped in an organized way. For each group, a rough estimate of the number of people is given, along with a brief account of some of the programs and services provided. In regard to kinds of help provided, emphasis is placed on large-scale federal programs, because these have become the vital bedrock of support for millions of Americans. You are encouraged to investigate some of the smaller target populations, as well as some of the local and private helping agencies, on your own.

AMERICA'S POOR

The United States is one of the wealthiest nations in the world; its gross national product (the value of all goods produced and services provided) is higher than that of any other country. Yet, despite this high level of affluence, millions of Americans are not sharing in the general wealth, as shown by the data in Chapter 1. Their relative deprivation affects the style and quality of their lives; it extends beyond mere distribution of income and includes inequality in education, health care, police protection, job opportunity, legal justice, and other areas.

There is continuing debate about the degree of hardship faced by the nation's poor people. Conservatives point out that many poor people receive noncash benefits such as food stamps, public housing subsidies, and health insurance, which help provide the necessities of life. Others charge that millions of Americans are so poor that they cannot make ends meet and that many are actually going hungry.

At present, it is difficult to know how many Americans are living in poverty because the number depends on the standard used to define poverty. Perhaps the most widely used measure is the threshold, or **poverty line**, provided by the Social Security

Administration and the Census Bureau. The threshold is used mainly for statistical purposes, for instance, preparing estimates of the number of Americans in poverty each year. All official poverty population figures are calculated using the poverty threshold. This figure is based on the fact that an average low-income family spends one-third of its total income for food. The poverty line, then, is the food budget for a family of a given size multiplied by 3. Adjustments are made for changes in the cost of living for a given year. Another consideration is whether the family lives on a farm. Farm families supply some of their own food and are therefore assigned a lower figure. The poverty line should be taken as a general measure of economic well-being. It is not necessarily the income level used to determine eligibility for government assistance, a figure that varies by locality. Another slightly different version of the federal poverty measure is the poverty guidelines. They are issued each year in the *Federal Register* by the Department of Health and Human Services. The guidelines are a simplification of the poverty thresholds used for administrative purposes to determine, for example, financial eligibility for certain federal programs. Some programs using these guidelines for eligibility include Head Start, the Food Stamp Program, the National School Lunch Program, the Low-Income Home Energy Assistance Program, and the Children's Health Insurance Program (*Federal Register*, 2009).

The official poverty threshold allows convenient comparisons of poverty levels from year to year. It is not implied that the family could actually live on that amount. If total family income was less than the appropriate threshold for that family's size, then that family was considered to be living in poverty (U.S. Census Bureau, 2009). Schwarz and Volgy (1992) proposed a more realistic alternative measure. Their self-sufficiency threshold is defined as an economic budget that would allow a family of four to purchase minimum but essential items for food, housing, clothing, transportation, and medical and personal expenses, and to pay taxes. In other words, a family of four actually needs about 150% of the poverty-line amount to get by. It is estimated that there are about 24 million persons among the working poor, that is, those who are employed full-time, receive no welfare benefits, and live below the self-sufficiency threshold.

Who Are the Poor?

Obviously, poor people are those with a relative lack of money, resources, and possessions. Beyond this shared characteristic, America's poor may have little else in common. One important subgroup of poor people consists of those who have suffered a temporary setback that has reduced their ability to be self-supporting. These groups include workers who have been laid off, partners who have been deserted by their spouses, and persons needed at home in a family crisis. Most of these people would be considered able-bodied poor because they are potentially employable. Not all people living in poverty are unemployed. Approximately 48% are poor because their work hours were reduced, and 18% became poor because of losing the family breadwinner through divorce (Oswald, 2005).

A quite different subgroup of poor, sometimes called the "deserving poor," is made up of people who are not able to be self-supporting. Included are the aged poor, young children of poor families, some discharged mental patients, and people who are permanently disabled.

According to Brieland, Costin, and Atherton (1980), this diversity among sub-groups of poor has been an obstacle in developing satisfactory programs to help the poor; programs that suit one group may be inadequate for another. For example, to encourage the able-bodied poor to enter the job market, an aid program should pay low benefits. However, low benefits would be an undeserved penalty to a person who could not work in any case. As the 8th edition of this text enters print, similar obstacles are still apparent in our human services delivery system, making it difficult to reach those most in need.

Chapter 1 points out that a disproportionate number of poor can be found among minority groups. The poverty rate for African Americans and Latinos is considerably higher than for whites. Women and children are also overrepresented among the ranks of the poor. In fact, the great majority of those living in poverty consist of women and children; they are the major recipients of welfare benefits, food stamps, and other programs for the poor.

WELFARE

The single most important weapon in President Lyndon Johnson's "War on Poverty," introduced in the 1960s, was public welfare. It is difficult to provide a clear picture of **welfare** because it was not one but many programs. Local, state, and federal governments were all involved in a complex, interlocking fashion. The basic responsibility rested with local (that is, county or city) governments, which determined who was eligible for welfare and what benefits would be given. There was great variation in benefits paid by the various states, even when differences in cost of living were taken into account. Southeastern states, for example, tended to pay much less than California or some northern industrial states.

Aid to Families with Dependent Children (**AFDC**), no longer with us, was the program most people meant when they referred to welfare. Before this program was enacted, few acceptable options were available to a parent with no means of supporting young children. One alternative was to turn the children over to an orphanage; another was to seek work outside the home, leaving the children unsupervised. Neither alternative was satisfactory to the family or to the community.

Some commentators blame welfare for the great increase in out-of-wedlock births to teenage girls. A teenage mother is much less likely to complete high school and is more likely to be poor in later life than is a mature mother. Babies born to teenage mothers are at relatively high risk of illness, low birth weight, and developmental delays (Ventura, 1994). Clearly, they are at risk to perpetuate the cycle of poverty and end up as welfare recipients themselves.

It is adult males, 20 and older, who are responsible for the majority of babies born to teenagers aged 15 to 17. What has changed in recent decades is that pregnant teenage girls no longer marry the would-be father. Although some girls choose older boyfriends whom they regard as mature, a sizable amount of teenage sex is not consensual. In some poor areas, teenage girls report high rates of rape and sexual abuse. Many of the fathers in depressed areas are not able to provide support for a family. In one study, 32% of the adult male partners of teenage girls were neither working nor in school at the time of the child's birth (Shapiro, 1995). Under these circumstances, it is not surprising that the girls seek welfare support.

Welfare Reform During 1995, there was a growing political consensus that the welfare system needed a complete overhaul. The welfare state was criticized for breaking up families (discussed in Chapter 1), rewarding irresponsible behavior, and minimizing work incentives for the poor. Democrats conceded that their party had failed to strongly support the federal safety net for poor people (Toner, 1995). Some Democrats admitted that they had failed to keep vigil over welfare programs with the result that the programs did not change with the times. Mario Cuomo said, "We blew it. We were in power for a long time. We didn't correct ourselves. We didn't stay up to date, and we paid the price" (quoted in Wines, 1995, p. E1). The result was that 87 of 100 senators, including 3 of 4 Democrats, voted to abandon the federal welfare system that had been in place for three decades.

With the passage of the Welfare Reform Act of 1996 (The Personal Responsibility and Work Opportunity Reconciliation Act of 1996), the states of the union now have primary responsibility for managing welfare programs. Increased money in the form of **block grants** is being sent from federal to state levels. In fact, many states seized the initiative in reorganizing welfare programs. The names of some of the newer state programs provide an explanation of the direction of the changes. Consider the Virginia Independence Program, Wisconsin's Work Not Welfare Program, and Colorado's Personal Responsibility and Employment Program.

In Massachusetts, the Department of Public Welfare became the Department of Transitional Assistance (1995). It seems obvious that recipients are being told to assume more self-responsibility, prepare to work, and not expect benefits for an extended period. In fact, as of 2006, the term *welfare* was phased out, being replaced by the phrase *welfare-to-work*.

AFDC was phased out in favor of a variety of **workfare** programs. In 1998, the mayor of New York City, Rudolph Giuliani, announced his goal for New York City's poor. The plan was to end welfare completely by the end of the century (Swarns, 1998). The old system would be replaced by a universal work requirement for anyone hoping to receive financial help from the city. New York City created experimental job centers to replace certain welfare offices. Welfare applicants were required to meet with a financial planner to help them find alternatives to aid from the city. They were given a five-year lifetime limit on welfare and advised that some form of work is mandatory in order to receive benefits. New York, like other states, must create alternative workfare jobs for such a system to be effective.

Under such policies, only the most seriously disabled people will continue to receive cash assistance without working. Critics of these new policies point out that drug addicts, the disabled, and new mothers must receive additional forms of help in order for them to convert to a work-for-welfare system. Additional child care systems must be made available for those taking workfare jobs to get public checks, and expanded drug treatment centers and job training programs must also be created. Thus, it is anticipated that restricting welfare further will actually increase spending on each recipient through the necessity to expand child care and other services. These policies of New York, modeled after similar initiatives in Wisconsin, have as their basis a universal work requirement.

Various other states have imposed a time limit on welfare benefits. The idea is to prevent welfare from becoming a permanent lifestyle. Other proposals aim at promoting socially desirable behavior. In Maryland, for example, there is a 30%

reduction in welfare payments unless parents prove they have paid rent, kept children in school, and obtained preventive health care (for example, vaccinations).
Other ideas are aimed at keeping the family together. For instance, some states
have a "wedfare" component that allows the woman to retain a portion of grants
after marriage (Schmolling, 1994).

In summary, it appears that the states now have greater freedom in designing
their own welfare programs. Ideally, they will use this freedom to develop innovative programs that successfully move recipients into productive lifestyles. There are,
of course, various dangers in turning welfare over to the states. One is the possibility of negative competition between states to see who can offer the lowest benefits,
the object being to discourage welfare migration into the home state. Advocates for
the poor have expressed concern about the fact that only one state, New York, has
a constitutional provision that guarantees aid to its poorest citizens. A state court
ruled that Connecticut has no such responsibility, paving the way for cutbacks in
benefits and the imposition of time limits on how long benefits may be received
(Rabinovitz, 1995). The idea that poor people are entitled to a guarantee of at least
minimal subsistence seems out of favor at both federal and state levels.

Liberal commentator Mark Rank argues that welfare reform does not address
the basic problem of poverty. Although no one doubts that some individuals abuse
the welfare system, it is important to remember that the majority who receive welfare do want to work. The real problem, he suggests, is that viable opportunities are
not available to everyone because low-paying and part-time jobs simply do not pay
enough money to provide for a family. Minimum-wage jobs such as fast-food, clerical, and cleaning positions do not pay enough to keep a family above the poverty
level (cited in Popple & Leighninger, 1990, pp. 243–244).

Let us now take a brief look at what has happened since the passage of the Personal Responsibility and Work Opportunity Reconciliation Act of 1996.

WELFARE REFORM—AGAIN In 2002, Congress and the Bush administration reevaluated
the Personal Responsibility and Work Opportunity Reconciliation Act of 1996.
The intent was to improve and renew it, for much of the law expired in 2002. It
is clear that three of the many major goals of the law were accomplished, but not
to the satisfaction of everyone.

The first goal was to turn responsibility of providing assistance to families
and individuals back to the states. This was accomplished by providing block
grants to each state, thus enabling them to develop and implement their own
programs to help the needy. The second goal was implied in the title to part of
the new law. It was named Temporary Assistance to Needy Families (TANF).
Temporary was the key word. The law was aimed at eliminating the "culture
of poverty" that was seen by conservatives, legislators, and others as an ongoing
never-ending process, one in which people would remain on welfare for years
and years with a concomitant increase in economic and social costs. This perceived problem was dealt with by setting a five-year lifetime limit on obtaining
benefits under the new law. The third goal was not only to get families and individuals off welfare rolls, but to make sure that those eligible and able and taking part in the program were engaged in work, training, and/or school. All
recipients were in fact required to be in an approved work setting within

twenty-four months. Teenagers were required to go to school and live at home or in some supervised setting.

Failure to reach the goals just described, as well as additional goals of the legislation, was partially due to incomplete data. For example, critics felt that the block grants to the states were not sufficient to meet the needs of those eligible—or not eligible but in need—for the vast variety of state programs. Some felt that there was little or no congressional oversight to assure that funds were used only for the stated purpose of the legislation. In addition, while it was clear that there was an overall 50% decrease in the welfare rolls (Toner, 2002), other critics raised significant questions regarding the level of jobs, training, benefits, and income obtained by those taken off welfare. As for the time limits, questions were asked about what happened to those who were not engaged in work activities within the twenty-four-month period and to those who required help after the five-year lifetime limit had passed.

OTHER PROGRAMS FOR THE POOR

The federal government supports a number of other programs for people with limited income. These include food stamps, free or reduced-price school lunches, housing subsidies, and medicaid benefits. Let's take a closer look at some of these programs.

Some low-income families are eligible for food stamps, which can only be used for the purpose of buying food in an authorized food market. They cannot be used for buying liquor, beer, cigarettes, soap, paper products, or other nonfood items. The stamps cannot be redeemed for cash. In 2000 about 17.2 million Americans received food stamps (U.S. Department of Agriculture, 2001).

Poor people may also be eligible for various kinds of help with housing. Some communities provide low-cost housing, often called projects, for poor people. In some cases, welfare provides a rent subsidy for those unable to pay the full amount of their rent. Homeless people are put up in low-cost hotels until a permanent place is found. Regardless of the form of housing, poor people tend to be placed together in ghetto-like environments where crime, addiction, and substandard conditions are common.

The federal government provides health care to those of limited income through medicaid, a system that offers an array of **inpatient** and **outpatient** medical services. Although it has helped poor people gain access to improved medical care, the program is riddled with abuses, especially in poor areas. Some unscrupulous people set up "medicaid mills" in poor neighborhoods, where the patient is routinely run through a lengthy series of tests and procedures, many of which are unnecessary. Another problem with the medicaid system is that many doctors simply refuse to accept medicaid patients because the level of reimbursement is too low.

Not all programs for the poor are concerned with basic survival needs. For example, many city and state governments provide low-cost or free college education for low-income students. Many of these colleges have an open enrollment policy and make some provision for the under-prepared student in the form of remediation courses.

Most of the programs just mentioned are means-tested; that is, only those whose total financial support falls below a certain level are eligible for benefits.

Although these and other programs have improved the quality of life for many poor persons, life for the poor is far from easy, one reason being that there continues to be a strong undercurrent of hostility toward the poor in this country. Many hard-working Americans, convinced that welfare recipients are lazy and/or immoral people, bitterly resent paying tax money to support them. The poor themselves sometimes have incorporated these negative attitudes into their own thinking. They feel ashamed of not being independent and self-reliant, values important to Americans. These attitudes may be shared by the politicians who establish budgets and eligibility requirements, as well as by the workers who administer the programs. It is not surprising that welfare recipients often band together into informal groups where they may find not only understanding and support but more practical kinds of help.

This section can best be closed by recalling Will Rogers's remark, "It's no crime to be poor, but it might as well be."

Suggested Class Assignment
Report on the welfare system in your state, answering the following items:

- What are the eligibility requirements for entering the program?
- Describe the benefits, including cash awards, housing subsidies, and other allowances.
- Describe the recipient population in terms of age, gender, race, and education.
- What arrangements are made regarding employment, job training, or education?
- What changes, if any, have been made in the system in recent years?
- How does this program compare with those of neighboring states?
- How do recipients feel about the program?
- How does the program deal with unmarried teenage mothers?

THE UNEMPLOYED

Let's begin our discussion of unemployment with some of the obvious benefits that typically come from having a steady job.

- It provides income needed for the necessities of life.
- It helps one to be independent and self-supporting.
- It helps one feel like a useful member of society.
- It structures time in a useful way.
- It provides social contacts with others.
- It may place one in a stimulating environment.
- It provides an opportunity to use and develop talents.

CONSEQUENCES OF JOBLESSNESS

The benefits that come from having a job obviously vanish when a worker is laid off or fired. Instead, there is often a sense of absence of control over one's life, coupled with a fear of having to depend on others. The unemployed person begins to feel cut off from the mainstream of life, a feeling that deepens as time goes on.

The devastating consequences of unemployment were highlighted in a study of white-collar men who had lost their jobs in the recession of the mid-1970s; they showed signs of severe psychological **stress** (Braginsky & Braginsky, 1975). Although many were college graduates and had held prestigious managerial positions, their self-esteem was sharply lowered by the experience. Most suffered deep shame, avoided friends, and felt isolated from society. They felt insignificant and suffered from the feeling that they had lost value in the eyes of family members. Another consequence of their prolonged unemployment was a deep cynicism toward established institutions.

Unemployment Rates

Each month, the U.S. Bureau of Labor Statistics reports the official rate of unemployment in the labor force. The labor force is defined as people 16 years of age or over who worked 1 hour for pay during one survey week or who did not have a job and were actively seeking work. The nation's official unemployment rate in recent years has ranged from 7.1% during the 1991 recession to 5.5% during the recovery of 1995 (Hershey, 1995) to 4% in 2000 and back to 5.7% in 2001 (*Bloomberg News*, 2001). This statistic does not include the estimated 1 million discouraged workers who are no longer even trying to find jobs. Nor does it include the underemployed people who are working part-time because they could not find full-time jobs. In 2009 the unemployment rate in the United States is the highest it has been in over a quarter of a century. As a result of this and other economic turmoil facing the United States, President Obama has proposed an expansion of unemployment benefits.

It is suspected that a disproportionate number of minorities are involved in the underground economy, a term that refers to exchange of goods and services—both legal and illegal—that are not regulated or taxed by government (Julian & Kornblum, 1986). This so-called underground economy includes income from drugs, prostitution, flea markets, and gambling, as well as employment with wages that are paid "under the table" or "off the books." By and large, those involved in these unrecorded activities are not eligible for social services or pension plans.

Unemployment Insurance

The unemployment **compensation** system is our society's way of helping people who have been laid off from their jobs. The states regulate **unemployment insurance** programs, which vary in rules and eligibility requirements. In most states, workers and employers contribute to the program. Often the amount and duration of payments are based on the individual's earnings history and length of employment. Most states pay benefits for up to 26 weeks and usually require some evidence that the person is actually looking for work. In addition, a federal-state extended benefits program is sometimes activated when unemployment rates become relatively high in a particular state; it provides up to 13 additional weeks of regular benefits. A further increase in the number of weeks of coverage has been provided by Congress during times of high unemployment. Even when maximum supplements are available, an unemployed worker runs out of benefits in 65 weeks.

Impact of Unemployment on Human Services

Increases and decreases in unemployment have a number of direct and indirect effects on human services. Various surveys, reports, and studies clearly show that negative economic changes result in increases in certain physical illnesses, elevated crime rates, and increased first admissions to both state prisons and mental hospitals. These and other negative effects of economic downturns may take several years to fully develop. It appears that the stress associated with loss of livelihood may have a long-term, insidious effect. It is equally clear that people react to this stress in very different ways. Some lash out with antisocial behavior, and others may suffer physical or mental breakdowns. The shock waves of unemployment ultimately reach mental hospitals, general hospitals, prisons, and a variety of other agencies.

CHILDREN IN NEED

Children are endangered not only by poverty but by illness, rejection, lack of understanding, the inability of parents to socialize them properly, and many other factors. Human services workers realize that children are a high-risk group for developing all sorts of physical and emotional problems. Children often haven't fully developed the skills and defenses needed to deal with the stresses of life. Although some remarkable children do well in spite of grave hardships, inadequate care, love, and guidance put most children at risk of developing a serious disorder.

Problems serious enough to require professional help include childhood psychoses and mental retardation. Milder disorders include school phobia, bed-wetting, and extreme shyness. These and other **dysfunctions**, fully described in abnormal psychology courses, will not be detailed here. Instead, the vulnerability of children in terms of the changing American family will be examined. There has been a great deal of recent public discussion about how these sweeping changes have affected children.

CHILDREN AND THE CHANGING AMERICAN FAMILY

Chapter 1 discussed the dramatic changes that have taken place in the American family in recent decades. It seems clear that, on average, American children are now worse off in some respects than children of the recent past. More children are growing up with fewer parental resources: less time, only one parent, stress due to separations (Wolfe, 1991). In addition, many children—about one in four—are living below the poverty line (Gannett News Services, 1995). Today's youngsters perform worse at school, are twice as likely to commit suicide, use much more alcohol and drugs, and are twice as likely to be obese as children of the previous generation (Fuchs, 1991).

CHILDREN OF SINGLE-PARENT FAMILIES

In 1960, 9.1% of America's children lived in single-parent families; the percentage increased steadily during the following decades, reaching approximately 27% in 2000 (U.S. Census Bureau, 2000). The Census Bureau also revealed that the percentage of children in these homes is disproportionately high in our central cities. The great majority of these homes are without a father.

As mentioned in Chapter 1, one of the disadvantages of single-parent families is the greater likelihood of children living in poverty. Mother-only families have very high rates of poverty. After a divorce or separation, the mother's earnings become the major source of family income, and usually, the post-divorce income of women is significantly lower than that of divorced men. For single parents of both sexes, there are likely to be problems associated with combining work with child rearing. Job mobility, earning power, freedom to work late, and job performance are all likely to be negatively affected (Grief, 1985, p. 181).

Children from single-parent families also have above-average levels of youth suicide, mental illness, violence, and drug use. When you add poor school performance to the list of problems, it becomes obvious that this population is likely to be in need of help from a range of human services agencies.

The psychological aspects of single parenthood are problematical in that the single parent must play both mother and father roles. In addition to providing love and nurturance, the single parent must represent the family interests to society at large, interpret society for the children, and be a figure of authority and discipline for them (Costin, Bell, & Downs, 1991, p. 137). For many single parents, the pressures of playing these roles, along with the need to make a living, create considerable stress.

Helping efforts for the children of single parents have been centered in the schools. One approach that has enjoyed some success is peer counseling in the form of "rap groups" for children. Whether sponsored by the school or a local counseling agency, these groups help the youngsters to ventilate strong feelings about their disrupted home life and also to reduce the sense of isolation that some feel. In the group setting, children realize that their feelings are shared by many others in similar situations.

In some cases, the child may be so disturbed that professional help is sought. Some community agencies, such as child guidance centers, offer individual or family therapy with a social worker, psychologist, or psychiatrist. Some of these agencies maintain a reference library of books, pamphlets, and films on death and divorce for use by clients and families of clients.

In addition to psychotherapeutic intervention, a great many other kinds of services may be available to these children and their families—so many, in fact, that only a brief listing is provided here:

- Daytime care programs for young children aim to foster optimal intellectual development and to help overcome some of the emotional effects of early deprivation.
- Parent-assistance programs are designed to help the inexperienced or overburdened parent to deal with some of the practical problems of child and home care.
- Socially supportive organizations such as Big Brothers/Sisters may help fill the gap in a child's life that was left by a departing parent.
- Family crisis intervention may combine the skills of police and human services workers to help resolve intense domestic disputes that require police intervention.
- Teenage mothers may be provided with programs to help them continue their education and also to instruct them about parenting, sexuality, and social services for which they may be eligible.
- Community centers may offer an array of useful services, including social and recreational programs for children at different ages.

ABUSED AND NEGLECTED CHILDREN

It is not known how much the recent changes in American family life have contributed to the apparent increase in **child abuse**. It is certain only that there has been a huge increase in the number of reports of abuse during recent decades. Some experts attribute part of the increase to intensive case finding and reporting, implying that similar cases existed in the past but were not reported. During recent decades, the media have reported many sensational stories, which have increased public awareness of the suffering of young victims of abuse. It is even possible that our concern for these youngsters has ushered in a phase of over-reporting of doubtful or unfounded cases of abuse.

Exactly how is child abuse or maltreatment defined? Abuse and neglect cases are so varied that they defy any simple or uniform definition. A preliminary definition would encompass maltreatment of a child in physical, emotional, or sexual areas. And, of course, each area has degrees of severity of maltreatment. In a given case, experts might disagree on whether a given treatment constituted abuse.

The following list offers an idea of the various types of maltreatment that have come to the attention of human services workers:

- Children have been physically assaulted, that is, beaten, kicked, slapped, punched, or shoved. In some cases, an implement such as a knife, whip, or strap has been used, and in still others, the child has been burned with a cigarette or scalded with a hot liquid.
- Sexual abuse of a child has involved a variety of acts ranging from fondling of genitals to penile penetration. The atrocious crimes of incest and child rape are included in this category.
- The abuse has taken the form of emotional assaults, such as threatening, belittling, or disparaging the child.
- In some cases, the child has been confined by being tied up, chained, or locked in a closet or room.
- Neglect of the child's needs may also be viewed as abusive. Examples have included outright abandonment of the child, failure to provide needed medical care, inadequate supervision, poor nutrition, inadequate clothing, neglect of the child's education, and disregard of the child's safety.

A distinction is usually made between abuse and neglect of a child. Abuse is usually an act of commission on the part of the caregiver, meaning a voluntary act, whereas neglect is an act of omission, in which some ingredient important to the child's welfare is not provided. Many instances of neglect are involuntary on the part of the parent or caregiver. Sometimes, the caregiver may be unable to provide for the child because of illness, incarceration, loss of income, or some other unforeseen event.

The number of cases of child abuse and neglect cannot be stated with certainty because estimates come from so many different sources. In 2000, 3 million referrals were made concerning the welfare of children (Children's Bureau, 2002). Of these about 879,000 were victims of neglect or abuse; 63% of the children suffered neglect, 11% physical abuse, 10% sexual abuse, and 8% psychological abuse. Professionals such as teachers, human services workers, and physicians made over half of the referrals. Families, friends, neighbors, and community members made the rest.

Although these data are the most comprehensive available, it should be kept in mind that they include only those cases that actually come to the attention of community agencies. Many cases probably go unreported. Some people who suspect that a child is being abused may decide not to make a report because they are afraid of retaliation on the part of the abuser, or perhaps doubt that the authorities will take any effective action. In addition, it is clear that false reporting of child abuse cases is a disservice to the children who are involved. They are forced to undergo the pressures of public hearings and are generally placed under great stress. Another problem is that the unfounded cases necessitate the waste of professional time, which could be put to better use in valid cases.

CAUSES OF CHILD ABUSE Many factors play a role in child abuse. Some have to do with environmental stress, whereas others involve the personality traits of the abusing caregiver. Abusive parents tend to be young, of lower economic-class status, frustrated, unemployed, alcohol abusers, and often suffer from marital discontent (Egeland, Clochetti, & Taraldson, 1976). Child abuse also takes place in middle- and upper-class homes, but the affluence of the parents is often used to prevent incidents from becoming known. Regardless of class, the abusing parents often take out their frustrations on their helpless children.

Very often, abusing parents lacked effective role models in childhood and were themselves abused or neglected. However, it would be a mistake to conclude that child abuse inexorably repeats itself in successive generations. Kaufman and Zigler (1987) warn against repeatedly telling adults who were maltreated as youngsters that they will abuse their own children, because for some it may become a self-fulfilling prophecy. These authors reviewed the child-abuse literature and concluded that about 30% of those who were abused as children complete the cycle with their own offspring. This rate is six times higher than the rate in the general population, but it is important to note that the vicious cycle is the exception, not the rule. The cycle is less likely to be repeated in adults who have a loving, supportive relationship with a spouse or a lover and who have relatively few stressful events in their lives. It also helps if the adult consciously resolves not to repeat the cycle of abuse and seeks counseling to discuss effective parenting.

Although abusing parents may come from any background, there is a very strong relationship between poverty and abuse. In fact, family income is probably the most powerful single indicator of child abuse and neglect (U.S. Department of Health and Human Services, 1988). Various studies from the Department of Health and Human Services point to the fact that maltreatment was much more likely to occur in families with an annual income under $15,000 than in families with an income above this figure. Nothing about this finding is very surprising, because poverty is likely to bring with it frustration, insecurity, and stress. People with low incomes tend to have more children than those from upper income levels while having fewer resources to take care of them. Substance abuse, criminal behavior, and high rates of mental illness are just a few of the other negative factors that tend to be prevalent in poor families and that contribute to abuse.

HELPING THE ABUSED OR NEGLECTED CHILD Many private and government agencies offer child protective services. Some of the most important are state social service agencies, which may be designated as the department of social services, the department of human resources, or the department of human services. These agencies process most of the cases of abuse and are responsible for making a determination of whether to accept the case for services.

If a case is accepted, the agency must decide what services are needed. Sometimes the parents will be helped to improve their level of care by means of counseling. However, if the abusing parents are not cooperative, the case may be referred to court, which may in turn assign legal custody to the agency. In these cases, parents are granted physical custody of the children only if they accept monitoring and services by the agency to make sure there is no further maltreatment of the child. Various community services, such as tutoring or recreation, may be provided to the children while the parents are taught the skills needed to be successful caregivers. In a minority of cases, the court and the agency may decide that the child would be seriously endangered by remaining in the home. Foster placement then becomes the option of choice.

An increased demand for placements, due to the spread of crack-cocaine use among women, has come at a time when fewer foster homes are available because more women have joined the workforce. This situation has prompted many state and local agencies to cut corners on foster home investigations. Children are sometimes placed in overcrowded homes with unsuitable guardians. Consequently, there have been many reports of children being raped, beaten, and neglected in their foster homes.

It should be pointed out that most foster parents are decent people who raise children for little monetary reward. States and localities are generally raising the amount paid to foster parents. Other steps taken to deal with the crisis in foster care are the recruitment of more (and better) foster parents, training of foster parents, increasing the number of caseworkers, and, when feasible, helping the abusive biological parents to keep their children at home.

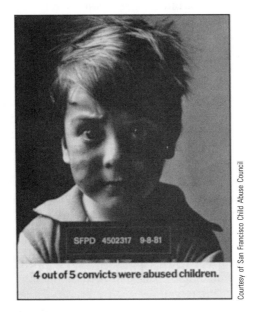

Courtesy of San Francisco Child Abuse Council

SFPD 4502317   9-8-81

4 out of 5 convicts were abused children.

This poster makes a powerful appeal on behalf of abused children.

The preferred approach is to hold the family together if that is at all possible and to give the parents the support they need to become adequate parents. Rather than to punish the parents, the goal is to help them break the cycle of abuse. One approach is to use groups to teach effective parenting to those whose own parents were usually disastrous role models. The abusing parents are encouraged to call the staff of the mental health agency when they feel the impulse to hurt their children. It must be understood by all concerned that effective parenting does not come naturally but must be learned in a step-by-step fashion. The study of child abuse makes it quite obvious that maternal and paternal "instincts" cannot be relied on to produce love and care for a child. Parenting involves a wide range of skills, attitudes, and knowledge that are normally acquired from one's own parents. Child abusers often fall into the pattern of imitating the abusive parents who raised them.

Another approach to treatment is the one adopted by Parents Anonymous (PA), a group founded in 1970. Being a self-help group, it avoids the angry feelings that are often generated by an outside authority intruding into a home. Often, the abusing parents feel guilty about their maltreatment of their children. They are very sensitive to being shamed and belittled by authorities, however much they may "deserve" it. In the PA meetings, modeled after Alcoholics Anonymous, the abusing parents voluntarily admit their tendencies to others like themselves.

With the support of the group, they struggle to control themselves and to find other ways of dealing with their children. Although it is too early for a definitive assessment of the effectiveness of this approach, it can be said that PA is growing in popularity, with more than 100 chapters in the United States.

CHILDREN ARE MEMBERS OF MANY TARGET POPULATIONS Additional references to children may be found in subsequent sections on people with disabilities, mental illness, and retardation.

SURVIVORS OF DOMESTIC VIOLENCE

Domestic violence, an increasingly common problem seen by mental health professionals, is abuse by one person of another in an intimate relationship. It can apply to people who are married to each other, living together, dating, in a heterosexual relationship, or part of a gay or lesbian couple. It can include physical or emotional abuse. Physical violence may take the form of slapping, kicking, hitting, punching, burning, throwing things, or any other behavior that is intended to physically hurt another. Emotional abuse is often a way in which a batterer attempts to control his or her victim by destroying that person's self-esteem with name-calling, ridicule, and shame. As part of emotional abuse, the abuser may withhold money; forbid the other from working, socializing, or seeing family; and threaten the victim with harm.

Sexual abuse is often part of the abuse picture. Forcing someone to have sex when she doesn't want to, or engage in sexual acts she does not like, forcing someone to have sex with others, are all forms of sexual abuse. Domestic violence has been described as any act that causes the victim to do anything that she or he does not want to do, prevents the victim from doing what he or she wants to do, or causes the victim to fear the abuser (Berry, 1996).

Who Are the Victims?

The number of women who are abused every year is staggering. Each year, millions are severely injured by male partners, and many die. Battering does not discriminate, as women from all ethnic backgrounds, cultures, and economic classes are victims of domestic violence. However, the poor and vulnerable are more likely to come to the attention of social workers and other mental health professionals, due to their limited resources.

Domestic violence is the leading cause of injury and death to American women (Gosselin, 2003). Three million women reported being abused in a year, and one in five reported being abused or raped in her lifetime (Gosselin). Estimates are that at least another 3 million batterings go unreported. When women do leave abusive relationships, they are most likely to be killed or injured when attempting to break off the relationship (Sonkin & Durphy, 1997).

Domestic abuse shelter.

Although most of the victims of domestic violence are women, and the majority of the perpetrators are men, husband battering does exist; as many as 24,000 men per year have reported being abused. Some of these men are in gay relationships, and some are in heterosexual relationships (Berry, 1996). Domestic violence in the gay and lesbian community is estimated to have similar **prevalence** rates as in heterosexual communities (Gosselin, 2003).

Victims may feel helpless, trapped, unable to escape their batterer. Some feel that they love their abuser and hope that they can change the abusive behavior. Others have been financially dependent while raising children. Some lack the skills necessary to work, as the abuser kept them from the workplace. Often the abuser isolates the victim from friends and family, so the victim has nowhere to turn for social support.

Some victims of abuse have a childhood history of abuse. Many do not. Some may be economically dependent, whereas others may be successful in their careers. In other words, the stereotype of the battered woman as passive and fragile is often untrue. Many do try to stand up to the violence but find that it is too difficult. Often survivors are too frightened to leave, having been threatened with death if they do. Indeed, when the batterer knows that the relationship is ending, there is an increased risk of severe and sometimes fatal injury to the victim.

THEORIES

Violence against women has existed for centuries. Even in the United States, wife-beating was legal until the late 1800s and early 1900s. In 1882 Maryland became the first state to pass a law that made wife-beating a crime, punishable by 40 lashes or a year in jail (Gosselin, 2003). By the beginning of the twentieth century, domestic violence was no longer legally sanctioned. However, courts rarely intervened in domestic matters, and what occurred "behind closed doors" was of little concern to the law. In the 1960s, domestic violence became a subject of both social and legal concern. In the 1980s mandatory arrests of batterers were found to be effective deterrents to future escalating violence (Gosselin). The National Center on Women and Family Law concluded that policies of mandatory arrest laws do result in increased arrests of batterers and enable victims to contact helping agencies, as well as promoting the message that domestic violence is a crime.

Early explanations for why women remained in violent relationships suggested that battered women were masochistic. That is, they were attracted to men who would cause them to suffer (Walker, 1979). Dr. Lenore Walker, an expert in the field of domestic violence, refuted that theory, stating instead that women feel powerless in domestic violence situations due to gender-role socialization. This powerlessness, or learned helplessness, explains why women see themselves as responsible for the battering and remain helpless to escape from the situation. This is part of the battered woman syndrome and an aspect of the cycle of domestic violence. There is almost never a single episode, but rather an ever increasing buildup of power and control on the part of the abuser, with concomitant denial and accommodation on the part of the victim (Walker, 1995). Kathleen Ferraro (1997) describes four phases of the abusive relationship.

Phase I: During the first six months of the relationship there is no battering. She enjoys time alone with her partner and does not see his desire for social exclusivity as oppression but as mutual affection.

Phase II: The first act of physical violence is met with disbelief. The woman rationalizes the assault and denies the uncharacteristic victimization. The perpetrator blames her through some imagined provocation. It is unlikely that the violence will be deterred by the minor sanctions of criminal justice action unless it occurs in the early stages and in certain types of battering relationships. Societal pressure frequently forces the woman into "making the best of it."

Phase III: A change in the severity or frequency of the abuse may trigger a transition into this stage. Defensive violence is one tactic that may be used to ward off attacks. The woman may attempt to leave the emotional and economic bond that had developed. Threats or psychological torture make early attempts difficult and often they return. About one-half of those who leave are successful in this attempt.

Phase IV: Convinced by threats from constant surveillance and punishments, women believe that they cannot get away. Failed attempts to leave reinforce the perception. This stage is horror-filled and may bring about depression and post-traumatic stress syndrome. Suicide may be contemplated. A severe altercation may lead to homicide as the final stage in what becomes a "kill or be killed" scenario. (Ferraro, 1997)

Studies report the incidence of post-traumatic stress disorder (PTSD) to range from 25% to 84% of women who suffer from physical abuse (Carlson & Choi, 2001). Symptoms of PTSD include depression, anxiety, nightmares, flashbacks, and generalized fear. Substance abuse has also been found to be a problem among battered women (Munoz-Kantha, 1996).

INTERVENTIONS

As awareness of domestic violence has increased, attitudes have changed. The women's movement was instrumental in bringing attention to this problem as well as to other often overlooked issues that affect women, such as rape and incest. Since the first hotline for battered women that was opened in 1971, there have been national and local hotlines to provide callers with information on resources for victims of domestic violence. The first shelter for battered women opened in St. Paul, Minnesota, in 1974 (Gosselin, 2003). More than 2,000 shelters exist across the United States, providing refuge and resources for battered women who have no other place to go.

Shelters usually assign women to counselors who assist the resident in obtaining needed services, such as legal services, finances, educational help for the children, emergency medical care for the family, and counseling services. There, residents learn about orders of protection, access custody information, obtain public assistance if necessary and learn about educational and/or vocational opportunities for themselves. Shelters usually conduct educational groups about domestic violence for their residents, consisting of information about the causes, impact, and cycle of battering and the consequences of remaining in a violent relationship. Most shelter stays are short-term, and residents are assisted in locating permanent housing. However, there are not enough shelters available to meet the needs of all battered women.

Unfortunately, the long waiting lists for housing and the lack of funds available to battered women have caused many women to flee their abuser, only to become homeless. This issue, along with the lack of coordination of services for battered women, has led to some changes in domestic violence policy and in the way in which domestic violence survivors receive help. In response to the fragmented and sometimes disjointed system of separate organizations attempting to coordinate services for victims of domestic violence, the President's Family Justice System Initiative was launched in October 2003. In 2005 the first Family Justice Centers were opened in the United States; these attempted to improve the lives of family violence victims through community collaboration and comprehensive services in one location. These centers, which have since opened in New York City, San Diego, San Antonio, and 12 other cities around the country, offer access to medical care, counseling, law enforcement assistance, social services, employment assistance and housing. They are, for the most part, drop-in centers, where no one is turned away. They are staffed by nonprofit agencies and supported by community leaders, government agencies, and caring individuals.

In spite of all the publicity that this population has received and the change in society's attitude about domestic violence, the numbers of domestic violence survivors continue to rise. Obviously, we have not done enough, as a society, to ensure that women are safe in their own homes. Some of these new programs are promising, but community support is crucial. Fewer people are asking, "Why doesn't she leave?" and instead are trying to find new ways to stop the violence by education, compassion, and action.

SENIOR CITIZENS

The 1980s saw a dramatic rise in the number of Americans aged 65 and older; the 1990 census counted 31.2 million Americans in this age group, a 22% increase since 1980 (Crispell & Frey, 1993). Senior citizens accounted for 13% of the entire U.S. adult population in the early 1990s, and this trend is clearly present in the early twenty-first century as well. It is expected that both the percentage and absolute number of senior citizens will continue to increase. By 2030 there will be about 65 million older people in the country.

This huge increase in the senior citizen population will have a profound influence on human services, because the chances of needing outside help increase sharply with age. The percentage needing the help of another person to perform personal care or home management is 14% for those aged 65 to 74, 26% for those aged 75 to 84, and 48% for those 85 and older. Older people account for a relatively high percentage of hospital stays, have longer hospital stays, and average more visits to the doctor than people under 65. Also to be considered is the fact that senior citizens suffer higher rates of depression and suicide than the general population.

Older people inevitably undergo physical changes that increase susceptibility to diseases such as cancer, heart disease, arthritis, and diabetes. As the body declines in vitality, it becomes less able to deal with stress and malfunction. Physical problems are compounded by social and psychological difficulties. For example, the senior citizen has to face up to the loss of loved ones as well as to the possibility of feeling less useful and more of a burden to others. Financial problems are also likely to come with old age. The majority of senior citizens leave the workforce, sometimes pressured to do so by rules and regulations of their employers. With retirement, income drops sharply. This explains why social security benefits are of such vital concern to many senior Americans.

SOCIAL SECURITY

The federal government plays a major role in providing for the needs of senior citizens. The Old-Age, Survivors, and Disability Insurance (OASDI) program, popularly known as social security, is the largest social welfare program in the United States. During 2000, 49.3 million individuals received OASDI benefits. The majority of the beneficiaries were retired workers and their spouses; a smaller number were disabled workers. The amount of money received is adjusted yearly and is pegged to the Consumer Price Index. The idea is to help beneficiaries keep up with the rising costs of living. In 2000, continued yearly increases raised the average monthly benefit to $845 for a single retired worker and to $1,420 for a retired couple (Social Security Administration, 2001).

News headlines have sometimes conveyed the impression that social security may be going broke. There is, in fact, no immediate problem. It is true that the funds will be exhausted by 2030 unless Congress takes action, for several reasons. The looming retirement of 70 million baby boomers (persons born during the late 1940s and early 1950s) is one factor. Another is that people are living longer and, consequently, collecting benefits for a longer time. Even more important is the fact that there will be fewer workers in the future to support more beneficiaries. In 1950 there were 16 workers for every person receiving benefits; today the ratio is 3:1, and by 2030 it will be 2:1. These figures again reflect the fact that the proportion of senior citizens in the U.S. population is increasing steadily (Carlson, 1995).

HOW ARE BENEFITS DETERMINED?   The amount received is based on a formula that uses average earnings over an individual's entire working life. The worker receives credits based on the amount earned each year. The amount it takes to earn one credit changes annually. In 1995 an individual received one credit for each $630 of annual wages up to a maximum of four credits a year. At this rate, it would take 10 years to earn the 40 credits needed to qualify for benefits.

There is no doubt that social security has transformed the way older Americans live. By helping them to be independent, it has also changed the lives of many of their children (Rovner, 1995). It is by far the nation's largest and most successful antipoverty program. In 1992 social security lifted the incomes of 9.6 million Americans over 65 above the poverty threshold. In effect, without social security, the senior citizen poverty rate would have been almost 50% instead of only 11.8%. Few people realize that 6 of 10 workers in private industry have no pension other than social security (Rovner).

Those who want to earn money in addition to their benefits by continuing to work are penalized by the system. Between ages 65 and 69, a recipient cannot earn more than a specified amount without losing some benefits. Non-wage income such as interest on savings may be earned in any amount without loss of benefits.

These regulations appear to favor affluent people who are likely to enjoy this significant non-wage income and penalize poorer individuals who need to work to supplement meager incomes.

Supplemental Security Income (SSI) is a federal program that pays monthly cash benefits to people who are 65 or older, are blind, or have a disability and who have limited resources and income. As of 1991, a person with unearned income of less than $4,884 was eligible (unearned income includes social security benefits, pensions, rent, and interest). A person may have a somewhat larger amount in wages, classified by the government as earned income, and still be eligible. A person is considered disabled if he or she is unable to work because of a physical or mental impairment, but, of course, the disability must be medically certified. The maximum monthly payment varies for an individual or couple. However, states may add to the federal SSI payments if they wish. Another benefit provided by SSI is a small payment per month to people living in institutions such as mental hospitals.

The eligibility rules and benefits are quite complex. The interested student is urged to visit a social security office to obtain further information. Several pamphlets containing useful information are usually available for the taking.

HEALTH CARE FOR THE AGED

"No longer will older Americans be denied the healing miracle of modern medicine. No longer will illness crush and destroy the savings they have so carefully put away over a lifetime." These words were spoken by President Lyndon Johnson in 1965 when medicare was created as an amendment to the Social Security Act (Connell, 1995, p. 3B).

At that time, only half of American seniors had any health insurance. In 1999 about 39.1 million held medicare cards. Medicare provides hospital benefits, operating room charges, regular nursing care, and medical supplies. It also covers some services at home such as part-time skilled nursing care for convalescents who no longer need to be in a hospital. However, the program does not cover all preventive services.

Medicare does not by any means pay all of the costs of medical treatment. There are significant deductibles and limitations of coverage. The deductible, now $100, is the amount the person must pay out of pocket per year before the insurance goes into effect. Once the deductible is met, medicare pays a set fee for covered doctor and hospital services and procedures. When all is said and done, medicare ends up paying about 45% of the actual expenses incurred (Connell, 1995). This is why many senior citizens buy private "medigap" insurance to help cover the costs not covered by medicare.

Providers complain about the complexity of the system and about the need to hire clerical staff to process the paperwork. Huge manuals, listing each procedure along with a designated fee and code number, must be consulted. Frustrating delays occur when a provider tries to get through to a representative to correct errors or resolve complaints. Some doctors do not "accept assignment," meaning they do not accept what medicare pays as full payment. The patient must then pay the difference. In fairness, it must be said that many of the same kind of complaints by providers are made about private medical insurers.

In spite of its limitations, medicare is a very popular program with senior citizens. Consequently, politicians who fear the wrath of the program's recipients at election time consider changes in the program with caution. However, it is widely accepted in Washington that changes are necessary.

Medicare is financed, in part, by a payroll tax that has been increased frequently since its inception. Some policymakers now feel that tinkering with the existing system will not solve the problem. They favor a complete redesign along the lines of a voucher system. Presently, the government acts as insurer, paying doctors and hospitals for covered services. Under one proposed plan, the government would contribute a fixed amount of money to each medicare beneficiary, who would then go into the marketplace to purchase his or her own insurance plan. Individuals could choose among different benefit packages and, of course, different premiums. They would receive cash rebates if they selected a plan charging less than the standard federal payment (Toner & Pear, 1995).

MEDICAID FOR SENIOR CITIZENS   Medicaid was created as part of the social security system at the same time as medicare. It was intended primarily to provide health insurance for people with low incomes or serious disabilities. In practice, senior citizens and people with disabilities consume two-thirds of medicaid's dollars, with poor, able-bodied individuals taking up the rest. A major expense is caring for senior citizens in nursing homes. Two of three nursing-home residents have their bills paid by medicaid (Connell, 1995). The remainder must "spend down" their savings until they have become paupers, at which point medicaid kicks in.

THE DEMENTIAS

Dementia is not one but a group of disorders caused by damage of brain tissue. Regardless of the specific type of damage, individuals suffering from any of these disorders tend to show similar deficits, such as short-term memory loss, reduced ability to learn new material, and difficulties in understanding abstract or symbolic ideas. Problems in concentration, judgment, and emotional control are likely to become more noticeable as the disease progresses. Eventually, the person may have difficulty in recalling words or the labels of common objects, or may begin repeating the same phrases over and over again. Finally, the victim may be unable to recognize friends and family.

Until recently it was assumed that these dysfunctions were in all cases due to arteriosclerosis, popularly known as "hardening of the arteries." We now know that this disease is responsible for only about 15% to 20% of dementia cases (Hooyman & Kiyak, 1991). In this form of dementia, certain areas of the brain show infarcts, or areas of dead tissue, the result of small strokes that damage blood vessels feeding the brain. Those with multi-infarct dementia, as this condition is called, often have a history of strokes and high blood pressure.

The most common dementia of later life is **Alzheimer's disease**, which accounts for over 50% of all cases of dementia. The **diagnosis** of Alzheimer's disease can be absolutely confirmed only after a patient has died and the brain tissue is examined: the typical features are neurofibrillary tangles (distorted nerve fibers) and senile plaques (nerve fiber lesions) in the brain tissue. However, early diagnosis can now be made with a high degree of accuracy, based on an extensive series of physical and psychological tests. The prevalence rates of this disorder tend to increase sharply with age. Although less than 2% of the general population under age 60 are afflicted, rates climb to 20% for those over the age of 80. Even higher rates have been reported for those over age 85 (Hooyman & Kiyak, 1991, p. 269).

Unfortunately, no completely successful treatments for dementia are available. However, many victims can benefit from changes in the environment aimed at helping them find their way around. Simplified routes from room to room can be indicated with tape or markers. Written schedules of activities and written directions for cooking, bathing, and taking medications can serve to support the victim's memory. It is also important to maintain a regular schedule and to keep the patient active (Hooyman & Kiyak, 1991). Victims of dementia are generally aware that something is wrong with them, so depression is a real possibility. Everything feasible should be done to help engage the person in recreational activities. Ideally, these kinds of therapeutic steps will help slow the rate of deterioration.

The dementias may have devastating consequences for the victims and their loved ones. It is estimated that some form of dementia, or senility, is involved in over 50% of admissions to nursing homes. For every American who suffers dementia, there are three close family members who are affected by the emotional, physical, social, and financial burdens of caring for the primary patient. Family caregivers often face the prospect of witnessing the gradual deterioration of a loved one's intellect and personal relationships. To make matters worse, health, social, and personal care services in the community are often unresponsive to the needs of patients and families, and institutional care is often characterized by a lack of thorough **assessment**, heavy reliance on convenient drug therapies, and little attention to psychological interventions that may help families to cope (Weiler, 1987).

The economic costs of the dementias are huge and steadily increasing. The total cost of caring for the disease per patient ranges from about $49,000 to $500,000, depending on the patient's age at the onset of the disease. These figures do not include lost productivity of afflicted people. Unfortunately, there is no way to fully insure against the economic costs of these disorders, and insurers and government programs have been reluctant to make chronic diseases eligible for any coverage. The families of victims must often pay thousands of dollars out of pocket.

Community Programs for Senior Citizens

Aside from social security, an array of programs help maintain the senior citizens in the community. Senior Americans with low income may be eligible for food stamps and low-cost housing. In addition, many communities have senior centers that offer a range of services, including social clubs, counseling, leisure-time skills training, and inexpensive meals. The general thrust of these programs is to reduce the isolation that many senior citizens experience, especially after the loss of a spouse. An attempt is made to connect the person with a lively social group and to enhance the sense of commitment to the community. Some agencies provide visitors for homebound seniors or escorts for those who need help getting to the doctor, bank, or market. Meals on Wheels provides hot meals to seniors who can't get out of the house.

Working with the elderly.

These programs provide the link between the person and the community, sometimes delaying or preventing institutionalization. Of course, not all seniors avail themselves of these programs, seeing themselves as extremely capable, not "old" at all, and resenting any implication that they need help.

NURSING HOMES

The great majority of senior citizens are able to live in the community, and only a small percentage live in institutions, including hospitals for the chronically ill, mental hospitals, prisons, and nursing homes. By far, the greatest number of institutionalized senior citizens are living in nursing homes. Nursing homes vary in the amount of skilled nursing care that they provide. Some care for significantly disabled individuals, whereas others cater to those with less severe limitations. It should be made clear that nursing homes are not hospitals—they do not provide service for the acutely ill. Rather, they maintain those with a chronic condition who do not require active medical intervention. These may be people with mild brain damage or physical handicaps that limit mobility.

What factors determine the need to place a senior citizen in a nursing home? Some of the most common are physical deterioration, lack of support services in the community, and the inability of the family to provide the level of care needed by the older person. There is little evidence to support the belief that large numbers of senior citizens are "dumped" into institutions. Usually, American families try to keep their older members in the community if at all possible. In fact, many senior citizen members with mild limitations do live with their relatives. However, sometimes the health of the senior citizen deteriorates to the point where round-the-clock care is required. As suggested before, the changing patterns of the family, especially the increase in working mothers, make it increasingly difficult to care for an infirm senior citizen at home.

The number of senior citizens living in nursing homes has increased in recent years. This rise may be in part owing to changing family patterns, but it is also related to the increased availability of nursing homes. This increase was spurred by federal funding for this purpose in the 1960s when it became clear that there was a shortage of facilities for senior Americans. The availability of medicaid in the mid-1960s also stimulated the growth of nursing homes. Most residents pay for their care through medicaid. The costs are so high that relatively few individuals could afford to pay out of their own resources.

The idea of putting an older person in a nursing home arouses strongly negative feelings on the part of all concerned. Some of this revulsion is due to horror stories about nursing homes that neglect or even abuse patients in their care. Some critics believe that many nursing homes are chiefly concerned with the profit and convenience of management. It is true that the nursing-home industry is composed largely of private, profit-making concerns, many of which are part of larger chains. There is no doubt that abuses do occur and that some nursing homes seem to be places where patients wait to die. The general trend, however, is that most homes provide adequate custodial care along with token recreation and **rehabilitation** programs.

Even in places where physical care is beyond reproach, the patients seem to spend inordinate amounts of time just sitting around. They are often babied to an unnecessary degree because it is faster and easier for staff to feed, bathe, and dress them than to wait for patients to do it themselves. The lack of therapeutic programs is due simply to the fact that it costs money to provide them. Many nursing-home administrators are unaware that improvements can be made with no increase in cost by training existing staff to encourage patients to function maximally.

WORKING WITH SENIOR CITIZENS

Older people who are active and in control of life are less likely to be depressed and are more successful in coping with problems. Although encouraging older people to be active is desirable, it must be kept in mind that older people may have some realistic limitations on their activities. These limitations might be due to irreversible physical deterioration or to loss of loved ones. Older people often need help in accepting their realistic losses before they can go on to develop new activities and new social relationships.

These realistic limitations only partly explain why some human services workers do not seek to work with the aged. This trend has been observed in social work, psychology, medicine, and other helping professions. Various studies have cited reasons for negative staff attitudes toward older clients. For example, senior citizens stimulate the workers' fears of their own old age and also arouse the workers' conflicts with parental figures. Some helpers believe that old people are too rigid to change their ways, and others are concerned about devoting a lot of time and energy to a patient who might soon die.

Those workers who put their fears and prejudices aside find that working with the aged can be very rewarding and enjoyable. The **prognosis** is not usually as negative as feared, and there are pleasures and delights to be derived from contact with old people. In our experience, student workers often begin fieldwork training with the aged with distaste but come away from the experience with positive feelings. Often, students are deeply touched by their contacts with senior shut-ins and nursing-home residents. They feel rewarded by the sense of really making a difference in a client's life.

PEOPLE WITH DISABILITIES

Included in the category of the disabled are people with a physical or mental impairment that limits one or more major life activities such as seeing, hearing, speaking, or moving. Thus, not only those who are blind, deaf, physically impaired, mentally retarded, or mentally ill are considered to be disabled, but also those with hidden impairments such as arthritis, diabetes, heart and back problems, and cancer. Some authors make a distinction between the terms *handicap* and *disability*. Disability refers to a diagnosed condition, such as blindness or deafness, whereas handicap refers to the consequences of the disability. The implication is that the consequences can be greater or lesser depending on various factors, such as society's attitude toward the disability in question.

There are no exact estimates of the number of people with disabilities, partly because of the uncertainty about including people with mild impairments. It is estimated that the total number of disabled in the United States is more than 36 million, or about 15% of the entire population. It has also been estimated that 10% of the children under 21 are disabled and that more than 50% of those 65 and over report various health impairments. By any estimate, the number of people with serious disabilities is awesome.

MAINSTREAMING PEOPLE WITH DISABILITIES

The history of society's treatment of the disabled can be summed up in two words: segregation and inequality (Burgdorf, 1980). People with disabilities have often been denied their rights and have not been readily admitted into the mainstream of American life. It is only in recent decades that this country has witnessed a wave of activism and accomplishment for these people. Various social and legal steps have been taken to help people with disabilities. For example, federal courts have issued landmark decisions that state that physical handicap is not a legitimate excuse for denying a person's constitutional rights. Congress passed the Rehabilitation Act of 1973, which prohibits discrimination against qualified handicapped people in regard to federal programs, services, and benefits. Perhaps even more important is the Education for All Handicapped Children Act of 1975, which calls for a free, appropriate education for children with disabilities in the least restrictive setting. Despite these positive steps, the struggle to admit people with disabilities into the mainstream of social and economic life has just begun.

The person with a disability who wishes to participate more fully in community life is often faced with a wide array of barriers. Some of these are physical or architectural. For example, a person in a wheelchair cannot climb stairs or may not be able to open a door without help. A person on crutches may not be able to use certain kinds of public transportation. Governments on all levels have taken steps to eliminate these architectural barriers. To an increasing extent, people with disabilities are being provided with ready access to public buildings. Ramps enable the wheelchair user to enter buildings with relative ease. Sidewalks are being modified to allow passage of wheelchairs, and doors and elevators are being changed to permit easier operation by the disabled. The considerable costs of these alterations have kept them from being instituted in some settings.

Despite legislation calling for the inclusion of children with disabilities in regular classrooms, some school systems have not fully complied with the law. It must be stated, however, that the special needs of disabled children do impose extra expenses on a school budget that may be tight in the first place. Aside from the costs of physical renovations, there may be additional expenses of providing special equipment and transportation. For example, visually impaired youngsters might need learning materials on tape or in Braille. Turnbill (1982) points out that court cases that establish the right of some children with disabilities to attend school 12 months a year, of deaf children to obtain interpreters during all aspects of their training, and of disabled children to obtain psychotherapy at school expense are costly not only in terms of money but also in terms of political capital. What Turnbill implies is that activists who fight for the rights of disabled children must show some reasonableness in the demands they make. If demands seem excessive to the citizens in a community, there is danger of a general loss of public support for services to people with disabilities.

The right of individuals with disabilities to equal opportunity in employment is clearly established. Yet, a problem centers around the fact that social security and medicare regulations tend to discourage disabled people from looking for work. Their support payments and medical benefits often exceed what they could earn after taxes, particularly if their jobs are not steady. If a person with a disability earns above a specified amount, she or he risks losing government support. There isn't much incentive to work under these conditions.

PSYCHOLOGICAL BARRIERS AGAINST PEOPLE WITH DISABILITIES

Negative societal attitudes are another obstacle that limits the **acceptance** of people with disabilities into the mainstream. American culture prizes competence, autonomy, and physical attractiveness. Americans are daily subjected to a media barrage of sexy, youthful, healthy people who entertain, sell products, and provide role models. In this atmosphere, it is inevitable that disability, particularly obvious disability, would have a negative impact on a person's sense of self-worth. Some people with disabilities have incorporated these negative cultural attitudes and made them the basis for self-defeating behaviors; in other words, they behave in such a way as to unnecessarily limit their participation in life roles and functions. Some may feel that there is no use in trying because they will not be accepted anyway.

Abundant evidence exists that people with disabilities arouse strong negative emotions in able-bodied people—in particular, anxieties about loss, vulnerability, and weakness. The able-bodied person may be repulsed or embarrassed by anything awkward or unusual about the disabled person. It is not surprising, then, that some nondisabled people prefer to avoid social contact with the disabled. When forced to interact, they may behave in unnatural ways. For example, the able-bodied person is apt to go to one of two extremes: either pretending that the disability doesn't exist and doesn't matter or feeling sorry for the disabled person and being excessively helpful. It is often difficult for the able-bodied person to get beyond another's disability and relate to that person on the basis of shared human feelings and desires (Asch, 1984a). In another work, Asch (1984b) contributed the following reflections about her experiences as a person with a disability:

Personal Reflections of a Blind Psychologist

Once, in a group dynamics program, I had to decide under which sign I would stand for an exercise in difference and group identification—white, straight, young, Jewish, woman, or disabled. Because many of the participants had focused on my disability in their dealings with me during the two-week program, because I had already revealed many aspects of myself, including my similarities with others (whether or not they had been seen), and because no other person with a disability was there to convey what it meant to be disabled, I stood under the disability sign.

An acquaintance overheard me say that it had been hard to decide whether to stand under the sign for disabled or that for woman. "If you hadn't identified as disabled," she said, "I would have said you were denying." With more honesty and irritation than tact, I replied, "It's for people like you that I have to stand under that sign. You and your attitudes have put me there, not my blindness itself."

Were it not a social problem, disability would require no discussion. In a more just world, disability might not be a social, economic, or political problem. It would not be a topic for meetings and discussions. I write out of conscience, anger, and disappointment that to live with myself, to better myself and others like me, I have no choice but to speak about what could have and should have been a rather inconsequential part of myself and my life. I write in neither pride nor shame, but simply because I have no other choice.

I long for the day when I, other disabled psychologists, and other disabled people will go into any room in any convention, any meeting, or gathering or job in the world and be greeted, evaluated, rejected, or accepted for who we are as total human beings. We need such a forum not because disabled people are so special, separate, or unique but because we must let people know of our desire and right to be part of the world from which we should never have been excluded. (pp. 551–552)

THE REHABILITATION PROCESS

The process of helping people with disabilities to achieve the highest possible level of productivity and independent functioning is a team effort in which many different professionals play a role. Clearly, the task of physicians, nurses, and other medical specialists is to help the person with a disability attain maximum use of self. This is one step in the process of rehabilitation. Psychological aspects of the process are of equal importance. In some cases, the person with a disability may become so discouraged as to be unresponsive to counseling. Some patients refuse to accept the seriousness of the disability or any limits that it may impose. The rehabilitation counselor helps the patient to deal with psychological obstacles, oversees the patient's progress, and is usually available to the client from the beginning to the end of the process.

In the rehabilitation agency, the patient's school and job history is reviewed in light of future job or training possibilities. A counseling psychologist may be asked to administer a battery of tests to reveal the person's abilities, interests, and aptitudes. Using all of the available information, a plan is developed that involves either training or actual placement on a job. Some large rehabilitation centers are equipped with workshops where clients can try various activities such as carpentry, clerical work, machine operation, and so on. Here, they are able to gain confidence by achieving success at various tasks. An occupational therapist may be assigned to help them increase skills and to build tolerance for sustained work. Even after the client is placed on a job or begins school in the community, follow-up interviews are arranged to resolve any problems that come up in the placement.

The disabled are often perceived by others in a somewhat distorted way. The disability tends to generalize in the minds of others to the whole person, that is, to induce others to see disabled people as more limited than they really are. In counseling, the person with a disability is helped to come to grips with these unrealistic perceptions of other people and the effect of these perceptions on the disabled person's self-image. The effective counselor recognizes that people with disabilities are more like the able-bodied than otherwise and works with their real strengths and assets.

PEOPLE WITH MENTAL ILLNESS

Physical illness is easier to define than **mental illness** because it involves bodily disorders that can be observed and measured in precise ways. Mental illness, on the other hand, involves feeling states, perceptions, and behaviors that sometimes depart only slightly from the normal range. To make matters worse, mental illness is sort of a catchall term that includes everything from temporary emotional upsets to long-lasting psychological breakdowns. An account of the heated controversies about the nature of mental illness will be reserved for Chapter 4.

The mentally ill are generally regarded as people with emotional and psychological problems who seek help from psychiatric and mental health facilities. More specifically, however, the interim report of the President's New Freedom Commission on Mental Health (Hogan, October 29, 2002) is focused on serious mental illness for adults and children under 18 years of age. Serious mental illness for adults is defined by federal regulations as any diagnosable mental disorder that affects work, home, or other areas of social functioning. Federal regulations define serious mental disorders for those under 18 years of age as any diagnosable mental disorder that severely disrupts social, academic, and emotional functioning. Further discussion of the report occurs later in this chapter and in greater detail in Chapter 8.

A DESCRIPTION OF ONE PERSON'S EXPERIENCE WITH MENTAL ILLNESS Houghton (1980) provided the world with a moving account of her mental illness as a young woman, when a psychotic episode struck her "with the force of a nuclear explosion." Joan Houghton's description of this experience follows:

The Crisis of Mental Ilness

All that I had known and enjoyed previously was suddenly transformed like some strange reverse process of nature, from a butterfly's beauty into a pupa's cocoon. There was a binding, confining quality to my life, in part chosen, in part imposed. Repeated rejections, the awkwardness of others around me, and my own discomfort and self-consciousness propelled me into solitary confinement. (Houghton, 1980, p. 8)

Joan remembered sitting with her mother in the waiting room of a mental hospital while her father investigated admission procedures. A young man was seated nearby. Perspiration dripped across his brow and down his cheeks. Joan took a tissue from her purse and gently wiped the moisture from his face. She tried to reassure him that everything would be fine. Joan was then ushered into a small room where she met a social worker and a psychiatrist. After a brief conversation, they presented her with a piece of paper and instructed her to sign. She signed "Saint Joan," without realizing that she had thereby admitted herself to a mental hospital. "My first psychotic episode appeared as a private mental exorcism, ending with the honor of sainthood and the gifts of hope and faith" (Houghton, 1982, pp. 547–552).

Joan was hospitalized for 5 weeks. Her recovery involved a struggle against her own body, which seemed to be drained of energy, and against a society that seemed to reject her. "It seemed that my greatest needs—to be wanted, needed, valued—were the very needs which others could not fulfill" (Houghton, 1980, p. 8).

Joan eventually recovered and was able to hold a job at the National Institute of Mental Health. An articulate young woman, she wrote eloquent accounts of her struggle with mental illness. It appeared that important unmet needs played a major role in precipitating her breakdown.

PREVALENCE OF MENTAL ILLNESS

In any given year, about 30% of the adults and 17% of the children and adolescents in the United States display serious emotional disturbances and are in need of treatment. These figures translate into millions of adults and children who are disabled by mental illness. More specifically, it is estimated that of every 100 adults,

- 13 have a significant anxiety disorder,
- 6 suffer from a serious depression,
- 5 display a personality disorder involving maladaptive tendencies that cause distress or impaired functioning,
- 1 is schizophrenic, that is, shows disorganized thinking and is out of touch with reality,
- 1 suffers from the brain disorder of Alzheimer's disease, and
- 10 abuse drugs or alcohol.

These data strongly suggest that psychological and behavioral disorders are a major problem in our society (Comer, 1995; Regier et al., 1993). Nationwide surveys of adults showed that between 16 and 22 million people in this country receive therapy for psychological problems in the course of a year (Narrow, Regier, Rae, Manderscheid, & Locke, 1993; Regier et al., 1993).

Most of those who seek psychotherapy on an outpatient basis suffer from anxiety or depression. One recent trend is that people with serious disorders such as schizophrenia are increasingly seeking psychotherapy, as are those with substance-abuse disorders. Another recent trend is that therapy is no longer a privilege of the wealthy. Owing in part to the expansion of medical insurance coverage, people at all economic levels, including minorities, are seeking treatment (Comer, 1995). Chapter 4 reviews the various theoretical models that guide treatment for psychological disorders.

TRENDS IN MENTAL HEALTH CARE

Dramatic changes have occurred in recent decades concerning the places where Americans are treated for serious mental illness. A basic reform in psychiatric care that started in the 1950s was to get mental patients out of institutions as quickly as possible and to treat them in community-based facilities. In 1955 there were 560,000 patients in state and county mental hospitals. The numbers living in mental hospitals steadily declined to 160,000 in 1978 (Coleman, Butcher, & Carson, 1984) and to a low of 69,000 in 1995 (Butterfield, 1995). As of 2006, it was estimated that the inpatient mentally ill population was still declining, with no **reliable data** available.

This decline in occupancy reflected increasing awareness among mental health experts that long-term hospitalization is not the best choice of treatment for many patients. For one thing, lengthy hospitalization tends to create a dependence on the institution that hampers the patient's reentry into the community. Another contributory factor has been the introduction of powerful tranquilizing medications. These new drugs help suppress the disturbed and agitated behaviors of some patients, thereby making it possible to treat them on an outpatient basis.

Patients admitted to mental hospitals do not stay nearly as long on the average as in the decades prior to the 1950s. However, it soon became obvious that many briefly treated patients are not able to live in the community without recurring episodes of acute disturbance. Their symptoms flare up periodically, and they have to be readmitted to the hospital. It is not unusual for some mental patients to have 10, 15, or even 20 brief stays at mental hospitals. Critics of the trend toward briefer hospitalizations point to the problems resulting from the "revolving door" effect, in which patients keep returning for hospitalized treatment because of inadequate care during prematurely terminated stays. They also charge that many mental patients are simply being "dumped" into communities without provisions for aftercare.

It might be useful at this point to take a closer look at the two parts of this intended reform of mental health care: the first is **deinstitutionalization**, which means getting patients out of long-stay hospitals, and the second is community-based treatment.

DEINSTITUTIONALIZING MENTAL PATIENTS The 1960s were years of rapid social change. Old ways of doing things were challenged in every area of life, including the mental health field. Social activists charged that large numbers of mental patients were being detained, often against their will, in huge, outmoded psychiatric hospitals. They further alleged that many of these patients were simply being warehoused in custodial wards and not getting much in the way of treatment. Very often, patients were not even asked how they felt about being in the hospital. There was a great deal of merit to these criticisms, especially in regard to the state hospitals. Many such hospitals were located far from the communities they served, making it difficult to reconnect patients with their former communities.

Meanwhile, civil rights attorneys were active in championing the rights of mental patients. They argued that mental patients were entitled to **due process** of law before being committed against their will. If hospitalized, the patients were to receive treatment in the least restrictive environment. These legal efforts finally culminated in the landmark Supreme Court decision in *O'Connor v. Donaldson* (1975), which held that it is unconstitutional to confine a non-dangerous person in a mental hospital against her or his will unless adequate treatment is provided.

COMMUNITY CARE FOR MENTAL PATIENTS   Of course, it was not enough simply to condemn the old approach to mental illness. In response to the pressures of social reformers, mental health experts began to implement a community-based approach to the problem that was designed to achieve certain important goals. One was to prevent mental disability whenever possible by fostering constructive social change. Another was to seek out people in need of help and treat them in the community. Still another goal was to facilitate the reentry of institutionalized people into the community.

The Community Mental Health Centers Act of 1963 was to provide the means of achieving these and other goals. This federal legislation provided for the establishment of a network of mental health centers throughout the nation. Each center was to provide an array of services to the community. Five basic services were to be offered:

1. *Inpatient care.* Each community mental health center was to have a hospital for seriously disordered mental patients. The plan was that patients would be treated as quickly as possible and returned to the community. Only patients who did not respond to treatment would be referred to long-stay institutions.
2. *Outpatient care.* The center was to provide psychological services through an outpatient clinic.
3. *Partial hospitalization.* A facility was to be provided to treat patients during the day but allow them to return home evenings and weekends. The intent of **partial hospitalization** was to prevent patients from becoming dependent on the treatment facility as they might be if confined on a 24-hour basis.
4. *Emergency care.* The center was to maintain a 24-hour crisis center to deal with psychiatric emergencies.
5. *Consultation, education, and information.* The center was to offer consultation, education, and information to others vitally concerned with mental health issues such as teachers, police and city officials, and probation officers. The idea was to facilitate social changes that might help prevent emotional disorders.

The act was subsequently amended to add several other desirable goals in addition to these **mandated programs**. These included rehabilitation in the form of vocational and physical training for patients as well as research and evaluation. For example, the center was to do research to evaluate its own effectiveness to explore the causes of psychological disorder.

The plan was a good one, but the community mental health centers have not been able to fully attain their goals. The original plan called for the establishment of 2,000 centers, each serving a specific catchment or health service area. By the mid-1990s, only about 600 centers were in full operation, which meant that only about 30% of the population in need was being served.

The deinstitutionalization of mental patients and the inability of community mental health centers to provide the services that would enable these individuals to become productive members of their communities have led to the reinstitutionalization of many of those patients. This time, however, many of these individuals find themselves not in psychiatric hospitals but, instead, in prisons. Current estimates are that approximately 500,000 of today's prison inmates have diagnosable mental disorders. Once in prison, their sentences are extended as a result of their illnesses, the symptoms of which may make it impossible for these individuals to adjust to prison life or to abide by prison rules. New mental health providers might consider this new population of mentally ill individuals as they prepare to enter the mental health field.

CURRENT PROBLEMS IN MENTAL HEALTH CARE

Bassuk and Gerson (1978) wondered how the well-intentioned reform of deinstitutionalization could have created so many problems. These authors assert that the discharged mental patient was to be supported by a full spectrum of aftercare services but that communities rarely provided such services. The living arrangements were often very poor. Many patients drifted to substandard inner-city housing that was unsafe, dirty, and overcrowded. Vocational training, job referrals, transportation, and recreational facilities were lacking. Aftercare agencies complained that they were not given sufficient funds to provide services needed by ex-patients.

By the mid-1980s, it was generally accepted by mental health professionals that deinstitutionalization had been a massive failure (Lyons, 1984). In retrospect, policymakers have placed the blame on three major factors. One was a tendency to view state mental hospitals as prisons that violated the civil rights of mental patients. As long ago as 1975, Paul Schmolling wrote an article entitled "Civil Rights for Mental Patients: The Road to Neglect?" that argued that while some of the early actions of the civil rights movement helped to publicize and correct long-standing abuses, the movement increasingly seemed to be in pursuit of goals that were ultimately detrimental to patient welfare. To an excessive degree, civil libertarians were operating under the influence of an analogy that equated mental patients with persecuted minority groups (Schmolling, 1975, p. 168). The author suggested that this analogy lent itself to rescue fantasies. Patients were prematurely considered "cured" and discharged from hospitals on a wholesale basis. Unfortunately, the extent of their social disability was often not recognized.

The second factor that led to the ultimate failure of this policy was the overselling of tranquilizing medicine. Scientific researchers had given us antibiotics and effective vaccines against certain diseases. It did not seem too much to expect that researchers would give us a pill that would revolutionize the treatment of the mentally ill. Tranquilizers were sold—by the carload—as a panacea for mental illness. Regretfully, the drugged patients did not do as well in the community as expected.

Although drugs may help a patient return to the community, they do not meet the same needs as do friends, family, a job, and continued support services.

The third factor was that deinstitutionalization was supported as a way to reduce the enormous costs of caring for patients on a round-the-clock basis. Ironically, the anticipated savings did not occur. The state hospitals tended to spend more and more as they cared for fewer and fewer patients. Johnson (1990, p. 103) presented data showing that the annual cost per mental patient nearly quadrupled between 1969 and 1977 and that some hospital systems showed large increases in overall costs as the inpatient population shriveled. One reason, among many others, for this is that the political power of the state employee unions enabled them to maintain high levels of staffing even though the patients were disappearing from the wards. Politicians went along with this policy because they anticipated the support of these employees at election time.

WHAT MENTAL HEALTH SERVICES ARE NEEDED?

Based on the commonsense ideas advanced by Johnson (1990), here is a partial list of the needs of mental health patients living in the community:

- *Housing.* The mentally ill need a place to live where their sometimes eccentric behavior will be tolerated. In other words, they need a safe haven where they will not be subject to hostile criticism by intolerant persons.
- *Outreach.* Mental patients often lack a clear sense of time and place and are likely to miss their appointments. It is very often useful for staff members to go visit patients in their residences and engage them in their own environment.
- *Hospitalization readmission.* The chronic mental patient requires occasional readmission to the mental hospital. Once patients become openly bizarre, delusional, or dangerous to themselves and others, it should be possible to readmit them without a lot of bureaucratic red tape. The readmission need not be viewed as a failure of the aftercare program, because these disorders are defined, in part, by a need for occasional removal to a safe inpatient setting. Sometimes staff members delay too long in arranging the hospitalization because of their own sense of personal failure.
- *Skills of living.* The chronic mental patient often needs help with the skills of daily living and interpersonal relations. Tasks such as personal hygiene, grooming, shopping, budgeting, traveling, and everyday conversation need to be practiced. As Johnson (1990) suggests, many therapists do not find this kind of educational activity very interesting and would prefer a deeper, more verbal kind of therapy. Again, the helper must decide if the patient's needs are best served with deep analysis or with instruction in the skills of daily life.

THE NEW CHRONIC PATIENT Since the early 1970s, when the policy to deinstitutionalize became dominant, the trend has been to provide acute hospital care for a few weeks to people with psychotic disorders and outpatient clinic treatment following discharge. The integration between hospital and clinic has often been inadequate. A number of younger Americans have become acutely, then chronically, ill during this era of limited care. They have gone from their twenties to their thirties living in the community in a way that Pepper (1987) describes like this:

> They do not carry shopping bags or wear three sweaters in the summertime. Most dress like their age-mates, aspire to hold a job, be in love, have children, take vacations, and in every other way fulfill the American dream. But living in the community also offers them the opportunity to drink alcohol, smoke pot, do cocaine, heroin, LSD, PCP—just like everybody else. Unfortunately, most of them respond to even small doses of drugs with psychosis, depression, or a worsening of their personality disorders. Most regrettably, public policy and practice in the last decade have further tended to separate drug and alcohol treatment services from mental health treatment. It is a rare community today that offers integrated treatment for such individuals, who now constitute a majority of the younger seriously disturbed population. (p. 454)

IS REINSTITUTIONALIZATION THE ANSWER? A backlash has resulted from the failure of deinstitutionalization to solve the problems of the mentally disabled. Some professionals have called for a halt to deinstitutionalization and a return to large-scale institutions. They point out that institutionalization is more humane than homelessness, hunger, and victimization. Plum (1987) argues that this is a shortsighted "solution" to the problem and that it would be preferable to develop better support systems in the community. She also recommends that we explore combinations of institutionalization and noninstitutional forms of mental health services. It is clear, though, that despite all the advances proposed and accomplished in coping with mental illness, and despite the increase in knowledge, skill, and expertise of therapists, mental illness is with us yet. In addition, it has become, according to the World Health Organization (2001), the single greatest cause of disability in the United States, Canada, and western Europe (Figure 2.1).

In a letter to President Bush in 2002, Hogan, chairman of the President's New Freedom Commission on Mental Health, provides some highlights in the commission's interim report. The major belief of the commission is that "America's mental health service delivery system is in a shambles." It found that the system is not capable of efficiently delivering and financing effective treatments such as medication, psychotherapies, and other services. These services are operated by a multitude of different agencies, programs, and levels of government. There are so many programs that they are most often operating with different rules and it is often impossible for families and consumers to find the care that they need. Further discussion of these issues is presented in later chapters.

SUBSTANCE ABUSERS

The term *substance abusers* refers to people who misuse certain substances for the purpose of altering mood or psychological state. The substances used for this purpose range from foods such as sugar and carbohydrates to alcohol and hard drugs such as heroin, amphetamines, and **barbiturates**. Virtually the entire adult population uses some of these substances at one time or another. What is the distinction between using and abusing a substance?

One important criterion is that the abuser employs the substance to avoid facing up to problems. When under stress, he or she "turns on" to the stuff in question

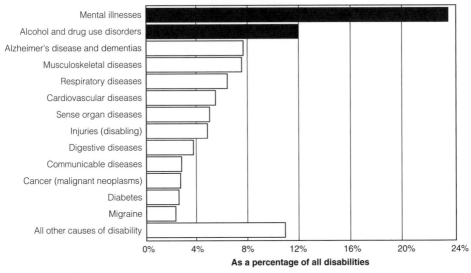

United States, Canada and Western Europe, 2000

As a percentage of all disabilities

FIGURE 2.1 | CAUSES OF DISABILITY IN UNITED STATES, CANADA, AND WESTERN EUROPE*

*Cause of disability for all ages combined. Measures of disability are based on the number of years of "healthy" life lost with less than full health (i.e., YLD, years lost due to disability) for each incidence of disease, illness, or condition. All data shown add up to 100%.

to feel better without doing anything about the troublesome situation. The abuser runs the risk of becoming addicted; this means that he or she may become both psychologically and physiologically dependent on the substance.

Certain drugs, including alcohol, alter body chemistry if taken to excess. Once addicted, the individual must continue to use the substance if unpleasant **withdrawal symptoms** are to be avoided. It is not practical to review all possible addictions in this section, so we will focus on three addictions that have received the most attention from human services: alcoholism, heroin abuse, and methamphetamine abuse. In addition, cocaine abuse is given coverage because it has become so prevalent in our society. For information on substance-abuse counseling, see Chapter 6.

ALCOHOLICS

Some experts believe that alcoholism is the number one public health problem in the United States today. The number of people who are psychologically dependent on alcohol has been estimated at anywhere from 8 to 20 million. The lack of precision in the count is due to difficulty in distinguishing between heavy drinkers and alcoholics, as well as the fact that many people abuse alcohol in secret. The majority of known alcoholics are adult men, but the number of adult women who drink to excess has increased in recent years. There is also significant alcohol abuse among teenagers and even among preteens.

Why are so many Americans dependent on alcohol? One important property of alcohol is that it helps the drinker to feel relaxed and uninhibited. Continued use,

REAL LIFE HUMAN SERVICES WORK

I didn't start out to be in the field. As an aspiring artist, my decision to attend college as an education major was a practical one. While waiting to become self-sufficient as a painter, I would teach art in public school, earn a living and gradually become a member of the art world. My education, however, led me in a different direction. First of all, I recognized that the 900 children I was seeing in the school system a week were responding to their art making, often, as a therapeutic activity. This led me to become a member of the American Art Therapy Association and to study art therapy at a graduate level. Then, I was asked to start an arts class at a residential program for substance abusers, heroin addicts, as a way of enriching the treatment experience for them. Although somewhat apprehensive about entering a setting in which I had no experience, I decided to try it. It totally changed my life. I began working with clients for whom the art experience was not only personally enriching, but also of therapeutic value. I worked with a psychiatrist and a social work supervisor in developing my skills in assessment and intervention and, when the program was closed, I moved on into the mental health arena. I went back to school for clinical psychology and became a mental health consultant, doing initial evaluations, short-terms interventions and running groups. This experience opened my awareness, especially to the plight of women substance abusers and their children, often neglected in the treatment process and consistently underserved as a population. I wrote a grant to establish a day program for these women and their children; it is funded by the National Institute on Drug Abuse and I became the program director. During this time, I also was tapped as an agency trainer and, together with a colleague, developed a year-long curriculum on counseling substance abusers to upgrade staff performance and effectiveness. Moving on from this agency, after a number of years, I became a program director in a free-standing residential program for women in a nearby state. I developed a clinical program to include those women who were indigent, those who were from rather wealthy backgrounds in the area, and those who were released from prison as part of a community-release project in the department of corrections. Substance abuse does not recognize economic differences. During this period, I became licensed as an alcoholism and drug abuse counselor by the state in which I then worked.

As a result of my experience, I was approached about a consulting position in an outpatient treatment center as a program developer, grant-writer and community relations person. Although not working with clients, this experience broadened my skill set as well as my networking opportunities. After several consulting years, I returned to my work with clients in a private practice administered by a licensed social worker. This was a challenging experience and required the acquisition of yet another set of skills; i.e., business management as a self-employed professional. During this period of about seven years, I was approached about becoming a staff training director for the same agency in which I had worked as an art therapist and mental health consultant so many years before. I left private practice to begin training others in the field to become effective, credentialed counselors. A new state credential in substance abuse counseling was created at the time I was training and I was granted that credential based on my past experience. So I now had the credentials from two states. After several years of doing this, a position came up in the criminal justice system which intrigued me: it was a clinical director spot in a newly formed drug treatment court. I had long been troubled by the lack of coordination between the courts and substance abuse treatment programs; this offered an opportunity to be on the cutting edge of a new concept: problem-solving courts.

(continued)

I took the position and helped to create a new modality within the criminal justice system that I believe continues to make a significant difference in the lives of criminogenic substance abusers. After this court was up and running, I was recommended for a position back into a program agency setting as an executive administrator of clinical treatment. This agency was in an extremely poor section of the city and had been known as a major force in the community's well-being, i.e., the immigrant community received not only treatment, but many other needed human services from this agency. I took the position, liking the opportunity to establish clinical guidelines and practice for an entire agency for several years until the opportunity to teach substance abuse counseling at the college level was offered.

Presently, I am directing such a program at a community college. In this setting, I have had the opportunity to design and develop the curriculum for the counseling program which is approved by the state education department and by the state's substance abuse services agency. I continue to provide special training, both in and outside the college to criminal justice agencies and treatment providers as a consultant, participate at the state level in the review of current practices in substance abuse education and sit on a state association board for the drug treatment courts. My hope for my students is that they see the limitless possibilities in pursuing the field in which I have spent [the] majority of my professional life. Through utilizing their creativity, passion and desire to perform good works, their career opportunities and goals can be furthered in an astonishing way.

Joan Standora, B.S., M.A., CASAC, Ph.D.

however, reduces motor coordination and causes a number of deficiencies such as blurred vision, thick speech, and the suspension of normal judgment. This combination of properties explains why the majority of serious auto accidents are alcohol-related. Most individuals are able to use alcohol in moderation to feel at ease in social situations. However, the alcoholic comes to rely on alcohol to help deal with stressful and difficult situations. At some point on the path to addiction, the alcoholic becomes unable to face difficulties without using alcohol as a crutch. Prolonged excessive drinking can lead to a variety of health problems, including serious damage to the brain or liver. On a social level, the alcoholic may jeopardize both employment and family life.

Treatment for the alcoholic has changed dramatically in this century. Throughout most of our history, alcoholism was seen as a kind of moral weakness. Drunks were either ignored or treated as criminals. During the first half of the previous century, it was common practice to jail alcoholics, particularly those of low social status. It became obvious that this punishment had no long-range effect on the alcoholic, who never seemed to learn the "lesson."

Alcoholics Anonymous (AA), founded in 1934, called for an end to punitive, moralistic approaches to the problem. Instead, alcoholism was to be regarded as an illness and treated as such. AA bases its program for helping alcoholics on group meetings during which members confess their dependence on alcohol. One basic tenet of AA is that alcoholics are not to think of themselves as cured at any time. They are simply trying to live one day at a time without alcohol. At the same time, they gain strength from meeting other people who are controlling their desire for alcohol. Added to this is the spiritual emphasis that is one of the pillars of the AA approach. The alcoholic calls on a higher power to help control the problem.

AA meeting in a women's prison.

It should be stressed that the organization was founded by and is run by alcoholics. As such, it is a self-help group and a model for similar groups such as Narcotics Anonymous and Cocaine Anonymous, established by drug addicts. AA is certainly the most popular of the self-help groups. As of 1995, it had more than 2 million members in 89,000 groups across the United States and nearly 100 countries (Comer, 1995).

Al-Anon is a related self-help group that provides support for people who live with alcoholics. Members share their experiences and learn how to cope with the effects of drinking on their lives. They may also learn how to stop reinforcing the drinking and related behavior of loved ones (Comer, 1995).

For various reasons, discussed by Comer (1995, p. 477), it is difficult to determine the success of self-help groups. Some keep no records of members who drop out of the program. Others may be distrustful of professional researchers and don't cooperate with them, although this attitude is beginning to change. Most of the evidence of success comes from testimonials of many thousands who believe they have been helped.

Psychotherapy by itself has not proved to be of great value in treating alcoholics, nor have strictly medical approaches been of lasting value. For many years, hospitals—both general and psychiatric—were reluctant to undertake treatment of alcoholics. It seemed futile merely to provide the alcoholic with a place to "dry out" when the benefits usually were temporary. Most mental health professionals now believe that treatment must be multifaceted. The first step is primarily medical because it involves detoxification, that is, removing the toxic substances from the body and restoring the body chemistry to normal. Medication is used to control withdrawal symptoms. Family and occupational counseling follows, aimed at helping the patient to function better in the community without resorting to alcohol. Follow-up counseling in the community might subsequently be coupled with continued membership in AA. Gradually, hospitals are beginning to establish special units for the treatment of alcoholism along the lines just suggested. Concurrently, there has been a trend to train human services workers in counseling alcoholics. For more information about alcoholism, see Chapter 8.

HEROIN ADDICTS

It is even more difficult to determine the number of heroin addicts than the number of alcoholics in the country because of the illegal nature of **heroin** use. Understandably, addicts are not eager to stand up and be counted. During the 1960s, heroin use increased so dramatically that the media began talking about the "heroin epidemic" (Bazell, 1973). Recent surveys show that heroin use continues at a high rate. Although it is difficult to gather precise data, the considered opinion among experts is that there are more than a million heroin addicts in the United States (Davison & Neale, 1996).

Whereas alcoholics are widely distributed throughout the range of social classes, heroin addicts tend to be concentrated in the lower socioeconomic classes, particularly among minority group members. Initially, narcotics addiction was seen primarily as a problem of the inner cities. However, during the last two decades, there has been a spread of heroin addiction to white suburban areas as well as to small towns and cities across America. In Ohio, for instance, heroin-related deaths spread into 18 new counties from 2004 to 2007, the latest year for which statistics are available (Archibold, 2009). Regardless of area, heroin addiction is most common in people in their late teens to early twenties. One other group with a high rate of addiction is that of physicians who have easy access to pure morphine and other narcotics; they typically become involved in drugs at a later age than street addicts and also seem better able to function on the job than street addicts.

A number of factors account for the appeal of **narcotics**, a class of drugs derived from **opium**, including heroin, morphine, and codeine. The immediate effect is a sense of euphoria, followed by a state of deep relaxation and contentment. This blissful state, which may last 4 to 6 hours, is followed by the unpleasant return to reality called "coming down." Frequent use of the drug for a month or so is sufficient to addict most people.

Addiction is both physiological and psychological in nature. Once addicted, users feel physically ill if they cannot get the drug. Unfortunately, larger and larger doses are needed to achieve the same effect. Drug addiction is then likely to become a way of life, with much time spent getting the money to feed the habit. The addict often turns to illegal means of raising the money, but reports of addicts turning to violence are greatly exaggerated. They are more likely to get involved in theft, burglary, and shoplifting because the income is more reliable. Another major source of income is selling drugs to others, thus perpetuating the problem. Female addicts often turn to prostitution to get money (Rorvik, 1979).

Aside from imprisonment, treatment for narcotics addicts has taken three basic forms: hospitalization, methadone maintenance programs, and self-help groups.

Until the 1960s, hospitalization under supervision was usually the only practical alternative. As might be expected, this approach is most successful in helping the addict to "detox," that is, to overcome the ill effects of withdrawal from heroin. However, the relapse rate is very high once addicts leave the hospital.

Methadone maintenance has been one of the most common approaches utilized for narcotic addiction. **Methadone** is a synthetic narcotic chemically similar to **morphine** that is itself highly addictive. The presumed usefulness of this drug is derived from its capacity to satisfy or reduce the craving for heroin. Methadone does not produce the stupor associated with heroin, nor does it require ever-increasing doses to be effective. It frees the addict of the necessity of raising money for heroin and opens the door to normal job and social routines. Unfortunately, most addicts cannot be tapered off to the point where they can go drug-free. In effect, they substitute one addiction for another, but from society's point of view, an addiction to methadone is preferable to an addiction to heroin because it decriminalizes the addiction.

The third major approach is based on intense group pressure brought to bear on addicts by their peers—reformed addicts. Synanon is perhaps the best known of these self-help groups for addicts. Founded in the 1960s, it grew to the point where it was able to maintain several residences for addicts in a number of cities. Similar groups began to mushroom in the late 1960s and early 1970s. The general approach is drug-free and stresses a tough-minded attitude toward the addict, who is seen as a dependent child with few redeeming qualities.

In some programs, the group assault appears designed to break down the defenses of the addict so completely that new behaviors become a necessity. Drug addicts point out that middle-class professionals are too soft to work effectively with addicts. Whereas this may or may not be true, there is little solid evidence that these self-help groups have found the formula for success. One unsolved problem of such programs is the high dropout rate; the most difficult cases often simply leave the group.

TREATMENT WITH DRUG ANTAGONISTS This refers to using drugs to change the effects of an addictive drug. One of the best known of these is disulfiram, usually known by its trade name, **Antabuse**. It is used to treat chronic alcoholic patients who need special help to remain sober. Taken by itself the drug has few negative effects, but if the patient drinks alcohol after taking Antabuse, he or she will experience nausea, vomiting, and other ill effects. The idea is that persons on Antabuse will avoid alcohol knowing the consequences. The obvious disadvantage of this treatment is that patients can simply decide not to take the drug if they plan to resume drinking.

Another type of treatment is based on the use of **narcotic antagonists** such as naloxone, cyclazocine, and naltrexone. These drugs do not have an aversive effect but deprive the narcotic addict of the euphoria usually produced by **opiates** such as heroin. Without the high, there would seem to be little point in continuing the use of the narcotic. It has been reported that these drugs may also block the high that alcohol creates. Comer (1995) cites some studies that suggest the possibility of promising results with drugs of this type. However, these drugs may cause negative **side effects** in some persons, including severe withdrawal reactions (Goldstein, 1994).

COCAINE ABUSERS

Cocaine abuse is prevalent on levels of the socio-economic ladder from the affluent of Hollywood to the poorer, inner-city neighborhoods. One reason for the spread of cocaine is that the supply has increased, resulting in lower prices.

Cocaine, a derivative of the coca plant, is sometimes called coke, snow, blow, toot, flake, or nose candy, among others. It is usually snorted into the nasal passages where it is readily absorbed. Some users melt the impurities, leaving pure cocaine or freebase, which is smoked for an intense high. Intravenous injection is the most hazardous way of administering cocaine; not only are the chances of addiction increased, but an additional danger comes from non-sterile needles.

In 1986 a new form of cocaine called **crack** became prevalent; it is a pea-size, crystallized form of the drug that is sold in small units for a relatively low price. Crack produces an intense high very quickly. This factor plus its low price account for its attractiveness to teenagers and people with limited income.

Cocaine increases alertness and brings about a heightened sense of well-being verging on euphoria. In heavy users, this cocaine high is followed by a rapid descent into pain, anxiety, and depression, which in turn compels the user to find and use more. Some end up using cocaine almost continuously until the supply is exhausted. This pattern, called a "run," may go on for a number of days. Repetitive use is a clear sign of addiction or **physical dependence** on the drug.

Large doses of cocaine, or prolonged use, may produce a state of paranoia. Heavy users may feel under threat of attack and may arm themselves accordingly. In some people, cocaine abuse may lead to hallucinations of touch, taste, and smell. One strange consequence of abuse is cocaine psychosis—the belief that bugs or snakes are crawling under the skin. Gallagher (1987) noted that one Hollywood actress required plastic surgery after she clawed her face open to kill imaginary bugs.

As yet no widely accepted specific treatments are available for cocaine abuse. Most treatment takes place in general drug and alcohol treatment programs that use the same methods in treating cocaine addicts as in treating other substance abusers. It should be kept in mind that the classification of abusers into discrete categories (that is, alcoholic, cocaine addict, and so forth) may sometimes be misleading, because many individuals abuse more than one substance.

Cocaine Anonymous is a self-help group that began as an adjunct to Alcoholics Anonymous and now has about 1,000 chapters nationwide. Like AA, it helps the user achieve sobriety on a day-to-day basis. Coke-anon (or Cocanon) is a companion organization for relatives and friends of the addict.

Some clinicians believe that cocaine abusers do not become motivated to stop their drug use until they "hit bottom" and lose everything. However, other experts in the field believe that this scenario can be avoided by means of a confrontation of the abuser by family and/or employer. At an intervention meeting, family members and friends may gather together with the abuser and a professional, typically a physician, psychologist, or social worker experienced in such work. They present the abuser with clear documentation of the results of the abuse, treatment options, and a statement of the family's response if she or he refuses treatment or continues the abuse.

These meetings are emotionally charged and may cause the abuser to defend against what seems like a general attack. But when it goes well, the impact may be great enough to convince the addict to enter treatment immediately. If the user continues to deny the seriousness of the habit, the family may resolve to stop enabling the addiction by covering it up, taking over the responsibilities of the addict, supporting the addict, and so on. Family members may go so far as to refuse to live in the same house with the addict. Instead, they focus on getting their own lives together.

Methamphetamine Abuse

Methamphetamine is a highly addictive stimulant that affects the central nervous system. It is classified as a Schedule II stimulant, which means that it has a high potential for abuse and is available only through a prescription that cannot be refilled. Currently, its medical uses are limited and has been indicated as a treatment for narcolepsy (a sleep disorder) and attention deficit hyperactivity disorder (Iritani, 2007; Ramson, 2007).

The drug was developed early last century from its parent drug, **amphetamine**, and was used originally in nasal decongestants and bronchial inhalers. One of the most common Food and Drug Administration (FDA)–approved uses of amphetamines is an appetite suppressant to treat obesity.

Amphetamines were used widely by soldiers during World War II, the Korean War, and Operation Desert Storm to counteract fatigue and heighten endurance.

Amphetamines were frequently prescribed in the United States in the 1950s and 1960s to patients who wished to lose weight or were depressed, and they continued to gain in popularity as drugs of abuse into the 1970s (Doweiko, 2009). It was at about this time that physicians more clearly understood the devastating side effects of chronic amphetamine abuse and how it would dominate the user's life. Amphetamines were classified as Schedule II substances in the Controlled Substances Act of 1970. Today, the use of amphetamines has still not disappeared from either the illicit drug trade or from certain medical practice (Hanson, Venturelli, & Fleckenstein, 2006). A variety of related drugs and mixtures are still prescribed by physicians.

Like amphetamine, methamphetamine causes increased activity and talkativeness, decreased appetite, and a general sense of well-being and euphoria. Methamphetamine, however, is a more potent stimulant and has longer lasting and more harmful side effects on the brain and the central nervous system, with a high potential for widespread abuse. Methamphetamine abuse can lead to significant and often irreversible medical, psychological, and social consequences. Adverse health effects include memory loss, aggression, malnutrition, severe dental problems, and addiction (Chang, Ernst, Speck, & Grob, 2005).

Methamphetamine is commonly known as meth, speed, or chalk. In its smoked form, it is often referred to as crystal, ice, crank, or glass, among a host of other street names. It is a white, odorless, bitter-tasting crystalline powder that dissolves easily into water or alcohol. It can be taken orally, intranasally (snorting the powder), by needle injection, or by smoking. With chronic use, tolerance for methamphetamine can develop. In an effort to intensify the desired effects, users may take higher doses, take it more frequently, or change the method of intake. In some cases, abusers can inject as much as a gram of the drug every 2 to 3 hours over several days (Center for Addiction and Mental Health, 2009.)

Crystal methamphetamine abuse is considered by many to be the fastest growing and most serious drug problem facing America today. One of the reasons for its popularity is that it can be produced by combining a specific set of chemicals, all of which can be legally obtained (United States Drug Enforcement Administration, 2009). The illicit manufacture of crystal methamphetamine is particularly dangerous because the process is toxic and potentially explosive. Traffikers and/or users of crystal methamphetamine have been known to create "batches" of the drug right in their own homes or garages. The bulk of production, however, is done by drug trafficking cartels in the United States as well as Mexico and Canada. In some areas of the country, especially on the west coast, methamphetamine abuse has outpaced the abuse of heroin and cocaine and in many western and midwestern states, methamphetamine is second only to alcohol and **marijuana** as the drug used most frequently (National Institute on Drug Abuse, 2009). According to the 2007 Monitoring the Future Survey conducted by the National Institute on Drug Abuse, an estimated 10.4 million people, age 12 or older (4.3% of the population) have tried methamphetamine at some time in their lives. Evidence from emergency departments and treatment programs attest to the growing impact of methamphetamine abuse in this country.

Methamphetamine abuse can be prevented and methamphetamine addiction can be treated. People do recover but only when effective treatments that address the multitude of problems resulting from abuse are readily available. Currently the most effective treatments are behavioral. An example of this approach is the matrix model, a comprehensive behavioral treatment approach that combines behavioral therapy, family education, individual counseling, 12-step support, drug testing, and support for non-drug-related activities. Another related approach shown to be effective are contingency management interventions, which provide tangible incentives in exchange for engaging in treatment and maintaining abstinence (Roll, Petry, Stitzer, Victor, & Sami, 2006). There are no medications available as of now approved to treat methamphetamine addiction.

CONFLICTING APPROACHES TO THE DRUG PROBLEM

What to do about drug addicts has been the subject of intense controversies during recent years. At least three different approaches can be identified, each of which has strong supporters. These are (a) legalization or decriminalization of drugs, (b) law enforcement, and (c) treatment for addicts.

Some Americans are so frustrated by the failure of our attempts to control narcotic abuse that they are ready to raise the white flag: legalize narcotics, they say, and be done with it (Kupfer, 1988). They are willing to risk greater drug use to reduce the crime associated with illegal drug traffic. The underlying idea is to take the profit out of the drug business. Law enforcement efforts tend to drive up the prices of illegal substances, making the business more profitable. If we eliminate the laws against the possession, sale, and use of drugs, according to this view, we will reduce the violence, corruption, and medical problems associated with their use. Lazare (1990) argues that instead of spending vast sums for police, prosecutors, judges, prison guards, and so on, we should tax the sale of previously forbidden drugs and use the money for drug treatment.

A case against legalization has been made by Schmolling (1993), who reviewed evidence showing that unregulated access to narcotics has led to disastrous results in the past. In fact, the Harrison Act of 1914, which outlawed self-administration of narcotics, was enacted because of the realization that cocaine and opiate addiction was causing crime and family instability (Musto, 1987). There is also reason to believe that legalization of narcotics would result in huge increases in the number of addicts (Wilson, 1990). Cocaine, for example, is intensely addictive and may produce a state in which other considerations such as job, family, children, sleep, food, and even sex go out the window. A policy of making cocaine freely available would undoubtedly increase the number of crack babies. Wilson states that the only way to be certain of the effect of easy availability of cocaine would be to try it and see, but he quickly adds that this is one social experiment we dare not make because the consequences would be devastating.

The second approach, law enforcement, is the chief weapon that the government employs in the war on drugs. This approach is based on a moral (or punitive) model that holds that individuals must be held responsible for violating the law. In this view, violators are capable of choice and must face the consequences if they break the law. During the 1980s, adherents of this model argued that we were losing the drug war because we were too soft on users and dealers. This led to more arrests, mandatory (and sometimes severe) sentences for dealers, and increased surveillance and interception of drugs smuggled into the country. The increased use of legal sanctions during the 1980s apparently had the effect of reducing drug use among casual users but had little effect on frequent users, defined as those who use drugs at least once a week (White House, 1989). Other consequences of the "get tough" approach are overcrowded court dockets, increased expenses associated with enforcement efforts, and, as documented in the next section, a huge increase in the prison population.

The third approach, treatment, is based on the medical model, described in detail in Chapter 4. The general idea is that addicts are suffering from an illness and should be treated rather than punished. In this view, abusers are victims of compulsive, self-destructive cravings and are in need of medical and psychological treatments. Although governments spend more on law enforcement than on treatment, drug treatment is nevertheless a major industry in this country. Five thousand drug agencies operate nationwide, including the following:

- Detoxification units that have the short-range goal of ending physical dependence on drugs.
- Inpatient units that offer detox with a beginning of counseling to be continued on an outpatient basis.
- Outpatient clinics providing support and therapy.
- Methadone units designed to maintain heroin addicts in the community.
- Residential, drug-free, therapeutic communities that help the addict develop a new lifestyle.

INTERACTIONS BETWEEN LEGAL AND THERAPEUTIC APPROACHES

In debates about drug policies, conservatives tend to argue in favor of intensified law enforcement, whereas liberals are more inclined to favor treatment approaches. The two approaches are often presented as though they are opposed to each other. In reality, there is an intimate connection between the two that is often overlooked. Legal pressures account for 40% to 70% of all referrals to community alcohol and drug treatment programs (Schottenfeld, 1989). Agency statistics probably do not reflect the true magnitude of coerced referrals. Many seemingly self-referred individuals are responding to outside pressures but were not referred directly by the courts. Some are pressured by child welfare agencies, and others by a spouse or employer. Every intake worker at drug treatment agencies has listened to earnest pleas for treatment followed by a request beginning, "By the way, I could use a letter showing I'm in treatment." The letter would be brought to court, to probation offices, or to an employer, or a welfare agency providing benefits. The proportion of genuinely voluntary referrals to drug treatment agencies is probably quite low. Despite abundant evidence to the contrary, many heavy users believe that they can "handle" their drugs of choice and perceive themselves to be recreational users rather than addicts. If it weren't for law enforcement and other forms of coercion, there would be little spontaneous demand for treatment aimed at a drug-free lifestyle.

Schmolling (1993) argues in favor of a more cooperative, rather than competitive, relationship between law enforcement and treatment agencies. Some existing programs involve what might be called a therapeutic use of law enforcement. The basic idea is to give addicts a clear choice; that is, personal freedom is made contingent on drug-free, responsible behavior. One model based on this concept is California's Civil Addict Program (CAP). As described by Anglin (1988), an addict convicted of property crimes or drug dealing could be committed to the program. The two-phase program consists of an incarceration period followed by monitored release in the community. A crucial feature of the program is that addicts can be reincarcerated for infractions, including drug use as determined by urine testing. The message of this program is clear: If you want your freedom, stay clean. Treatments that enhance social and vocational competence help the addict move toward a more productive way of life. Relatively few addicts choose conventional criminal processing over participating in this sort of program.

CRIMINALS

The United States has a relatively high rate of criminal activity compared to other affluent nations. Our homicide rate leads the industrialized world, owing, in part, to the drug problem and ready availability of handguns. How do we know how much criminal activity is taking place? There are two main sources of information: police reports and victim surveys. The FBI's *Uniform Crime Reports* (Federal Bureau of Investigation, 1995), issued annually, is based on crime reports contributed by more than 16,000 law enforcement agencies. These reports tell us what crimes have actually been reported by citizens to the police. A victim survey is quite different because it is derived from a household poll in which people are asked whether they have been a victim of a crime during a given time period.

The best known victim survey is the National Crime Survey, which is a poll of about 160,000 people in 84,000 households. This survey has been issued annually since its inception in 1973. The victim surveys reveal much higher rates of crime than do the police reports. The reason is obvious: many crime victims do not file a complaint with the police. Why not? It may be that the perpetrator is a close friend or family member. Other victims do not want the nature of the crime to be made public, and still others may feel that "nothing will be done about it anyway, so why bother?" There is also the possibility of reprisals against the person bringing charges.

The data on crime must be viewed against the background of a major shift in the political environment that began in the 1980s, bringing with it changing policies related to crime and imprisonment. The previous emphasis on rehabilitation gave way to a more punitive approach. The public wanted more effective crime control and rewarded politicians who promised to get tough on criminals. Another reason for the change in policy was that a series of experimental studies raised serious doubts about the effectiveness of rehabilitation (Blumstein, 1995, p. 395). The dominant finding was that no particular approach consistently works in reducing post-release criminal behavior. It appeared that the characteristics of offenders and the environment to which they return have more influence on recidivism than any special program. The major impact of the new policies was a huge increase in prison population. The United States is second in the world, behind Russia, in rate of incarceration and has a rate 4 times that of Canada and 14 times that of Japan. Our high rates are due largely to violent crimes as opposed to property crimes. According to Holmes (1994), surveys of state prisoners have found that 94% had previous convictions or are in prison for violent crime; the data showed that when they were free, they committed violent and repeated crimes. The public is concerned about the recycling of these violent offenders back into the community.

Considering that an increasing number of people with criminal tendencies were in prison, it seems logical to expect the crime rate to go down. Actually, the *Uniform Crime Reports* showed a stabilization in reported crime rates but not a significant decline. An analysis of the data by Freeman (1995) resulted in the chilling conclusion that the "propensity for crime among noninstitutionalized men increased immensely during the 1980s" (p. 175). In other words, the fact that massive incarceration did not reduce crime rates means that there are more criminals out there. Some surveys indicate that the crime rate has rapidly increased in several rural states and is higher than in some urban states such as New York and New Jersey.

To understand some of the causes of this propensity to crime in the United States, it would help to look at the youngsters—the juveniles—who are just beginning their criminal careers. Most criminal careers begin in the juvenile years.

JUVENILE OFFENDERS

The general public does not fully realize that juveniles, defined by most states as persons younger than 18, commit a large percentage of serious crimes. During the mid-1980s, persons under 18 accounted for about one out of every three arrests for robbery, about half of all arrests for property crimes, and about one of six arrests for rape. Each year, more than a million juveniles are arrested by the police in the United States. This alarmingly high rate of criminal activity among youngsters is by no means confined to inner cities. Similarly high rates have been reported for youngsters from suburban and rural areas.

One repeated finding of studies both here and abroad is that 6% of the boys of a given age will commit half or more of all serious crimes in that age group. According to Wilson (1995), these young chronic offenders tend to

- Have criminal parents.
- Be low in verbal IQ and do poorly in school.
- Live in emotionally cold, discordant families.
- Be emotionally cold themselves.
- Be impulsive.
- Reside in poor, disorderly communities.
- Begin their misconduct at an early age.
- Use drugs and alcohol.

These findings are in line with a number of other factors that have been identified as contributing to delinquency. Perhaps most basic is a home life characterized by insecurity and rejection of the youngster. Delinquent youths are likely to come from homes disrupted by divorce rather than by the death of a parent. Inconsistent discipline is another contributing factor. Parents are likely to alternate harsh punishment with periods of neglect or disinterest. The delinquent generalizes contempt for the parents to other authority figures, including teachers and police.

Usually, delinquents do not receive the kind of parental help and encouragement that is needed for success in school. Various studies demonstrate quite clearly that inner-city delinquents have little confidence that they can achieve success in our society. They anticipate dropping out of high school and, at best, being stuck in a low-level job, and they sometimes feel justified in breaking the rules because the system is so much against them.

The courts have generally treated juveniles differently from adult offenders. The juvenile court system was designed not so much to punish but to protect the best interests of the child. However, this approach is now under attack by citizens who feel that the courts are too lenient with dangerous juveniles. The argument is that teenagers who commit adult crimes (for example, rape, assault, and murder) should be treated as adults and dealt with severely. The courts are caught between the interests of an outraged community and the rights of the youngster.

JUVENILE CORRECTION PROGRAMS A variety of programs are used to treat juvenile offenders. For juveniles whose crimes are not very serious, and who have supportive families, the court may recommend some form of in-home supervision. Informal probation, intensive supervision, mentoring programs, and after-school programs are some of the programs that may be considered.

For youngsters who pose greater risk but are not considered extremely dangerous, placement in group homes, foster care, and other community-living situations are the programs of choice. For those who represent the highest risk to the community, most states provide a continuum of increasingly restrictive settings ranging from isolated wilderness camps to high-security locked facilities.

According to Greenwood (1995), recent decades have seen a trend away from the large, traditional training schools where most serious juvenile offenders were once placed. These institutions were criticized for offering sterile and unimaginative programs and for allowing abuse and mistreatment of the weaker juveniles. In place of these institutions, many states are substituting smaller, often privately run, community-based settings. These community programs at least present the hope of offering a wider range of rehabilitative programs.

An exception to the general trend toward community-based facilities is California, which continues to rely on large, secure training schools. These institutions house from 700 to 1,500 youthful offenders. One reason for this preference is that California is inundated with juvenile offenders, accounting for 20% of the youth locked up in the entire nation (Greenwood, 1995). Many other state systems are struggling with reduced budgets to handle an increasingly difficult and dangerous population. This sometimes results in the provision of custodial care with little money left over for therapeutic programs.

ADULT OFFENDERS

What should we do with those who violate the law? This is an intensely controversial issue that generates widely divergent answers from liberal and conservative commentators. Some believe that we are too soft on criminals and that many criminals escape prosecution on legal technicalities. Others argue that the entire system is heavily biased against poor people and minorities. For prosecutors, the central questions are how to allocate limited resources in regard to a bewildering variety of cases involving street crime, domestic violence, drug violations, child abuse, white-collar offenses, and repeat offenders (Forst, 1995).

There is intense conflict about imposing mandatory minimum sentences in drug cases. Indeed, some judges are now refusing to try minor drug cases. Judge Jack Weinstein (1993), for example, has argued that our justice system is in crisis largely because of drug prosecutions. He points out that, nationwide, over one-third of all new inmates are drug offenders. Because of mandated sentences, he continues, drug smugglers and dealers are serving longer prison terms, sometimes 10-year minimums, than was previously the case. The resulting overcrowding in our prisons is wasteful and self-defeating because it deters no one from dealing in drugs.

Former Texas senator Phil Gramm (1993), on the other hand, was among those in favor of tough sentencing for drug dealers. He stated his belief that most criminals are rational men and women who commit crime because they think it pays. And in the United States, they are right; crime does pay because there is a low expectancy of actually being arrested, convicted, and imprisoned. "When a potential criminal knows that if he is convicted he is certain to be sentenced, and his sentence is certain to be stiff, his cost-benefit calculus changes dramatically and his willingness to engage in criminal activity takes a nose dive," argued Senator Gramm (1993, p. A19). We have witnessed a dramatic increase in crime since the 1960s, he said, because we have treated criminals as victims of dysfunctional families, of capitalism, and of society at large. Instead, we should, in his opinion, keep criminals off the streets and keep them from harming our children.

PROBATION   Some offenders receive suspended sentences and are placed under the supervision of a probation officer. Many of those on probation are nonviolent offenders with no prior convictions. About 80% of probationers complete their terms without a new arrest (Clear & Braga, 1995). However, the public is rightly concerned about a subgroup of offenders who have high rates of criminal activity.

An important recent trend in probation is the push toward better classification of probationers so that those who pose the greatest risk to the community receive more supervision. In the past, too little time was devoted to serious offenders. Now, cases are assigned "work units" in accordance with need, and each probation officer is responsible for a certain number of work units (Clear & Braga, 1995).

PRISON AND CORRECTIONAL PROGRAMS   The finding that prisoners are not being rehabilitated in significant numbers is not surprising in view of the fact that most prisons provide little more than custodial care. Relatively little effort is devoted to treatment and job training. Life in prison is routinized, time is structured, and the social system is completely authoritarian. It is not the kind of place in which one can learn to function adaptively in a free society. Although incarceration undoubtedly has the effect of deterring some prisoners from future crime, it is also true that others become hardened by their total immersion in a society of criminals.

Inciardi (1987, p. 580) states that each of the present correctional strategies—vocational training, education, penitence through prayer, recreation, group therapy—seems to work for somebody. The difficulty is that we do not know which approach is most effective for whom. Perhaps the greatest problem is in the selection of offenders for participation in a particular rehabilitative program. Inciardi suggests that we need to do a better job in the screening of offenders and that we should admit that some offenders cannot be helped by any known program. Improvement is also needed in determining when an offender has received maximum benefits from any given technique. All of this means that correctional programs should learn to be more efficient and cost-effective.

ALTERNATIVES TO INCARCERATION   Although some Americans believe that incarceration is the only adequate moral response to the suffering imposed upon innocent victims by criminals, various alternatives are being put into practice in many parts of the country. The high costs of incarceration, the overcrowding in prisons, and the lobbying of penal reformers are some of the factors that account for increasing the number of offenders who are assigned to some form of nonincarceration program (DiIulio, 1991). Here are brief descriptions of some approaches that are now being tried.

House Arrest with Electronic Monitoring   In the case of house arrest with electronic monitoring, the offender, usually an adult who has committed property crimes or white-collar crime, is required to stay in or around home except to participate in court-approved activities. She or he is required to wear an electronic monitoring device, usually in the form of an ankle bracelet, that enables corrections officers to know where the offender is at any time. The offender is incarcerated if there are any violations.

Community-Service Sentences   Another alternative to incarceration, a community-service sentence, involves placing offenders in their own community under close supervision, where they are required to perform some socially useful task (for example, painting buildings or cleaning vacant lots) to help pay part of the cost of their supervision. Usually, the offenders work in small groups supervised by a corrections officer.

Intensive-Supervision Programs   In an intensive-supervision program, participants must either work or go to school, submit to random drug and alcohol tests, and reside in a community center with strict rules about chores, curfews, and social interactions. In addition, they may be required to make restitution to victims.

Early results showed high rates of failure for these programs. These offenders did not seem to do better in terms of arrests and other measures than those on routine supervision such as that used in conventional probation and **parole** (Clear & Braga, 1995).

Boot Camps   The idea of immersing offenders in a military-style experience similar to basic training is another type of program. It is hoped that this program will instill some pride and self-discipline in the offender. There is no evidence that these programs either deter or rehabilitate prisoners.

More assessments of these innovative approaches are needed before any final conclusions can be drawn.

PEOPLE WITH MENTAL RETARDATION

It is apparent that some children are not able to learn as quickly as their age-mates. In fact, the first **intelligence** tests were designed to identify children who could not accomplish age-appropriate tasks. These tests measure the child's ability to memorize, concentrate, grasp verbal abstractions, do arithmetic, and perform other skills. By definition, the child who is average in ability for a particular age has an **intelligence quotient** (IQ) of 100. Those who score significantly below average in ability are classified as persons with retardation. The precise cutoff score is arbitrarily selected, and there is variation among scaling systems. However, most authorities consider individuals with IQs below 70 to be mentally retarded.

CAUSES OF RETARDATION

Few people realize that most individuals with **mental retardation** show no evidence of brain injury or defect but that, rather, environmental factors account for the majority of cases. These factors include a destructive or abusive home life, parents who are dysfunctional and poor role models, and limited **learning** opportunities during infancy and early childhood. The myth that learners with retardation are brain injured has been an obstacle to setting higher expectations for these individuals (Borich & Tombari, 1995, p. 525).

Certain genetic disorders may cause below-average functioning in learning and achievement. Phenylketonuria (PKU) is an example of a single-gene disorder that may cause severe retardation. Babies with PKU appear normal at birth but are unable to metabolize an amino acid called phenylalanine, which then accumulates and converts to toxic substances. Fortunately, infants can now be screened for PKU. If diagnosed early and started on a low-phenylalanine diet, they may develop normally.

Chromosomal disorders take place during formation of the egg or the sperm and are not hereditary. The best known of these disorders is Down syndrome, named after Langdon Down, the British physician who first identified it. About 1 of every 800 live births results in this syndrome, with the incidence increasing with the mother's age. Persons with Down syndrome have a distinct appearance, with a small head, flat eyes, high cheekbones, and sometimes a protruding tongue. Several of these features suggested an Asian appearance and led to the condition being called Mongolism, a term that is now completely out of favor. Most persons with this syndrome range in IQ from 35 to 55, with some having IQs close to 70. Until the 1970s, clinicians were pessimistic about the potential of children with Down syndrome, but they are now viewed as capable of learning and accomplishing many things in their lives (Comer, 1995, p. 682).

Prenatal complications are another possible cause of retardation. Most brain growth takes place during fetal development, that is, before birth. Many difficulties may affect brain development during this phase, including decreased oxygen supply to the developing fetus and exposure to alcohol, drugs, and other toxins. In the case of fetal alcohol syndrome, for example, the infant weighs less than normal, develops slowly, and may show other deficits. The brain of the fetus or infant is also vulnerable to viral infections such as measles, rubella, mumps, HIV, and herpes, which may impair cognitive processes (Borich & Tombari, 1995).

CLASSIFYING PEOPLE WITH MENTAL RETARDATION

Cases of mental retardation are diagnosed and classified on the basis of both intelligence tests and tests of adaptive functioning. The latter measure the extent to which a person has learned basic skills such as personal care, feeding, toileting, language, pedestrian skills, and skills having to do with getting along with other people. These adaptive skills are learned by most people without formal training (Borich & Tombari, 1995). Most states rely more on the IQ score in diagnosing mental retardation than on measures of adaptive behavior (Morgenstern & Klass, 1991).

There is wide variation in intellectual ability within the group of persons classified as retarded. They are subdivided into four groups: the mildly, moderately, severely, and profoundly retarded. As shown in Table 2.1, the large majority are classified as mildly retarded. These individuals can learn basic adaptive skills, such as dressing and feeding themselves, and can perform many kinds of work tasks. They can marry, live independently with some supervision, and hold jobs. For example, McDonald's has found that these workers can do many kinds of routine jobs.

As we go down the scale, individuals are less capable and require more help and supervision. There is also greater probability that the person will show some physical defect or deformity. Persons who are profoundly retarded may have limited mobility, and communication is generally limited to some simple gestures and vocal intonations. Some of these individuals are cared for in large institutional settings, but there is a trend toward placing them in smaller group homes with 15 to 20 residents. See Table 2.1 again for further information about the expected performances of individuals at various levels of retardation.

The education of persons with retardation begins with a mapping out of target behaviors. Self-care, social behavior, and basic academic and vocational skills are usually the main areas of concentration. Within each area, specific skills are divided into simple components that the person is capable of learning. Learning then proceeds in a step-by-step fashion, gradually building the simple components into more skilled performance (Coleman et al., 1984). The advantage of this gradual approach is that the person experiences success frequently in the learning process.

It should be stressed that most persons with retardation can learn a variety of social and vocational skills and need not be institutionalized. Those with mild retardation are the most capable, and they are taught within the public school system. Others may be placed in special schools in the community. At school, they are taught elementary reading, writing, and arithmetic to the fullest possible extent. The less capable students may devote relatively more time to learning the basic skills of daily living such as washing, eating, brushing teeth, buttoning buttons, and so on. Some are eventually placed in sheltered workshops where they may do light assembly, packaging, and other jobs for modest pay. Often, payment is on a piecework basis. Nevertheless, the jobs are real jobs, and the pay is real money. This means that the worker can experience the satisfaction that comes from making a contribution to society.

In the recent past, many children with retardation were considered uneducable, and little effort was put into teaching them academic skills. Educators are now coming around to the view that we should avoid a pattern of very low expectations for these students. Dover (1990) recommends that certain principles be followed with regard to instruction. The first of these is that programs focus on instructional goals as primary objectives and that medical and psychological goals be provided only when there is a clear need for them. In other words, learning comes first. The failure to learn should lead to a search for better techniques of instruction.

Another principle is that the goal of instruction should be independence. Dover also suggests that communication training receive heavy emphasis. Students must learn to communicate if they are to gain access to desired activities, make their needs known, or get the attention of teachers and other individuals. Perhaps the main idea is that exceptional learners should be classified primarily on their needs to learn certain skills. This means that children are not blind, deaf, mentally retarded, or learning-disabled but instead are students who need instruction in mobility, pedestrian skills, signing, reading recognition, money management, and so on.

The outlook for persons with retardation has improved significantly since 1970 when the President's Committee on Retardation concluded that the potential contribution of many such persons was being wasted because of a shortage of adequate schools and facilities. Since then, the number of retarded people simply being warehoused in large custodial institutions has decreased dramatically. Increasingly, persons with retardation are included in regular schools and in community programs.

TABLE 2.1 | BEHAVIORAL EXPECTANCIES OF INDIVIDUALS WITH RETARDATION BY LEVEL OF SEVERITY*

Level of Retardation	Percentage of the Retarded	Preschool Behavior (under Age 6)	School Performance	Adult Functioning	Social Adjustment
Mild IQ Range 50–69	85%	Slightly slow in walking, taking, and caring for self, but not very different from average children; often not identified as retarded before entering school	Can learn academic skills at between the third- and sixth-grade level	May become self-supporting and has potential for sheltered or competitive employment; some supervision may be needed	Able to interact with others but with some poor social skills; makes friends; marriage a possibility
Moderate IQ Range 35–49	10%	Noticeably slow in learning self-help skills, but eventually learns to walk and talk on a simple level	Can learn academic tasks up to second-grade level; survival skills can be learned	Capable of employment in highly supervised settings; very rarely suitable to independent living; live in supported settings	Can interact with others but may appear awkward and slow to understand; marriage rarely attempted
Severe IQ Range 20–34	4%	By age 6, may have learned to walk and feed self; speech limited; may not be toilet trained at this phase	May be able to learn basic self-care skills and some speech	Capable of simple tasks in home or sheltered workshop; some permanent care is needed.	Social interactions generally very limited
Profound IQ Below 20	1%	May have some minimal ambulatory skills at age 6; communication usually by nonverbal techniques; may not be toilet trained	May be able to learn some basic movements and positions; some are bedbound, helpless	Not capable of employment; permanent care needed; may be institutionalized	Little or no social awareness

*Based on various sources, including Patton, Payne, and Beirne-Smith (1990).

THE HOMELESS

For most people, home is associated with warmth, protection, and sharing life experiences with loved ones. It is a place of safety, a refuge from the pressures and demands of the outer world. The thought of being homeless, of having no place to call one's own, is almost inconceivable to most of us. Nevertheless, this is precisely what has happened to thousands of Americans. Men, women, and children all over the country are finding shelter in bus and train terminals, parks, alleyways, abandoned buildings, caves, packing cases, and other unlikely places. The more fortunate among them spend the night in a mission or Salvation Army shelter where a shower and hot meal are provided.

McKinney (1994) defined a homeless person as one who "lacks a fixed, regular, and adequate night-time residence; and ... has a primary night time residency that is: (a) a supervised publicly or privately operated shelter designed to provide temporary living accommodations ..., (b) an institution that provides a temporary residence for individuals intended to be institutionalized, or (c) a public or private place not designed for, or ordinarily used as, a regular sleeping accommodation for human beings." There may be other definitions, but this one is part of federal law and therefore is sufficient for our purposes.

Homelessness in the United States is an embarrassment, considering that it exists in the context of great wealth. Although some homeless have always been with us, their numbers have increased dramatically since the mid-1980s. As rapidly as shelters opened, they were filled to capacity. In New York City, a "right to shelter" policy threatened to drain the budget (Bassuk, 1995, p. 318). Santos and Ingrassia (2002) describe the recent sudden increase of homelessness in New York City. Since 1998, the number of families living in shelters almost doubled, to 8,400 from 4,400. In 1998, there were 21,172 people in city shelters; in 2000 that number increased to 35,164. The increase continues today. In addition, they claim that 15,000 children bed down each night in 1 of approximately 70 shelters or other temporary housing. They point out that the challenges are not unique to New York—homelessness is increasing throughout the nation. In fact, as of 2006, sweeping new legislative policies are being debated in San Francisco due to a growing homeless population in that city. Policymakers across the country want to know how many people need shelter, but attempts to count the homeless yield widely divergent results.

Why do the numbers differ so much? The counts vary depending on several factors. One factor is who does the counting. It appears that government agencies may produce low numbers to minimize the extent of the problem. Advocacy groups, on the other hand, may tend to exaggerate the numbers to dramatize the problem and, possibly, increase public support to help the homeless. This is not a suggestion that anyone is actually making up numbers. The fact is that researchers may use different techniques for counting the homeless and may define homelessness more or less stringently. In any case, the homeless are somewhat elusive in the sense that they move from street to shelter to housing in a nomadic fashion. Some homelessness consists of brief episodes, but other cases constitute virtually permanent lifestyles. And we should not forget the "couch people" who have moved in with friends and relatives and who are not included in the homeless tallies (Daley, 1987).

It may not be possible to come up with an exact number due to all of these variables; the Urban Institute estimates that as many as 3.5 million people experience homelessness in the course of a year (Burt & Laudan, 2000).

WHY ARE PEOPLE HOMELESS?

The National Coalition for the Homeless (1999) asserts that poverty and lack of affordable rental housing are some of the major causes. Others at high risk include persons who are victims of domestic violence, the mentally ill, senior citizens, those with addictive disorders, the unemployed and underemployed, and those who lack affordable health care.

Another category of homeless has been identified as the situationally homeless. These are people "whose homelessness has resulted from a change in circumstances, such as eviction, or urban redevelopment" (Breakey, 1987, p. 42). Their problems are chiefly financial and stem from difficult circumstances rather than major disabilities such as alcoholism or mental illness.

A major and continuing problem is the dramatic reduction in low-cost housing due in part to the process of gentrification—the redevelopment of rundown areas of our cities so as to attract middle- or upper-class residents. Low-cost housing is converted to high-priced condominiums, old hotels that once catered to transients are torn down or upgraded, and so on. The problem reflects a limitation of our capitalist system: It is not profitable to build new low-cost housing, so it doesn't get done. Without government subsidy, it is unlikely that the need for low-cost housing will be met.

ATTITUDES TOWARD THE HOMELESS

Americans tend to divide society into winners and losers. The homeless are even bigger losers than those consigned to the welfare system. Often they are seen as lazy, weak, defective persons who are content to live off of handouts from hardworking, decent people. It is not surprising, then, that homeless people are sometimes treated with contempt. Some towns have passed ordinances, making it illegal for the homeless to sleep at night in public places. In other communities, the police tell the homeless to move on, sometimes even providing one-way bus tickets to facilitate the move.

Although negative feelings toward the homeless may prevail, they are by no means universal. Some express a deep compassion for the plight of the homeless. Marin (1987) listened to the life stories of the homeless and found a pattern that usually began with ordinary life. Then a catastrophic event occurred, which in turn led to a series of smaller events until homelessness became inevitable. In this view, the homeless are not different from the rest of us. They have suffered a loss or injury and have had homelessness thrust upon them.

HELPING THE HOMELESS

The system of services for the homeless as it existed in the 1970s was totally insufficient to meet the growing need. For example, rescue missions were set up 50 or more years ago, when most clients were male alcoholics. Rescue missions are shelters supported by religious groups that typically operate under a rigid set of rules. They vary greatly in size, ranging from 15-bed shelters to huge barracks-style arrangements that accommodate hundreds. Except for some large Salvation Army shelters that have hired social workers, missions are generally staffed by religious converts who are intent on saving others from perdition as well as alcoholism.

The voluntary sector also provides a network of shelters run by churches, synagogues, and nonprofit community agencies. As the need for shelters increased, many congregations decided to open church doors to those who needed a place to sleep. From these sorts of informal beginnings, some churches went on to set up formal shelters that sometimes provide supportive counseling. Voluntary groups such as Traveler's Aid and the YWCA and YMCA have also provided shelters. Shelters run by churches and **voluntary agencies** always seem short of funds; some shelters close during the summer months, and others have had to close their doors permanently.

During the early 1980s, it became increasingly obvious that private voluntary agencies could not by themselves do the job of helping the homeless. Nevertheless, municipal governments showed a marked reluctance to increase expenditures for this purpose. Vigorous activity on the part of **advocates** along with glaring publicity was required to prod cities into action. New York, Los Angeles, Philadelphia, Washington, DC, Chicago, and other large cities all acted to support additional shelters. Typically, the city selects unused public buildings and then contracts with a private group to actually run the shelter. In practice, city shelters are thought to be larger, more violent, and more bureaucratic than private ones. They also tend to cost more to operate than private shelters.

Additional help for the homeless was provided by the federal government in 1983. After prolonged prodding by advocates, Congress appropriated $100 million for emergency services to be dispensed by the Federal Emergency Management Administration (FEMA). Lesser amounts were appropriated in subsequent years. Some of the money goes to soup kitchens and other forms of emergency help. FEMA also distributes grants to voluntary umbrella organizations such as the United Way and the National Conference of Catholic Charities. Most of those who work with the homeless believe that federal funding, although welcome, has been grossly inadequate.

In summary, it seems fair to say that the services provided to the homeless were late in coming, still have the quality of hasty patchwork, and remain inadequate to meet the need. It can also be said that the underlying problems have not been addressed in a large-scale way. Hope and Young (1986) argue that the rights to life, liberty, and the pursuit of happiness are empty abstractions unless animated by rights to housing and basic sustenance. A true safety net, they maintain, should be a first step.

Currently, the general public does not appear to be greatly concerned about the plight of the homeless. The term *compassion fatigue* has sometimes been applied by the popular press to describe prevailing public attitudes. As Bassuk (1995) notes, "Regardless of the numbers, the very existence of people on the streets in a society as affluent as ours is a travesty. As the homelessness epidemic has become a chronic disfigurement, the public has increasingly inured itself to the desperate plight of the growing numbers of individuals and families" (p. 319). The "insidious spread" of homelessness, Bassuk continues, "should cause at least enough alarm to make us question our priorities."

Working with South African black children with AIDS.

PEOPLE LIVING WITH HIV/AIDS

Although AIDS, an acronym for acquired immune deficiency syndrome, does not presently claim nearly as many lives as do heart disease and cancer, no other disease raises such intense fears and concerns among the general public. The threat of AIDS, a contagious disease, has altered patterns of sexual activity and is the center of intense controversy about what steps should be taken to prevent the spread of the disease.

WHAT IS AIDS?

AIDS is a serious viral disease that damages the body's natural immune defenses. The disease begins when the human immune deficiency virus (HIV) enters the bloodstream, but this cannot be detected for six weeks or even longer in some cases. At this early stage, many infected people experience no ill effects, although some show mild symptoms such as fatigue, swollen glands, and possibly a rash. These initial symptoms disappear, but the virus quietly multiplies.

During the middle stage of the disease, which may begin after five years, the **immune system** declines in strength, and treatment with AZT, DDI, and other antiviral drugs may be started. Years may elapse before the final or terminal phase is reached. This final phase occurs when the immune system is weakened to the extent that it can no longer fight off invading bacteria, viruses, and parasites. Death may be caused by pneumonia, unusual cancers, or any of a variety of other "opportunistic" diseases. For years, people weren't considered to have AIDS until they showed overt signs of serious illness, but the federal government has revised its standards to include those whose blood tests show a serious level of deficiency but who are as yet symptom-free (Enkholm, 1991).

THE AIDS EPIDEMIC

Within a period of a few years, AIDS grew from a clinical oddity to a major epidemic. When the first cases of AIDS were reported in 1981, epidemiologists at the Centers for Disease Control (CDC) in Atlanta began tracking the disease. They determined that the first cases of AIDS probably occurred in 1977. By 1982, the syndrome had appeared in 15 states, with the majority of victims being homosexual or bisexual men (Institute of Medicine, 1986). As of 1993, the World Health Organization (1993) estimated that over 13 million people worldwide had become infected with HIV. This included over 1 million in North America, 500,000 in western Europe, and another 1.5 million in Latin America and the Caribbean. Hardest hit was Africa, with over 8 million infections. The data suggested that an increasing number of infections were due to heterosexual intercourse (Merson, 1993).

There were an estimated 40.3 million people living with AIDS/HIV at the end of 2005. Of these, 10 million were young people between the ages of 15 and 24. Close to 5 million people were newly infected with the AIDS virus in 2005 (UN-AIDS/WHO). Sub-Saharan Africa remains the hardest hit by the AIDS epidemic, as two-thirds of all people living with AIDS/HIV are in this region. The number of women who are affected continues to increase. In 2005, 17.5 million women were living with AIDS, 1 million more than in 2003. Thirteen million of those live in sub-Saharan Africa. There has been a tremendous increase in AIDS/HIV in eastern Europe and central Asia as well.

In the United States, the cumulative number of persons reported with AIDS to the CDC through 2001 was 793,026. They consisted of 649,186 males, 134,845 females, and 8,994 children under 13 years of age. Total deaths were 457,667, including 5,168 children under 15 years of age (Centers for Disease Control, 2002). The CDC estimates that there were 1 million people living with AIDS in the United States in 2005, but up to one-third did not know that they were infected (World Health Organization, 2005). In 2006, 35,314 new cases of HIV/AIDS in adults, adolescents, and children were diagnosed in 33 states. Almost three-quarters of diagnoses among adolescents and adults were for males. Persons aged 25 to 44 accounted for the largest proportions of newly diagnosed HIV/AIDS cases (Centers for Disease Control, 2008; http//www.CDC.HIV/AIDSSurveillanceReport2008).

WHO ARE THE VICTIMS OF AIDS?

The victims of AIDS fall into the following categories:

- Sexually active homosexual and bisexual men
- Present or past users of intravenous drugs
- Homosexual and bisexual men who are also intravenous drug users

- People with hemophilia or other coagulation disorders
- Heterosexual contacts of someone with AIDS or at risk for AIDS
- Infants born to infected mothers (1%)

The remaining cases do not fall into any of these groups, but researchers believe that transmission occurred in similar ways.

Individuals who are HIV-positive are more likely to be people of color, residents of inner cities, and economically disadvantaged than is the general population. They include women, mainly African American or Latino, who did not insist on condom use and were infected by a male lover.

How Is the Disease Transmitted?

It seems clear from the categories of victims that the major means of transmission is sexual contact, particularly anal intercourse and other sexual practices that may result in semen-to-blood or blood-to-blood contact. Anal intercourse is a high-risk activity because the lining of the rectum is thinner and more easily torn than the thicker protective lining of the vagina. Anal intercourse can therefore result more easily in direct semen-to-blood exchange. Although in a small percentage of cases the virus has been transmitted from an infected male to a female, it is not known if these cases involved oral or anal intercourse.

Needle sharing among intravenous drug users is another major means of transmission. This practice can result in small amounts of blood from an infected person being injected directly into the bloodstream of the next user. The risk of contracting AIDS through a blood transfusion has been significantly reduced since May 1985 by screening all blood donations for the AIDS virus.

Preventing the Spread of AIDS

Educational campaigns about AIDS by private and government agencies are aimed at both the general public and those in high-risk groups. The intent is to encourage people to discontinue practices that spread the disease. Specifically, sexually active people are being advised to refrain from sexual contact with those whose health status is unknown and to avoid practices that may result in blood-to-blood or semen-to-blood exchanges. Male homosexuals who have had contact with a number of partners are being advised to assume that they have been exposed to the virus and to refrain from sexual contact involving the exchange of bodily fluids. Drug users are being urged not to share needles and to enter treatment programs that will help them become drug-free (New York State Department of Health, 1986). Some state agencies are offering voluntary free testing for those who wish to determine whether they have been exposed to the AIDS virus. Another preventive effort, which has aroused much controversy, is the campaign to encourage the use of condoms in sexual intercourse. Schools are making greater efforts to educate children about the dangers of sexually transmitted disease and, in some areas, are actually dispensing condoms to students. At the same time, the media are considering lifting the ban on the advertising of condoms.

Merson (1993) argued that prevention is the key to reducing the horrific effects of AIDS. At the World AIDS Conference, various speakers pointed to the fact that increasing evidence shows that condoms for men and women, sex education, public information campaigns, needle exchange programs for users of injectable drugs, and other strategies can prevent HIV infection (Altman, 1998). At the same time, we have to face the fact that our prevention message is not getting through to young adults. Recent data have shown that among persons between 18 and 25 there was actually an increase in the rate of HIV infection between 1986 and 1992 (Rosenberg, 1995). During the same period, the rate for older white males leveled off.

What is disturbing about the data is that the risks are well known to younger adults. Apparently, many are choosing to engage in unsafe sex even though the methods of preventing infection are understood and widely publicized. There are, however, differences in reported AIDS rates throughout this country. For example, in 2006 one in five black men in New York City between the ages of 40 and 49 had HIV or AIDS. Black women, meanwhile, accounted for 34% of new AIDS cases, up from 12% 20 years ago. Furthermore, heterosexual sex has now replaced drug use as the most common means of transmission of the virus, creating a more difficult terrain for health care workers (Santora, 2006). Clearly, we must redouble our efforts to persuade young adults and minorities to avoid unsafe sexual practices.

CARE FOR PEOPLE WITH AIDS

A wide spectrum of human services has been developed for people with AIDS, including the following:

- Informational hotlines—for example, the CDC National Hotline (800-322-7514)—that give out information on community AIDS groups around the country
- Educational materials provided by federal, state, and local governments
- Counseling for AIDS patients, families, and those at risk for AIDS
- Assistance in locating medical, dental, and other health services
- Transportation to medical care
- Assistance with insurance coverage, housing, and civil rights issues

Walker (1987) points out that every AIDS patient has an average of eight close relatives and intimates. This means that millions of lives have already been disrupted by AIDS in one way or another. There is clearly a great need to provide support not only to the AIDS patients but also to their close associates. Across the country, approximately 100 community-based organizations have started to provide support groups for patients' families. The Gay Men's Health Crisis in New York City has programs for both the parents and partners of those with the disease. Similar support groups exist in Minneapolis, Denver, San Francisco, and other large cities. Some groups are without formal leaders, whereas others are led by trained mental health professionals.

Families have a difficult time dealing with any seriously ill patient, but AIDS families are particularly hard-hit. Walker (1987) observes that some families are shocked to learn that a member has been leading a secret life. The links to homosexuality and drug abuse cause some family members to feel **stigmatized**, secretive, and possibly angry at the victim. Health officials who have been tracking the disproportionate AIDS death rates among minorities over the last several years say those rates stem from a failure to identify the sick and get them into treatment, as well as a failure to keep them in care, and the strong stigma that AIDS carries in many minority neighborhoods (Santora, 2006). Families must learn to live with grief, cope with feelings of shame, and address their anger at the patient. The act of talking is the beginning of the process of working through these intense feelings.

AIDS AND THE HEALTH CARE SYSTEM

The increasing number of AIDS patients is taxing the capacities of public hospitals and clinics, especially in larger cities. The high costs of taking care of AIDS sufferers are due, in part, to these factors:

- The illness tends to require the services of diverse medical specialists because so many bodily systems may be affected.
- The medications used are themselves costly, and, in addition to that, may cause side effects that, in turn, need to be treated with additional costly therapies.
- Home care for the dying becomes difficult or impossible because potential caregivers may also be debilitated, leading to sometimes lengthy hospitalization.
- AIDS victims are living longer, with the course of the disease running about twelve years from initial infection to terminal phase.
- The illness does not run a smooth course. Symptoms may come and go in an unpredictable fashion, and there may be stable periods. This pattern means that the victim may require multiple hospital admissions (Strauss, Fagerhaugh, Suczek, & Weiner, 1991).

In short, it appears that AIDS is developing many of the cost factors associated with other chronic diseases such as cancer and heart disease. The cumulative effect of these chronic diseases is to tax the health care system beyond its present capacity. This situation has put various subgroups of health care consumers in competition with one another for the limited funds available for research and treatment. AIDS victims are placed at a disadvantage in this competition because they are perceived by some as having made personal lifestyle choices that brought about their present predicament. The argument runs that the rest of us should not be required to pay for the consequences of their choices. Well aware of negative public attitudes, AIDS activists have created a powerful national lobby devoted to increasing government and private investment in AIDS research and treatment.

In an ideal world, all human lives would be treated as equally valuable and, therefore, be regarded as deserving the same quality of medical care. It is unlikely that this ideal will be realized any time soon in the United States. It runs counter to the values of many Americans, who would provide better care to those who are perceived as most deserving, that is, those who make an economic contribution to the community. A more practical problem is that we may not have the resources to provide high-quality medical care for everyone. The sharing of available resources would mean a reduction of services for those now enjoying high-quality care. It seems doubtful that the affluent will be willing to do this for the sake of homeless people, addicts, or AIDS patients.

We believe that we must take steps to slow the development of all chronic diseases, including AIDS, and do our utmost to prevent these diseases from occurring in the first place. This means the development of programs of prevention aimed at improving the environment and at altering our behavior to stop the spread of disease.

SUMMARY

This description of some target populations gives an idea of the magnitude of the task facing human services today. Of course, one cannot add up the number of people included in each population because there is overlap among the groups. An individual may be poor, physically disabled, a senior citizen, and an alcoholic. In fact, there is a strong tendency for poverty and advanced age to be disproportionately associated with both mental and physical disorders. A member of a low-income family is twice as likely to become disabled as a member of a middle-class family. It is also true that nearly half of the adult disabled population is at or near the poverty level. Even more alarming is the increase in the number and percentage of Americans who are chronically ill, over 65, or disabled.

It is not known how the United States will respond in the future to this greatly increased need for services. It is apparent that a distinct shift in national priorities has occurred during the past decade. The earlier commitment to solve social problems, particularly those associated with poverty and racism, has given way to a focus on other priorities. The prevailing trend is to hold down or reduce spending for social programs. In one sense, the pattern is a familiar one. Historically, periods marked by concern for the less fortunate members of society have alternated with periods of relative neglect. No one knows how long the current trend will continue. Certainly, many programs have been cut, and the impact has been keenly felt by human services workers and the populations they serve.

One possible approach to reducing the costs of human services involves the increased use of prevention programs. Millions of dollars are spent on facilities and services for criminals, mental patients, alcoholics, and drug addicts, yet relatively little money is invested in programs designed to prevent individuals from joining these target groups in the first place. Similarly, larger sums are spent on welfare benefits than on programs that might keep some people off the rolls.

Obviously, a person who has been trained for a well-paying job is unlikely to need long-term welfare support. The initial cost of a successful prevention program would be more than made up in the long run. Unfortunately, politicians and others concerned with funding have proved very resistant to investing in prevention programs. These issues will be discussed in more detail in Chapter 8.

It is likely that new approaches to target populations will increase proportionately with the growth in population. However, some groups, particularly senior citizens and the disabled, will increase at a disproportionate rate. The net effect is that a greater percentage of the population will be in need of services, which will be provided by a relatively smaller number of human services workers. This is the dilemma that will face human services in the near future.

ADDITIONAL READING

Abadinsky, H. (1997). *Drug abuse: An introduction*. Chicago: Nelson-Hall.

Comer, R. J. (1996). *Fundamentals of abnormal psychology*. New York: Freeman.

Corey, G., Corey, M. S., & Callanan, P. (1998). *Issues and ethics in the helping professions* (5th ed.). Pacific Grove, CA: Brooks/Cole.

Costin, L. B., Bell, C. J., & Downs, S. W. (1991). *Child welfare: Policies and practices* (4th ed.). New York: Longman.

Davison, G. C., & Neale, J. M. (1996). *Abnormal psychology* (6th ed.). New York: Wiley.

De Genova, M. K. (1997). *Families in cultural context: Strengths and challenges in diversity*. Mountain View, CA: Mayfield.

Dell Orto, A. E., & Marinelli, R. P. (Eds.). *Encyclopedia of disability and rehabilitation*. New York: Macmillan.

Ferraro, K. (1997). Battered women: Strategies for survival. In A. Cardarelli (Ed.), *Violence between intimate partners: Patterns, causes and effects*. Needham Heights, MA: Allyn and Bacon.

Jacobs, E. E., Mason, R. L., & Harvil, R. L. (2009). *Group counseling: Strategies and skills* (6th ed.). Belmont, CA: Thomson Brooks/Cole.

Jansson, B. S. (2000). *The reluctant welfare state*. Belmont, CA: Wadsworth.

Mehr, J. J. (2001). *Human services: Concepts and intervention strategies*. Boston: Allyn and Bacon.

REFERENCES

Altman, K. A. (1998, June 29). At AIDS conference, a call to arms against runaway epidemic. *New York Times*, pp. 61, B5.

Anglin, D. M. (1988). The efficacy of civil commitment in treating addiction. *Journal of Drug Issues, 18*, 527–547.

Archibold, R. C. (2009, May 31). In Heartland Death, Traces of Heroin's Spread. *New York Times*, pp. 1, 24.

Asch, A. (1984a). The experience of disability: A challenge for psychology. *American Psychologist, 39*, 529–536.

Asch, A. (1984b). Personal reflections. *American Psychologist, 39*, 551–552.

Bassuk, E. L. (1995). Dilemmas in counting the homeless. *American Journal of Orthopsychiatry, 65*, 318–319.

Bassuk, E. L., & Gerson, S. (1978). Deinstitutionalization and mental health services. *Scientific American, 238*, 46–53.

Bazell, R. J. (1973). Drug abuse: Methadone becomes the solution and the problem. *Science, 179*, 772–775.

Berry, D. B. (1996). *The Domestic Violence Sourcebook*. Los Angeles: Lowell House.

Bloomberg News. (2001, December 27). American companies had nearly a million layoffs this year. *New York Times*, p. C6.

Blumstein, A. (1995). Prisons. In J. Q. Wilson & J. Petersilia (Eds.), *Crime* (pp. 387–419). San Francisco: ICS Press.

Borich, G. D., & Tombari, M. L. (1995). *Educational psychology: A contemporary approach*. New York: Harper-Collins.

Braginsky, D. D., & Braginsky, B. M. (1975, August). Surplus people: Their lost faith in self and system. *Psychology Today*, pp. 68–72.

Breakey, W. R. (1987). Treating the homeless. *Alcohol Health and Research World, 11*, 42–46, 90.

Brieland, D., Costin, L. B., & Atherton, C. R. (1980). *Contemporary social work* (2nd ed.). New York: McGraw-Hill.

Burgdorf, R. L., Jr. (Ed.). (1980). *The legal rights of handicapped persons*. Baltimore, MD: Paul Brookes.

Burt, M., & Laudan, L. (2000, February). America's homeless II: Populations and services. Oral presentation at the Urban Institute First Tuesday's Forum, Washington, DC.

Butterfield, A. (1995). *Changing asylums*. Upper Saddle River, NJ: Prentice Hall.

Carlson, B. E., & Choi, D. (2001). Intimate partner abuse. In A. Gitterman (Ed.), *Handbook of Social Work Practice with Vulnerable and Resilient Populations*. New York: Columbia University Press.

Carlson, E. (1995, June). CHATER sees no crisis now, but warns of strain in next century (AARP Bulletin, Special Report). Washington, DC: American Association of Retired Persons, Centers for Disease Control. (2008). *HIV/AIDS surveillance report, 2006* (Vol. 18). Atlanta: U.S. Department of Health and Human Services, CDC.

Center for Addiction and Mental Health. (2009). Retrieved March 30, 2009, from http://www.camh.net.about addiction.

Centers for Disease Control. (2002). Basic statistics, cumulative AIDS cases. Atlanta: Division of HIV/AIDS Prevention, CDC.

Chang, L., Ernst, T., Speck, O. & Grob, C. S. (2005). Addictive effects of HIV and chronic methamphetamine use on brain metabolite abnormalities. *American Journal of Psychiatry, 162*, 361–369.

Children's Bureau. (2002, April). Summary of key findings from calendar year 2000. Washington, DC: National Child Abuse and Neglect Data System, Administration for Children and Families.

Clear, T. R., & Braga, A. A. (1995). Community corrections. In J. Q. Wilson & J. Petersilia (Eds.), *Crime* (pp. 421–444). San Francisco: ICS.

Coleman, J. C., Butcher, J. N., & Carson, R. C. (1984). *Abnormal psychology and modern life* (7th ed.). Glenview, IL: Scott, Foresman.

Comer, R. J. (1995). *Abnormal psychology* (2nd ed.). New York: Freeman.

Connell, C. (1995, July 28). Worried about Medicare. *Standard Star*, Gannett Suburban Newspapers, p. 3B.

Costin, L. B., Bell, C. J., & Downs, S. W. (1991). *Child welfare: Policies and practices* (4th ed.). New York: Longman.

Crispell, D., & Frey, W. H. (1993, March). American maturity. *American Demographics*, pp. 31–42.

Daley, S. (1987, June 17). "Couch people": Hidden homeless grow. *New York Times*, pp. B1, B4.

Davison, G. C., & Neale, J. M. (1996). *Abnormal psychology* (6th ed.). New York: Wiley.

DiIulio, J. J. (1991). *No escape: The future of American corrections*. New York: Basic Books.

Dover, R. B. (1990). Defining mental retardation from an educational perspective. *Mental Retardation, 28*, 147–154.

Doweiko, H. (2009). *Concepts of chemical dependency* (7th ed). Belmont, CA: Brooks/Cole/Cengage Learning.

Egeland, B., Clochetti, D., & Taraldson, B. (1976). Child abuse: A family affair. In *Proceedings of the N. P. Masse Research Seminar on Child Abuse*, Paris, France (pp. 28–52), Cambridge Press.

Enkholm, E. (1991, November 17). Facts of life: More than inspiration is needed to fight AIDS. *New York Times*, pp. E1, E3.

Federal Bureau of Investigation. (1995). *Uniform crime reports*. Washington, DC: U.S. Government Printing Office.

Federal Register. (2009). *Vol.* 74, No. 14, January 23, pp. 4199–4201.

Ferraro, K. (1997). Battered women: Strategies for survival. In A. Cardarelli (Ed.), *Violence between intimate partners: Patterns, causes and effects.* Needham Heights, MA: Allyn and Bacon.

Forst, B. (1995). Prosecution and sentencing. In J. Q. Wilson & J. Petersilia (Eds.), *Crime* (pp. 363–386). San Francisco: ICS.

Freeman, R. B. (1995). The labor market. In J. Q. Wilson & J. Petersilia (Eds.), *Crime* (pp. 103–105). San Francisco: ICS.

Fuchs, V. R. (1991). Are Americans underinvesting in their children? *Society, 28,* 14–22.

Gallagher, B. J. (1987). *The sociology of mental illness* (2nd ed.). Upper Saddle River, NJ: Prentice Hall.

Gannett News Services. (1995, September 27). Census: 1 in 7 were poor in 1990. *Standard Star,* p. 22A.

Goldstein, A. (1994). *Addiction: From biology to drug policy.* New York: Freeman.

Gosselin, D. K. (2003). *Heavy hands: An introduction to the crimes of family violence.* Upper Saddle River, NJ: Prentice Hall.

Gramm, P. (1993, July 8). Mandatory jail sentences work. *New York Times,* p. A19.

Greenwood, P. H. (1995). Juvenile crime and juvenile justice. In J. Q. Wilson & J. Petersilia (Eds.), *Crime* (pp. 445–488). San Francisco: ICS.

Grief, G. L. (1985). *Single fathers.* Lexington, MA: Lexington Books.

Hanson, G. R., Venturelli, P. J., & Fleckenstein, A. E. (2006). *Drugs and society* (9th ed.). Sudbury, MA: Jones and Bartlett.

Hershey, R. D. (1995, November 4). Job growth was sluggish last month. *New York Times,* p. A37.

Holmes, S. A. (1994, October 28). Ratio of inmates reach one million in a 2-decade rise. *New York Times,* pp. A1, A25.

Hooyman, N. R., & Kiyak, H. A. (1991). *Social gerontology: A multidisciplinary perspective.* Needham Heights, MA: Allyn & Bacon.

Hope, M., & Young, J. (1986). *The facts of homelessness.* Lexington, MA: Lexington Books.

Houghton, J. F. (1980). One personal experience: Before and after mental illness. In J. G. Rabkin, L. Gelb, & J. B. Lazar (Eds.), *Attitudes toward the mentally ill: Research perspectives* (pp. 3–10). Rockville, MD: National Institute of Mental Health.

Houghton, J. F. (1982). First-person account: Maintaining mental health in a turbulent world. *Schizophrenia Bulletin, 8,* 547–552.

Inciardi, J. A. (1987). *Criminal justice* (2nd ed.). New York: Harcourt Brace Jovanovich.

Institute of Medicine, National Academy of Sciences. (1986). *Mobilizing against AIDS: The unfinished story of a virus.* Cambridge, MA: Harvard University Press.

Iritani, B. (2007, July). Addiction (Vol. 102, pp. 1102–1113). News Release. Bethesda, MD: National Institute on Drug Abuse, National Institutes of Health.

Johnson, A. B. (1990). *Out of bedlam: The truth about deinstitutionalization.* New York: Basic Books.

Julian, J., & Kornblum, W. (1986). *Social problems* (5th ed.). Upper Saddle River, NJ: Prentice Hall.

Kaufman, J., & Zigler, E. (1987). Do abused children become abusive parents? *American Journal of Orthopsychiatry, 57,* 186–192.

Kupfer, A. (1988). What to do about drugs. *Fortune, 117,* 39–41.

Lazare, D. (1990, January 23). The drug war is killing us. *Village Voice,* pp. 22, 24–26, 28–29.

Lyons, R. D. (1984, October 30). How release of mental patients began. *New York Times,* pp. C1, C4.

Marin, P. (1987, January). Helping and hating the homeless. *Harper's Magazine*, pp. 39–49.

McKinney, S. B. (1994). Who is homeless? Fact Sheet Number 3. Washington, DC: National Coalition for the Homeless.

Merson, M. H. (1993, May 28). Slowing the spread of HIV: Agenda for the 1990s. *Science, 260*, 1266–1268.

Morgenstern, M., & Klass, E. (1991). Standard intelligence tests and related assessment techniques. In J. L. Matson & J. A. Mulnick (Eds.), *Handbook of mental retardation* (2nd ed., pp. 195–210). New York: Pergamon.

Munoz-Kantha, M. (1996). Domestic violence, battered women, and the dimensions of the problem. In H. Harris & D. C. Maloney (Eds.), *Human services: Contemporary issues and trends*. Needham Heights, MA: Allyn & Bacon.

Musto, D. F. (1987). *The American disease* (expanded ed.). New York: Oxford University Press.

Narrow, W. E., Regier, D. A., Rae, D. S., Manderscheid, R. W., & Locke, B. Z. (1993). Use of services by persons with mental and addictive disorders: Findings from the N.I.M.H. epidemiologic catchment area program. *Archives of General Psychiatry, 50*, 95–107.

National Coalition for the Homeless. (1999). Why are people homeless? Fact Sheet Number 1. Washington, DC: National Coalition for the Homeless.

National Institute on Drug Abuse. (2009). Info facts—Methamphetamine, retrieved March 5, 2009, from http://www.NIDA.nih.gov./infofacts/methamphetamine.html

New York State Department of Health. (1986, March 1). Acquired immune deficiency syndrome: 100 questions and answers (pamphlet). Albany, NY: Department of Health.

O'Connor v. Donaldson, 422 U.S. 563 (1975).

Oswald, W. T. (2005). *Broadening our approach: Attacking poverty at its roots.* Paper presented at the Western Regional Conference of the National Organization of Human Services, Fullerton, CA.

Patton, J. R., Payne, J. S., & Beirne-Smith, M. (1990). *Mental retardation* (3rd ed.). Columbus, OH: Merrill/Prentice Hall.

Pepper, B. (1987). A public policy for the long-term mentally ill: A positive alternative to reinstitutionalization. *American Journal of Orthopsychiatry, 57*, 452–457.

Plum, K. C. (1987). Moving forward with deinstitutionalization: Lessons of an ethical policy analysis. *American Journal of Orthopsychiatry, 57*, 508–514.

Popple, P. R., & Leighninger, L. H. (1990). *Social work, social welfare, and American society*. Needham Heights, MA: Allyn & Bacon.

Rabinovitz, J. (1995, June 20). Court allows welfare cuts in Connecticut. *New York Times*, pp. B1, B5.

Ramson, R. (2007, July). Addiction (*Vol 102*, pp. 1021–1022). News Release. Bethesda, MD: National Institute on Drug Abuse, National Institutes of Health.

Regier, D. A., Narrow, W. E., Rae, D. S., Manderscheid, R. W., Locke, B. Z., & Goodwin, F. K. (1993). The de facto U.S. mental and addictive service system: Epidemiologic catchment area prospective 1-year prevalence rates of disorders and services. *Archives of General Psychiatry, 50*, 80–94.

Roll, J. M., Petry, N. M., Stitzer, M. L., Victor, K., & Sami, R. (2006). Contingency management for the treatment of methamphetamine use disorders. *American Journal of Psychiatry, 163*, 1993–1999.

Rorvik, D. M. (1979, April 7). Do drugs lead to violence? *Look*, pp. 58–61.

Rosenberg, P. S. (1995, November 24). Scope of the AIDS epidemic in the United States. *Science, 270*, 1372–1375.

Rovner, J. (1995, June). Social security lauded for its achievements—But what of the future? (AARP Bulletin, Special Report). Washington, DC: American Association of Retired Persons.

Santora, M. (2006, February 4). City AIDS report highlights risk to black men and women. *New York Times*, pp. B1, B4.

Santos, F., & Ingrassia, R. (2002, August 18). The face of homelessness has changed. *New York Daily News*, pp. 12–13.

Schmolling, P. (1975). Civil rights for mental patients: The road to neglect? *Hospital and Community Psychiatry, 26,* 168–170.

Schmolling, P. (1993). Social policy issues in narcotics abuse. *Journal of Health and Social Policy, 5,* 49–65.

Schmolling, P. (1994, January 16). States are on right welfare track. *Standard Star,* Gannett Suburban Newspapers, p. 3E.

Schottenfeld, R. S. (1989). Involuntary treatment of substance abuse disorders—Impediments to success. *Psychiatry, 52,* 164–176.

Schwarz, J. E., & Volgy, T. J. (1992). *The forgotten Americans.* New York: Norton.

Shapiro, J. P. (1995, August 14). Sins of the fathers. *U.S. News and World Report,* pp. 51–52.

Social Security Administration. (2001). *Statistical abstract of the United States.* Washington, DC: U.S. Government Printing Office.

Sonkin, D., & Durphy, M. (1997). *Learning to live without violence: A handbook for men.* Volcano, CA: Volcano.

Strauss, A. L., Fagerhaugh, S., Suczek, B., & Weiner, C. (1991). AIDS and health care deficiencies. *Society, 28,* 63–73.

Swarns, E. (1998, July 21). Ending welfare. *New York Times,* pp. 14, B2.

Toner, R. (1995, July 16). Resolved: No more bleeding hearts. *New York Times,* pp. 1, 16.

Toner, R. (2002, March 3). Helping the poor in the post-welfare era. *New York Times,* pp. 21–22.

Toner, R., & Pear, R. (1995, July 23). Medicare, turning 30, won't be what it was. *New York Times,* pp. 1, 24.

Turnbill, H. R. (1982, August). Oversight on Education for All Handicapped Children Act, 1982. Testimony before the Senate Subcommittee on the Handicapped, 97th Congress. Available from the Senate Committee on Labor and Human Resources, Washington, DC.

United States Drug Enforcement Administration. (2009). Retrieved March 13, 2009, from http://www.usdoj.gov/dea/concern/meth.html.

U.S. Census Bureau. (2009). *Statistical Abstracts of the United States.* Washington, DC: U.S. Government Printing Office. Retrieved March 26, 2009, from http://www.census.gov/hhes/poverty/povdef.html

U.S. Department of Agriculture. (2001). *Statistical abstract of the United States.* Washington, DC: U.S. Government Printing Office.

U.S. Department of Health and Human Services, National Center on Child Abuse and Neglect. (1988). *Study findings: Study of national incidence and prevalence of child abuse and neglect.* Washington, DC: U.S. Government Printing Office.

Ventura, S. J. (1994, October). Data on teenage pregnancies. *Statistical Bulletin, 75,* 10–17.

Verhovek, S. H. (1995, September 21). States are already providing glimpse at welfare's future. *New York Times,* pp. A1, B10.

Walker, L. (1979). *The battered woman.* New York: Springer.

Walker, L. (1995). Battered women and learned helplessness. In J. Makepeace (Ed.), *Family violence: Readings in the social sciences and professions.* New York: McGraw-Hill.

Walker, L. (1987, June 21). What comforts AIDS families? *New York Times,* pp. 16–22, 63, 78.

Weiler, P. G. (1987). The public health impact on Alzheimer's disease. *American Journal of Public Health, 77,* 1169–1175.

Weinstein, J. B. (1993, July 8). The war on drugs is self-defeating. *New York Times*, p. A19.

White House. (1989, September). *National drug control strategy*. Washington, DC: U.S. Government Printing Office.

Wilson, J. Q. (1990). Against the legalization of drugs. *Commentary, 89,* 21–28.

Wilson, J. Q. (1995). Crime and public policy. In J. Q. Wilson & J. Petersilia (Eds.), *Crime* (pp. 489–507). San Francisco: ICS.

Wines, M. (1995, September 24). The social engineers let welfare go unfixed. *New York Times*, pp. E1, E14.

Wolfe, B. L. (1991). Treating children fairly. *Society, 28,* 23–28.

World Health Organization. (1993). The HIV/AIDS pandemic: 1993 overview. Geneva: Author.

World Health Organization. (2001). The cost and toll: 2001 overview. Brietland: Author.

World Health Organization. (2005). Joint United Nations Program for HIV/AIDS, United Nations/World Health Organization, AIDS epidemic update, December 2005, http://www.UNAIDS.org/en/publications

Yoshikawa, H. (1994). Prevention as cumulative protection: Effects of early family support and education on chronic delinquency and its risks. *Psychological Bulletin, 115,* 28–54.

CHAPTER 3

HUMAN SERVICES IN HISTORICAL PERSPECTIVE

CHAPTER CONTENTS

INTRODUCTION

Who is responsible for helping the disadvantaged within a society? the family? religious organizations? the government? Should helping be viewed as a basic human right or as a societal gift? Throughout history, societies have responded to these questions in various ways. If a society does accept some responsibility for helping its disadvantaged, additional questions quickly emerge. Which groups of people and types of problems should be helped, to what extent, and how?

How a given society answers these questions is based on its dominant values, attitudes, and beliefs. If a society believes that its poor or senior members should be helped, then it will develop some system or method to provide the needed care for these target populations. Another society may give priority to its physically or mentally disabled members and develop services focused on these groups but exclude others.

The present range and diversity of human services are quite large. Throughout history, many people and events have influenced the development and direction of the field. As societies have changed through the ages, values and beliefs have often been replaced by new ones or at least modified. The developing human services systems of today are, to some extent, an outgrowth of our previously held societal values and beliefs concerning helping. It is likely that the quality, methods, and availability of human services in the future will be greatly influenced by current attitudes toward helping. Through knowledge of the past, we can better understand the present and also be in a more favorable position to shape the future.

For clarity and better understanding of the historical development of the interrelated aspects of the human services field, this chapter is divided into several sections. The first sections provide a general overview of the historical roots of the human services field by tracing the development of early societal beliefs and helping practices. The next section traces changing societal attitudes and helping practices that have contributed to the development of human welfare services. Next we examine the historical development of mental health services. The chapter concludes with a brief discussion of future trends in the human services field.

PREHISTORIC CIVILIZATIONS

The earliest records of helpful treatments can be traced back to the Stone Age of approximately half a million years ago. Through cave drawings and the remains of primitive skulls, scientists know about a medical treatment called **trephining**. In this procedure, a small section of the skull was bored out, probably by means of sharp stones or other such crude instruments. This hole cut from the skull was supposed to allow a route of escape for the evil spirits believed to inhabit the afflicted person's body, thereby curing the person. Scientists have surmised that this treatment was administered to people who evidenced certain forms of observable deviant behavior. It should always be remembered that what constitutes deviant behavior is a product of what the norm for behavior is at a given point in time.

In this early era, most human problems were attributed to devils, demons, or other evil spirits. Belief in the supernatural or **demonology** was the dominant belief system of the age, and various procedures or rites were used to exorcise evil spirits. These ideas arose from early humans' attempt to explain the universe. All natural phenomena such as earthquakes or floods were attributed to the work of evil spirits. These ancient people also accepted the related belief, called **animism**, that spirits inhabit various inanimate objects such as rocks, trees, or rivers. The shaman, or medicine man, who performed rites of exorcism, can now be viewed as the earliest human services worker. It was commonly believed that these individuals understood the secrets of the supernatural and possessed certain religious or mystical qualities that enabled them to help afflicted individuals.

Life during prehistoric times was at best a matter of pure survival against the hostile environment. Human problems centered on gathering food and having a relatively safe place to sleep. Poverty meant being unable to locate or secure food, and weaker individuals were sometimes simply left to perish. In situations involving the physically disabled or infirm elderly, the tribe or extended family unit would usually share or provide for these individuals. However, the afflicted person's importance to the tribe often determined the amount of assistance received. In some instances, tribes took in and befriended individuals separated from other tribes. Newcomers usually had to prove their worth in some manner in order to be allowed to stay with the tribe.

The family was the primary source of help for these ancient people, but religion would play an increasing role in the evolution of human services.

EARLY CIVILIZATIONS

Prior to 450 B.C., the world was widely believed to be governed by supernatural spirits. There were no major organized attempts to understand human problems and behavior from a scientific point of view. However, significant changes in beliefs were about to emerge that would alter the earlier supernatural explanations for human behavior.

During the Golden Age of Greece, a number of philosophers began to put forth new beliefs concerning human nature. One of these was the Greek physician Hippocrates (460–377 B.C.), who disagreed with the belief that supernatural spirits were the sole cause of human disease. He believed, rather, that most diseases were chiefly physiological or organic in origin. He shared the point of view earlier postulated by Pythagoras that the brain was the center of intelligence and that mental disorders were due specifically to the malfunctioning of the brain (Coleman, 1976).

Another contribution made by Hippocrates was his development of a system of psychiatric labels for patterns of deviant behavior. These labels included melancholia, mania, and epilepsy. To appreciate more clearly the radical change in belief advocated by Hippocrates, one must consider that the previous explanation for epilepsy was that it was a sacred or divinely ordained disease. Hippocrates claimed this disease was caused by a blockage of air in the veins due to secretions of the brain (Hoch & Knight, 1965). The treatments advocated by Hippocrates differed considerably from the earlier skull-cutting procedures. His treatments often involved vegetable diets, exercise, and a tranquil lifestyle.

Whether Hippocrates had the correct physiological explanation or treatment is not of critical historical importance here. The theory that diseases could be explained by natural—as opposed to supernatural—causes is of major importance. This change in belief systems regarding the origin of diseases influenced another significant change. Because deviant behavior or psychological problems could now be viewed as diseases of organic origin, they could now be considered part of the domain of medicine (Rimm & Somervill, 1977). As such, these conditions could be treated by physicians, rather than priests, medicine men, or other religious healers. This separation of treatment responsibilities was one of the first steps toward developing the system of specialization that has continued to the present time in human services.

In the ancient Rome of 150 B.C., another physician, the Greek-born Asclepiades, advocated treatment procedures for mental disorders that stressed a medical and humane approach. His recommended treatments often involved massages and baths to soothe excited or nervous patients, with wine to calm the nerves. He actively denounced the cruel and severely harsh treatments that were still popular at this time, such as housing patients in totally dark cells, beating them with chains, bloodletting, castrating, and subjecting patients to prolonged periods of starvation.

Galen (A.D. 130–200), a Greek medical writer, was able to compile, systematize, and integrate a considerable amount of material from many complementary fields. His topics included medicine, anatomy, physiology, and logic. In addition, he made a major contribution to the understanding of abnormal behavior by developing a system of classifying the causes of mental disorders. He believed all disorders were either physical or mental. He felt these disorders could originate from such things as injuries to the head, fear, shock, or emotional disturbances.

The early civilizations presented some striking contradictions in helping attitudes and services. Although many advances were being made and many individuals were attempting to struggle against fear, ignorance, and superstition, the use of cruel treatment procedures was still prevalent. Even as many advocated more humane and philosophical beliefs concerning the nature of people, the practice of buying and selling slaves still existed, and the poor and disabled often begged for alms along city streets. Although physicians were available for the sick, only those who could pay had access to them. The Romans and the Greeks viewed physical weakness or disability with little tolerance. Often the physically ill were taken out of towns to uninhabited areas or deserted islands where they were left to struggle by themselves or die. Of course, these practices pertained predominantly to the poor or those without resources or family protection. As in most societies, the rich were treated one way and the poor another.

The period A.D. 200–475 marked a steady decline for civilization. As major plagues killed thousands upon thousands of people between the first and fourth centuries A.D., intense fear and anxiety spread throughout Europe and the Middle East. In this climate of fear, Christianity emerged and developed a large and zealous following. Medicine could not stop the plagues, so people turned to the comfort and solace offered by Christianity, which became the prime religion of the Western world. Religious figures replaced medical figures as the saviors from illness. The causes of disease were again explained in terms of loss of faith and the influence of demons. Evil spirits were viewed as the cause of most human misfortunes.

MIDDLE AGES

The Middle Ages date from the fifth century with the collapse of Rome at the hands of the barbarians advancing from the east. During this time, exorcism reemerged as the prevalent treatment for most disorders. The medical advances achieved by

Greece and Rome were mostly forgotten (Fisher, Mehr, & Truckenbrod, 1974). Christianity became the dominant power throughout the Middle Ages.

As the Church became steadily more powerful and organized in the early part of the Middle Ages, it developed and provided a variety of human services. Monasteries often served as sanctuaries, refuges, and places of treatment for the mentally ill. The Church established institutions for the poor, provided residences for people with disabilities, sponsored orphanages, and founded homes for the aged. Initially, these services were housed within church facilities, but later other, nonreligious sites were founded.

In its earliest beginnings, the Church espoused the belief that the wealthy or those with adequate resources had a responsibility to help the less fortunate. The less fortunate, in turn, began to expect assistance as an obligation from the wealthy. Both the rich and the poor developed social roles and expectations for one another, and a clear distinction between the two classes was evident. It is important, however, to note that assistance given to the poor was set at the lowest subsistence or survival level. Much of contemporary human services philosophy can, in fact, be traced back to these early interpretations of religious values and teachings.

During this period, there was little interest in finding out why the disadvantaged were disadvantaged. The causes of poverty, for example, were of little interest to those providing human services. The rights and obligations for each class of society were clearly spelled out, and no further understanding seemed necessary.

Initially, people believed that giving to the disadvantaged was important simply because others were deserving of and needed help. The Church gradually began to lose this emphasis on helping out of humanitarian concerns and replaced it with the notion that helping had to be done if one wanted to ensure salvation and a peaceful afterlife. The Church preached that giving was a means of salvation, a means to an end. People would be rewarded in an afterlife for fulfilling their obligations in this life. Giving was seen as a necessary duty of the wealthy that they often fulfilled reluctantly.

As the Church developed human services, the overall climate of the Middle Ages was marked by chaos and extreme cruelty toward unbelievers. During the period 1200–1400, the belief in witchcraft greatly increased, and in certain regions mass outbreaks of flagellation (whipping) rituals occurred (Russell, 1972) in attacks against accused witches.

Although the Church tried to control all opposing beliefs and alternative religious movements, it was not completely successful. As people became disillusioned with the ability of the Church to protect them from misfortune, a variety of fanatical sects emerged throughout medieval Europe, and fear of witchcraft became a mass **obsession**. As Rimm and Somervill (1977) point out,

> Witches were viewed not only as degenerate beings in league with devils, but also as causes of sickness, disease, personal tragedies, and the stealing and killing of children. They were perceived as vicious instigators of terror, highly dangerous to a threatened and unstable society. (p. 16)

In the Middle Ages, the growth of fanatical sects represented a form of extremism, an impulsive act often characteristic of youth. In fact, the Europe of the Middle

Ages was a youthful society. The death rate was extremely high, and people did not often survive past 40 years of age.

Beginning in the thirteenth century under Pope Innocent III, a religious tribunal was established. This tribunal, referred to as the **Inquisition**, was given the responsibility of seeking out and punishing any and all crimes associated with witchcraft or other forms of heresy. The methods employed by this ecclesiastical body to obtain confessions for accused crimes included intimidation, burning, boiling suspects in oil, cutting their tongues out, and other forms of torture. Although the Inquisition used cruel and inhumane measures, the Church espoused the belief that it was providing a service to society by getting rid of the causes of disease and famine. It also served as a means for the Church to exert its power and encourage loyalty by threatening those who did not conform to stated policies and beliefs.

Throughout the Middle Ages, a major power struggle existed between Church and state. Each faction wanted more power to govern without interference from the other. The Church developed a steady source of income by demanding that its parishioners donate approximately 10% of their incomes for church-related activities. The state viewed this steady source of income as a threat to its own base of power and sought many times to make it illegal to give money or services to those who could work.

Gradually, the disadvantaged came to be classified according to whether they physically could work or were unfit for work, such as the disabled, senior citizens, and children. Those individuals deemed legitimately unfit for work came to be known as the "worthy poor," whereas the others were looked upon as being lazy and unworthy of assistance. Even though this steady clash for power existed, the Church was successful through most of the Middle Ages at preserving its domain, especially as far as providing human services to "worthy" individuals.

RENAISSANCE

As Europe emerged from the Middle Ages, it entered a period of rapid and turbulent change marked by the end of the feudal system, the birth of **industrialization**, and a decline in the power of the Church. As the government became more powerful and influential, individual states, cities, and towns developed more power. The middle class, composed mainly of tradespeople, grew, prospered, and became a more visible and distinct part of society.

By the sixteenth century, the previously established religious, social, and economic order had changed significantly. The government, the Church, and newly emerging business leaders shaped the nature and direction of societal change. Unfortunately, the rationale for change is often based on the priorities and complex concerns of those in power and does not necessarily benefit all in society. These changing societal forces had a tremendous influence on the direction and quality of human services. It is important to realize that the current system, providing an enormous range of services for the welfare of human beings from birth until death, started out by simply providing food or shelter as a form of social welfare.

Having now provided a general overview of the early development of human services philosophy and practice, we will examine the subsequent growth of human welfare services and then that of mental health services.

HUMAN WELFARE SERVICES SINCE THE RENAISSANCE

During the sixteenth century, the Protestant Reformation escalated the many struggles for power between Church and state. By the end of that century, the state had
finally established authority over the Church. As a result of diminished Church
power, it became incumbent upon the state to take over many services formerly
provided by the Church, which included providing for human services.

Under Henry VIII of England, the government formally took over the human
services functions of the Church to provide for people who were not self-sufficient
and established a system of income maintenance and public welfare. The official
policy mandating this transition of power was outlined in the statutes of 1536 and
1572. In 1601, the **Elizabethan Poor Laws** established a system that provided shelter
and care for the poor. This law also specified local responsibility for the poor and
disadvantaged. It was first the responsibility of the family to provide for all human
services. If the family could not provide such services, it then became the state's responsibility to provide for disadvantaged individuals within their communities.

Although the Poor Laws involved some people with good intentions, these laws
were not initially created as a generous humanitarian gift from the state to aid its
disadvantaged citizens; rather, they were a means of social control following an
era of mass frenzy, disease, famine, and economic instability that threatened to
break apart the existing social structure.

As a result of the Poor Laws in England, a system for classifying the disadvantaged into three categories was established: (a) the poor who were capable of work;
(b) the poor who were incapable of work because of age, physical disability, or
motherhood responsibilities; and (c) orphaned or abandoned children who became
wards of the state. The poor who could work were forced to work in state-operated
workhouses. Massive overcrowding, filth, and inadequate food made these workhouses barely tolerable. If the individual was incapable of work and in need of
food or shelter, he or she could be sent to an **almshouse (poorhouse)**. The living
conditions there were similar to those of the state workhouses.

By comparison to the almshouse or workhouse, a more tolerable alternative
was available for the more "fortunate" of the disadvantaged. In certain communities it was possible for individuals or families to remain in their own dwelling and
receive contributions of food and other items from their community. This circum-
stance was far less common than the other methods of providing services. Money
was never given directly to the poor family, and many other essential services,
such as medical care, were not generally available.

As this early, often crude human services system evolved, procedures and rules
were more clearly established and defined. Policies were established to decide who
would be eligible for available services and who would have the authority to decide
who got what and who went where. As the programs became more complicated,
the government created a subsystem with sole responsibility for overseeing its public welfare system. Each community had its specified government welfare administrator, who made the local decisions regarding a person's eligibility for services. As
the number of individuals needing assistance increased, the local community bureaucracy became more impersonal. Indeed, this is still a problem with modern welfare systems. The form of welfare bureaucracy created in England during this

period became the early forerunner of our modern welfare system in the United States.

INDUSTRIAL REVOLUTION

By the 1800s, the Industrial Revolution was developing momentum. The Industrial Revolution began with the invention of a few basic machines and the development of new sources of power. The advent of industrialization created the mechanization of manufacturing and agriculture, changed the speed and methods of communication and transportation, and began the development of factory systems of labor. These events, in turn, caused dramatic changes in economic systems (Perry & Perry, 1988).

Large populations of unemployed individuals moved from rural areas to urban centers in search of work. Although new forms of labor were needed and work was available for some, the great majority of people still found themselves in poverty. As a result of the swell in the disadvantaged population within urban areas, many public institutions were created. The majority of the urban poor found themselves facing worse conditions than those they had left behind. Adequate living space was scarce, producing overcrowded and unhealthy conditions. Food was in short supply, and the urban environment provided little room to grow crops. Families often found themselves separated as members left in search of work.

Workers were generally seen by businessmen as commodities, to be used only when needed and disregarded when work was not immediately available. It was during this time that workers started banding together to share and provide what they could for one another. This banding together for the collective benefit of all resulted in the development of the early guilds and unions. In an effort to deal with the perceived threat to the social order brought on by these large numbers of disadvantaged people in urban areas, the government created more workhouses, debtors' prisons, houses for delinquents and orphans, and mental institutions.

The Industrial Revolution brought about a new social philosophy that had a strong influence upon society's attitude toward the poor and disadvantaged. This new social philosophy, known as the **Protestant work ethic**, reinforced a set of values supporting the virtues of industrialization and condemned idleness as almost sinful.

Hard work, and thereby the accumulation of wealth, was interpreted as God's reward for leading a virtuous life. On the opposite end of this philosophy, poverty was often viewed as a form of punishment from God. This philosophy, as most notably preached by John Calvin, supported the notion that poverty-ridden individuals should remain in their disadvantaged conditions because God had divinely ordained this condition for them.

It was during the 1830s in England that the concept of **less eligibility** was established. This concept set forth the guideline that any assistance given to the disadvantaged must be lower than the lowest wage paid to any working person. Work was seen as an ultimate good, and its absence, for any reason, was to be looked down upon. In theory, this concept sought to provide an incentive for all to work.

Another corresponding influence on society's attitude toward the disadvantaged was the concept of the **laissez-faire economy**, introduced by the Englishman Adam Smith in 1776. In his book *The Wealth of Nations* he argued for an economy in which government had virtually no influence and placed no restrictions on

Immigrants within a large city during the 1800s.

the free marketplace. According to Smith, without government control, society would grow and prosper by itself based on people's individual merit and hard work. Supporters of this concept saw human services not as a right but as a misguided societal gift—a gift that they perceived would actually hinder overall economic production.

As previously described, many of these events and philosophies developing in England and Europe had a strong influence on societal attitudes toward helping in the United States. The economic value system emerging from England was again reinforced in the United States by the writing of another Englishman, Herbert Spencer. It was Spencer who interpreted Charles Darwin's writings on evolution in a provocative manner. His ideas, which came to be known as **Social Darwinism**, applied theories of animal behavior to human behavior. Using Darwin's biological premise in regard to natural selection and coupling it with an economic argument, Spencer espoused the idea that those disadvantaged people who were unfit for society should not be helped; it was the natural order of things for them to help themselves or perish, as in nature. This, it was felt, would provide another incentive for people to work. Of course, this theory did not take into consideration those individuals who, for physical or other reasons, were unable to work. Additionally, this theory did not consider the many individuals who wanted work but for whom no work was available. In essence, Social Darwinism only served to foster an attitude of indifference toward the poor.

EARLY REFORM MOVEMENTS IN THE UNITED STATES

As the many institutions for the disadvantaged grew in size, workers were needed to supply the various types of helping services, and the result was to formalize the system of "professional" helpers. Conditions within institutions were intolerable. The large number of people housed in small spaces created unbearable overcrowding. Lack of heat in winter, instances of brutality, inadequate food, and many other examples of inhumane treatment generated a good deal of concern by private citizens and led to a series of attempts at social reform.

Many of the social reformers of the mid-nineteenth century did not focus their efforts on a single injustice but instead called for a voice of reason and humane concern in every area of human welfare. In the late 1800s and early 1900s, the movement toward human welfare made great advances. In this period of heavy immigration to the United States, many thousands of newly arrived immigrants found themselves homeless and displaced in their new country. It was during this time that settlement houses were developed to provide immigrants with the essentials of life and to help them get a foothold in American society.

The **settlement house movement** was a reflection of early human services philosophy. Settlement house workers embraced the view that it was the responsibility of society to help the poor and disadvantaged. They also advocated a major shift in helping attitudes and human services thinking to the belief that many of the problems confronting individuals are created by environmental circumstances rather than by personal inadequacy. This point of view has come to be known as the human services perspective. The founders of the movement expressed the idea that one must work toward improving social conditions. To accomplish this goal, a system providing for basic human services must be created to facilitate an adequate quality of life. It was further believed that a truly successful human services system should provide opportunities for all people to improve their lives and realize their potentials.

One notable early settlement house was Hull House, founded in Chicago by Jane Addams. It was here, many historians believe, that contemporary social work was born. Using Hull House as the primary hub of her human services activity, Addams managed to create a small but comprehensive network of human services in her Chicago neighborhood that included basic adult education classes, kindergartens, and an employment bureau. In the following years, many other settlement houses were founded throughout the country. They served as a training ground for those providing social work services.

The early 1900s in the United States marked the resurgence of another significant human services movement. Often referred to as the progressive or social justice movement, its aim was to bring about social change through political action and legislative reform. This movement, which reflected liberal reform ideas, was embraced by many factions of society, including the unions. Accepting the earlier idea that the social environment is a major factor in creating people's problems, the reformers advocated a series of economic reforms including a minimum-wage standard, a pension system for older workers, an eight-hour day and a six-day workweek, as well as laws providing for unemployment insurance and the regulation of child labor. Many successful changes occurred despite the prevailing conservative outlook. The government began to assume greater responsibility for the provision of human services. During this period, a growing number of Americans became aware that a system of human services is integrally connected to the economic system and the role of the government. A comprehensive system providing for human services requires the support and interconnectedness of all institutions within society.

The Depression and World War II

The stock market crash of 1929 and the Great Depression dramatically changed the lives of many Americans. With huge numbers of unemployed workers and a depressed economy, the need for expansion of human services was evident. With millions of people unemployed, the relationship between environmental circumstances and human problems could not have been more clear.

The federal government under the direction of President Franklin Delano Roosevelt established a series of government aid programs called the **New Deal**. These programs attempted to make work available where possible and to provide direct assistance to those people incapable of work. Examples of such programs were the Works Progress Administration, which provided jobs; the Civilian Conservation Corps, which provided training; and Aid to Dependent Children, which provided direct government aid.

In 1935 a major government response to the existing social conditions was the Social Security Act. This legislation established a form of social insurance and protection for individuals against an unpredictable economy. It not only helped alleviate the current social conditions but was also calculated to aid and protect future generations. Social security subsequently provided for a wide array of health and social welfare services.

It has happened throughout history that people's attitudes change but are sometimes difficult to completely erase. There are always those who cling to previous ideas and attitudes for both good and bad **motives**, as well as those who advocate change for similarly varied reasons. The 1940s in the United States witnessed a reemergence of the trend toward conservatism. Public criticism was again heard, denouncing the government system of providing for human services as helping create a form of "welfare state." Conservatives felt that too much aid would rob people of the incentive to help themselves. However, as conservatives and liberals debated how much assistance is beneficial, returning World War II veterans created a further need for a variety of human services. As indicated in Chapter 1, this clash between conservative and liberal thinking is still very evident today.

The 1960s through the 1980s

The 1960s were characterized by social unrest in the United States. The Vietnam War was being waged overseas, and many Americans at home participated in marches and demonstrations to protest the ills they felt existed within the system. This was a turbulent, sometimes violent period marked by protests at many college campuses across the country. Widespread and organized efforts of this kind resulted in an eventual end to the war and advanced the civil rights movement and the War on Poverty. These latter movements were successful in bringing national attention to the plight of minorities and the poor. New legislation was enacted that resulted in the establishment of many programs and services. Although the civil rights movement and the War on Poverty did create increased economic and educational opportunities for the disadvantaged, they did not eliminate poverty and discrimination in the United States.

In the 1970s and 1980s, human welfare services in the United States grew considerably. A massive number of programs were developed to provide for human services throughout the life cycle. In the midst of such an array of services, the need for services of these types still remains great. Debates continue to rage over which programs are truly helpful and worthy of funding and which should be trimmed from our federal or state budgets. This controversy over social policy is discussed in more detail in Chapter 7.

MENTAL HEALTH SERVICES SINCE THE RENAISSANCE

In certain instances, the historical development of our system of mental health services paralleled the development of our system of human welfare services, as previously described. It is now apparent that having an adequate food supply, shelter, income, and other necessities of life has a direct bearing on one's mental health. Of course, contemporary knowledge and understanding of how environmental factors influence human problems are much better than they were in the past. Previously, individuals deemed mentally ill faced a grim future without any substantial alternatives. The following sections examine the people and events that have helped shape societal attitudes and treatment of the mentally ill.

EARLY MENTAL ASYLUMS

Early institutions created to house the behaviorally deviant were commonly referred to as asylums. The word **asylum**, when used in this context, refers to a place of refuge that provides protection, shelter, and security. Although many mental patients did view the asylum as a place of refuge or safety, a good number probably did not. It was society that viewed the asylum as a form of protection and shelter from those labeled as deviants.

The early public mental institutions in Europe and the United States were located within communities, and the community was primarily responsible for the governance and maintenance of the institution. As communities tend to be different from one another, so too did these institutions differ from one another. No universal guidelines for patient care or procedures were established among this broad network of community mental institutions, and mistreatment and abuse frequently occurred.

One noteworthy exception, among others, to the generalized inhumane treatment and lack of concern toward the mentally ill was the mental hospital established in 1409 in Valencia, Spain. This hospital is probably the oldest mental hospital still functioning today (Andriola & Cata, 1969). As a rule, patients were readily discharged after they were deemed able to return to society. Patients were treated with relative dignity, and a system of voluntary admissions was established. The example set by this hospital is even more striking when one considers that the Inquisition and witch-hunting **mania** were also prevalent during this era.

One of the earliest public asylums and the one most typical of the overall character of these institutions was **St. Mary's of Bethlehem** (Bedlam), created in 1547 in England. Although originally intended to be humanitarian in nature, this institution, as well as others to follow, was little more than a dungeon in which the

Early mental asylum.

behaviorally deviant were locked up and subjected to cruel, often ghoulish, treatment. Inadequate food, insufficient clothing, filth, infectious disease, and overcrowding were commonplace. The more difficult patients were subjected to treatments that consisted of days, weeks, or months spent in mechanical restraints or chained to the walls and denied food or water. The majority of patients were either mentally retarded, aged, physically ill, or accused or convicted of crimes. Little attention was given to individual cases, and the patients could just as easily have been sent to a prison or poorhouse as to a mental institution.

ERA OF HUMANITARIAN REFORM

During the next 200 years, similar conditions existed in institutions for the insane in this country, such as Pennsylvania Hospital founded in 1752 and Williamsburg Hospital founded in 1773 (Bloom, 1977). During the late 1770s and early 1780s, a reform movement began that would alter significantly, although briefly, the existing conditions in mental institutions. This movement toward humane treatment of the insane has been referred to as the era of humanitarian reform and the moral treatment movement. This movement, which had its earliest beginnings in Europe, had great influence on institutions in the United States in the late eighteenth and early nineteenth centuries.

Following the French Revolution in 1792, physician Phillipe Pinel became the director of **La Bicêtre**, a mental institution in Paris. It was here that Pinel, inspired by the idea that the insane might be curable, unchained some prisoners and provided adequate food, clothing, and other necessities of life. Although reform was clearly evident, Pinel and other early reformers still advocated the use of harsh measures as sometimes-useful tools of treatment. However, the reforms of Pinel are considered by many to be the first major revolution in mental health care (Wahler, Johnson, & Uhrich, 1972).

This reform movement, begun in France, spread to England. In 1813 the British physician Samuel Tuke, the director of the York Retreat, initiated a similar series of reforms. In the United States other physicians also advocated similar improvements. It was during these early years of reform that physicians gained most in prestige and prominence in their evolving interest and later specialization in treating the behaviorally deviant.

Even though the early reforms advocated by Pinel, Tuke, and others had an impact on the institutions of the day, by the middle 1800s in the United States, public awareness and interest in the plight of the mentally ill had waned. Without such interest, the institutions once again fell back into a period characterized by neglect and widespread mistreatment.

It was in the mid-nineteenth century that Dorothea Dix became a prominent figure in the evolution of human services. Through her efforts, the earlier reform movement that had begun in Europe and lost temporary impetus in the United States was again revived and gained its greatest foothold in the United States. Dorothea Dix was instrumental in gathering enough public support to make greatly needed changes in the inhumane conditions of the asylums, as well as in prisons and many poverty-related shelters. Following a personal investigation of asylums and prisons throughout the country, Dix wrote many newspaper articles outlining the plight of the disadvantaged. She contacted legislators and began a successful lobbying effort to inform and educate the public concerning these conditions within the institutions. As Bloom (1977) notes,

> Before [Dix's] career came to an end, 32 state mental hospitals had been built in the United States, care of the mentally ill had been removed from the local community, and the professional orientation toward the insane had been changed from seeing them as no different from paupers or criminals, to seeing them as sick people in need of hospital care. (p. 11)

The creation of a system of large state psychiatric hospitals to replace predominantly poorly run smaller community institutions was seen as an improvement in care for the mentally ill. However, this progress was followed by new problems. Believing the large psychiatric hospital to be the answer, the public seemed to lose concern for this population. In the following years, a gradual and steady rise in new admissions to these hospitals once again resulted in overcrowding, mismanagement, and mistreatment.

During the early 1900s, advocates of the social justice movement, who had been active earlier in other areas of human welfare, turned their attention to abuses within mental institutions. Having no desire to dismantle these institutions, they sought rather to change the system of patient treatment and procedures.

New policies creating individual treatment plans were established. Such individualized plans, taking into account each patient's personal history, appeared to be a more humane and responsible way to administer treatment. This policy seemed a step in the right direction, but it unfortunately created other abuses within the system. Too much arbitrary power and authority were given over to the professionals and bureaucrats overseeing these systems. Of course, some patients benefited from more individualized consideration, but generally the large and unchecked state system often ignored individuals' rights and denied the possibility that the state could be wrong in certain instances.

Freud's Influence

By the 1920s and 1930s, Sigmund Freud's classic theories concerning human behavior were well established and widely accepted. Having had to endure considerable criticism in the earlier years of his developing work in response to his emphasis on human sexuality, his later, refined theories had a major impact on most facets of society. Although Freud did not work directly in institutions, he had a strong influence on the prevailing treatment approach. His theories were so widely accepted by the public that the mental institutions of the 1930s adopted his approach to treatment and became psychoanalytically oriented. His contributions were so influential that many consider the second mental health revolution to have begun with public acceptance of his work (Wahler et al., 1972).

As discussed in Chapter 4, many criticisms of certain aspects of Freud's theories continue today. One such criticism by those who employ a human services perspective is that Freud's psychoanalytic theories focus too narrowly on the inner person, excluding the environmental factors that influence human behavior. Freud's impact, though considerable, did not lead to significant changes in the institutional system of care for the mentally ill. Steady deterioration in this system continued. Although there were exceptions, most hospital staffs were generally overworked, understaffed, and poorly trained. Patients were often neglected, and many remained in hospitals for years.

Trend Toward Deinstitutionalization and Decentralization

In the early 1950s, certain changes began to develop in several hospitals as the result of growth in the field of **psychopharmacology**. It was now possible through the use of drugs to effectively reduce a patient's bizarre behavior, thereby affording other opportunities for treatment. Many patients previously viewed as untreatable were now able to return to the community while continuing with drug treatments at home (Pasamanick, Scarpitti, & Dinitz, 1967). Many controversies surfaced regarding the alleged widespread misuse or abuse of such drugs. Critics claimed that patients were controlled by routinely giving them unneeded drugs. Others pointed out that drugs may cause side effects as bad as the illness being treated.

Deinstitutionalization became a major policy during this time. There was a growing belief that people could be treated more successfully in familiar community settings. Some felt that deinstitutionalization was implemented more because of financial concerns than for treatment reasons. It was felt that it was just too expensive to keep people institutionalized on a round-the-clock basis, and treatment was initially thought to be less expensive in community settings.

Another change appearing at this time in the large state hospitals was **geographic decentralization**. This procedure, which initially began as a change focused on administrative admissions procedures, was eventually to have a significant effect on the role of mental patients and their communities. Through this new administrative procedure, patients were placed in hospital wards based on their place of residence prior to admission. Patients were housed and treated with other patients from their own communities rather than dispersed throughout the hospital system. Prior to this change, state hospitals generally remained isolated and removed from the communities they served. Through geographic decentralization, communities became more aware of the patients residing therein. Many problems have resurfaced regarding this issue, as many communities have openly voiced fear and dissatisfaction with having mental health facilities or programs located within their borders.

COMMUNITY MENTAL HEALTH MOVEMENT

The 1960s were an important era for the field of mental health. Many professionals have, in fact, referred to this decade as the one that saw the third mental health revolution (Hobbs, 1964; Wahler et al., 1972). The changes occurring in this period marked another significant shift in human services philosophy as characterized primarily by the **community mental health** movement.

To appreciate more fully the sweeping changes advocated by the community mental health movement of the 1960s, one must look at the various issues that prompted this movement. A growing disenchantment with the traditional large state psychiatric hospital system of the 1950s was based on the following problems with that system:

1. The traditional system focused exclusively on the treatment and rehabilitation of existing mental illness rather than on its prevention.
2. Many of the state psychiatric hospitals were too far away from the communities in which their patients resided.
3. Services were fragmented, with poor coordination between hospital and community agencies.
4. The traditional system emphasized long-term individual therapy to the exclusion of innovative clinical strategies, such as outreach programs, crisis hotlines, and family therapies, which might have helped a greater number of individuals.
5. Nontraditional sources of personnel, such as generalist human services workers, were not being used despite a growing worker shortage.

The Joint Commission on Mental Illness and Health (1961, p. 2) evidenced the thrust of the community mental health movement as it recommended that the objectives of modern treatment should be the following:

1. To save patients from the debilitating effects of institutionalization as much as possible

2. If patients required hospitalization, to return them to home and community life as soon as possible
3. Thereafter, to maintain them in the community as long as possible

In 1963 the Community Mental Health Act was signed into law. This legislation reflected a growing philosophy that mental health services should be located in the community with the government allocating funds for the creation of these comprehensive community mental health centers. Chapter 2 examines the specific services offered by these centers. Deinstitutionalization was encouraged, resulting in a major shift of mental patients from the large mental hospitals to these community mental health centers.

The community mental health movement has its advocates and its opponents. Some assert that although the number of patients in the large institutions has decreased and the average length of stay has been reduced considerably, the tendency to readmit patients over and over again to the institutions has correspondingly grown (Wahler, 1971). Other watchful observers of the movement have pointed to instances in which patients have been placed in community settings without adequate supervision. Opponents of the movement indicate that the initial community centers often resembled the traditional hospital organization. The difficulty of developing new mental health services grew out of a situation in which the workers were already socialized and evolved from the old hospital system (Perlmutter & Silverman, 1972).

Advocates of the movement point to the healing power of the community and the need to normalize the method of treatment as much as possible. If the goal of treatment is eventually to return the patient to a functioning life in the community, the community must be an integral part of the treatment.

ADVENT OF GENERALIST HUMAN SERVICES WORKERS

Another important development in the 1960s was the formal recognition of the role of **generalist human services workers** as reflected in the new careers movement. The

 REAL LIFE HUMAN SERVICES WORK

The colorful history of the human services agency I've worked with for over ten years is attached to a famous event in America's history. There was a festival in 1969, and this festival was called "Woodstock" although the site was more than an hour west of the sleepy little town with the actual name. Regardless, the town became instantly famous, and with this fame came buses and carloads of America's youth, searching for a utopian existence and escaping the confines of the world they were living in. Unfortunately, the once quiet little town of Woodstock was becoming overwhelmed with young people sleeping on benches in the town's well known "green," people hitchhiking in and out of the town, camping in parking lots, and seeking out food and clothing. One member of the town—Gail Varsi—recognized that there was a problem. Ms. Varsi opened her home and her phone line to these people; the famous Family of Woodstock Hotline still maintains the same number that was Ms. Varsi's home telephone number in 1969. With the

help of local businesses, clergy and residents, she organized food drives, clothing exchanges, and often transportation back to where many of these young people came from. These are the roots of Family of Woodstock, Incorporated. Today, the agency services all of Ulster County, running programs such as the only domestic violence shelter in the county, a teen runaway shelter, several homeless shelters, several walk-in centers (still maintaining a "free store" and a food pantry) and case management services for adults and adolescents.

Family of Woodstock, Inc., was born when a community need was recognized and addressed; continuing in this line of thinking was the reasoning for the MidWay Program.

There is a clear age of adulthood, and many of the young people the agency was working with, although adults at the age of 18, were unable to live independently and did not possess the skills necessary to maintain a manageable lifestyle. The agency was confronted with young people who were not technically "runaways" in the classic sense, but were homeless due to many circumstances; some were victims of domestic violence and sexual assault in their homes, some had parents who were unable to care for them because of financial restraints, substance abuse issues, [or] incarceration, and some just wound up with nowhere to go. Many fell through cracks that were not as prevalent before the early 90's when divorce became common place, opening the door for this new concept of the "blended family" and many of these kids became unwanted as younger children took their place in the new family structure. These kids were the basis for MidWay.

I am the director of "the Midway Program." I oversee two houses, one in Ellenville, New York, and one 28 miles away in Kingston, New York. The Kingston House was the site for the original MidWay. Family of Woodstock, Inc. owns the house where the program stands in a small residential neighborhood, close to the center of the small city. The Ellenville site exists in the small, rural village of Ellenville, also in a quiet residential neighborhood. Both sites are home to 6 adolescents, ranging in age from 16–20. The program is co-ed, and can manage 3 parenting teens in each program. The length of stay in the program is 18 months, or up to 24 months if the participant enters the program at age 16 in order to allow them to complete high school while in the program. Participants in the program are offered their own room, furnished and complete with cable television; they share a kitchen, two bathrooms, and a common area with one another. There is a staff member in the program 24 hours a day. From 9 to 5 there is a case manager, available for consultation, transportation, assistance with appointments and referrals. There is a Life Skills Manager from 4:30 to 9:30, available for assistance with imperative daily living skills, like budgeting, laundry, grocery shopping, and other skills such as communication and relationship building. There is also an overnight shift, [starting at] 9:00 in the evening, [and] ending the following morning. Although there is only one staff member on at a time, there is what is referred to as a "cross over," where the staff leaving the program provide the staff coming on shift with a summary of the events taking place on the previous shift.

As the director of the program, I conduct interviews with the referrals the program received from sources including probation, hospital social workers, school guidance counselors and social workers, and other shelters in the area such as domestic violence shelters. The clients I interview for the program are frequently dealing with issues such as substance abuse or mental illness, and often a combination of the two. The clients accepted into the program are referred to local service providers for mental health and substance abuse counseling. Although the clients the program serves are high need and may not be able to live independently, the MidWay Program can maintain these clients with the appropriate support and care from other service providers.

On a daily basis, I communicate primarily with the case managers of the two programs, receiving updates on the status of the resident[s]. There is a behavioral modification system used in the program; the residents are on different levels based on their

(Continued)

accomplishments and behavior. The residents sign and receive a contract when they enter the program. Their status is tracked and discussed in a bi-weekly case conference where all of the staff of the program, the program director, and a mental health consultant meet to communicate the events of the program from the previous week. When a resident of the program is doing poorly, [he or she] schedule[s] a meeting with the program director to decide whether or not [he or she] will remain in the program.

The residents are expected to maintain their house; they have evening chores, checked nightly by the two residential counselors of the program. In addition, they are responsible for the condition of their rooms. They are assisted in grocery shopping, but cook their own meals, often together because [of] the "home-like" environment the program strives to create.

The residents also create schedule[s], crafted for every individual with [his or her] specific needs in mind with the help of the case manager. We develop schedules to occupy approximately forty hours a week of the residents' time; the schedule contains work, school (sometimes college, high school, or a GED course), substance abuse and mental health treatment, or any combination of these. As the director of the program I oversee and approve these schedules. I also meet with the kids regularly to discuss their experiences and feelings about the program; I have a background in direct care, so this is one of the most rewarding parts of my job. I discuss their status in the program and if a resident is not doing well in the program, I discuss the potential of [his or her] being asked to leave the program; [he or she] may be asked to write what is referred to as an appeal letter to explain why there should be another chance for [him or her] to remain in the program. We like to run the program with the assumption that the staff and the program [are] performing the roles that parents would take in a healthy family atmosphere; we think of the program as an opportunity for the residents to experience a healthy and supportive family environment.

Kimmer Gifford, MSW

title *generalist human services worker*, most recognized and used today, was originally *paraprofessional worker* in the 1960s. In addition, several other titles were also popular during this period, including *lay therapist* and *new professional*. The 1964 Economic Opportunity Act and the Schneuer Subprofessional Career Act of 1966 provided the impetus and the government funds to recruit and train entry-level workers for a range of positions within the human services field. These related legislations, coupled with other antipoverty amendments, created approximately 150,000 jobs for generalist human services workers (Reissman, 1967).

The rapid growth of the paraprofessional movement arose from a perceived worker shortage as the new community health centers sought initially to use personnel in more innovative ways. Albee (1960) pointed out the critical shortage of trained mental health professionals. He predicted an even greater shortage in the future and advocated the creation of a new kind of generalist mental health worker who could be educationally prepared in a shorter period of time. Through the creation of two- and four-year training programs based in colleges, it was believed that aspiring workers could receive enough broad-based education and general human services skills to function on a generalist level alongside the more highly trained professionals. Many of the basic tasks previously performed by psychologists, psychiatrists, or social workers—such as intake interviewing and setting fee schedules—could be delegated to the generalist human services worker, thus freeing the professional to focus selectively on more advanced clinical aspects of treatment and diagnosis that often required more extensive graduate preparation.

Although no single description would adequately encompass the diversity of roles of generalist human services workers, there is agreement on the following important common characteristics of the generalist:

1. Working directly with clients or families (in consultation with other professionals) to provide a variety of services
2. Able to work in a variety of settings that provide human services
3. Able to work with all of the various professions in the field, rather than affiliating with any one of the professions
4. Familiar with a variety of therapeutic services and techniques, rather than specializing in one

Some of the more common work activities of generalist human services workers include, but certainly are not limited to, the following:

- Helping clients in their own environments with various services
- Helping people get to existing services (as in simplifying bureaucratic regulations and acting as client advocate)
- Acting as assistants to various specialists (for example, psychiatrists, psychologists, nurses)
- Carrying out activities for agencies and programs, such as budgeting, purchasing, and personnel matters
- Gathering information and organizing and analyzing data
- Providing direct care for clients who need ongoing services
- Working with various community groups to create needed programs and develop resources

Since the 1960s, new and expanded roles have been created for generalist human services workers. Gartner (1971), Wahler et al. (1972), and Alley, Blanton, and Feldman (1979), among others, have traced the evolving functions and roles of these workers. The role of the generalist human services worker, once narrowly defined as merely custodial in nature, had grown by the 1970s to include a wide range of therapeutic activities. As Minuchin (1969) noted, the paraprofessional movement initiated a reexamination of professional roles and tasks, which resulted in a renewed interest in environmental factors as opposed to the intrapsychic view of maladaptive behavior. As a result, the human services field of the 1970s through today emphasizes the use of generalist human services workers in roles reflecting the importance of a patient's social and environmental needs.

Chapter 6 provides a closer examination of the diverse functions and roles of generalist human services workers. Table 3.1 lists legislations in the mental health movement through history.

FUTURE TRENDS

The many tasks and problems facing our human services system today are similar to those faced previously. Poverty, unemployment, and mental illness, among other problems, still exist. What is different, however, is that new methods and approaches

Table 3.1	Highlights and Legislation in the Mental Health Movement
800–1300s	Church becomes major provider of services to the mentally ill.
1409	Oldest mental hospital still functioning today is established in Valencia, Spain.
1752	Pennsylvania Hospital for the Mentally Ill is founded.
1792	Phillipe Pinel, director of a French mental institution, believes the insane might be curable and initiates reforms.
1800s	Dorothea Dix and other social reformers help to establish the state psychiatric hospital system in the United States. National Society for Mental Illness (Hygiene) is established to study the care of the insane.
1920–1930s	Freud's theories concerning human behavior gain widespread acceptance.
1935	Aid to Families with Dependent Children and Social Security Act.
1937	First International Committee for Mental Hygiene is formed. Hill-Burton Act provides funds for building psychiatric hospital units.
1946	National Mental Health Act establishes federal funds to develop training programs for mental health professionals.
1948	World Federation for Mental Health is formed.
1950s	Major advances are made in the field of psychopharmacology.
1955	Congress creates Joint Commission on Mental Illness and Health. This committee evaluates the needs of the mentally ill and seeks to make resources available.
1961	World Psychiatric Association is formed.
1963	Mental Retardation Facilities and Community Mental Health Centers Construction Act is passed. Trend begins toward community care for the mentally ill and decentralization of the mental health system.
1964	Economic Opportunity Act is passed. Passage of Schneuer Subprofessional Career Act gives impetus and funds to recruit generalists for training in human services and mental health field.
1967	Federal government provides money for the staffing of mental health centers.
1968	Community Mental Health Centers Act provides for comprehensive services for the mentally ill.
1970	Comprehensive Alcohol Abuse and Alcohol Prevention, Treatment, and Rehabilitation Act is passed.
1973	Rehabilitation Act provides access to vocational rehabilitation services for adults.
1974	Juvenile Justice and Delinquency Prevention Act is passed.
1975	Education for All Handicapped Children Act and Individuals with Disabilities Education Act ensure right to education in least restrictive environment.
1979	Mental Health Systems Act establishes bill of rights for the mentally ill and the right to refuse medication.
1984	Office of Prevention is established within the National Institute of Mental Health.

(Continued)

TABLE 3.1	CONTINUED
1986	Protection and Advocacy for Mentally Ill Individuals Act is passed.
1987	McKinney Act created for job training, child care, and literacy programs for poor and homeless.
1990	Americans with Disabilities Act is signed into law. It prohibits discrimination against people with disabilities.
1996	The Personal Responsibility and Work Opportunity Reconciliation Act replaces Aid to Families with Dependent Children.
2005	The Deficit Reduction Act requires states to engage more TANF cases in productive work activities leading to self-sufficiency.
2009	American Recovery and Reinvestment Act provides increased funds for Medicaid, food stamps, health care, and increased unemployment benefits and TANF (public assistance) funding.

are needed to deal with them in our highly complex and technological society. The rate of change is so rapid and the changes so complex today that new levels of stress, anxiety, and insecurity have been created for many.

Along with the trend toward increasing specialization, more and more people find that their previously acquired skills are rapidly becoming obsolete. Although scientific achievements have increased our life span, war, increased terrorism, economic upheavals, the AIDS epidemic, the massive drug problem, and other troubles have given rise to widespread concerns about what type of future awaits us and our children.

In an effort to keep pace with a changing society, the human services system must also change and grow. For example, agencies must develop new sources of funding, such as grants from government, foundations, and other private groups. In addition, more agencies are reaching out to attract volunteers to help maintain various programs and services. As indicated in Chapter 7, the shortage of funds has become an increasingly large issue in the early 2000s and will continue to be an issue in the future. And as our earlier discussion in Chapter 1 indicated, the movement toward privatization of service agencies is yet another trend that continues.

Over the past forty years, with the change from hospital care to community care for the mentally ill, there has been a dramatic increase in the use of **paraprofessionals** or generalist workers in the human services field. At present, they are the single largest group delivering direct care to the mentally ill. One of the more recent trends, likely to continue for quite some time, is the establishment of bachelor's degree, master's degree, and doctoral degree programs in human services. Many programs formerly titled "mental health technology" or "mental health assistant" have been changing to adopt the more generic title of "human services."

New trends in the licensing of human services professionals are appearing throughout this country. A number of state governments have passed legislation (and some are currently in the process of doing so) that benefits individuals whose education and/or professional training did not meet that state's requirements for licensure in any of the mental health fields discussed earlier in this chapter. This new legislation expands the number of professional titles under which mental health workers may work. In New York State, for example, the title of "mental health professional" was created. Individuals who met the specific requirements for any of the four areas within this title (that is, creative arts therapy, marriage and family therapy, mental health counseling, and psychoanalysis) began their professional careers as licensed practitioners in 2005. To obtain one of these licenses, the applicant must possess a minimum of a 45-credit master's degree and between 1,500 and 3,000 hours of supervised counseling experience, depending upon the specific license (New York State Education Department, 2005a,b,c,d). In the first year of their existence, mental health professional licenses were granted to 462 individuals in New York State (New York State Education Department, 2006).

Current population trends indicate an increase in immigration into the United States. U.S. Census figures predict that sometime between the years 2030 and 2050, racial and ethnic minorities will become the majority population (Sue, 1996). Our human services system will be hard-pressed to meet the needs of this culturally diverse population, many of whom will possess little or no formal education and will see no immediate job opportunities. The great diversity in cultural backgrounds has already initiated many changes in the provisions of services and has caused a reexamination of the roles of Western and non-Western helping strategies. Multicultural programs and ethnic sensitivity training are already a part of our current training system, and they are likely to continue on a larger, more formalized scale in the future. There will be increased importance placed on having (a) knowledge about other cultures, (b) the skills necessary in working with diverse populations, and (c) the proper attitudes when working with individuals of varying cultural backgrounds (Neukrug, 2008). Chapter 5 examines the various issues of multicultural awareness in further detail.

Another important demographic trend is what many gerontologists refer to as "the graying of America." This refers to the growing number of people 65 years of age and older. Over 15% of the population is currently over 65 years of age and estimates indicate that by the year 2040, more than 25% of the population will be in that category (Harris, 1990). To understand this trend more clearly, consider that there are currently more people living in the United States over the age of 65 than the total population of Canada. The growth of the aged population indicates an increasing need to provide specialized services to meet the physical and emotional needs of later life. Programs for senior citizens can include day treatment programs within community mental health centers, programs housed in senior care retirement settings, long-term care facilities such as nursing homes, or a variety of other services offered through senior centers throughout the country.

It is clear that as people live longer, quality of life issues will receive more attention. Thus, the growing emphasis on community-based services will continue. Moreover, an increased focus on prevention and wellness, rather than the emphasis on illness and treatment, will occur. This rise in the senior citizen population will create an increased need for more people trained to provide service. An increasing number of undergraduate and graduate programs are offering specialized gerontological coursework and internship training opportunities working with the senior citizen population.

Advances in computer technology have changed our society. Such technology has affected the delivery of human services as well. Human services agencies are turning to technology to help them provide better quality care in a more cost-effective manner. These new technologies have altered the very nature of communication within the field. There is an increasing reliance on electronic mail (e-mail) for immediate discussions and consultations with colleagues in other work-related activities. The Internet serves as an invaluable resource to quickly obtain information or conduct research to aid in planning and implementing programs to help those in need. For example, we are witnessing the growth of counseling online in which people can receive immediate assistance from within the privacy of their homes.

Computer technology continues to transform information management as all intake interviews, billing, assessment results, treatment, planning, and other client record keeping can be coordinated, stored, and transmitted almost instantaneously.

Software programs are now being used for the training of human services professionals. Interactive videos, CD-ROMs, and other interactive multimedia tools can provide specific training in a variety of selected topics. In addition, software programs are emerging for use with clients. These tools are designed to help clients gain knowledge and skills in areas such as parenting, adult daily living skills, vocational skills, or substance awareness and prevention strategies. Very clearly, the need for trained human services personnel with computer technology skills is growing.

Another very important trend within the field is an increasing emphasis on advocacy and on the need for human services workers to develop competency in the use of advocacy. Advocacy, as we know, occurs on many levels. One can represent a client within an agency in an attempt to gain additional services for the client; represent an agency within the political system to fight for increased funding of social service programs; or lobby for new state or national legislation to benefit an underserved population or group, such as the poor or homeless. As Chapter 5 examines more closely, advocacy work is becoming increasingly vital to this field.

As the human services profession continues to evolve and expand, the need for insuring minimal levels of competency will increase. The National Organization for Human Services and the Council for Standards in Human Service Education are two organizations, among others, working toward this and other goals. Competency guidelines now exist, as do ethical standards of practice, skills standards, and training-program standards.

Historically, human services have been focused on client populations in need of basic services such as food, shelter, or financial support. As discussed earlier, the scope of human services has in recent decades expanded beyond the goal of providing basic services. Another trend likely to continue well into the future finds human services programs expanding into corporate America. Employers have recognized that workers who have fewer psychological problems are more likely to be effective and productive workers. Industry has encouraged its workers to seek help, and many large corporations have responded by creating employee assistance programs. A variety of services are available to employees, which may include drug and alcohol abuse counseling, marital counseling, stress management, and many other types of personal intervention strategies requiring trained human services personnel. Human services workers will find increased employment opportunities within this sector.

As the managed-care approach continues to dominate the delivery of human services in America, the expanded role of case management will likely increase. More and more human services workers will find themselves functioning as case managers within this diverse service system. The devastating aftermath of natural disasters over the past several years, along with the omnipresent threat of terrorism, has heightened the need for greater preparedness. The federal government, as well as many local governments and relief organizations, has created larger, more comprehensive disaster response services. These services focus upon the physical needs of those most affected as well as the emotional side effects. As a result, there will likely be an expanded role and need for specially trained human services personnel to function as members of these response teams throughout the country.

ADDITIONAL READING

Corey, M. S., & Corey, G. (1998). *Becoming a helper* (3rd ed.). Pacific Grove, CA: Brooks/ Cole.

Hampton, J. K. (1991). *The biology of aging.* New York: Brown.

Harris, H. S., & Maloney, D. C. (Eds.). (1996). *Human services: Contemporary issues and trends.* Boston: Allyn & Bacon.

Iglehart, A. P., & Becerra, R. M. (1995). *Social services and the ethnic community.* Boston: Allyn & Bacon.

Neukrug, E. (2004). *Theory, practice and trends in human services: An introduction.* Pacific Grove, CA: Thomson Brooks/Cole.

Popple, P. R., & Leighninger, L. (1993). *Social work, social welfare and American society* (2nd ed.). Boston: Allyn & Bacon.

Sheehy, G. (1995). *New passages: Mapping your life across time.* New York: Ballantine.

Vissing, Y. M., Salloway, J. C., & Siress, D. L. (1994). Training for expertise versus training for trust: Issues in rural gerontology. *Educational Gerontologist, 20*(6), 797–808.

Ward, M. J. (1946). *The snake pit.* New York: Random House.

Woodside, M., & McClam, T. (1998). *An introduction to human services* (3rd ed.). Pacific Grove, CA: Brooks/Cole.

REFERENCES

Albee, G. W. (1960). The manpower crisis in mental health. *American Journal of Public Health, 50,* 1895–1900.

Alley, S., Blanton, Jr., & Feldman, R. (Eds.). (1979). *Paraprofessionals in mental health: Theory and practice.* New York: Human Sciences Press.

Andriola, J., & Cata, G. (1969). The oldest mental health hospital in the world. *Hospital and Community Psychiatry, 20,* 42–43.

Bloom, B. L. (1977). *Community mental health: A general introduction.* Pacific Grove, CA: Brooks/Cole.

Coleman, J. (1976). *Abnormal psychology and modern life.* Glenview, IL: Scott, Foresman.

Fisher, W., Mehr, J., & Truckenbrod, P. (1974). *Human services: The third revolution in mental health.* New York: Alfred.

Gartner, A. (1971). *Paraprofessionals and their performance.* New York: Praeger.

Harris, D. K. (1990). *Sociology of aging* (2nd ed.). New York: Harper & Row.

Hobbs, N. (1964). Mental health's third revolution. *American Journal of Orthopsychiatry, 34,* 822–833.

Hoch, P. H., & Knight, R. P. (Eds.). (1965). *Epilepsy: Psychiatric aspects of convulsive disorders*. New York: Hafner.

Joint Commission on Mental Illness and Health. (1961). *Action for mental health*. New York: Basic Books.

Minuchin, S. (1969). The paraprofessional and the use of confrontation in the mental health field. *American Journal of Orthopsychiatry, 34,* 722–729.

Neukrug, E. (2008). *Theory, practice, and trends in human services* (4th ed.). Pacific Grove, CA: Thomson Brooks/Cole.

New York State Education Department, Office of the Professions (2005a). Creative arts therapy license requirements. Retrieved February 12, 2006, from http://www.op.nysed.gov/catlic.htm

New York State Education Department, Office of the Professions (2005b). Marriage and family therapy license requirements. Retrieved February 12, 2006, from http://www.op.nysed.gov/mftlic.htm

New York State Education Department, Office of the Professions (2005c). Mental health counseling license requirements. Retrieved February 12, 2006, from http://www.op.nysed.gov/mhclic.htm

New York State Education Department, Office of the Professions (2005d). Psychoanalysis license requirements. Retrieved February 12, 2006, from http://www.op.nysed.gov/psyanllic.htm

New York State Education Department, Office of the Professions (2006). License statistics. Retrieved February 12, 2006, from http://www.op.nysed.gov/mhpcounts.htm

Pasamanick, B., Scarpitti, F. R., & Dinitz, S. (1967). *Schizophrenics in the community*. New York: Appleton-Century-Crofts.

Perlmutter, F., & Silverman, H. A. (1972). C.M.H.C.: A structural anachronism. *Social Work, 17,* 78–84.

Perry, J. A., & Perry, E. K. (1988). *The social web* (5th ed.). New York: Harper & Row.

Reissman, F. (1967). Strategies and suggestions for training paraprofessionals. *Community Mental Health Journal, 3,* 103–110.

Rimm, D. C., & Somervill, J. W. (1977). *Abnormal psychology*. New York: Academic Press.

Russell, J. B. (1972). *Witchcraft in the Middle Ages*. Ithaca, NY: Cornell University Press.

Sue, D. W. (1996). The challenge of multiculturalism: The road less traveled. *American Counselor, 1*(1), 6–14.

U.S. Department of Labor, Bureau of Labor Statistics. (1999, March 20). Occupational outlook, http://www.stats.bls.gov/oco/ocos0.59.htm#outlook

Wahler, H. J. (1971). What is life all about, or who all needs paraprofessionals? *Clinical Psychologist, 24*(3), 11–14.

Wahler, H. J., Johnson, R., & Uhrich, K. (1972). *The Expediter Project: Final report to National Institute of Mental Health*. Seattle, WA: Department of Social and Health Services.

CHAPTER 4

THEORETICAL PERSPECTIVES

CHAPTER CONTENTS

INTRODUCTION

A theory is a statement that attempts to explain connections among events. It is not in itself a fact but a concept that brings facts together into a sensible overall picture. There is nothing mysterious about the process of making, testing, and using theories. Even quite young children construct useful theories about events in their daily lives. These take the form of ideas such as, "If I say I'm sorry, Mommy won't hit me," or "If I do well at school, my parents will give me a present." These ideas are based on observations of previous events. On a simple level, they enable the child to understand, predict, and sometimes control the environment.

The process of theory making goes on throughout life. The fact is that the individual is constantly being bombarded with incoming stimuli. Without mental structures to classify and organize these events, the individual would be overwhelmed and unable to function in an organized way. In this sense, theory making is absolutely essential to successful living.

Just as personal theories enable the individual to function effectively, scientific theories enable the human services worker to function effectively. This chapter examines a number of major theories that help workers understand the causes of disorders and plan effective action to either prevent or treat these disorders.

SCIENTIFIC THEORY

There is no hard-and-fast distinction between personal and scientific theories. All theories are intended to help us make sense of the world around us. The distinguishing features of scientific theories are that they are consciously formed, tested, and shared with other researchers. One purpose of scientific theories is to serve as a guide to future research. Ideally, theories should be continually tested and modified to fit newly discovered facts.

Of course, scientists often fall short of this ideal. Many theories once accepted by reputable authorities are now completely discredited. Sometimes incorrect theories are based on faulty, or limited, observations. For example, a number of early investigators attributed criminal behavior to inherited tendencies (Lombroso-Ferrero, 1911). In this view, the criminal was a "born type" who could be distinguished from "normals" by certain physical traits, such as a low forehead, an unusually shaped head, eyebrows growing together above the bridge of the nose, and protruding ears. Modern investigators found that this theory did not account for criminals who lacked these physical characteristics and that it ignored data that linked criminal behavior to poverty and certain social conditions.

Because theories often serve as guides to action, the blind acceptance of an incorrect theory may have harmful consequences. The only remedy against the hazards of bias is to be receptive to all of the relevant facts in a situation.

THEORIES ABOUT HUMAN DISORDERS

Now that a general idea of what theories are and what purposes they serve has been presented, focus shifts to the main concern of this chapter: theories about human disorders. Very simply, these are theories that try to explain why and how certain disorders come about. Based on this understanding, each theory proposes certain treatments designed to alleviate the disorder in question. Theories, then, are not merely matters for dry academic discussion; they also have a powerful impact on what the helper does for or to the client.

Traditionally, human disorders are divided into two main types: physical and mental (or psychological). The latter will be emphasized because these types are of main concern to the human services worker. All of the major theories to be reviewed offer reasonable explanations of how and why psychological disorders occur. However, the explanations are quite different from one another. Why are there so many different explanations? There are several possible answers to this question. One is that human behavior is so complex that no single theory can explain every disorder. Another answer is that each theory tends to focus on certain kinds of abnormal behavior. A third point, related to the other two, is that different theories tend to focus on different levels of observation. To better understand the base of the various theoretical helping models most often utilized today, one needs an understanding of the historical underpinning of these contemporary approaches. Before proceeding to the specific theories, it is necessary to clarify what is meant by levels of observation.

THREE LEVELS OF OBSERVATION

Each theory tends to focus on one of three general levels of observation: (a) biological, (b) psychological, or (c) social. In other words, researchers are apt to specialize in the study of events at one particular level.

From the biological point of view, an organism is viewed as a physical or biochemical system. Disease, physical damage to the body, or inadequate development of internal organs may all hamper an individual's ability to get along in the outside world. For example, some forms of mental retardation are due to abnormal development of the brain and nervous system. It is also known that one form of senility is due to a breakdown in the blood vessels of the brain. It is now accepted that conditions previously thought of as psychological in nature, such as alcoholism and schizophrenia—a serious and persistent mental illness—have genetic components. In addition, research has suggested that the brains of individuals who suffer from schizophrenia are anatomically different from the brains of those without the illness. As a result, many disorders that are conceptualized as having biological components, such as schizophrenia and depression, are treated by utilizing the medical model, explained and discussed in detail a little later in this chapter. Treatment in the medical model often involves medication, or what is referred to as psychopharmacological intervention. Psychopharmacology is the study of the effects of any **psychoactive drug** that acts upon the mind by affecting brain chemistry. Medications have been developed to treat many categories of mental disorders, including psychoses, mood disorders, anxieties, and even substance abuse. Physical abnormalities are the main province of medical science. The medical approach to treatment (to be described) employs medication, surgery, and other physical methods to cure, or at least ameliorate, disorders.

From the psychological point of view, the individual attempts to gain gratification of needs and goals by interacting with the outer environment. To adapt successfully, the person must behave in ways that suit the immediate situation. The person's skills, motives, needs, emotions, and ways of handling stress all play a role in this adaptive struggle. Obviously, some individuals are more successful than others in attaining satisfactions. Some of the psychological problems familiar to the human services worker are clients' low self-esteem, lack of skills, and self-defeating ways of trying to achieve stated goals in life.

The social level refers to the powerful influences of family, school, neighborhood, and society. The majority of social service work is accomplished within this social domain. Human services professionals, social workers, and counselors help to empower those who are marginalized by society. They help clients obtain affordable housing, make home visits to determine whether children are safe, counsel victims in domestic violence shelters, and become community advocates. Current research suggests that the quality of our social relationships has a major impact on our physical functioning, including our cardiovascular, immune, and hormonal systems (Gilbert, 2002). Whether individuals grow up in warm and loving homes or in abusive and neglectful environments seems to affect such things as brain maturation, the ability to fight disease, a tendency toward depression, and poor recovery from stress (Schore, 2002).

Controversy and some confusion exist about applying these three levels of observation to specific disorders. Biological, psychological, and social theories have been put forward about alcoholism, schizophrenia, criminality, and many other disorders. Various investigators proclaim that one level is more important than the other two in causing these disorders. There is, for example, intense debate about the relative importance of inherited physical traits in predisposing an individual toward one disorder or another. The fact is that all three levels may be involved in the development of a certain disorder. This premise serves as the basis for the following model, which integrates all three points of view.

BIOPSYCHOSOCIAL MODEL

Mental disorders have many causes, or are multi-determined. It is important to develop an understanding of how different aspects or levels of functioning interact with one another to create or cause problems. The biopsychosocial model takes into account the influences of each domain or level of functioning of the individual: the biological (or physical), the psychological, and the social. It helps us understand the influences of the biological realm, including genetic makeup, the disease process, immune system and hormone functions, and more. Plus, it helps us see how these systems impact the psychological and social areas of the individual. It also sheds light on the influence of the psychological, such as the effect of anxiety and stress on a person's physical well-being. In addition, the social environment in which a person lives, such as not having access to quality health care or decent housing conditions, can also affect the other two areas. Most mental health professionals agree that human disorders come about as a result of a disruption in at least one of these systems, and that healthy functioning is a result of a successful integration of all three.

POLITICAL IMPLICATIONS OF THEORY

The controversies among theories are not merely matters of factual evidence but also involve underlying political and economic factors. For example, it makes a difference whether the behavior problems associated with poverty are attributed to (a) psychological defects, such as laziness or lack of intelligence, or (b) the impact of society, which has stacked the cards against the poor. In the first case, the individual is held fully responsible for his or her poor circumstances. In the second, the person is seen as the victim of social and economic factors beyond his or her control. Obviously, a more sympathetic response goes along with this second point of view.

MODELS OF DYSFUNCTION

This brief introduction to theory paves the way for discussion of two general models of dysfunction: the medical model and the **human services model**. The term *model* in this context refers to a general theoretical point of view about the causes of disorders. Perhaps the earliest model was the religious or magical perspective, which emphasized evil spirits as the cause of illness. The medical model, with its scientific focus, gradually replaced the spiritual notion of causation. The medical model emphasizes biological factors, such as bacterial, viral, or genetic agents, in causing diseases. More recently, the human services model, with its focus on social factors, has challenged the medical model. We will first take a detailed look at the medical model.

MEDICAL MODEL

As applied to psychological disorders, the **medical model** stresses the causative role of factors within the individual. Adherents of the medical model do not claim that all so-called mental disorders are due to biological or organic factors. In fact, they make a distinction between organic and functional disorders.

The organic disorders are caused by physical abnormalities of the brain, nervous system, and other internal systems. Epilepsy, senility, some kinds of retardation, and certain psychotic states are examples of disorders in which some physical abnormality has been found to play a role. Organic disorders may be caused by inherited defects, chemical imbalances, viral infections, malnutrition, and various drugs and poisons. Disorders associated with physical damage are likely to be long-standing, whereas those associated with drugs may represent temporary disorders of brain function.

The functional disorders, in contrast, are due to psychological factors operating within the individual. These might include poorly controlled drives and impulses, unrealistic ideas, and unresolved conflicts. Addictions, antisocial tendencies, neuroses, and some psychotic reactions are classified as functional disorders. This means that the major causes are presumed to relate to the personality of the individual rather than to any physical defects. Some disorders, such as the schizophrenias, cannot be classified with great confidence because of doubt about the causes.

Medical Procedure

Regardless of whether a disorder is organic or functional, the procedures of medical practice can be applied to it. This means that a certain psychological disorder can be approached as though it were a physical disorder, such as measles or tuberculosis. The first step in medical and psychiatric practice is to arrive at a diagnosis, which means to classify and label the disorder according to the presenting symptoms. Next comes the formulation of a treatment plan, which may include medication, shock therapy, psychotherapy, and/or confinement to a mental hospital. The treatment is related to the prognosis, which is an educated guess about what degree of recovery can be expected for the patient.

For example, a young man became despondent over losing his fiancée to someone else. He made the rather dramatic suicidal gesture of threatening to jump from the roof of an apartment building but let himself be talked down by the police. He was taken to a community mental health center and admitted to a ward for observation and treatment. He was diagnosed as suffering from a depressive reaction. The treatment plan included brief counseling sessions to help ventilate his feelings of hurt, loss, and anger. In addition, he was put on a mood-elevating drug. In view of his history of good functioning, the prognostic outlook was favorable. This is the medical model in action: a psychological or emotional reaction is handled with the basic procedures of medicine.

TREATMENT APPROACHES OF THE MEDICAL MODEL

Because the medical model is accepted by many professionals employed in mental hospitals, prisons, schools, mental retardation centers, and other settings, the human services worker needs to understand something about the treatments derived from this model.

By far the most common treatment approach is drug therapy, sometimes called chemotherapy. Recent decades have seen the development of a wide variety of powerful drugs that are capable of modifying mood and emotional states. The **major tranquilizers**, for example, are a class of drugs first introduced to the United States in the 1950s. They quickly became a major treatment modality in psychiatric clinics and hospitals when it was found that they suppress or ameliorate some of the disturbed behavior of psychotic patients. They are likely to be used when a patient shows extreme tension, aggressiveness, delusions, hallucinations, or insomnia. Although they do not produce a cure, they usually make the patient more manageable by staff. Thorazine, Mellaril, and Stelazine are the trade names of three of the most frequently used tranquilizers.

Another popular treatment approach involves the use of **minor tranquilizers** to reduce tension and anxiety. In the 1960s, Roche Laboratories introduced two drugs that were members of the chemical family called **benzodiazepines**: Librium and Valium. These drugs soon captured a large share of the market for psychotropic medications, prompting other drug companies to produce and market similar drugs (Lickey & Gordon, 1991). In 1975, about 85 million prescriptions for benzodiazepines were written in the United States. This trend was followed by a wave of concern in the medical community about the possible overprescription of these medications. As professionals became worried about the risks of abuse, including addiction and dependence, the rate of prescription began to decline. It was found that withdrawal from the drugs may bring serious complications, including an anxiety state more severe than the original anxiety disorder (Miller & Mahler, 1991). However, during the 1980s and 1990s, there was a gradual return to high consumption of these drugs. Most of the prescribing is done by general practitioners rather than by psychiatrists. The drugs provide a handy means of pacifying patients who complain of tension, anxiety, mild depression, and insomnia.

Another relatively recent drug therapy is the use of **lithium carbonate** for people suffering from manic-depressive disorders. It is particularly useful in controlling the excessive elation, irritability, and talkativeness of the manic phase. Still another group of mood-altering drugs are the **antidepressants**, which have been effective in combating certain types of severe depressive states.

Table 4.1 lists the generic and brand names of some frequently prescribed psychotherapeutic medications. New drugs are constantly being marketed, and it is likely that the table will need updating by the time you see it. All human services workers in medical settings are advised to prepare their own table of medications commonly used in their service. An essential reference book is the *Physicians' Desk Reference* (1996), a comprehensive text on all kinds of drugs that is updated annually. It is suggested that students learn how to use it.

Table 4.1 | Major Types of Psychotherapeutic Medications

Type of Drug	Generic Names	Brand Names	Major Uses	Possible Side Effects
Major tranquilizers	Chlorpromazine Phenothiazines Haloperidol	Thorazine Stelazine Mellaril Prolixin Compazine Haldol	Sometimes called antipsychotics, these medications help control severe anxiety, agitation, delusions, hallucinations, hostility, and hyperactivity associated with schizophrenia and other psychotic states.	Confusion, restlessness, insomnia, euphoria, exacerbation of psychotic symptoms, muscle weakness, and fatigue. Prolonged use may result in tardive dyskinesia, a neurological disorder featuring involuntary muscular movements.
Minor tranquilizers	Benzodiazepines Meprobamates	Valium Librium Serax Restoril Xanax Miltown Equanil	These antianxiety medications are widely prescribed by primary care physicians when anxiety, irritability, and agitation—symptoms often related to situational stress—become severe enough to interfere with daily functioning.	Drowsiness, dizziness, headache. Since these drugs depress the central nervous system, reflexes are slowed. Caution must be taken when driving and operating machinery. Dangerous when used in combination with alcohol and other CNS depressants. Some patients may become addicted to these drugs.
Antidepressants	Tricyclics	Elavil Sinequan Tofranil Aventyl	These medications generally lift mood and are used to combat severe depressions. They have been found to be particularly	Anxiety, restlessness, exacerbation of psychosis, dry mouth, blurred vision, skin rash, fatigue, sensitivity to sun.

(continued)

TABLE 4.1 | CONTINUED

Type of Drug	Generic Names	Brand Names	Major Uses	Possible Side Effects
	MAO inhibitors Combination agents	Nardil Parnate Limbitrol Triavil	effective in endogenous depression—having no apparent situational cause. The MAO inhibitors are often used for patients who do not respond favorably to treatment with tricyclics.	
Second-generation antidepressants	Fluoxetine Sertraline Paroxetine	Prozac Zoloft Paxil	Although the major use is still to elevate mood, these medications are increasingly being used to treat eating disorders, including obesity, and obsessive-compulsive disorders.	May cause nausea and headaches but are reported to have fewer undesired effects than the earlier antidepressants.
Antimanic	Lithium carbonate	Eskalith Lithane Lithonate	Primarily used to treat manic episodes and bipolar affective disorders. It is also being used in some cases of schizophrenia.	Levels of lithium in the blood must be monitored and carefully regulated, as it can act as a toxic agent impairing various bodily processes. Overdosage may produce serious complications and may be lethal.
Sedative-hypnotic	Barbiturates	Triazolam Halcion	Used to produce a calming effect and to induce sleep. Can	Extreme dullness and drowsiness. May be deadly when taken with

	Phenobarbital Seconal Amytal Nembutal Pentothal	be used to treat convulsive disorders.	alcohol or other CNS depressants. May be habit forming.
Anticonvulsant	Phenytoin sodium Primodone	Dilantin Mysoline	Used to help control epileptic seizure disorders.	Insomnia, nervousness, motor twitchings, headache, nausea, vomiting, and many other symptoms.
Stimulant	Amphetamines	Benzedrine Dexedrine Methedrine Ritalin	Used in treating overweight and narcolepsy (uncontrolled fits of sleep) to allow under-functioning areas of the brain to increase their function, thereby helping to control hyperactivity and inattention.	Insomnia, restlessness, talkativeness, loss of appetite, paranoid ideation, and possible aggression and anxiety.
Antialcoholic	Disulfiram	Antabuse	Used as an aversive therapy in treatment of alcoholism. When alcohol is taken while a person is using Antabuse, a potent negative reaction occurs, including nausea, vomiting, racing heart, and flushing.	Use is contraindicated in people with certain physical disorders; may be carcinogenic with prolonged use, and may cause nervous system toxicity.

OTHER MEDICAL TREATMENTS

Drugs are only one type of medical model treatment. A number of convulsive therapies have been developed for use with psychiatric patients. The most common of these in current use is the famous (or infamous) **electroconvulsive therapy** (ECT). Used extensively in private psychiatric hospitals, it involves administering an electric shock at the patient's temples for a brief (0.1- to 0.5-second) duration. Treatments are given several times a week and may continue for 5 or 6 weeks. ECT is used mainly to treat patients who are depressed, especially when there is no obvious external stress such as divorce, death, or loss of job. Probably no other form of therapy evokes such negative feelings as this one. Despite modern trappings, it appears to many to be some kind of medieval torture. During the 1950s, there were many reports of abuse and sloppy administration of the procedure. It was used with a wide variety of disorders, and results were often unfavorable. Recent refinements of the technique have reduced side effects and increased its effectiveness.

Another medical-type treatment, called **psychosurgery**, has also been sharply criticized by human services workers. The most frequently used procedure of this type is **lobotomy**, which involves cutting nerve fibers connecting the frontal lobes to other parts of the brain. Literally thousands of these operations were performed on mental patients during the years before the introduction of major tranquilizers. It was used mainly with patients who were so aggressive that they presented severe management problems. Unfortunately, the procedure often produces serious irreversible side effects such as lethargy, childish behavior, and mental dullness.

Valenstein (1986) has provided a fascinating history of psychosurgery. He tells the story of how it came about that "tens of thousands of mutilating brain operations were performed on mentally ill men and women in countries around the world" (p. 3). By the 1960s, it was apparent that these lobotomies were causing severe damage to the victims. These operations, now thought bizarre and obsolete, were part of the mainstream medicine of their time. Their popularity was due in part to many psychiatrists' readiness to believe in simple, biological approaches to the treatment of the mentally ill. Valenstein also shows that the physicians who developed and promoted the lobotomy were driven by intense ambition to deceive themselves and others about the value of their "cure." These events clearly show the need for clinical testing of new, potentially harmful procedures before they are allowed to be used on a large scale.

Other therapies related to medical approaches, such as rehabilitation and occupational therapy, are described in Chapter 6.

CRITICISMS OF THE MEDICAL MODEL

A number of authors have cried out against the injustices that arise from the medical/psychiatric approach to mental illness. Szasz (1973), for example, charged that his psychiatric colleagues were guilty of persecuting mental patients under the guise of treating them. In particular, he questioned the validity of labeling certain individuals as mentally ill when, in fact, they were merely suffering from problems in living. Mental illness, he stated further, is a myth, not a genuine disease at all. The underlying purpose of labeling (diagnosing) certain people as mentally ill, he suggested, is to provide society with a convenient means of getting rid of undesirable deviates. These are typically people who have committed no real crime but are bothersome, annoying, or frightening to other people.

Along the same lines, Kovel (1980) charged that psychiatry's focus on the psychological aspects of the patient "is a handy way of mystifying social reality" (p. 73). The same author argued that psychiatrists exert social control over social misfits by telling them they have a case of this or that and then imposing a treatment plan. What is left out of the process, said Kovel, is acknowledgment of the damaging role of poverty, poor housing, lack of opportunity, unemployment, and other social ills.

Some of the most vocal critics of the medical model are those who claim that psychotropic medications are effective only because of their ability to interfere with normal brain functioning. Symptom control is the primary goal of the treatment—not treating the disorder itself or enabling the mentally ill to more effectively address the environmental factors that may be responsible for their disorders. And symptom control is achieved in the medical model by rendering portions of the brain inactive or, as the most extreme of these critics say, by "killing" brain cells (Whitaker, 2002).

HUMAN SERVICES MODEL

The human services model received its major impetus during the 1960s. It was closely associated with social movements devoted to bettering the lives of oppressed minority groups. Human services workers thought of themselves as warriors and sometimes even as revolutionaries. Impatient with the medical model and its emphasis on the inner person, these workers wanted to bring about great social changes by improving the environment. In particular, they focused on the harsh external conditions that oppressed the lives of the poor. These workers were not interested in formulating complex theories. Their attitude was pragmatic, that is, based on a spirit of practical problem solving. The idea was, if a therapy worked, use it.

The basic assumption of the human services model is that maladaptive behaviors are often the result of a failure to satisfy basic human needs. The first step in intervention is not diagnosis but an assessment of the victim's life situation to discover what needs are not being met. Some people may be in need of decent housing, medical attention, a job, or a more adequate diet. Others may be lacking these essentials and may also be extremely lonely and in need of social interaction. It is not surprising that emotional problems are intensified by factors such as unemployment, loneliness, and low social status. Society, not the individual, is seen as the culprit. Therefore, society must be prodded to provide the needed goods and services.

HANSELL'S THEORY

One of the most elaborate theories used by human services workers is Hansell's motivation theory (Hansell, Wodarczyk, & Handlon-Lathrop, 1970). Hansell and his colleagues theorized that people have to achieve seven basic attachments to meet their needs. If they do not achieve each attachment, they go into crisis, or a state of stress. Here is a list of the seven basic attachments, along with signs of failure of each one:

1. Food, water, and oxygen, along with informational supplies. Signs of failure: boredom, apathy, and physical disorder.

2. Intimacy, sex, closeness, and opportunity to exchange deep feelings. Signs of failure: loneliness, isolation, and lack of sexual satisfaction.
3. Belonging to a peer group such as social, church, or school group. Signs of failure: not feeling part of anything.
4. A clear, definite self-identity. Signs of failure: feeling doubtful and indecisive.
5. A social role that carries with it a sense of being a competent member of society. Signs of failure: depression and a sense of failure.
6. The need to be linked to a cash economy via a job, a spouse with income, social security benefits, or other ways. Signs of failure: lack of purchasing power, possibly an inability to purchase essentials.
7. A comprehensive system of meaning with clear priorities in life. Signs of failure: sense of drifting through life, detachment, and alienation.

HUMAN SERVICES INTERVENTIONS

Hansell's scheme readily lends itself to the task of helping the client in practical ways. The worker needs to find ways to satisfy some of the client's unmet needs. The client's complaints are related to the signs of failure just described.

Sometimes the nature of the unmet need is blatantly obvious; at other times it may be quite subtle. The client is not always able to cooperate with the helper. For example, the client may deny having a certain need or may feel demeaned by accepting the kind of help available. The aim of human services counseling is usually to link the client with sources of satisfaction. This might involve helping the client secure welfare benefits, find a job, join a club or social group, return to school, or locate a temporary shelter. The focus is on solving problems here and now. Past problems and bad experiences may be discussed, but they are not the main focus of counseling.

The human services worker is usually a generalist trained to work in a variety of agencies to provide across-the-board services to clients and their families (Southern Regional Education Board, 1978). By definition, a generalist is familiar with a variety of therapeutic approaches rather than specializing in one or two areas. The main goal of intervention is usually to identify the needs and problems of the client and then provide resources to meet the needs and solve the problem. Of course, the worker is not usually able to meet needs in a direct, personal sort of way but is familiar with service providers in the community and can recommend them. These service providers would include doctors, ministers, lawyers, police officers, parole officers, mental health professionals, and just about anyone else who may be able to help the client. If needed services are not available, the worker may be able to influence the community to set up new programs, a subject that is discussed in Chapter 8.

A wide variety of roles may be played by the human services worker, each calling for special skills. The worker may be an advocate, a mobilizer, a teacher, or an administrator. The skills required by these activities are discussed in further detail in Chapter 5. The immediate point is that the underlying purpose is usually the same: identifying and meeting the needs of clients.

Human services workers have sometimes criticized mental health professionals (psychiatrists, clinical psychologists, and social workers) for overlooking obvious practical solutions to human problems. One reason for this oversight is that these professionals are often trained in intricate psychological theories and treatment methods. They tend to see problems as reflecting deep emotional conflicts rather

■ | REAL LIFE HUMAN SERVICES WORK

"What you are is God's gift to you, what you make of yourself is your gift to God!" I was raised on this anonymous quote. It's this quote that would take me from the land of architecture to the land of teen violence prevention. My name is Kimberly Dilosa and I am the founder/development director of YOUTHanasia Foundation Inc., the foundation that "kills what's killing Greater New Orleans teenagers". The foundation cures teen violence by 1) consuming the deadly idle time of teenagers, 2) inspiring youth-led intervention and prevention programs and events for youth ages 13–18, and 3) educating community stakeholders on the correlation between mental illness and teen violence. I am a teen mentor and community organizer! I founded YOUTHanasia Foundation in 1997, and in 2006 became a national award winner of The Robert Wood Johnson Foundation. RWJF awarded me $120,000 which I used to open the Teen Center for Non-Violence in the summer of 2007. The Teen Center for Non-Violence is a safe haven for teen hurricane survivors struggling with the mental effects of Hurricane Katrina. Do you know 4 years after the storm, there are kids who still cannot verbally communicate and/or are afraid to think of what they went through during Hurricane Katrina?

Although I am the winner of numerous awards I am simply a teen mentor and community organizer! I spend my days working to cure teen violence as a sickness versus fixing it as a problem. Thus, I tackle teen violence from the social and emotional side—a side traditional law enforcement and politicians fail to understand. My days are filled with grant writing, emails, meetings, volunteer drives, etc. My Saturdays are filled with loving "my babies," the teen members of The Teen Center for Non-Violence.

My work is the most important in a community still struggling to recover from the worst natural disaster in U.S. History. I nurture the future—if there are no inhabitants to carry Greater New Orleans forward, why rebuild? The Greater New Orleans community is currently losing 1–3 teenagers a day to homicide, suicide or arrest. Traditional law enforcement officials and politicians are running around in circles and the problem is getting worse. On August 29, 2009, the 4th Anniversary of Hurricane Katrina, I unveiled "The Campaign to Rebuild a Teen-Friendly Greater New Orleans." I created this campaign to permanently cure teen violence in Greater New Orleans through interactive community mapping, the creation of teen-friendly events and programs, and the redirection of funds from teen-friendly corporations to be used in the rebuilding of Greater New Orleans.

My work literally speaks for me! The very first group of teens I have ever mentored is now the Board of Directors of YOUTHanasia Foundation. Another mentee, Frank Delaney, is now the Executive Director of the agency. So many success stories have come out of my unconventional box, and the kids never leave me. They come back to volunteer, serve as guest speakers, etc. I started mentoring teenagers when I was 22 years old. I am now 34 years old. I'm married to John Dilosa Jr., and have 2 kids—KaJa, 5 and Jahari, 2. I earned a degree in architecture from Tuskegee University in 1997.... [L]ittle did I know I would be designing human lives!!

Kimberly Dilosa

than poverty and other external factors. Psychoanalytic theories in particular confer status and prestige on therapists. One author has suggested that the mundane problems of poverty hold little fascination for the middle-class professional, who would prefer to psychologize about the poor and prescribe the latest fashion in psychotherapy (Pelton, 1978).

ISSUES UNDERLYING CONFLICT BETWEEN MODELS

The conflict between adherents of the medical and human services models goes far beyond disputes over theory. A host of issues related to power, money, and licensing have not been fully resolved. For example, human services workers maintain that the criteria for delivering service should center on competence to do the job. They point out that **indigenous workers** who live in the community served are often more effective in helping residents than highly educated professionals. They also point out that generalist human services workers are often able to perform counseling and therapy just as effectively as traditional professionals.

Without denying the usefulness of indigenous workers and paraprofessionals, traditional mental health professionals are likely to emphasize the importance of advanced academic training, degrees, and licenses in determining job duties, salaries, and responsibilities. They see themselves as supervisors of workers with less academic training. Each side accuses the other of basing claims on narrow self-interest rather than considering the needs of the clients.

Although this topic is discussed further in subsequent chapters, it can be stated here that human services workers are steadily growing in numbers and assuming more and more responsibility for delivery of services. With this growth has come an increased desire for professional training and status. What is emerging is a new breed of professionals, trained not in medical model disciplines but in human services.

HOLISTIC TREND IN MEDICAL THEORY

As we have seen, the traditional medical model views disease as a departure from a biological norm and, accordingly, stresses biological, or physical, approaches to treatment. Increasingly, this model is being criticized for its limited scope and for overlooking the social settings in which disease occurs. The holistic approach, which considers all aspects of a person's life, is gaining favor among both physicians and human services workers as an alternative model. It is based on the idea that environmental, social, and psychological factors may all contribute to illness or to health. It follows that health promotion need not be limited to biological or physical interventions. Practitioners of holistic healing attempt to find a balance between a person's mind, body, and spirit in a given environment. In specific cases, the holistic ideal may translate into any of the following kinds of treatment: changes in diet, meditation, relaxation, **biofeedback**, and stress reduction (Popple & Leighninger, 1990). Because it emphasizes lifestyle factors, the holistic approach lends itself to prevention of illness. Holistic programs, aimed at promoting healthier lifestyles, have been established in industrial, hospital, and school settings.

PSYCHONEUROIMMUNOLOGY A new field of study that has already provided evidence supporting the basic ideas of the holistic model is psychoneuroimmunology (PNI). PNI attempts to find connections among psychological states, the nervous system, and the immune system. To use somewhat outdated terminology, it is the study of interactions between the mind and the body. As Lerner (1994) explains, "emotional states and behavior patterns may profoundly affect not only our symptoms but the progress of our disease itself" (p. 137).

Experimental studies have shown that acute stressors (for example, electric shock, bright lights, extreme temperatures, or overcrowding) often cause suppression of the immune system in animals. The immune system is our first line of defense against disease; it consists of complex mechanisms that detect and destroy foreign invaders such as bacteria and viruses. It also defends against cancer cells that originate within the body. Early findings reviewed by Lerner indicated that humans under stress also undergo a weakening of the immune system, putting them at increased risk of infectious disease and tumor growth. These findings help explain the repeatedly found connection between disease and stressful life events, as discussed in Chapter 1. Lerner (1994) expresses astonishment at the lack of attention paid to emotional factors by some conventional doctors in the treatment of cancer and other serious disorders.

ALTERNATIVE MEDICINE Payer (1988), a leading medical journalist, compared medical practices in the United States with those of several modern European nations. She found that American medicine is more aggressive than that of England, France, and Germany. American doctors perform more invasive diagnostic examinations and more surgery than others. Up to one-third of American patients have been seeking alternative methods. Some seek **alternative medicine** when they have not been helped by traditional medicine, but an increasing number are simply bypassing the regular doctor. Still other patients seek alternative treatments for certain conditions and regular treatment for other conditions (Ricks, 1995).

There is a large menu of unconventional methods from which to choose. For example, asthma, chronic pain, drug addiction, and other disorders may be treated by means of **acupuncture**, a traditional Chinese method in which needles are inserted into the skin at certain critical points. Chinese doctors believe that a system of meridians, or energy pipelines, runs through the body. The points at which the needles are placed are like valves where the energy levels can be adjusted. Although some may question whether these meridians really exist, there is little doubt that acupuncture has proved its value in controlling pain and nausea. Other uses are now being seriously researched (Lerner, 1994). Also growing in popularity is Chinese herbal medicine, which has a very long history of use in the Far East.

A number of doctors are now providing nutritionally oriented alternatives to more conventional drug-oriented approaches. Medical schools have long been criticized for failing to educate doctors in nutrition, but they are beginning to make up for this deficiency. It is well known that poor nutrition, particularly the high-fat/high-sugar diet of Americans, contributes to heart disease, high blood pressure, diabetes, and other ills. Thus, it makes sense to seek improved health through better nutrition.

Visualization, or imagery, therapy has received a good deal of attention in the popular media. In this form of therapy, patients are first taught to relax and then to develop their own images for fighting the disease. Apparently, this technique makes use of the power of suggestion. There is much evidence from religious healing, experimental studies, and other sources that our expectations can sometimes be used to alleviate anxiety and promote healing (Frank & Frank, 1991). The so-called placebo effect refers to the strong influence that inactive "medications," such as sugar pills, may have on a patient's condition. Again, it is the patient's expectations that may influence the effect of a given pill.

So many other alternative approaches are available—such as homeopathic medicine, Hindu methods of healing, and aromatherapy—that it is not possible to detail them all here. Critics have conceded that some of the alternative methods have been proven to be effective, but they maintain that others may have dubious value in regard to a particular disorder. It is up to the consumer to carefully evaluate the evidence pertaining to a particular therapy before getting involved with it.

The holistic trend in medicine may provide the means of reconciling the medical model with the human services model. This is because the holistic approach recognizes the importance of environmental factors in human disorders. On a practical level, the acceptance of alternative methods of healing will mean a greater role for nonmedical therapists in the treatment of physical illnesses.

SCHOOLS OF THERAPY

The perspectives most commonly used in group and individual approaches to psychological problems are the psychoanalytic, the humanistic, and the behavioristic schools, or systems, of therapy. A "school" in this context is a group of workers who study certain disorders and use similar methods of study. Although the members of a school may disagree about various points, they share certain basic ideas about the causes of psychological disorders. These basic beliefs, in turn, dictate their approach to helping.

PSYCHOANALYTIC VIEWPOINT

The development of **psychoanalysis** is very much associated with Sigmund Freud and his followers. Actually, many of Freud's insights, such as the idea of the unconscious mind, had already been discovered by others (Murray, 1988). There is no doubt, however, that Freud was responsible for shaping psychoanalysis into a coherent system of thought. Under Freud's direction, psychoanalysis became one of the influential movements of modern times.

Psychoanalysis is based upon the observation that individuals are often unaware of what underlies their emotions and behavior. These "unconscious" factors may contribute to their unhappiness and frustration, and may lead to the development of symptoms, such as anxiety or depression, or difficulties in their interpersonal relationships.

MAJOR FREUDIAN CONCEPTS

The major idea that evolved from psychoanalysis was that neurotic symptoms are the result of conflicts within the patient. Neurotic symptoms include **phobias**, which involve an intense fear of a specific stimulus such as enclosed places; obsessions, which involve the repeated intrusions of certain unwanted thoughts into consciousness; and **compulsions**, which require the patient to repeatedly perform some ritualistic act such as hand washing. These and similar complaints are the result of a conflict between a person's sexual and aggressive urges on one hand and society's demands for control of these impulses on the other (Maddi, 1972). The neurotic symptoms represent attempts to resolve the conflict.

Sigmund Freud

In Freudian terms, the personality is made up of three subsystems: the **id**, the **ego**, and the **superego**. The id is the seat of primitive instincts such as sexual and aggressive drives. This part of the personality wants what it wants now. It is the first system to appear in the development of the child. The ego is gradually developed to help the child attain gratification in a realistic and socially acceptable manner. The ego employs reason and logic and is concerned with helping the person survive in the world. The superego, similar to the conscience, is an outgrowth of the taboos and moral values of the society as interpreted by the parents. It aims to inhibit desires that are regarded as wicked or immoral. These three forces are in constant interaction, one factor that makes the theory very complex.

When the ego, the "executive" of personality, is confronted with id impulses that are threatening to get out of control, anxiety and guilt feelings are aroused. In some instances, the anxiety is reduced by coping with the impulses in a satisfactory way. A young person may, for example, decide to gratify sexual urges in the context of marriage. When a realistic resolution of conflict is not available, the ego employs a **defense mechanism** to reduce tension. For example, the entire conflict may be repressed, that is, blocked from awareness. Or the desire may be expressed in some disguised or symbolic way. For example, aggressive urges may be discharged in sports and games, or erotic feelings may be expressed in artistic pursuits.

THERAPEUTIC CONCEPTS

Early in his career, Freud began to work with Josef Breuer, a Viennese physician who pioneered in treating neurotics. Breuer treated a number of patients whose symptoms were "hysterical" in nature, that is, due to emotional rather than physical factors. Some of these patients suffered memory losses or paralysis of certain organs but had no physical defect that could account for the symptoms. Breuer treated them with hypnosis, the method used by earlier therapists. Under hypnosis, patients were often able to recall painful experiences, called traumas, associated with the onset of the symptoms. Breuer found that if the patient could relive the painful emotions associated with the trauma, the symptoms often disappeared. This was the beginning of the "talking cure," a method based on uncovering feelings and experiences buried in the unconscious.

FREE ASSOCIATION Freud carried on the talking cure with new patients. He gradually developed the technique of **free association**, in which the patient lies on a couch and is encouraged to say anything that comes to mind, no matter how embarrassing it may seem. The basic aim was to bring into conscious awareness any memories or thoughts that had been repressed, that is, pushed into the unconscious because of their threatening nature. While free associating, clients sometimes "blocked," or became unable to bring emotionally charged thoughts into conscious awareness. Freud regarded this as a sign of resistance, which can be defined as any tactic or behavior that works against the production of unconscious material. All clients resist therapy at one time or another. Freud recognized that resistances must be approached with caution because they protect the patient from unbearable anxiety. Overcoming resistances became a regular part of analytic therapy.

Transference Freud found that during therapy his clients sometimes experienced feelings, attitudes, and defenses toward him that were derived from previous significant relationships. These feelings and attitudes seemed to have been transferred from the past to the present. The client reacted to Freud as though he were the client's mother, father, or some other important figure. Occasionally, patients seemed to fall in love with him and wanted very much to please him. Or sometimes the client would be very hurt if strong feelings were not reciprocated.

According to Freud's theory, **transference** reactions imply that the client is generalizing from past experience. If the mother was warm and overprotective, the client assumes that the analyst will also behave in this way. Over the years, analysis of transference became a central feature of psychoanalysis because it provided a vehicle for resolving old conflicts. Analysis of transference made it possible for analysts to work toward a radical change in the client's personality.

The goals of psychoanalytic therapy have changed greatly over the years. The aim of the early work was simply to relieve neurotic symptoms, whereas later analysts aimed to bring about significant personality change. In this sense, psychoanalysis is the most ambitious system of therapy and one reason that therapy may take many years.

Psychoanalytically Oriented Psychotherapy

The form of treatment developed by Freud came to be known as classical or orthodox psychoanalysis. It required three, four, or even five sessions a week and could go on for many years. Free association, dream analysis, and analysis of transference were the major technical methods. As the analytic movement grew and its practitioners emigrated to America and to other parts of Europe, the treatment was adapted to different cultures. Psychoanalysis became very popular in the United States during the 1930s and 1940s, but it was streamlined to suit American needs and tastes. The number of sessions was reduced to one or two a week, an armchair was usually substituted for the couch, and there was relatively greater emphasis on solving present-day problems as opposed to delving into the past. Many psychiatric clinics and mental hospitals employed this modified analytic approach in treatment and training.

Modern psychoanalytic theory and practice has come a long way since Freud. New psychoanalytic perspectives include interpersonal, relational, and self-psychology. Psychoanalysis has evolved into a more active experience, where the relationship between therapist and client is emphasized and, although understanding the past is still important, the present is a focus as well. The next generation of psychoanalytic thinkers included Karen Horney, Erich Fromm, Erik Erikson, and Harry Stack Sullivan. Though they remained in the psychoanalytic tradition, each departed considerably from the Freudian model.

The theories of these neo-Freudians are too complex to be presented in detail. However, some of their major ideas can be briefly reviewed. The neo-Freudians highlighted social factors in the development of personality. Horney (1950), for example, believed that the child's dominant motive is not gratification of instincts but a striving for security and acceptance by others. When important people in the family are perceived as hostile and ungiving, the child experiences painful feelings of anxiety.

Horney discerned three major trends or tactics that children use to reduce this anxiety and increase security. In one pattern children find moving toward others makes them feel safe. These children may become submissive and self-effacing in their dealings with others. The second pattern shown by some youngsters is a moving away from others. These children seem to act on the premise that if they don't get too close to others, they won't get hurt. The third pattern is moving against others, which may take the form of rebellious and antisocial behavior. The other neo-Freudians developed somewhat different ideas but agreed with Horney's emphasis on social interaction.

The new revisionists all doubted Freud's assumption that adult personality was shaped by early childhood experiences. For example, Sullivan (1953), who founded the interpersonal theory of psychiatry, believed that experiences during the juvenile and adolescent phases could have a profound impact on personality. He felt that it was crucial for a youngster to have close friends and confidants during these difficult periods of life.

Along with the other neo-Freudians, Erikson (1963) stressed the social aspects of human development. He taught that in each stage of life, the person tries to establish an equilibrium between the self and the social world. At each phase of development, the person is faced with a task or a crisis to be resolved. For example, the infant's basic task is to develop a sense of trust in self, others, and the world. Obviously, the infant is totally dependent on others for survival. In an atmosphere of insecurity, the child may develop a sense of mistrust that can retard progress and color later relationships with others. At each later phase, the person is faced with another crisis. Obviously, it would be helpful for the human services worker to have an understanding of the developmental tasks faced by clients at various stages. It is sometimes important to examine the choices a client made at previous stages of life and to consider how these affect current functioning.

CRITICISMS OF PSYCHOANALYSIS

No other psychological theory has been subjected to such intense criticism as has psychoanalysis. Some of the early attacks were harsh and highly emotional in tone and may have been triggered by Freud's exposure of sexual problems in Victorian Europe. The day is past when professionals are shocked by frank discussions of sexual matters. However, certain other criticisms are based not on outraged sensibilities but on serious doubts about the scientific credibility of psychoanalysis.

Many critics have noted that analysts often base conclusions on what patients remember about their past experience. As Freud himself discovered, there is no way to be sure whether the anecdotal reports represent real events, fantasies, or some combination of fact and fancy. Rarely does any independent verification exist of the events reported by patients. Thus, there is some basis for the criticism that psychoanalysts have built a huge theoretical structure on a weak foundation.

Another serious criticism is that analytic theory lacks predictive value and relies on after-the-fact explanations (Hall & Lindzey, 1978). For example, it is not very helpful to be informed that a client attempted suicide due to a strong death wish because that "explanation" is circular. In other words, the strong death wish is inferred from the behavior itself. Other behaviors are explained in terms of complex interactions between id, ego, and superego. If a patient gives in to sexual impulse, this might be interpreted as a victory for the id over the superego. If the impulse is repressed, the superego has won. The problem is that psychoanalysis does not provide clear rules for predicting in advance whether one or another part of the personality is going to dominate future behavior.

Another type of criticism centers around the general failure of analysts to report on the effects of their therapy. Considering the popularity of analytic thinking during the 1920s to mid-1950s, there were very few reports of the outcomes of the treatment. Those reports that did surface usually did not include a control group, that is, a comparison group of patients who received no treatment or some other treatment. Prochaska (1984) reviewed some of the relevant studies and concluded that there is still insufficient evidence to judge the effectiveness of analytic therapy.

Perhaps the most scathing denouncements of Freudian theory have come from those with a human services orientation. Certain implications of Freudian theory can be seen as harmful to the interests of disadvantaged individuals. For example, Freud's idea that the child develops an irrational, unconscious mind early in life seems to imply that behavior is largely determined by unconscious forces. Maladaptive or antisocial behavior is seen as the outcome of internal forces beyond rational control, which downplays the role of here-and-now environmental events. These and other aspects of the analytic approach were simply unacceptable to the social activists of the 1960s. They wanted to help people now, and they wanted to do it primarily by changing the environment rather than by changing the person.

Some Useful Applications of Psychoanalytic Concepts

Psychoanalysis seems here to stay. Although no longer predominant, it is one of several therapeutic approaches actively competing for students, adherents, and clients. Certain analytic ideas have withstood the test of time and may be useful to human services workers.

The concept of defense mechanisms is probably the most widely used concept in **psychotherapy**. It is often useful to consider how a client reacts to anxiety and guilt feelings and perhaps to discuss some alternative ways of dealing with these painful emotions. It is also helpful to the client to review those unpleasant past experiences that may be interfering with present functioning. Without becoming bogged down in the past, it may be important for both worker and client to understand how the client got into his or her current predicament. This review of the past may reveal some self-defeating behaviors that the client needs to modify in the future.

Regardless of theoretical bias, counselors and therapists acknowledge that certain Freudian themes come up again and again in therapy. These themes include the client's desire to be preferred by the parent of the opposite sex, sibling rivalry, guilt feelings about sex, and fear of closeness or intimacy with another. The therapist can benefit from psychoanalytic insights about these issues without accepting them as doctrine.

HUMANISTIC PERSPECTIVE

The **humanistic perspective** emphasizes the unique qualities of humans, especially their capacity for choice and their potential for personal growth. A major assumption is that the individual is free to choose alternatives in life.

Humanists deny the psychoanalytic belief that human behavior is dominated by animalistic drives. There is always a capacity for free will and choice even if the person feels trapped by circumstances or compulsive drives. A related assumption is that the person strives toward the highest possible fulfillment of human potentialities. There is potential for growth, or some kind of forward movement, in every human being. In this sense, humanists share a generally optimistic view of human nature.

The humanist position is to some extent a reaction against the methods of modern science. Existentialists, in particular, argue that science tends to dehumanize people by regarding them as mechanical devices. In this view, science tends to pull people apart in a misguided attempt to see how they work. The person is divided into sensations, feelings, drives, perceptions, thoughts, physical systems, and so on. In this process of analysis, critics claim, the unique quality of the individual is lost.

Furthermore, humanists maintain that this unique person cannot be understood by a distant objective observer. Real understanding requires getting into the frame of reference of the other person, that is, understanding how the other experiences and perceives the world. Some sort of dialogue between two persons is necessary for the understanding to come about. It is also assumed that both individuals engaged in a dialogue are likely to influence and change each other. The human being is never seen as a finished product but as always changing. The following section goes into more detail about some of the concepts and treatment applications devised by humanistic theorists.

HUMANISTIC APPROACH TO HELPING

Humanists take a **holistic perspective** toward understanding their clients. This means that they want to understand the person as a whole, as opposed to breaking the personality into its components. The focus is on an individual's private view of the world rather than on objective reality. What a person believes to be true, whether it is really so or not, influences behavior. If you are convinced that a person dislikes you, for example, this belief governs how you relate to that person even though the other person may not really dislike you.

The humanistic therapist helps the client clarify feelings, think more deeply about problems, and explore all important aspects of the current life situation. The helper provides an atmosphere in which this kind of exploration can safely

Carl Rogers

take place. Unlike other significant people in the client's life, the therapist has no desire to push the client in one direction or another. In other words, the helper does not want to mold or shape the client into some preconceived image. Clients are therefore free to search for their own special meanings and directions in life.

Implied in what has been said is that humanists are not sympathetic toward the therapist who plays the role of doctor-expert. Humanistic counseling is less directive than other approaches, but more focused upon a "strengths" orientation with the client. Counseling is a dialogue between two individuals, each with his or her unique experiences and perceptions. The helper does not have instant remedies or solutions to life's problems but helps clients struggle toward their own answers.

SELF-ACTUALIZATION The humanistic approach to helping is based on the concept that self-actualization is a primary motivating force in human behavior. Rogers (1959) defined this motivational force as "the inherent tendency of the organism to develop all its capacities in ways which serve to maintain or enhance the organism" (p. 196). Crystals, plants, and animals grow without any conscious fuss; the same kind of natural ordering process is available to guide the development of the person (Whyte, 1960). Very often, however, the forces of self-actualization bump up against conditions that others impose (Meador & Rogers, 1984). In other words, the child may be loved and approved only when behaving in certain specified ways—for example, when good, cheerful, productive, successful, or competitive. These conditions begin to warp the natural process of self-actualization. Often, the child totally accepts these conditions because she or he has no basis on which to question them. In therapy, the person has the opportunity to resume growth in the atmosphere of acceptance provided by the therapist.

Maslow's (1954) concept of self-actualization is contained in the following sentence: "What a man can be, he must be" (p. 46). This means that individuals must do what they are best equipped to do. One can maximize one's potential as a secretary, administrator, artist, politician, or mechanic. Skills, interests, background, and inherited tendencies all need to be considered in determining areas of maximal fulfillment. Serious difficulties may arise if the drive for self-actualization is thwarted. For example, if a person who wants to help disadvantaged people must work as an accountant, or if someone with artistic ability is employed as a salesclerk, the need to fulfill potentials is not being satisfied. The individual may feel out of place and may be haunted by a sense of self-betrayal.

RESPONSIBILITY Many people who seek counseling have been thwarted in their push for self-actualization by a tendency to live for others. All too often, they have been influenced by parents, teachers, or peers to pursue goals that are uncongenial to their true natures. Often, the growing child seeks approval from elders by living up to their demands and expectations. Some adults who seek help remain stuck in patterns of childish dependence. They have not fully accepted responsibility for finding their own paths in life. Perls (1969) suggested that a prime goal of therapy is "to make the patient not depend upon others, but to make the patient discover from the very first that he can do many things, much more than he thinks he can do" (p. 29). He added that frustration is essential for growth because it helps individuals muster their own resources to discover that they can do well on their own. The therapist has to be alert to the manipulations of clients who may try to get the therapist to tell them what to do. The general thrust of humanistic therapy is to get the client to assume responsibility for thoughts, feelings, and direction in life. Only then is the person really free to pursue self-actualization.

THE SELF-CONCEPT   The **self-concept** is the core, or center, of the personality around which experiences are organized and interpreted. The "I," or the "self," includes how we see ourselves, how we think others perceive us, and how we would like to be. The self-concept begins to develop early in life. Children begin to evaluate certain experiences as good or bad and, quite naturally, take on the values of parents, teachers, and peers. However, values imposed from the outside may require them to ignore inner feelings. For example, if they learn that anger or sexual urges are bad or not valued, they may block these urges from awareness.

Rogers (1951) suggested that maladjustment occurs when a person denies awareness to significant experiences that do not fit the self-concept. When one's behavior and experiences do not mesh with the way one sees oneself, there is a lack of "congruence," which may lead to tension and anxiety. One goal of therapy, then, is to help the client face and accept these denied experiences. The client may, for example, come to accept hostile feelings as okay in some situations. The hope is that this acceptance will reduce the tension and conflict.

CRITICISMS OF THE HUMANISTIC APPROACH

Some critics believe that humanists exaggerate the benefits of the therapist's accepting attitude. It may take more than an attitude of positive regard to transform the client into a self-actualizing person. When Rogers (1967) attempted to treat schizophrenics with this approach, the results were not especially impressive. It may be unrealistic to expect one caring relationship to overcome years of negative life experiences.

Nor is it always helpful to emphasize that people have choices. Many poor, discouraged people do not see themselves as having numerous choices, and they really do not have the range of options available to affluent persons. They may need some practical kinds of help and some new opportunities before they can experience their potential for growth.

The humanistic approach does not seem to apply to patients who are not intellectually capable of making their own decisions. Young children and many retarded people and mental patients are not really able to make decisions about direction in life. The major decisions must be made by those responsible for their care. Although every client can be treated in a respectful way, it often doesn't make sense to treat the client as an equal. The behaviorist approach (to be discussed) seems to lend itself more effectively to treatment of people with limited potential.

POSITIVE ASPECTS OF THE HUMANISTIC APPROACH

The most useful aspect of the humanistic perspective is that it provides the human services worker with a sophisticated understanding of the helping relationship. Humanistic therapists have gone far beyond armchair speculation on this issue. Credit must be given to Rogers, his associates, and other humanists for providing solid research evidence about qualities in a relationship that facilitate positive change. Because this evidence is discussed in Chapter 5, it need not be reviewed here. Suffice it to say that humanists have contributed significantly to improving the tools and skills of the counselor.

BEHAVIORISTIC MODEL

Unlike psychoanalysis, **behavior therapy**, or behaviorism, did not begin as a method of treating psychological problems but has its roots in experimental studies of animal and human behavior. Dating back to the 1800s, it began as a reaction against psychological studies in which human subjects were asked to report on their sensations and perceptions. The early behaviorists felt that psychology wasn't getting anywhere by gathering vague reports of conscious experience. They argued that there was no way to verify a person's private experiences. They proposed, instead, that psychology be put on a firm scientific footing by studying overt behavior under such conditions that two or more observers could agree that a particular action or response had taken place.

   The early behaviorists believed that important laws governing behavior could be revealed by studying the behavior of animals—cats, dogs, rats, pigeons—in carefully controlled experimental situations. The emphasis was on conditioning, which involved situations that brought about a change in the behavior of the organism. Two general kinds of conditioning were identified and were designated as classical and operant conditioning. It is important for the counselor-therapist to understand both types because therapeutic approaches have been derived from each.

CLASSICAL CONDITIONING

Classical conditioning involves the study of reflexes, that is, responses elicited by certain stimuli in an automatic fashion. Such responses do not have to be learned or acquired by the individual. For example, an animal or person will respond with an eye blink if a puff of air is applied to the eye. Another automatic response in some creatures is to salivate when eating or chewing. Pavlov's (1927) studies of this salivary reflex in dogs are among the best-known experiments in the field of psychology. The basic experimental approach was as follows: Before conditioning, surgery was performed on the dog's cheek so that the saliva could be collected and measured precisely. During training, a bell, buzzer, or some other neutral stimulus was sounded just before food was given to the dog. As it ate, saliva would naturally begin to flow. The neutral stimulus and the food were presented over and over on subsequent feedings. Eventually, the dog salivated to the neutral stimulus even when no food was presented. Pavlov had succeeded in conditioning the response to a stimulus that would not elicit it before training. He observed that this conditioned response would eventually fade away—become extinguished—if the food were no longer presented.

Classical conditioning would be of limited interest if it applied only to dogs or salivary responses. Its importance stems from the fact that conditioning occurs in many real-life situations. In particular, the laws of classical conditioning seem to underlie the fear response. Many of us have been conditioned by life events to fear certain objects and situations such as dogs, water, examinations, snakes, or enclosed spaces. Fears can also become associated with social situations involving persons of the opposite sex, authority figures, crowds, and so on. Once a fear has become associated with a particular situation, it may not help very much to be told that the fear is irrational or exaggerated. Behaviorists have developed some useful techniques, to be discussed, for helping people overcome their fears.

OPERANT CONDITIONING

The other major type of conditioning, called either operant or instrumental, usually involves responses that are under voluntary control. This is in contrast to the involuntary reflex involved in the classical method. In the operant approach, the animal or person is moving freely in the environment.

Courtesy of the Skinner Institute

B.F. Skinner

Skinner (1971) is probably the best-known investigator of operant behavior. The basic principles can be demonstrated in the lab by means of the Skinner box. This is nothing more than a chamber with a lever and a food tray. A hungry rat placed in the box first explores its surroundings. Eventually, it pushes down the lever, which causes a pellet of food to drop into the cup. The rat soon begins to press the lever more and more frequently because this response is reinforced, that is, followed by a desirable or gratifying outcome.

In everyday life, our behavior is constantly influenced by patterns of rewards and punishments. Children are trained by parents and teachers by means of good things to eat, grades, and expressions of approval. "Bad," or socially unacceptable, behaviors may be followed by either punishment or the removal of desired rewards. The general pattern continues into adult life when others shape our behavior by rewarding certain performances with paychecks, promotions, or verbal praise, while discouraging other actions with various punishments and deprivations. The principles of **operant conditioning** have been applied to a number of therapeutic goals. Some will be reviewed in a subsequent section, but first we look at some early attempts to apply behaviorist principles to therapy.

JOHN B. WATSON AND LITTLE ALBERT

John B. Watson was an American psychologist who coined the term *behaviorism* and did much to make the new approach known to the general public. In his book *Psychology from the Standpoint of a Behaviorist*, which appeared in 1919, and in numerous magazine articles, he argued that the social environment was a powerful factor in conditioning personality and behavior. He boasted that given control over a child's early environment, he could produce a lawyer, doctor, Indian chief, criminal, or just about any kind of adult.

John B. Watson

The immediate importance of Watson is that he advanced the idea that behaviorism could be applied to the understanding and treatment of psychological disorders. His experiment with Little Albert, an 11-month-old boy, attracted a good deal of attention (Watson & Rayner, 1920). The purpose of the experiment was to show that an irrational fear, or phobia, could be acquired through conditioning. The experimental procedure was designed to condition a fear of a white rat in Little Albert, who previously was fond of rats and other animals. The experimenter, standing behind the boy, struck a steel bar with a hammer when Albert reached out to touch the white rat. The loud noise frightened the child and made him cry. After this procedure was repeated a few times, Albert became very fearful at the sight of the animal even without the loud noise. His newly acquired fear of white rats generalized to rabbits and other furry animals as well as to white furry objects such as a lady's muff.

Later, one of Watson's associates devised a method of treating such fears. Jones (1924) first conditioned a fear of a white rabbit in a child named Peter. She then presented the white rabbit at a distance when Peter was enjoying something to eat. Gradually, she brought the animal closer and closer, taking care not to evoke the fear response. The boy's fear was gradually eliminated, presumably because the once-feared stimulus was progressively associated with pleasant feelings.

BEHAVIORISTIC VIEW OF ABNORMAL BEHAVIOR

Phobias and other types of abnormal behavior might be the result of learning and conditioning. The implications of these discoveries had a profound impact on the way behaviorists view abnormal behavior and "mental illness." They concluded that there is no basic difference between abnormal and normal behaviors because all behaviors are acquired by the same processes of learning and conditioning. The terms *abnormal* and *maladaptive* are simply labels applied to behaviors that are ineffective, self-defeating, or unacceptable to society. For example, one person may have learned through painful experience that stealing is followed by unpleasant consequences. Another person may have learned that stealing pays because the rewards are immediate and the punishment uncertain, absent, or tolerable. It merely clouds the issues to label some behaviors as antisocial or maladaptive. It is even worse to label certain persons as mentally ill or sick because it implies that they suffer from some mysterious defect of mind or spirit. Rather than labeling people, it might be more constructive to help them unlearn undesirable patterns of response and substitute new, more adaptive patterns.

In addition to Watson and his associates, a number of other workers began to apply behaviorist ideas to treatment. By and large, however, behavior therapies remained in the shadow of analytic approaches until about the mid-1950s. Since that time, the behaviorist approach has shown extraordinary growth and combined with a cognitive component may soon become the dominant psychological approach to therapy.

Behavioral techniques have been employed in almost every kind of human services facility, including mental hospitals, community mental health centers, correctional facilities, family service agencies, schools, and community settings (Sundel & Sundel, 1982). Behavioral therapies have been developed to treat a variety of problems including obesity, smoking, substance abuse, speech difficulties, bed-wetting, tics and similar nervous habits, sexual dysfunctions, and a variety of psychosomatic problems such as ulcers and high blood pressure.

Before describing some of these techniques, the assessment procedure that precedes treatment should be addressed.

BEHAVIOR ASSESSMENT In treatment based on behavior assessment, the origin of the problematic behavior is considered along with the factors that currently maintain the behavior. This assessment leads to the establishment of behavioral objectives— in other words, specifying the behaviors to be changed and the new behaviors to be acquired. Behaviorists ridicule the pursuit of vague goals in therapy. For example, if a client complains of a lack of self-confidence, the behaviorist attempts to pin down exactly how the client behaves in specific social situations. The therapist might ask how the client would behave if he or she were a self-confident person. These behaviors then become the target behaviors, and a program is set up to help the client acquire them. One advantage of the behavior-assessment approach to therapy is that the therapist and the client have a clear idea of what they are trying to do.

The following sections describe some of the treatment methods devised by behavior therapists.

SYSTEMATIC DESENSITIZATION An often used behavioral intervention called **systematic desensitization** is probably the most widely used therapy based on classical conditioning. As currently practiced, it is an elaboration of the previously discussed method of treating fears and phobias developed by Watson and his associates. Of modern investigators, Wolpe (1958, 1969) did the most to refine the technique and to establish its therapeutic usefulness.

Treatment begins with an assessment of the stimuli or situations that evoke the fear response in the client. Water, open spaces, dogs, spiders, snakes, high places, and enclosed areas are some of the specific things or situations that may cause intense fear. The method can also be applied to social fears such as that of being rejected or criticized by certain people.

During initial sessions, the client is taught some variant of the progressive relaxation technique originally developed by Jacobson (1938). This technique helps the client learn to relax by alternately tensing and relaxing the major muscle groups of the body. The next phase of treatment involves making up an anxiety hierarchy—a series of scenes related to one of the client's fears. The scenes are graded in terms of how much fear they evoke. For example, a student who is fearful of examinations might use a hierarchy in which the first scene involves being told by the professor that an exam is scheduled in 2 weeks. Further scenes bring this dreaded event closer and closer, until the final scene in which the student imagines receiving the exam itself. In treatment, each scene is imagined and paired with the relaxation procedures. When the client can imagine the least-threatening scene without tension, the next scene is presented. Eventually, the client is able to imagine every scene in a relaxed manner.

The results of systematic desensitization have generally been quite positive, showing that the treatment generalizes to real-life situations. In some applications, the therapy takes place in real-life situations rather than in the therapist's office. For example, clients who are afraid to fly in an airplane may be taken through a real-life hierarchy of situations that ends with them actually getting into a plane and flying. Regardless of where treatment takes place, the basic aim of systematic desensitization is to substitute a desirable response (relaxation) for an undesirable response (tension/anxiety) in a gradual, step-by-step process.

Token Economies   Perhaps the most ambitious use of positive **reinforcement** is the **token economy**, which has been used in residential settings, prisons, classrooms, and even in homes as a means of encouraging positive behavior in children. The aim is to encourage desirable behaviors by following those behaviors with a reward. The first step is to establish target behaviors. Depending upon the setting, these may be self-care, grooming, completing homework, doing chores, or exhibiting socially appropriate behaviors—any behavior that one wishes to increase. Tokens would be earned for each desired behavior. The task and the rewards are displayed on a chart. Tokens can then be redeemed for something of value, such as a special dessert, toy, trip, or a special privilege, depending on the setting and the population.

Ayllon and Azrin (1965) described a token economy at a state mental hospital that was highly effective in modifying social and work behaviors in the patients. There is evidence that longer-term benefits also occur. Another reason for the increasing popularity of the approach is that the principles underlying the treatment are easy to understand. Workers and therapists can learn to apply the methods after a brief training program.

Cognitive Behavioral Therapy   The cognitive, or thinking, model, which posits that the way in which we perceive the world affects our emotions, is the basis for **cognitive behavioral therapy** (CBT). Stressful life events, anxiety, and depression can all create distressing thoughts that may be distorted in some way. Cognitive therapy helps the individual identify these thoughts and learn to evaluate how realistic they are. Once they are identified, these therapists believe, the individual can then change the distorted thought pattern, which leads to feeling better and initiating behavior change.

As in behavioral therapy, CBT does not concern itself with the causes of problems. Nor do unconscious motivations of behavior have a place in CBT. The therapist addresses the conscious problem in a clear-cut and supportive manner. For example, when working with a severely depressed patient, the cognitive therapist, rather than ask about early experiences, will work with the patient to identify the distorted thinking that may be undermining the patient's functioning and creating feelings of poor self-esteem, possibly causing the patient to feel unworthy of a happy life. After exposing these distortions, patients are taught to retrain their thinking.

CBT was introduced in the late 1960s by Aaron Beck as a technique for the treatment of depression (Beck, 1970). Many responded to this new therapy with cynicism. At the time, most therapists believed that in order to solve psychological problems, it was necessary to develop a deep understanding of the sources of the problems. However, after years of research, it has been demonstrated in rigorous outcome studies that CBT is extremely effective in the treatment of many psychological disorders (Beck, 2005). CBT has successfully treated phobias, eating disorders, and anxiety. This is an appealing therapy for many, as it is relatively brief, making it cost effective and accessible.

CRITICISMS OF BEHAVIORISTIC APPROACHES

Behavior therapy has been sharply criticized by civil rights advocates, who point out that prisoners and mental patients have sometimes been subjected to behavior modification programs against their will. In some instances, inmates in institutions have been pressured to "volunteer" for such programs and have been given the distinct impression that noncompliance would be viewed as a failure to cooperate. This kind of threat must be taken very seriously when authorities have the final say about matters of parole or discharge. Even when participation is truly voluntary, the goals of treatment—the desired behavioral changes—are selected by staff, often with little or no input from the "subjects." Humanists doubt that a person can grow toward maturity and self-responsibility by being treated like a robot. Behaviorists view the matter of choice and free will in quite a different way than humanists. Skinner's (1971) *Beyond Freedom and Dignity* elaborates this view that freedom is an illusion.

POSITIVE ASPECTS OF BEHAVIORISTIC APPROACHES

Despite these and other criticisms, behavior therapy is growing rapidly in popularity, is the object of intensive research efforts, and has produced useful treatments for a variety of human illnesses and problems. Certain behavioristic ideas can be usefully applied by human services workers dealing with different kinds of problems. One useful idea is simply the notion of establishing clear-cut behavioral objectives for the helping process. What is the goal of a session with a client? What objectives is a community organization trying to attain? What would have to happen to solve the problem or meet the need? If an unproductive situation seems resistant to change, it may be worthwhile to discover the reinforcing agents that maintain the situation. Once clear-cut objectives are established and a strategy for meeting these goals is decided on, it is relatively easy to measure progress toward the goal. Whenever possible, it is helpful to gather solid facts and data that indicate this progress.

WHICH THEORY IS BEST?

Instead of asking which theory is best, it might be better to ask which theory and treatment are the most useful in regard to a particular human problem.

Theories are conceptual tools designed to help us understand complex situations. The best tool must be selected for the task at hand. Most helpers agree that certain theories seem to fit a particular client better than others. Probably the majority of skilled helpers are eclectic in approach. This means that they make use of several theories or parts of theories in their work rather than remain firmly devoted to one approach. From the eclectic point of view, it is acceptable to use the concept or treatment that seems appropriate to a particular situation. There is no requirement to be consistent in approach from case to case.

You may now feel somewhat bewildered by the variety of theoretical approaches that can be used in the helping process. Table 4.2 provides a condensed overview of the theories discussed in this chapter. It compares the five major theoretical perspectives along certain dimensions. In other words, it highlights, perhaps exaggerates, the differences between theories. It should help clarify the main points of comparison between these approaches.

ALTERNATIVE THERAPIES

In addition to the more established theoretical perspectives, a growing number of new and exciting therapies challenge traditional viewpoints by integrating the psychology of the mind with bodily responses. Embracing the holistic, or integrative model, these therapies take into account all aspects of a person's life, not just the "psychological" or the "biological." They view all processes as working together as a unified system. Body-mind therapies combine the strengths of "talk therapy" with bodywork, such as touch or exercises to increase body awareness. Individuals become more aware of their physical sensations, such as breathing, as well as their emotions, mental images, and behavior. This increased awareness about how the body is affected by physical stress and emotional injury enables the individual to work through patterns that are not resolved when only talking about their problems. By working on the relationship between the body and the emotional processes of the client, body-mind therapy is able to address emotional concerns that are not as likely to be resolved through talk therapy alone—such as recovery from traumatic life events. Since there are too many therapies to describe in this chapter, only some of the most widely practiced and best known among them will be mentioned.

One of the most successful body-mind therapies is **eye movement desensitization and reprocessing (EMDR)**. Accepted by mainstream organizations such as the American Psychological Association, the American Psychiatric Association, and many others, this form of therapy is extremely effective in treating victims of trauma (Davidson & Parker, 2001). Developed by Shapiro (2001), EMDR integrates psychodynamic therapy, cognitive behavioral therapy, and body-centered therapy in an eight-phase approach. The client focuses on a disturbing visual image while the therapist's fingers move across the visual field for 20 to 30 seconds. This process is repeated in several sessions as the client's emotional reactions to the trauma become less intense and more manageable. After EMDR processing, clients

TABLE **4.2** | A COMPARISON OF MAJOR THEORETICAL APPROACHES

	Medical Model	Human Services Model	Psychoanalytic Model	Humanistic Model	Behavioristic Model
Complexity of Theory	Complex	Simple	Very complex	Moderately complex	Relatively simple
Past/Present Emphasis	History used to arrive at diagnosis	"Here and now" solutions sought	Strong historical emphasis	"Here and now" emphasized	Present relearning
Assumed Causes of Disorder	Physical, bodily malfunctions	Unmet human needs	Internal conflict/instinct versus morals	Experiences that blocked self-actualization	Determined by previous conditioning
Therapeutic Approach	Medication, surgery, and physical treatments	Connect person with source of need satisfaction	Make conflict conscious	Create climate for growth, self-exploration	Change specific behaviors, habits, and thoughts
Length of Treatment	Varies depending on diagnosis	Short term preferred	Very long term (years)	Short to intermediate (months)	Usually short term

report that the emotionally distressing memory is eliminated and cognitive insights remain.

Peter Levine developed **somatic experiencing (SE)** by observing how animals in the wild discharge energy after encountering life-threatening situations. Humans, on the other hand, become traumatized because they do not discharge the residual trauma energy from their bodies. The energy remains trapped in the nervous system where it can wreak havoc on a person's mind and body. Humans, just like animals, have the ability to learn to release, renegotiate, and heal the trauma (Levine, 1997). Learning how to do this is the basis of SE. SE procedures are taught face-to-face through interaction with the practitioner and a client, one who has experienced either single-episode trauma, such as rape, or developmental trauma, meaning trauma issuing from interruptions in psychological development.

Additional therapies found to be effective are hypnotherapy, sensorimotor psychotherapy, the Rubenfeld synergy method, and polarity and integrative body therapy. All share a physiological or body component as well as a psychological one. Body-mind therapies have been especially valuable where talk therapy or other traditional therapies have not been successful, as in treating post-traumatic stress disorder (PTSD), and other resistant disorders.

SYSTEMS THEORY

A major development in recent decades has been the widespread application of **systems theory** to scientific problems. A system, living or nonliving, can be defined as a group of related parts having some function or purpose in common.

Miller (1978), in applying systems theory to living organisms, proposes that **living systems** are part of a sequence of larger systems, for instance, family, community, and nation; they are also composed of a series of smaller subsystems such as organs, tissues, and cells. Each system has a measure of independence from the larger system of which it is part, but it is also dependent on the larger system in some ways. Thus, an individual has some independence from family but also remains part of the family in important ways. Each system has a boundary, transfers energy and information across the boundary, and is controlled by some decider system such as parents in a family (Baruth & Huber, 1984). Feedback mechanisms adjust the behavior of the system in somewhat the same way that a thermostat regulates the temperature in a heating system. By these mechanisms, individuals interact with one another so that each influences the others.

Perhaps the major application of systems theory to psychological treatment has been in the field of family therapy. It became apparent to the family therapists of the 1950s and 1960s that traditional theoretical approaches were of limited use in understanding family interactions. It was sometimes observed, for example, that when one member of the family showed improvement, another got worse. The traditional therapies, which had been developed largely in one-to-one treatment, did not provide clear explanations for these kinds of complex interactions. Systems theory did, and it soon became the dominant approach in the field of family therapy.

Systems therapists began to question the prevailing view that the member of the family with the presenting complaint or symptom was the sick one. They also doubted that this symptomatic member, usually a child or adolescent, should be the major focus of treatment. They viewed the identified patient as reflecting disturbances in the entire family system. Rather than focusing on a disturbed family member, these therapists treated the entire family and sometimes even brought in members of the extended family, since it was found that present-day conflicts in the family sometimes reflected unresolved issues of previous generations.

One important application of systems theory to the understanding of family dynamics is the notion of circular causality in the family system, meaning that interactions between members take place in a circular manner: The behavior of one influences a second, which in turn may influence a third, which may then return to affect the first (Baruth & Huber, 1984).

The usefulness of systems theory is by no means confined to family therapy. Glasser (1981) is one of several authors who have applied systems to individual therapy, and there have been numerous applications of this approach to specific clinical problems. Human services workers should also be aware that systems theory can illuminate their understanding of large organizations. After all, many human services workers spend much of their professional time as part of a service delivery system. An instructive and amusing introduction to understanding organizations from a systems point of view is provided by Gall (1977).

Systems theorists are inclined to believe that their model will eventually come to dominate the behavioral sciences. This remains to be seen. There is no doubt that the influence of this approach is spreading rapidly.

ADDITIONAL READING

Durand, V. M., & Barlow, D. H. (2000). *Abnormal psychology: An introduction* (2nd ed.). Pacific Grove, CA: Brooks/Cole.

Frank, J. D., & Frank, J. (1991). *Persuasion and healing* (3rd ed.). Baltimore, MD: Johns Hopkins University Press.

Goldenberg, I., & Goldenberg, H. (1996). *Family therapy: An overview* (4th ed.). Pacific Grove, CA: Brooks/Cole.

Jung, C. (Ed.). (1964). *Man and his symbols*. Garden City, NY: Doubleday.

Ornstein, R. E. (1976). Eastern psychologies: The container vs. the contents. *Psychology Today*, pp. 36–43.

Prochaska, J. O., & Norcross, J. C. (1999). *Systems of psychotherapy* (4th ed.). Pacific Grove, CA: Brooks/Cole.

Rogers, C. R. (1977). *Carl Rogers on personal power*. New York: Delacorte.

Rosen, R. D. (1977). *Psychobabble*. New York: Atheneum.

Shulman, L. (2009). *The skills of helping individuals, families, groups and communities* (6th ed.). Belmont, CA: Brooks/Cole, Cengage Learning.

Skinner, B. F. (1971). *Beyond freedom and dignity*. New York: Knopf.

Sullivan, H. S. (1953). *Interpersonal theory psychiatry*. New York: Norton.

Welfel, E. R., & Patterson, L. E. (2005). *The counseling process: A multi-theoretical integrative approach*. Belmont, CA: Thomson Brooks/Cole.

REFERENCES

Ayllon, T., & Azrin, N. H. (1965). The measurement and reinforcement of behavior of psychotics. *Journal of the Experimental Analysis of Behavior, 8,* 357–383.

Baruth, L. G., & Huber, C. H. (1984). *An introduction to marital theory and therapy.* Pacific Grove, CA: Brooks/Cole.

Beck, A. T. (1970). Cognitive therapy: Nature and relation to behavior therapy. *Behavior Therapy, 1,* 184–200.

Beck, A. T. (2005). The current state of cognitive therapy: A 40-year retrospective. *Archives of General Psychiatry, 62,* 953–959.

Davidson, P., & Parker, K. (2001). Eye movement desensitization and reprocessing (EMDR): A meta-analysis. *Journal of Consulting and Clinical Psychology, 69,* 305–316.

Ellis, A. (1973). *Humanistic psychotherapy: The rational-emotive approach.* New York: Julian.

Erikson, E. H. (1963). *Childhood and society* (2nd ed.). New York: Norton.

Frank, J. D., & Frank, J. (1991). *Persuasion and healing* (3rd ed.). Baltimore, MD: Johns Hopkins University Press.

Gall, J. (1977). *Systemantics: How systems work and especially how they fail.* New York: Quadrangle New York Times Books.

Gilbert, P. (2002). Understanding the biopsychosocial approach: Conceptualizaton. *Clinical Psychology, 14,* 13–17.

Glasser, W. (1981). *Stations of the mind: New directions in reality therapy.* New York: Harper & Row.

Hall, C. S., & Lindzey, G. (1978). *Theories of personality* (3rd ed.). New York: Wiley.

Hansell, N., Wodarczyk, M., & Handlon-Lathrop, B. (1970). Decision counseling method: Expanding coping at crisis in transit. *Archives of General Psychiatry, 21,* 462–467.

Horney, K. (1950). *Neurosis and human growth.* New York: Norton.

Jacobson, E. (1938). *Progressive relaxation.* Chicago: University of Chicago Press.

Jones, M. C. (1924). A laboratory study of fear: The case of Peter. *Journal of Genetic Psychology, 31,* 308–315.

Jung, C. (Ed.). (1964). *Man and his symbols.* Garden City, NY: Doubleday.

Kovel, J. (1980). The American mental health industry. In D. Ingleby (Ed.), *Critical psychiatry.* New York: Pantheon.

Lerner, M. (1994). *Choices in healing: Integrating the best of conventional and complementary approaches to cancer.* Cambridge, MA: MIT Press.

Levine, P. (1997). *Waking the tiger.* Berkeley, CA: North Atlantic Books.

Lickey, M. E., & Gordon, B. (1991). *Medicine and mental illness: The use of drugs in psychiatry.* New York: Freeman.

Lombroso-Ferrero, G. (1911). *Criminal man.* New York: Putnam.

Maddi, S. (1972). *Personality theories: A comparative analysis.* Belmont, CA: Wadsworth.

Maslow, A. H. (1954). *Motivation and personality.* New York: Harper & Row.

Meador, B. D., & Rogers, C. R. (1984). Person-centered therapy. In R. J. Corsini (Ed.), *Current psychotherapies* (3rd ed., pp. 142–195). Itasca, IL: Peacock.

Miller, J. G. (1978). *Living systems.* New York: McGraw-Hill.

Miller, N. S., & Mahler, J. C. (1991). Addiction to and dependence on benzodiazepines. *Journal of Substance Abuse Treatment, 8,* 61–67.

Murray, D. J. (1988). *A history of Western psychology* (2nd ed.). Upper Saddle River, NJ: Prentice Hall.

Pavlov, I. P. (1927). *Conditioned reflexes* (G. V. Anrep, Trans.). London: Oxford University Press.

Payer, L. (1988). *Medicine and culture: Varieties of treatment in the United States, England, West Germany, and France.* New York: Holt.

Pelton, L. H. (1978). Child abuse and neglect: The myth of classlessness. *American Journal of Orthopsychiatry, 48,* 608–617.

Perls, F. (1969). *Gestalt therapy verbatim.* Moab, UT: Real People Press.

Perry, H. S. (1982). *Psychiatrist of America: The life of Harry Stack Sullivan.* Cambridge, MA: Belknap.

Physicians' desk reference (50th ed.). (1996). Montvale, NJ: Medical Economics.

Popple, P. R., & Leighninger, L. H. (1990). *Social work, social welfare, and American society.* Needham Heights, MA: Allyn & Bacon.

Prochaska, J. O. (1984). *Systems of psychotherapy: A transtheoretical analysis* (2nd ed.). Belmont, CA: Wadsworth.

Ricks, D. (1995, January 31). Alternative medicine attracts people of all ages. *Standard Star,* Gannett Suburban Newspapers, p. 6C.

Rogers, C. R. (1951). *Client-centered therapy.* Boston: Houghton Mifflin.

Rogers, C. R. (1959). A theory of therapy, personality, and interpersonal relationships, as developed in the client-centered framework. In M. S. Koch (Ed.), *Psychology: A study of a science* (Vol. 3, pp. 112–116). New York: McGraw-Hill.

Rogers, C. R. (Ed.). (1967). *The therapeutic relationship and its impact: A study of psychotherapy with schizophrenics.* Madison: University of Wisconsin Press.

Schore, A. (2002). The effects of early trauma on right brain development, affect regulation and infant mental health. *Infant Mental Health Journal, 22,* 201–269.

Shapiro, F. (2001). *Eye movement desensitization and reprocessing: Basic principles, protocols and procedures* (2nd ed.). New York: Guilford.

Skinner, B. F. (1971). *Beyond freedom and dignity.* New York: Knopf.

Southern Regional Education Board. (1978). *Staff roles for mental health personnel: A history and rationale for paraprofessionals.* Atlanta, GA: Author.

Sundel, M., & Sundel, S. S. (1982). *Behavior modification in the human services* (2nd ed.). Upper Saddle River, NJ: Prentice Hall.

Szasz, T. (1973). *The myth of mental illness* (rev. ed.). New York: Harper & Row.

Thorndike, E. L. (1913). *Educational psychology: The psychology of learning* (Vol. 2). New York: Teachers College Press.

Valenstein, E. S. (1986). *Great and desperate cures: The rise and decline of psychosurgery and other radical treatments for mental illness.* New York: Basic Books.

Watson, J. B., & Rayner, R. (1920). Conditioned emotional reactions. *Journal of Experimental Psychology, 3,* 1–14.

Whitaker, R. (2002). *Mad in America: Bad science, bad medicine, and the enduring mistreatment of the mentally ill.* Cambridge, MA: Perseus.

Whyte, L. (1960). *The unconscious before Freud.* London: Tavistock.

Wolpe, J. (1958). *Psychotherapy by reciprocal inhibition.* Stanford, CA: Stanford University Press.

Wolpe, J. (1969). *The practice of behavior therapy.* New York: Pergamon.

THE HUMAN SERVICES WORKER

- Clarifying
- Problem Solving
- Interviewing
- Report Writing

Factors That Influence the Use of Skills

- Values
- Professional Codes of Ethics
- Physical and Emotional Well-Being/Stress and Stress Management
- Environmental Factors
- Multicultural Awareness
- Prior Training
- Crisis Intervention
- Crisis Intervention Strategies

Human Rights, the Law, and Human Services

- Voluntary and Involuntary Services
- The Right to Refuse Services
- Due Process
- Least Restrictive Alternative

The Worker in Group Settings

- Definition of a Group
- Group Leadership Skills

The Worker in the Community

- Advocacy
- Community Organizing
- Community Outreach
- Case Management
- Providing Information

Additional Reading

References

INTRODUCTION

Chapter 4 discussed the major theories of the human services/mental health field. This chapter begins with the premise that theoretical knowledge alone is not sufficient for effective helping. Some workers know their theory but are ineffective in applying it. Other helpers seem to work well with clients but have very little theoretical background. In short, there is no definite relationship between the effectiveness of helpers and their knowledge of theory. Besides, it often happens that workers using the same theoretical approach vary greatly in effectiveness. What makes one helper more effective than another?

This question will be explored in terms of the characteristics that have been shown to contribute to successful helping. These characteristics, attitudes, and skills have been identified mainly by humanistic psychologists, who have done a great deal of research on the nature of the helping relationship. Empathy, genuineness, and self-awareness are some of the helper characteristics that contribute to a good relationship with a client. In addition, this chapter reviews some of the basic skills, such as the ability to listen and communicate effectively, that are vital to the helper's success. The chapter closes with a discussion of the special skills required in group and community settings. Throughout this chapter, worker, helper, counselor, and therapist are used interchangeably, much as in the real world, where human services workers who perform similar work are referred to by different terms, depending on their location and setting.

DIFFERENT STYLES OF HELPING RELATIONSHIPS

As you will recall, the psychoanalytic, behavior, and humanistic therapies each have different goals, and each places emphasis on different aspects of the helping relationship. The therapist's use of the concept of "self" will vary greatly, based on the choice of theoretical model and therapy utilized. To explain this more fully, the relationship between therapist and client in each of these perspectives will now be examined.

THE RELATIONSHIP IN PSYCHOANALYTIC THERAPY

Psychoanalysis seeks to bring unconscious material into the conscious mind and to strengthen the ego so that behavior is more reality-based and less driven by primitive instinctual desires. The emphasis is on exploring the client's early past experiences in the hope of achieving a deeper level of self-understanding and insight (Kohut, 1984). The therapist who practices classical psychoanalysis seeks to maintain a sense of neutrality and objectivity with the client. There is very little self-disclosure by the therapist. The anonymous stance assumed by the therapist, sometimes called the blank-screen approach, is considered essential to the psychoanalytic method. The purpose is to develop a transference relationship, in which the client will project onto the therapist unresolved feelings that originated in the client's past significant relationships. It is believed that if the therapist remains neutral, the feelings that the client develops toward the therapist must be derived from the client's past relationships (Corey, 1991). For example, the client may begin to see the therapist as a stern, cold, controlling authority figure as a result of transferring to the therapist unresolved feelings derived from previous experience with his or her father.

In psychoanalysis, the client usually does most of the talking. The therapist's primary role is to listen, understand, and eventually interpret the meanings of the client's experience. A major purpose of this process is to uncover unconscious motives and to help clients achieve insight into their problems. The attainment of insight through the analysis of the transference is assumed to be necessary for the client to change in meaningful ways.

THE RELATIONSHIP IN BEHAVIOR THERAPY

Behavior therapy is a direct, active, and specific problem-solving approach to treatment. The focus is on clients' current problems and life situations as opposed to their past history. Clients learn new coping skills and are urged to take specific action to reach desired goals rather than to reflect passively on prior experiences. Behavioral practitioners do not view the development of special client-therapist relationships as being central or all-important to this treatment approach. Instead, they contend that factors such as warmth, empathy, authenticity, permissiveness, and acceptance are necessary—though not sufficient by themselves—for behavior change to occur (Corey, 1991). The relationship is viewed primarily as a setting for the use of various behavioral strategies and techniques. The client becomes actively involved in the selection of her or his own goals, and the therapist applies specific techniques to help the client achieve those goals.

The helping relationship in this form of treatment has been characterized by critics as being somewhat rigid, overly directive, impersonal, and manipulative. However, many behavioral practitioners believe that establishing a good interpersonal relationship is highly desirable. Spiegler (1983) emphasizes that a good therapeutic relationship increases the chances that the client will be cooperative and receptive to therapy. Cormier and Cormier (1985) also stress that the behavioral approach should be based on a highly collaborative relationship between client and therapist. In fact, they view the process of selecting and achieving goals as a mutual, socially influenced process in which relationship variables are involved.

Girl listening to therapist.

THE RELATIONSHIP IN HUMANISTIC THERAPY

The humanistic approach places a great deal of emphasis on the client-therapist relationship as a catalyst for personality change. The focus is on clients' current life situations rather than on helping them come to terms with their personal pasts (May & Yalom, 1989). Humanistic therapists practice a client-centered approach in which the therapist does not actively establish goals or provide specific advice or direction to the client. The basic premise is that clients are capable of self-directed growth and have a great potential for resolving their own problems if provided with a helping relationship that facilitates such growth.

The underlying belief of this approach is best summarized by Rogers (1961) when he states, "If I can provide a certain type of relationship, the other person will discover within himself the capacity to use that relationship for growth and change, and personal development will occur" (p. 33). The use of any directive techniques designed to get the client to "do something" are, at best, considered secondary to the development of this unique client-therapist relationship. This approach places great emphasis on the "personhood" of the therapist. Not only does the therapist need effective helping skills, but she or he must also have the ability to create a growth-producing environment and must possess the personal characteristics and attributes amenable to these conditions.

REAL LIFE HUMAN SERVICES WORK

I am a licensed clinical social worker and the Director of Social Services at a skilled nursing facility and rehabilitation center in western New England. The facility has 136 beds with three separate units. In addition to supervising two other social workers, I carry a caseload of 60 residents on the long term care/dementia unit. Long term care is changing and so is the typical nursing care resident. Many residents are not elderly, but instead suffer with a major mental illness which prevents them from living independently. Some of these residents were patients in psychiatric institutions, group homes or other residences. Others lived at home with family members, now either deceased or unable to continue to care for them. These residents present social work and other disciplines with many unique challenges, including providing appropriate nursing care, recreations programming, and appropriate behavioral interventions.

My day begins with a morning meeting, which is comprised of the administrator, the director of nursing, the assistant director of nursing, nursing unit managers, social workers, and the directors of food service, maintenance, and housekeeping. We discuss nonclinical issues as well as review a report which is generated on each unit as to significant events that have occurred over the past 24 hours, including any deaths, accidents, incidents, or clinical concerns that have occurred on each unit.

New admissions take place almost daily and it is my responsibility to obtain a comprehensive psychological assessment on each admitted resident. Depending on the cognitive skills level of the resident, the history is obtained either from the resident him- or herself, [from] a family member, or from information that arrives prior to admission. A mental status exam is administered, which determines the short/long term memory impairment and level of cognitive skills. I assess the resident for signs of delirium, cognitive

(Continued)

impairment, and mood or other behavioral symptoms. Drawing on the history obtained from the resident's package, or from the family member or resident's report, I must determine the resident's health care proxy, durable power of attorney, and [whether] the resident had advanced directives, such as DNR or DNI orders. I plan an extended family meeting for the first week. This initial meeting is often heartbreaking as I watch the family surrender the care of their loved one to our institution. Often, family members did not know just how impaired their loved one was and how dangerous it was for them to live alone. In other cases it became too difficult for the family to care for their relative because of their own unrealistic expectations and now the guilt and the self-doubt continues to haunt them as they relinquish care to the nursing home.

During the entire stay of the resident, I monitor the resident for adjustment, mood, and behavioral or cognitive decline. I provide ongoing support and advocacy on behalf of my residents with regard to quality of life; support the rights of residents to retain their autonomy, [and] dignity and their right to a meaningful existence. In addition to these responsibilities, I am sometimes called upon to advocate on behalf of the resident to any indifferent nursing staff, mediate between families and nursing staff, residents, and kitchen staff, as well as with any [other] staff that provides services to residents. In addition, I interact closely with the psychiatric consultant and am often the person [who] identifies mental status changes. I make referral to hospice when a resident declines and continue to work closely with the hospice worker.

A huge segment of my day is spent helping family members negotiate the transition of their loved ones into this institutionalized setting and sometimes cope with the loss of a loved one who is still living and ultimately with [her or his] death. Often the most difficult process to witness is when the resident still recognizes [her or his] family members [and] knows [that she or he is] not at home and the family attempts to leave. In these case the resident cries, screams, and calls out to be taken back home by [the] family. This is still an upsetting and painful process to watch.

One of the saddest aspects of my experience in long term care that I struggle with is the frequent deaths of residents. Sometimes they are gradual and expected and other times they appear to be sudden. One of the traditions that I hope to reestablish in my nursing home is having a memorial service when a resident dies. This will, hopefully, provide a sense of closure for the surviving residents and facilitate a significant and necessary grieving process for residents and staff alike.

Another large part of my time is spent helping family members deal with the financial burden of long-term care and the Medicaid process. I often go to court to represent residents without families and apply for guardianship for them.

I facilitate residents, families, and staff in-services, attend many daily meetings as well as direct and supervise two additional social workers. Although [it is] at times challenging, painful and difficult, I feel that it is an honor to do this work. I advocate for those who cannot speak for themselves and help families, often at their most stressful and vulnerable time. Working with those in need in long-term care helps me understand how very fragile life is, and enables me to appreciate my own life so much more.

Francine Licata, C.S.W.

CHARACTERISTICS OF EFFECTIVE HELPERS

Although research has not yet indicated a "correct" method of helping, it has identified certain characteristics of helpers that are associated with successful helping. For example, the findings of Avila, Combs, and Purkey (1978), Brammer (1981), Brill and Levine (2005), Kottler (2008), Truax and Carkhuff (1967), and Rogers

(1961) indicate that effective workers possess certain personal characteristics that contribute to success, namely, empathy, genuineness, objective/subjective balance, self-awareness, acceptance, desire to help, and patience.

EMPATHY

Empatheia is a Greek word that refers to affection plus passion, touched by the quality of suffering. In Latin, the word *pathos* is analogous to the Greek *patheia*, with the added dimension of "feeling." Through the years, this somewhat vague meaning has evolved into a more comprehensive definition of **empathy**. For example, Brammer (1981) views empathy as the ability to appreciate and understand the client's perspective. More simply, empathy is the ability to see things from another's point of view, to imagine what it is like to "walk in the other guy's shoes."

Empathy is viewed by many professionals as the most important characteristic in a helping relationship. It serves as a basis for relating and communicating. When clients feel understood, they are generally more willing to risk disclosure of their inner feelings. Carkhuff and Berenson (1967) conclude that "the therapist's ability to communicate at high levels of empathic understanding involves the therapist's ability to allow him or herself to experience or merge in the experience of the client" (p. 109). The helper need not have undergone the experiences of a client to understand the client's feelings. Feelings are universal, and different experiences often generate similar feelings. For example, death of a loved one and divorce may both generate feelings of loss and anguish.

For empathy to be constructive, it must be expressed. Thus, if a client says he recently lost his father to cancer, the empathetic helper might respond, "That must be a very painful experience, causing you to feel angry, sad, and abandoned."

GENUINENESS

Genuineness is the expression of true feelings. In a helper, genuineness involves self-disclosure, a willingness to be known to the client. Genuineness is important because in most types of helping relationships, a certain degree of modeling behavior takes place in which the client tries to emulate the characteristics of the helper. If the helper is genuine, free, and expressive, the client is also free and able to express authentic feelings.

Schulman (1991) adds two dimensions to our examination of this characteristic by introducing parallel elements: "Two words are closely related in explaining the meaning of genuineness—*congruency* (when one's words and actions correspond) and **authenticity** (when one is him- or herself, not a phony)" (p. 307; emphasis added). Being genuine, however, is not free license for the helper to do or say anything to the client on a whim. Helpers are not "free spirits" who inflict themselves on others. Being genuine does not necessarily mean expressing all of one's thoughts to the client.

Helpers can be genuine without being hostile or hurtful to the client. For example, a client may ask the helper, "What do you really think of me?" Assuming that the helper has negative feelings at the moment toward the client's behavior, these feelings could be openly expressed in a variety of ways without appearing as a direct attack on the client. The helper might express disappointment at the client's unwillingness to attempt to change her or his behavior. In other words, one can dislike a person's rigidity but still respect the person as an individual.

Sharing personal experiences with the client can sometimes be helpful. For instance, the counselor may be helping someone come to grips with problems generated by a recent divorce. The helper may have been divorced and can therefore understand the range of the client's feelings on a personal level. In this instance, it may be appropriate to share experiences with the client and disclose how one worked toward resolving and understanding those feelings. Of course, it is possible for helpers to share emotions and feelings without discussing specific events or circumstances in their lives.

OBJECTIVE/SUBJECTIVE BALANCE

Subjectivity refers to private, personal, and unique ways of experiencing situations. Being subjective means one's experience is unique and not directly observable by another person. It is a private reaction to or feeling about someone or something. This reaction tends to be biased because it pertains only to the individual's experience.

Objectivity emphasizes verifiable aspects of an event. Objectivity involves the noting of facts without distortion by personal feelings or prejudices. It stresses description of what can be seen, heard, touched, and so on. An objective statement based on verifiable evidence might be, "Bill is 5 feet, 6 inches tall, weighs 145 pounds, and has blue eyes," whereas a subjective statement of these same conditions could be, "Bill is too short, overweight, and has unattractive, weird-looking eyes."

Subjectivity and objectivity represent opposite ends of a continuum. In the helping process, there are disadvantages to each quality when carried to extremes. The helper who is too subjective can become too emotionally involved with the client, as in the case of taking sides in marital counseling. In this sense, the helper can run the risk of losing the ability to make appropriate decisions or judgments.

Pure objectivity alone is also not a desired quality. As objectivity requires a detachment from one's personal feelings, the purely objective helper can run the risk of being viewed by the client as cold, uncaring, aloof, and uninterested in the client's well-being. This can cause obvious difficulties in communication and can build up feelings of resentment on the part of the client.

Either quality, when carried to extremes, can lead to difficulty in understanding people. The quality to be desired is an objective/subjective balance. A helper must have the ability to stand back and view a situation accurately but without becoming detached from personal feelings. Human services helpers need a blend of both subjectivity and objectivity.

SELF-AWARENESS

Self-awareness is the quality of knowing oneself. It includes knowledge of one's own values, feelings, attitudes and beliefs, fears and desires, and strengths and weaknesses—in other words, one's thoughts about oneself. This means that there are literally hundreds of ideas and images that make up the sense of self. Specific values, beliefs, ideas, and images become clear when one asks questions such as, "What's important to me?" and "What aspects of myself do I like or dislike?" The self-concept can be regarded as the inner world in which one lives. In the helping process, the helper often helps make this inner world visible to the client.

The effective helper must be aware of what messages are being transmitted to the client through both word and action. It is only through self-examination that we can begin to understand what aspects of ourselves would be most beneficial to the helping process. As Combs, Avila, and Purkey (1978) explain,

> Professional helpers must be thinking, problem-solving individuals. The primary tool with which they work is themselves. This understanding has been referred to as "the self as instrument" or "self as tool" concept. In the human services a helping relationship always involves the use of the helper's self, the unique ways in which helpers are able to combine knowledge and understanding with their own unique ways of putting them into operation. (p. 6)

Many professionals generally accept that if one wants to become more effective as a helper, it is necessary to start with self-awareness. Helpers who aspire to use self in an effective way must be aware of their patterns of personality and their own needs. They have a responsibility to be conscious of the ways in which their personality and behaviors affect others. Their beliefs, values, and attitudes can have a powerful effect on the helping process.

ACCEPTANCE

Acceptance is demonstrated by letting clients know that their feelings, attitudes, and opinions are worthy of consideration. The accepting helper sees each person as having a fundamental right to think, act, and feel differently from others (as long as there are no infringements of other people's rights, of course). From the humanistic perspective, communicating acceptance of the other person is vital to developing and maintaining the helping relationship, since it leads to feelings of psychological safety on the part of the client. In this setting, clients believe that no matter what they disclose, the counselor will not reject them.

As an accepting person, the helper recognizes the uniqueness in each human being. Brill (1998) suggests that the basis of any good relationship is mutual acceptance of each other's right to existence, importance, and value. Knowing one is accepted should encourage freedom to be oneself—to express one's fears, angers, joy, rage, and to grow, develop, and change without concern that doing so will jeopardize the relationship.

A major problem with understanding the quality of acceptance is that one can confuse acceptance of a client with approval of the client's behavior. Accepting a person does not imply that one likes or approves of all the values or behaviors of that person. Suppose a counselor is working with a heroin addict. The counselor can accept the client's feelings, experience, and beliefs without approving of heroin addiction. When a helper says, "I can accept anyone except a child abuser," she or he is judging the behavior as a total representation of the client. Individuals are made up of numerous values, attitudes, and behaviors—no single one represents the total individual.

DESIRE TO HELP

Many proponents of the humanistic perspective believe that effective helpers have a deep interest in other people and a desire to help, which allows them to receive satisfaction in promoting the growth and development of others. The feelings of self-satisfaction derived from seeing others make positive changes in their lives are a basic reward to the helper. This sincere desire to help is displayed and becomes readily observable in the helper's attitude toward his or her work. Just as people respond more favorably to salespeople who evidence enthusiasm and interest in the product they are selling, so clients respond more favorably to helpers who are enthusiastic about and interested in helping. One caution should be noted in this regard: Sometimes a helper's desire to help can extend too far, creating unnecessary client dependence on the helper.

Helpers accept as a social value the belief that people should help one another. Moreover, people who devote time and energy to helping others demonstrate a basic belief that those being served do have the fundamental ability to change (Cowen, Leibowitz, & Leibowitz, 1968). Many professionals agree that a desire to help people and the belief that people can change are characteristic of those who enter the human services field.

PATIENCE

Patience is the ability to wait and be steadfast; it is refraining from acting out of haste or impetuousness. As a helper, one may often feel that it would be beneficial to a client to do a particular thing, confront a situation, and so on, but patience requires that the helper not try to force a client to act. Patience is based on the understanding that different people do things at different times, in different ways, and for different reasons according to their individual capacities.

Frequently a helper must wait for a client to be ready to take a next step toward resolving a particular problem or toward achieving a desired goal. For example, helping a **developmentally disabled** individual to use eating utensils is a task that involves a lot of repetition over a long period of time. People do not always proceed on a prescribed timetable. Human beings can be awesomely frustrating creatures who often resist change even though the change is recognized as ultimately beneficial. An effective helper must have the patience to allow for the client's development and growth according to the client's needs and abilities.

BASIC HELPING SKILLS

Human services professionals must master certain basic skills to be successful. A skill is an ability to perform a particular task in a competent fashion. People are not born with the skills that are essential for relating effectively to other human beings; they are learned through training. Some helpers do, however, have more natural abilities than others in this area. Effective helpers continue to acquire additional skills and strive to refine already existing skills.

Because each individual is different, each helper must develop his or her own style and way of using these helping skills, which become the "tools of the trade."

The nine basic helping skills discussed here are listening, communicating, giving feedback, observing, confronting, clarifying, problem solving, interviewing, and report writing.

LISTENING

To listen means to pay attention to, to tune in to, or to hear with thoughtful consideration. Skillful listening is as important as talking and acting. It is through listening that helpers begin to learn about their clients and how those clients see the world and themselves. Helpers need to listen attentively to all messages from clients about matters such as how the clients view their problems and what they expect the helper to do about them. Without listening, all forms of potential help may become misguided.

To be effective as a listener, one must become aware of more than just the words that are spoken. There is a basic difference between hearing words and listening for the full meaning and message of the words. It is often not what clients say but how they say it that is important. Their body posture, tone and pitch of voice, silences and pauses, and speech patterns are all significant in understanding what they are trying to communicate. A phrase spoken in a sarcastic tone means something different from the same phrase spoken in a voice filled with cheer and lightness. Effective listening requires sensitivity to inconsistencies between a person's words and actions. The client who says "I'm fine" while tears begin to well up in her eyes is obviously communicating a contradictory message.

When listening to clients, the helper must recognize both the cognitive and affective content of what is being communicated. Cognitive content refers to thoughts and ideas. Affective content refers to the feeling tone of the message. When we watch a mime perform on stage, no words are spoken, but the mime's actions convey a full range of feelings and behaviors. The affective content sometimes differs from the cognitive content and is often less apparent. Responding accurately to a client's statement depends on the helper's ability to hear and understand what is being said and to perceive the underlying message. Helpers must ask themselves, "Does the client's behavior fit his words?" and "What is the client really trying to communicate?"

Another aspect of listening is the concept of selective perception, which means that individuals sometimes hear only the aspects of another's message that they wish to hear and disregard the rest. For instance, a helper might ignore the message conveyed by a client's tone of voice and respond only to the usual meaning of the words spoken if that is what the helper is hoping is true or thinking should be true. Johnson (1986) adds the following:

> There is considerable evidence that you will be more sensitive to perceiving messages that are consistent with your opinions and attitudes. You will tend to misperceive or fail to perceive messages that are opposite to your opinions, beliefs, and attitudes. If you expect a person to act unfriendly, you will be sensitive to anything that can be perceived as rejection and unfriendliness. (p. 93)

The helper's beliefs and attitudes can distort the message being received. When listening to others, it is essential to be aware of the possibility of selectivity in what you hear and perceive. Effective helpers are always listening for the full message.

COMMUNICATING

Communication is the process of transmitting feelings or thoughts so that they are understood. This process involves conveying information verbally or nonverbally through a variety of means such as body movements, facial expressions, and gestures. To communicate, there must be both a sender and a receiver of a message. Generally speaking, all behavior transmits certain information and may, therefore, be involved in communication.

Many aspects of human services work require the ability to communicate. Indeed, communication is an integral part of human services. It often focuses on transmitting specific information, as when a helper is counseling individuals facing retirement and must discuss financial planning, housing needs, or social or emotional concerns. At the other end of the life cycle, helpers working in children's human services programs may focus the content of their communication on the development of basic life skills. Communicating effectively with clients and responding appropriately to them are usually key factors in the success of any helping effort.

The complexity of communication is well illustrated by the game of passing a single message through a series of individuals who whisper it to one another in turn. When the last person tells the entire group his or her version of the message, it is usually significantly different from the original message. How do messages become distorted when conveyed to another person? To understand this, we must look at the various factors involved in communication and understand the obstacles and barriers that can distort even the simplest of messages.

Accurate communication occurs between people when the receiver interprets the sender's message the way the sender intended it. Difficulties in communication

Family communication within the therapy session.

arise when the receiver imparts to the message a meaning that was not intended. When the sender attempts to convey a message, the receiver must interpret the message before she or he can respond to it. All forms of communication require some degree of interpretation, meaning that an individual must construe, understand, and attach individual meaning to a message. It is through this act of interpretation that communication can become distorted.

The process of interpretation is always filtered through our individual biases, expectations, and prejudices. When information is transmitted, the listener tends to accept what seems to fit into his or her belief system and sometimes rejects or distorts information inconsistent with those beliefs. Also, people are sometimes so sure they know what the other person is going to say that they distort the incoming message to match their expectations. For example, if a man who has very low self-esteem asks his boss for a raise, he may take the boss's statement "I'll have to give it some thought" as a sign of refusal even though the boss does not mean for him to take it that way.

A common problem in communication occurs when the receiver understands the words of the message but fails to recognize the sender's underlying meaning. For example, a person might say "Sure is a rainy day" in an attempt to change the subject, but the receiver might assume the person is really concerned about the weather. Another example is the client who sits in the office looking down, arms crossed, slouched deeply in her chair, and responds to the question "How do you feel?" by saying "Fine." This client's nonverbal behavior, consisting of posture, eye contact, and facial expression, indicates the opposite of "fine." Which message does one respond to? The answer is both. The helper must hear the words but also be aware of additional information conveyed in the communication.

Helpers must have an awareness of their own styles of communication so that they can know when they might be creating difficulty in communication by sending out conflicting verbal and nonverbal messages to the client. Obviously, the quality of self-awareness enhances the skill of communicating effectively.

Inappropriate use of language can also lead to mishaps in communication. The helper should avoid using words the client may not understand or may find objectionable. In other words, the helper's vocabulary must be understandable to the client. Because words do not mean the same things to all people, the helper must sometimes provide clear definitions and examples of meaning. If the client's message is unclear, the worker has the responsibility of helping the client clarify its meaning.

Giving Feedback

Giving **feedback** is the process in which helpers convey to clients their perceptions, feelings, observations, or other information concerning the clients' behavior. Feedback basically represents an individual opinion or evaluation of the client by the worker. It helps clients become aware of how they are perceived by others. Clients can then decide to correct errors in judgment, change undesirable behaviors, and establish goals.

People do not operate in a social vacuum. We often seek out other individuals to give us their evaluation of how well we accomplish a particular task or perform a certain job. For example, many actors and actresses anxiously await the theatrical reviewer's evaluation of their latest performances. In the same manner, children proudly display their latest work of art to their parents and await the parents' praising comments. Feedback is a basic requirement of human beings in many aspects of life.

For the human services worker, learning how to provide feedback effectively is an essential task. Danish and Haner (1976) state that "to be helpful, the feedback must be given in such a way that the receiver (a) understands clearly what is being communicated; and (b) is able to accept the information" (p. 14). Timing is an important factor in the appropriate use of feedback. Is the client receptive to another point of view at this time? Sometimes clients are not receptive because they are in a highly emotional state. The relationship between worker and client is another critical issue in the use of feedback. If one respects and values the opinion of the other, one is more likely to accept what is offered.

The worker has to exercise judgment in regard to clients' abilities to accept feedback concerning their behavior or problems. Consider the example of the client who thinks she has a wonderful sense of humor, yet people tend to shy away from her when she jokes around. Several individuals may already have informed her that her jokes are not funny, but she may ignore these people, claiming they have no sense of humor. If in the worker's judgment the client would be more receptive to feedback from a helper, the worker can point out to the client that her sense of humor tends to be sarcastic and hurtful, which may be why people shy away from her.

Feedback serves many purposes. It can reaffirm what the client already believes and feels. It can inform clients of aspects of their behavior of which they were not previously aware. It can provide motivation for change and can also be a source of support during difficult times.

OBSERVING

For the purpose of this discussion, the definition of observing is the process of noting or recognizing an event. The event in question could be almost anything from the weather to the facial expression of a particular individual. Observing occurs in two stages: receiving sensory input and giving meaning to the information.

The human services worker always looks for signs or clues to understand more of what is going on with the client emotionally, such as the following:

- Facial expressions
- Vocal quality
- Body posture
- Gestures
- Clothing
- General appearance
- Eye contact
- Distance between worker and client

Workers usually rely on the sense of sight to provide them with basic information. The sense of hearing is equally important, however. In fact, all the senses receive messages that can supplement, confirm, or negate the initial impression derived from sight.

For example, the worker notes that the client is slouched in his chair, apparently at ease. However, as the interview progresses, the worker hears the client's rapid speech and intermittent stuttering, indicating tension. In effect, the worker's initial impression of the client as being relaxed has now been negated by other sensory information. This example also illustrates that an important aspect of observation is interpretation, or attaching individual meaning to an occurrence. Another helper might come up with a different interpretation of the behavioral clues.

CONFRONTING

In the context of the helping profession, **confrontation** can be defined as calling to the attention of the client discrepancies in the client's thoughts, attitudes, or behaviors (Ivey, Ivey, & Simek-Downing, 1987). A confrontation is actually an invitation to the client to become more aware of and to examine more fully certain aspects of behavior that seem to the counselor to be harmful or self-defeating. It is through the process of confrontation that clients are made aware of specific obstacles that have impeded or could prevent their reaching desired goals. Optimally, confrontation helps clients accept responsibility for their behavior.

Importantly, though, confrontation need not focus exclusively on negative aspects of clients' behavior. It can be used to show them some strengths and resources that they have overlooked. Such knowledge is usually welcomed, but the worker should be warned that sometimes it is not: the acknowledgment of strengths can produce anxiety in clients, because they realize that more can be demanded of them. Thus, confrontation involves challenge even when a positive aspect of behavior is pointed out. Before individuals can change, they must perceive a need for change. Confrontation provides one stimulus for change.

Constructively challenging a client can take various forms. Counselors can call attention to their self-defeating attitudes, point out discrepancies between what they say and what they actually do, focus on various manipulations or forms of game playing, or, as mentioned previously, address unrecognized areas of strength. Following are some examples of the use of confrontation in counseling.

EXAMPLE A

CLIENT: I am not really interested in a better-paying job. It will probably demand more of my time, and I will have to learn new skills and even wear a tie and jacket to work.

COUNSELOR: You say you are not interested in a better job, yet you have spent several sessions talking exclusively about it. Is it possible you really want to go after the better job and are afraid of failing, so you have convinced yourself that you really do not want the job? Are you possibly afraid of new demands that could be placed on you?

This confrontation addresses the client's incongruent behavior.

EXAMPLE B

CLIENT: I am really concerned about the shape of the world today. People do nothing to change the situation. People are starving. Trash is scattered all over the streets, crime is everywhere, and people do not get out and talk to one another anymore.

COUNSELOR: You say you are a concerned person, but the bulk of your time is spent sitting in front of the television and drinking beer.

This confrontation focuses the client on the discrepancy between what he claims concerns him and what he actually does about it.

The misuse of confrontation can have negative effects on clients. If the client is not ready to accept the challenge of the offered information, the confrontation is not helpful. The counselor must time the confrontation so that it is most helpful.

CLARIFYING

The basic purpose of clarifying is to make clear what information is being conveyed by the client and how it is being received by the counselor. Sometimes difficult situations and painful emotions can create problems with communication. When the counselor clarifies aspects of the client's message, the client knows how the message has been received. The process of clarifying often involves using the skills of paraphrasing, highlighting, and summarizing.

PARAPHRASING When the counselor **paraphrases** a client's message, he or she rewords it. In doing so, the counselor attempts to focus the client's attention on the main element of an immediate message. Through the use of paraphrasing, the counselor conveys to the client that the meaning and the feelings of the message have been received and understood. Consider the following example:

CLIENT: Even though I feel I have a lot of friends, I feel as if no one understands me or really wants to. My mother and father don't listen to me. My teachers ignore me, and my girlfriend says I'm no fun to be with anymore.

COUNSELOR: It sounds as if you feel that you have no one you can really talk to.

CLIENT: Yeah, I guess that is how I feel.

In this example, the counselor rewords and restates the client's message and pinpoints the basic feelings. This serves to focus the client on the main areas of concern in addition to conveying to the client that the counselor understands what is being expressed.

HIGHLIGHTING The technique of highlighting is very similar to paraphrasing but has a slightly different purpose. Paraphrasing is often done as a response to the client's immediate message. Highlighting, however, is not an immediate response and does not necessarily follow the sequence in which the client is expressing the message. Highlighting is an attempt to capture the recurring theme of messages during a counseling session. In this way, the counselor emphasizes the main aspects of what the client is expressing over a short time. This serves to focus the client's train of thought and draws the client's attention to the main areas of concern being expressed.

Following the previous example, the counselor has just spent 20 minutes listening to the client's appraisal of himself and his many friendships. The counselor is now attempting to highlight the major theme and feelings expressed by the client.

COUNSELOR: Even though you say you have many friends, you still feel that no one really understands you.

The counselor has now identified the major theme of the client's message and is again drawing the client's attention to what he has already expressed as his main concern.

SUMMARIZING Like paraphrasing and highlighting, summarizing is a means of giving back to clients the essence of what they have been trying to convey. The distinction between these terms concerns the amount of material covered. Paraphrasing and highlighting concentrate on the immediate aspects of client messages during parts of a single counseling session, whereas summarizing involves restating the chief elements of the client's message over one or a series of counseling sessions (Schulman, 1991). When the worker **summarizes** the major points of information and recurring themes brought forth by the client over several sessions, the client can develop a broader perspective on and deeper understanding of the depth and significance of specific problem areas. This process brings to the client's attention changes in feelings and attitudes that may have gone unnoticed. It enables clients to develop a frame of reference in which to see where they were, where they are now, and where they would like to be.

PROBLEM SOLVING

Problem solving is the process of identifying problems and the ability to resolve them in a systematic and constructive manner. Within the helping relationship, the worker's goal is not to just fix the problems for the client but rather to teach the problem-solving process. This way the worker is helping to equip the client with the skills necessary to develop alternatives, clarify issues, and resolve future problems as well. When workers model this process and help people work through their problems, they are assisting them to be more confident and independent. Furthermore, when clients have had some successes with managing problems, they are more likely to feel competent to manage future crises (Poindexter, Valentine, & Conway, 1999).

One of the basic beliefs of human services is that fundamental change must come from within. The helper's role, then, is to facilitate this process. In the midst of a crisis, people often develop a narrow view of their situation and usually perceive only a scarcity of available choices. Increasing problem-solving skills helps people gain greater control of their situation and begin to see more alternatives.

Various approaches to problem solving are commonly utilized within the human services field. The following six-stage process represents only one of the many possible problem-solving approaches. It contains elements drawn from various models and can be useful in various settings.

1. *Engagement.* Determine the person's feelings about the situation. Become involved, and establish constructive communication.
2. *Defining the problem.* Gather the facts, and assess the scope of the problem situation. Assess the level of severity. Who and what are involved, what resolutions have been attempted in the past, what has worked in the past, and what is the desired outcome?

3. *Developing alternatives*. Brainstorm. Be creative and resourceful. Think of options without immediately deciding on their practicality. List options and desired outcomes.

4. *Setting goals*. Evaluate all the available options, and list their potential for success. Prioritize the most important and desired outcomes. Break down the various components/issues into smaller, more manageable parts.

5. *Selecting the alternative*. After evaluating all possible alternatives, select an approach that can be tried or tested. Decide whether this alternative is workable and consistent with the person's feelings and desired outcome.

6. *Taking action*. Outline the necessary steps to implement the strategy and reach the desired goal.

INTERVIEWING

Interviewing is a common and essential process carried out by human services workers regardless of their professional discipline. To interview means to confer, consult, hold a dialogue, or talk (Samantrai, 2004). Interviews are usually considered to be face-to-face interactions that have a planned purpose, structure, and goals. They generally involve two or more people.

Within the broad field of human services, the purpose and goals of interviewing can be quite varied. For example, a helping interview can be conducted for the purpose of obtaining or conveying specific information, resolving a dispute, providing emotional support, problem solving, counseling, or assessing the needs of an individual. A helping interview is different from an informal conversation in that it contains a structure, goals, and specific roles. The roles of the worker and client differ, with the worker carrying the major responsibility for establishing communication and for being sensitive to the client's needs (Brill & Levine, 2005). Helping interviews are usually planned, the relationship is of a limited duration, and there are ethical guidelines that provide structure.

The interview should begin with the establishment of a common understanding and, in an ongoing contact, be related to what has happened before. It should continue through the work of weighing and considering feelings, behavior, and events. Finally, it should conclude with a summing-up of what has taken place and agreement on what the subsequent activity will be (Brill & Levine, 2005).

A variety of theories, techniques, and principles are available for effective interviewing. Elements common to most of these strategies are

- Nonjudgmental attitude
- Expression of feelings
- Rapport building
- Problem solving
- Confidentiality
- Reassessment
- Limited emotional involvement
- Acceptance

Most human services training programs, regardless of discipline, will likely provide a framework for acquiring these and other essential skills for interviewing.

REPORT WRITING

Report writing is a means of recording the interactions between clients and events. Most reports concern client behavior and progress. Report writing is not generally perceived as one of the more exciting skills to acquire within the human services field; nevertheless, it is one of the most practical and valuable. All professionals and institutions require a consistent method of keeping track of what happens to whom, when, and why, although specific methods and styles of report writing vary.

Report writing in one form or another is necessary in many aspects of the human services field. Agencies often use a standardized form for the various types of reports. Obviously, writing clearly and using language accurately are important. More specifically, reports are usually compiled with two basic objectives in mind: to establish a documented record for future reference and to convey current information regarding a specific case or event (Wicks, 1979).

A counselor working with many clients must keep an accurate report of each one's progress. Clients may be taking medication, which necessitates a consistent and accurate report on the type of medication, dosage, and consequent reactions. If a client changes counselors, the report of the previous counselor may be requested by the new counselor as a means of gaining background information on the client. In many clinics it is mandatory to keep reports of patient contacts, diagnoses, and treatments. Very often these reports are monitored by state and federal agencies to ensure a continuous level of compliance with state and federal regulations.

Reports are crucial when professionals evaluate or consult with public or private agencies, institutions, or schools. For instance, a human services specialist might be brought in to evaluate the effectiveness of a specific program or service. The evaluator would rely heavily on the records and reports submitted.

FACTORS THAT INFLUENCE THE USE OF SKILLS

This chapter has so far described a variety of skills and characteristics needed for effective helping. A number of factors can influence the way in which the worker applies these skills and characteristics, including values, professional codes of ethics, physical and emotional well-being, environmental factors, multicultural awareness, prior training, and crisis intervention.

VALUES

A person's sense of right and wrong, likes and dislikes, and standards of appropriate behavior are all a part of values. Personal, professional, and societal values develop through experiences with family, peers, and culture. Of immediate relevance to this text is the fact that the individual's values guide behavior in professional or working relationships. How a worker reacts to a particular client, situation, or problem is partly determined by the worker's values. Most workers of the humanistic orientation accept the principle that helpers should not try to impose their values on clients but should help clients clarify their own values. To be effective, workers must fully understand their own values and respect the client's right to have different values.

Consider the example of a human services worker who has strong personal values against abortion. The worker is asked to counsel a pregnant teenage client who is unsure about having the child. Obviously, the worker's personal values could have a strong influence on the way he or she goes about the helping process. If the worker pressures the client to make a decision in line with the worker's values, the client may later feel that she betrayed her own sense of what was right in this situation.

How can you as a beginning worker avoid placing values on others? It may help to think about the influences that shaped your values and beliefs. This reflection will help you to appreciate the fact that people who come from different backgrounds may have values different from your own. Other people feel that their values are "right" just as your values feel "right" to you.

To begin the process of clarifying your values, you might answer these questions:

- What values underlie your desire to help others?
- What social issues do you feel strongly about?
- Which client behaviors would you have trouble accepting?
- Which of your values would you like to change?
- What would you like to accomplish in human services?
- How do you go about solving personal problems?
- Do you readily seek help from others when you need it?

PROFESSIONAL CODES OF ETHICS

The development of professional codes of ethics involves the concept of "moral correctness." Deciding what is morally correct for everyone all of the time is a difficult, if not an impossible, task. One needs only to read a newspaper or listen to a TV news report to hear of the major battles fought daily in our elected legislative bodies over issues such as abortion, homosexuality, obscenity, premarital sex, or **euthanasia**. Certainly, the religions of the world vary in their views toward these and other issues. Even the law of the land varies considerably in different sections of the country regarding each of these issues. In 1973 the U.S. Supreme Court in the case of *Miller v. California* stated that local municipalities have the right to set their own standards concerning what is obscene, for instance.

Those charged with the responsibility of developing professional codes of ethics face difficult challenges. How can a particular set of guidelines or set of principles encompass everyone's varying beliefs? At present there is no single **code of ethics** that applies to all careers or disciplines in the broad field of human services. Rather, the professional organizations that represent individual careers have established separate codes of ethics to provide guidance and direction for their own members. Some professional organizations that have established such codes are the American Psychological Association (APA), the National Association of Social Workers (NASW), the American Medical Association (AMA), the Council for Standards in Human Service Education (CSHSE), the National Organization for Human Service Education (NOHSE), the American Counseling Association (ACA), the American Association for Marriage and Family Therapy (AAMFT), and the National Academy of Certified Clinical Mental Health Counselors (NACCMHC).

The general guidelines offered by professional codes of ethics could not possibly instruct the practitioner on what to do or how to behave in all professional situations. Ethical codes do, however, serve various important functions. For example, codes define minimal standards of professional conduct and attempt to ensure that workers meet various standards, requirements, or levels of competency (Corey, Corey, & Callanan, 1993). Ethical codes also define the scope of responsibilities for individuals and help clarify various common issues of major concern within a particular field. Van Hoose and Kottler (1986) cite additional reasons why such codes exist: (a) they are self-imposed as an alternative to having regulations imposed by legislative bodies, (b) they are designed to prevent internal bickering and disagreement within the profession, and (c) they are designed to help protect the practitioner in areas of malpractice.

Many areas of overlap exist among the various codes of ethics. The issue of client confidentiality and the right to privacy is one such area. The concept of confidentiality serves to protect the client from any unauthorized use of information by the human services worker without the informed consent of the client. In general, confidentiality can be viewed as a safeguard for clients' rights. The issue of client termination is another example. When is it considered ethically appropriate to terminate work with a client? Another important issue is, what responsibilities does the worker have to the community at large when working with dangerous or high-risk clients?

The Code of Ethics of the National Association of Social Workers (1982) addresses the issue of confidentiality in this manner:

H. Confidentiality and Privacy—The social worker should respect the privacy of clients and hold in confidence all information obtained in the course of professional service.

1. The social worker should share with others confidences revealed by clients, without their consent, only for compelling professional reasons.
2. The social worker should inform clients fully about the limits of confidentiality in a given situation, the purposes for which information is obtained, and how it may be used.
3. The social worker should afford clients reasonable access to any official social work records concerning them.
4. When providing clients with access to records, the social worker should take due care to protect the confidences of others contained in those records.
5. The social worker should obtain informed consent of clients before taping, recording, or permitting third party observation of their activities.

The "Ethical standards of human services professionals" (National Organization for Human Services, 2000) also address client confidentiality:

The Human Service Professional's Responsibility to Clients

Statement 1: Human service professionals negotiate with clients the purpose, goals, and nature of the helping relationship prior to its onset, as well as inform clients of the limitations of the proposed relationship.

Statement 2: Human service professionals respect the integrity and welfare of the client at all times. Each client is treated with respect, acceptance, and dignity.

Statement 3: Human service professionals protect the client's right to privacy and confidentiality except when such confidentiality would cause harm to the client or others, when agency guidelines state otherwise, or under other stated conditions (e.g., local, state, or federal laws). Professionals inform clients of the limits of confidentiality prior to the onset of the helping relationship.

Statement 4: If it is suspected that danger or harm may occur to the client or to others as a result of a client's behavior, the human service professional acts in an appropriate and professional manner to protect the safety of those individuals. This may involve seeking consultation, supervision, and/or breaking the confidentiality of the relationship.

Statement 5: Human service professionals protect the integrity, safety, and security of client records. All written client information that is shared with other professionals, except in the course of professional supervision, must have the client's prior written consent.

Statement 6: Human service professionals are aware that in their relationships with clients power and status are unequal. Therefore they recognize that dual or multiple relationships may increase the risk of harm to, or exploitation of, clients, and may impair their professional judgment. However, in some communities and situations it may not be feasible to avoid social or other nonprofessional contact with clients. Human service professionals support the trust implicit in the helping relationship by avoiding dual relationships that may impair professional judgment, increase the risk of harm to clients, or lead to exploitation.

Statement 7: Sexual relationships with current clients are not considered to be in the best interest of the client and are prohibited. Sexual relationships with previous clients are considered dual relationships and are addressed in Statement 6 (above).

Statement 8: The client's right to self-determination is protected by human service professionals. They recognize the client's right to receive or refuse services.

Statement 9: Human service professionals recognize and build on client strengths.

As discussed, in many instances professional codes of ethics can be very helpful to practitioners in their own fields. As with any set of guiding principles, the limitations are also apparent. Mabe and Rollin (1986) point out some of these limitations as follows:

1. Some issues cannot be suitably covered within the context of a code.
2. Enforcement of codes is sometimes difficult.
3. Conflicts are possible between two codes, between the practitioners' values and the code requirements, and between the code and institutional practice.
4. A code may conflict with the results of a court decision.

For additional information concerning the various professional codes of ethics, refer to the listing of professional organizations at the conclusion of Chapter 6. You can write directly to a professional organization and request a copy of its code of ethics.

Physical and Emotional Well-Being/Stress and Stress Management

Although no one expects the worker to be perfect, it stands to reason that workers will be more helpful to clients when they are psychologically intact and not distracted by their own problems (Hackney & Cormier, 2009). Even relatively mild physical maladies such as a cold, a toothache, or an upset stomach can alter or diminish one's ability and efficiency in **attending** to others. While experiencing physical discomfort, we tend to be more focused on ourselves than on other people. In addition to distracting us, physical discomfort can distort the accuracy of sensory information we receive. In addition to the aspect of physical discomfort, many human services workers can experience considerable stress in relationship to their job. Stress is a normal part of everyday life. Chang (2005), however, points out that stress is an inevitable consequence of pressure-laden jobs. Human services workers often witness some of the saddest sides of humanity, such as working with the homeless, abused or neglected children, or those who have experienced a recent loss. It is not easy and oftentimes impossible to leave at work feelings and concerns for our clients. As a result of this difficult work some human services workers experience "burnout." Burnout is job-related anxiety and fatigue and a reaction to chronic stress on the job (Kanel, 2008). Symptoms of stress and burnout can impair one's judgment at work and affect one's personal life and emotional stability as well as manifest in a host of physical symptoms.

Human services workers must be especially vigilant in attending to their own physical and emotional well being. As human services workers we must learn to manage our stress. For instance, healthy workers are aware of their physical well-being by trying to eat well and take care of their bodies through exercise, meditation, or other related activities. Some attend to their emotional well-being by seeking out, when necessary, counseling for themselves (Neukrug, 2008). There are a number of ways of keeping oneself healthy. It must, however, be viewed as a necessary part of human services work. Your effectiveness as a human service professional will be greatly influenced not only by the acquisition of training skills and knowledge but also by your ongoing physical and emotional well-being.

ENVIRONMENTAL FACTORS

Physical space influences both the worker and the client. For example, arrangement of furniture influences behavior. Barriers placed between individuals, such as a desk separating a worker from a client, create a more formal, businesslike, less personal style of interaction. This physical separation of several feet is analogous to keeping someone "at arm's length." Many large organizations serving the public often use barriers such as desks or counters with large plastic windows to create this type of environment. Acting in an intimate, personal, or less formal manner in this type of setting is often considered inappropriate. Removing the barriers and consequently becoming more physically accessible and closer to others create a different set of behavioral expectations. The worker should consider these factors.

MULTICULTURAL AWARENESS

In the United States, immigration patterns continue to add to the mosaic of a culturally diverse population in which many different ethnic groups exist side by side. U.S. Census figures predict that sometime between the years 2030 and 2050 racial and ethnic minorities will become the majority population (Sue, 1996). Within the human services field, it is increasingly likely that human services workers and their clients will have cultural backgrounds that differ. Understanding and working with cultural diversity have always been a part of the training of human services workers; however, their importance has become increasingly obvious, as current population data confirm.

Culture controls our lives and defines reality for each of us, with or without our permission and/or intentional awareness (Pedersen, Draguns, Lonner, & Trimble, 2008, p. 5). One's culture has a major influence on how one sees and experiences the world. Culture creates and shapes just about every aspect of a person's life, including language, beliefs, values, leisure activities, food consumption habits, clothing preferences, attitudes toward time, eye contact, gestures and body movements, facial expressions, and even attitudes toward life and death. As Zunker (2008) cautions, "be aware that observed differences in some clients should not be considered abnormal but can best be accounted for as part of the norms or practices of a particular culture." Does a human services worker need a thorough knowledge of every client's cultural background in order to be effective? Current research findings differ somewhat on the answer to this question. For example, would any Native American counselor need to fully understand Chinese culture in order to work effectively with any Chinese client? Lewis, Lynch, and Munger (1977) found that counselor and client ethnic identity may have little relationship to the counselor's overall effectiveness. On the other hand, Dillard (1987) concluded that to work effectively with clients of different cultures, counselors need to understand the social and psychological forces that affect their clients' verbal and nonverbal behavior.

Cultural diversity is a fact of life in today's world. Pedersen (1990) makes the point that counselors have two choices: to ignore the influence of culture or to attend to it. Either way, culture will still influence both the clients' and the counselors' behavior. Pedersen believes that the focus on cultural diversity is the most important development in the counseling profession in the past decade. Although various research studies ascribe different degrees of importance to the need for multicultural awareness, a sensitivity toward and a knowledge of a client's cultural background can only serve to make the human services worker more effective.

Most people identify with a religion or have a religious conviction (Shebib, 2002). Often clients' spiritual and religious beliefs are an important part of their cultural identity. Their religious beliefs may inform their values and the important decisions they make in life, such as who they will marry, how they relate to their family, and so on. Sometimes religious people feel that their problems need to be solved by a greater participation in their religious practices such as going to church more often, following religious laws more scrupulously, or praying. It is not uncommon for people who are connected to their religious institution to believe that their problems should be addressed by their clergy rather than a human services worker. Clients with strong religious convictions who seek counseling can best be helped by professionals who are aware of their spiritual orientation and beliefs; therefore, human services professionals should become informed about clients' spiritual backgrounds as well as their cultural backgrounds.

Educational systems and human services training programs should embrace a **multicultural perspective** and structure new policies and practices that are responsive to all groups in society. Depending on the cultural perspective from which a problem is considered, there can be various solutions (Corey, Corey, & Callanan, 1998). Pedersen (1990), Sue (1996), and Corey et al. (1998) indicate that the majority of the techniques and practices associated with most models of professional helping are derived from the point of view of Western culture. This can, of course, present some very real problems when you consider that Eastern cultural values present a different worldview. Ho (1985) and Saeki and Borrow (1985) illustrate this contrast by pointing out that Western culture stresses individuality, encouraging expression of one's feelings, self-assertion, and the fulfillment of individual needs. Eastern culture emphasizes interdependence, compliance, conformity, cooperation, collective goals, and acceptance of one's environment. Helpers will increasingly come into contact with client populations who do not share their worldview; therefore, culturally diverse approaches to helping become mandatory.

Guidelines for practice and culturally diverse perspectives have already been added to various professional codes of ethics, including those of the American Psychological Association, the American Counseling Association, and the National Organization for Human Service Education. Axelson (1985, p. 17) strongly suggests that all human services workers

- Become knowledgeable about several cultures.
- Study differences and similarities among people of different groups and their special needs and problems.
- Gain an understanding of how the individual relates to important events in life, what his or her personal values and morals are, and how they are constructed to form his or her worldview.

Skilled human services workers are aware of how their own background influences the application of their skills. Brill (1995, p. 251) stresses that workers should discover how their personal attitudes, biases, beliefs, and knowledge about different ethnic groups might affect their ability to consider problems objectively, define them accurately, make valid assessments, and present acceptable solutions. They should be particularly conscious of the ever-present danger of using stereotypes and generalizations as explanations of behavior.

Workers must also consider the impact that conflicting demands have on people of one culture who are trying to adapt to life in another culture. Conflict can arise between family loyalties that may require a person to select a mate from within his or her original cultural group as opposed to the new environment, which offers many other possibilities. It is therefore essential that helpers resist making value judgments for their clients.

PRIOR TRAINING

As indicated in Chapter 4, various theoretical approaches to helping are prevalent in the human services field. The approach a worker follows can influence how he or she perceives the client and therefore can affect which aspects of behavior the worker notes with particular emphasis. For example, the worker who employs a behavioral approach to helping might be more apt to notice and emphasize the client's overt physical manifestation of symptoms such as insomnia, weight loss, or nervous habits. This behaviorally oriented worker might not pay attention to certain aspects of the client's life history that could indicate an early childhood trauma. The psychoanalytically oriented worker, on the other hand, would be much quicker to notice and emphasize the client's earlier life experiences. Thus, strict adherence to a specific theoretical approach can limit the scope of one's skills.

CRISIS INTERVENTION

As discussed in Chapter 1, crisis intervention is a special form of help designed to meet the needs of a person faced with an unusually difficult life situation. It is a timely and skillful intrusion into a personal crisis to diffuse a potentially disastrous situation before physical or emotional destruction occurs (Greenstone & Leviton, 2002). A crisis is a perception of an event or situation as an intolerable difficulty that exceeds the resources and coping mechanisms of the person (Galliland & James, 1988).

Crisis intervention is a helping process that occurs at a much faster pace than other treatment modalities, such as case management or counseling, where weekly, monthly, or quarterly contact is sufficient (Poindexter et al., 1999). The goal is problem management, not problem resolution. The primary focus is to make all supportive services available immediately.

RECOGNIZING CRISIS   Crisis results from stress, either as an accumulation of events or a sudden experience. As stress mounts, the individual's normal coping mechanisms may become ineffective, and the potential for crisis increases. The crisis is an individual's emotional and physical reaction to the event, not the event itself.

TYPES OF CRISES   Research in the field of crisis intervention has indicated that crises can be classified into two major types: developmental and situational.

Developmental Crises   Erikson (1963) was one of the first to describe developmental crises resulting from the psychosocial maturational process. As we chronologically age, we undergo periods of major transition from childhood to puberty, into adolescence and then adulthood and old age. Each of these periods of transition in life requires a role change and the introduction of new tasks and brings its own unique conflict situations. For example, teenagers seek to further develop their identities, adults choose career paths, and older adults seek to redefine their lives upon retirement. It is the short periods of psychological upset that occur during a critical transition point in the normal development of a person that will be a major focus for the crisis worker (Kanel, 1999). It is generally accepted that individuals are more vulnerable to crisis at these pivotal points in life.

Situational Crises   Unlike crises that may arise during major transition stages of life, situational crises do not occur with any regularity. Often this type of crisis is sudden and is caused by specific traumatic events. Examples of situational crises are numerous and may include losing a job, physical abuse, rape, alcohol or chemical dependency, death of a relative or close friend, divorce, or experiencing a natural disaster or act of terrorism. These types of events create heightened stress and anxiety and increased psychological, emotional, or behavioral imbalance, which can cause a crisis. The chief characteristics that differentiate situational from developmental crises are (a) sudden onset, (b) unexpectedness, (c) emergency quality, and (d) potential impact on the community (Slaikeu, 1990, pp. 64–65).

Therapy in a rape crisis center.

CRISIS SYMPTOMS   As discussed, individuals react to crisis situations in a variety of ways. Clearly, one's past experiences play an important role in how one may react to any given event. There are, however, certain behavioral characteristics that may make an individual more prone to crisis, namely, low self-esteem, unresolved prior crises, a lack of meaningful personal relationships, and lack of social support or family systems.

Hoff (1995) describes four identifiable stages of crisis development:

1.   The individual reacts to a situation with heightened anxiety and attempts to utilize prior problem-solving skills.
2.   The individual's usual problem-solving skills are ineffective in resolving the situation, and the anxiety increases.
3.   All attempts at the resolution of the problem have failed.
4.   Tension and anxiety overcome the individual as the situation remains unresolved.

As an individual moves through the stages of crisis development, common signs and symptoms will become more apparent. Greenstone and Leviton (2002) list the following common emotional, cognitive, and behavioral symptoms:

Emotional	Cognitive	Behavioral
Generalized anxiety	Confusion	Sleep disturbance
Shock	Poor attention span	Withdrawal

Denial	Loss of trust	Change in appetite
Insecurity	Difficulty making decisions	Crying
Fear		Increased irritability
Panic		Change in level of activity
Despair		Regression
Depression		Unresponsiveness
Anger		
Grief		
Outrage		

CRISIS INTERVENTION STRATEGIES

Considerable research has been done in the field of crisis theory and intervention strategies since the pioneering works of Lindemann (1944), Erikson (1963), and Caplan (1964). Currently no single intervention strategy has proved effective in all types of crisis situations. Therefore, rather than present a single model of crisis intervention, or even multiple models, we will examine six points of an eclectic intervention model drawn from the works of Hoff (1995), Kanel (1999), Poindexter et al. (1999), and Greenstone and Leviton (2002).

1. *Attending to the person.* Actively listen to what the person is trying to communicate both verbally and nonverbally. Remain calm, supportive, and try to quickly establish and maintain a rapport. Try to identify the precipitating events. Act to relieve anxiety and try to prevent further disorientation.
2. *Assessment.* Accurately assess and clarify the source and meaning of the stress and anxiety of the person. Ascertain the level of intensity, and decide whether the situation warrants other supportive services or appropriate referral immediately. Decide which problems should be handled first, second, and so on.
3. *Provide structure.* Establish what you can do for the person, and define goals and objectives for her or him. Explore options. Think creatively. Allow the person to rely on you until he or she can gain control.
4. *Identify strengths and resources.* Communicate to the person that you believe him or her to be a capable person who is momentarily in a difficult and stressful situation. Explain that anxiety and stress are normal and expected reactions to an unusual situation. Help the person to identify other people or personal resources in her or his life that may be of assistance.
5. *Evaluation.* Decide what is the appropriate next step for the person. Consider additional help and referral sources. Develop a plan of action. Consult a supervisor or agency guidelines, if needed.
6. *Follow-up.* Contact the person within a few days to check whether referral to the specialist or agency was appropriate. Check whether the person contacted the referral sources in a timely manner. If necessary, contact the referral source directly to check whether the person has engaged the service.

CRISIS OUTCOMES   The outcome of a crisis can take various forms. Some view a crisis as an opportunity for growth. Whether people come out of the crisis state productively or unproductively depends on how they deal with it (Kanel, 1999). If they are able to develop and integrate the problem-solving skills learned as a result of the crisis, they can eventually function at a higher level than prior to the crisis. The acquisition of new problem-solving skills and coping mechanisms can facilitate growth of the individual, with an increase in self-confidence.

While many individuals do learn to cope with and resolve crises, some do not. For these individuals, unresolved problems may cause increased deterioration—such as antisocial behavior, depression, or withdrawal—leading to further problems associated with alcohol or chemical dependency.

HUMAN RIGHTS, THE LAW, AND HUMAN SERVICES

The laws of society affect all areas of human behavior in that they require the members of a society to learn what is acceptable (that is, legal behavior) and what is unacceptable (that is, illegal behavior). By defining the rights of individuals and society's obligations to its members, the legal system has a direct influence on the provision of human services. As society becomes more complex, the interaction between the law and the human services system tends to increase. Slovenko (1973) has highlighted several of the more significant areas of interaction:

- In some instances, human services have assumed the role of religion or law in explaining the causality of behavior. Behaviors previously viewed as sinful or unlawful may now be attributed to physiological or genetic causes. As a result, individuals may not be held responsible for their actions. Our discussion of the medical model in Chapter 4 highlights this point.
- Human services tend to emphasize rehabilitation rather than retribution. The idea is that offenders should be helped through our human services system rather than punished through our legal system.
- Since the state can intervene in the lives of those considered unable to handle their own affairs and who might present a problem to society, human services professionals are concerned that some persons judged by the courts to be suffering from mental illness might be deprived of their rights.

The law can override the values of a professional code of ethics of a particular profession. This might occur when deemed legally necessary to protect the health, safety, and welfare of the public. For example, one such situation involves client confidentiality. The need for confidentiality is outlined in various professional codes of ethics and considered necessary to ensure the effective treatment of clients. However, the law may require the disclosure of client information in an effort to prevent harm to others.

An illustration of this issue of confidentiality is the California Supreme Court decision in the case of *Tarasoff v. Regents of the University of California* (1976). The court stated that when therapists or counselors determine that a patient presents a serious danger to another, they have a "duty to warn" the intended victim. They are to apprise the victim of the danger, notify police, and take whatever other steps are reasonably necessary to protect the potential victim. Mehr (1995) expands these issues further when he points out the increased concern with the constitutional rights in regard to issues such as involuntary treatment, incarceration, and protecting the public.

As discussed, working within the complexities of our human services system requires a basic knowledge of the law. Specifically important is the relationship of law to various human rights issues. Further examination of some of these more common and controversial issues follows.

VOLUNTARY AND INVOLUNTARY SERVICES

As Mehr (1995) suggests, the concept of **voluntary services** generally embraces some of the following guidelines:

1. The client decides that some form of help is needed and contracts with the service provider for help.
2. The client takes part in creating the objectives and goals of treatment.
3. The client can discontinue or terminate the treatment if desired.

The concept of involuntary services is quite the opposite. Services are assumed to be involuntary based on these guidelines:

1. An individual or agency other than the client decides that a service is necessary. For example, the police or courts might require a homeless person to leave a public area and go to a shelter.
2. Various authorities (for example, courts, legal guardian, therapist) require the client to obtain a particular service.
3. Various individuals other than the client set treatment goals.
4. The decision to terminate the service is determined by someone other than the actual client.

These concepts are examined more closely in Chapter 2, in our discussion of drug-treatment programs.

THE RIGHT TO REFUSE SERVICES

As helping professionals, we assume that our actions toward our clients are in their best interests. Consequently, it has sometimes been assumed that we can successfully administer services even if the clients resist our efforts. Clients' resistance has been, in the past, regarded as a function of their particular disorder and therefore not heeded. The philosophy was that the helping professional knows what is best for the client. Under current law, however, clients do have the right to refuse services.

Consider the case of a patient in a mental hospital who refuses to take a particular medication prescribed by a physician. The courts have stated that it is illegal to force the patient to take the medication—unless a judge declares the specific patient to be legally incompetent. Each situation must, of course, be individually reviewed. People can still be committed to hospitals against their will and be required to receive treatment for specified periods of time. This issue is a multifaceted, controversial problem. The limits of the law relating to the extent to which patients can refuse certain types of treatment are currently being reexamined.

DUE PROCESS

The Constitution of the United States contains a provision under the Fifth and Fourteenth Amendments that government activities depriving people of liberty or property must be done with due process of law. Put quite simply, if you feel that you have been treated unfairly and would like the opportunity to state your position in court and rectify the wrong, you are seeking due process. For example, before a client can be committed for **involuntary service** for an unspecified period of time, the law provides for a hearing before a judge. Within a school setting, the right to due process may take the form of requiring school administrators to specify in writing various offenses for which a student can be disciplined. They must notify the children and their parents when rules are violated and then conduct a hearing.

Due-process procedures can be either full or partial. Full due-process procedures usually involve representation by a lawyer, a hearing before an impartial judge and jury, the right to present evidence and have witnesses, and the right to a written statement of findings. This type of procedure is most common when a person might be seriously damaged by a particular decision.

In certain situations, when there is less potential for harm, the law provides for partial due-process procedures. Partial due-process procedures are usually less formal and may involve an administrative hearing rather than trial by jury. In these circumstances, a notice of the charges and some type of assistance might be given in the preparation of a case.

Human services organizations most commonly are involved with partial due-process proceedings in disputes with clients. In this instance, the client has a right to appeal an organization's decision. An administrative hearing may be requested in which the client is allowed a legal advocate and an opportunity to state his or her case.

LEAST RESTRICTIVE ALTERNATIVE

Clients have a right to the **least restrictive alternative,** meaning treatment in settings that are the "least restrictive" to their personal freedoms and liberties. For example, as Mehr (1995) points out, if clients can receive proper outpatient treatment while residing in a community setting, then they should not be hospitalized, because hospitalization would deprive them of more personal freedom than necessary. Many individuals, however, remain in institutional settings, such as mental hospitals, mental retardation facilities, or nursing homes, because there may not be a less restrictive alternative available to them in a particular community.

THE WORKER IN GROUP SETTINGS

The responsibilities of a human services worker very often involve working with groups. They work in settings such as settlement houses, community centers, educational institutions, hospitals, and Ys, among others. This section will focus on the basic skills necessary to facilitate work with groups. It is an introduction for the beginning human services student to many additional concepts, skills, and techniques that can be acquired through advanced training in group work.

DEFINITION OF A GROUP

Some human services workers define a group as a collection of individuals who share a common purpose and work together to achieve their goals. Another definition is one provided by Brown (1991): "A group is considered a small face-to-face collection of persons who interact to accomplish some purpose." Either definition is useful.

There are two basic categories of groups: natural and formal. Natural groups include those consisting of families, friends, people with shared interests, gangs, and sometimes people in self-help gatherings, among others. These types of groups most often do not have a human services worker to help or guide them, and they generally do not meet in a human services agency or setting. The second category, formal groups, includes those aimed at therapy, personal growth, counseling, and sometimes self-help. They often meet in a human services agency or setting and are led by a worker assigned by the agency or setting. Some groups fit into both categories. Human services workers are concerned mostly with formal groups meeting in a human services setting.

GROUP LEADERSHIP SKILLS

Group leaders share many traits with orchestra conductors (Benjamin, 1978). Both help their group to develop their pace and tone in order to achieve their respective goals. According to Garvin (1981, pp. 113–114) group workers "use the group approach to accomplish the goals common to all social work activities: (1) to prevent

© David Harry Stewart/Stone/Getty Images

Group therapy.

members from developing dysfunctional ways of coping with their situation; (2) to enhance members' engagement in a creative use of artistic, social, intellectual, and other endeavors; and (3) to rehabilitate members who have developed handicaps in their social and personal functioning."

In this context, Goroff (1983, pp. 29–31) introduces certain principles that deal with how to help groups reach their goals. He states that "being responsible to and not for" a group is a basic principle of group work. Other principles are "not taking the power many people seem ready to give up" and "not [doing] for others that which they must do for themselves." To ignore these principles is in effect telling the group and individual members that they are not capable, equipped, or ready to take responsibility for their decisions or actions. Instead, the worker must continually recognize and affirm the individuals' strengths, dignity, worth, and integrity. Such leadership is required for the group to achieve its goals.

SELECTING GROUP MEMBERS In many groups, especially in therapy or counseling groups, the selection of group members is an important consideration. Establishing a balanced group is often desirable. The leader might want to provide a varied mix of young and old, male and female, or talkative and quiet members. Information about each individual is obviously necessary for deciding on each one's suitability to participate in the group.

ESTABLISHING GOALS Once the group is established, it must determine its goals. Goals are based on the members' overall level of functioning. In a group with a very low level of functioning, the goals are set primarily by the leader. However, the leader should provide every opportunity for the group members to express their views concerning the goals. Whether these goals are specific or general, they must be clearly defined and agreed upon by group members.

ESTABLISHING NORMS Establishing a clear set of rules, or norms, at the beginning of the group formation helps its members proceed more effectively toward the group's goals. The leader helps the group determine and establish such guidelines. One important rule would address the issue of confidentiality by having participants agree to discuss group matters only within the confines of the group. Another would determine how the group should make decisions. Still another rule might involve allowing each member to finish talking without interruption.

INTERVENING The human services worker intervenes by stepping in and attempting to help the group change something when necessary. Essentially, she or he points out a problem when it arises. **Intervening** is focused on behaviors, decisions, and discussions, both positive and negative, in order to help the group reach its goals. For example, the leader might intervene between two clients who are arguing over a particular issue or when a member violates the established rules of the group.

Sometimes groups get stuck. The leader might intervene when a discussion has reached an impasse, suggesting additional or alternate ways of viewing the situation or problem. Leaders might also intervene by introducing a specific therapeutic technique, such as role playing, to help clarify and bring additional insights to a particular problem that a client or group may be experiencing. Knowing how and when to move in—that is, to take action—is as important in group work as it is in interviewing and helping clients.

PROMOTING INTERACTION   The group leader acts as a facilitator by helping to promote, or bring about, interaction among the group members. Promoting interaction can lead to establishing clear channels of communication among clients. When group members are linked to one another, they begin to work together and relate personally. To be effective as facilitators, workers need to be insightful and sensitive. They have to find ways of relating the concerns of one individual to the concerns of others. This process provides further opportunities for mutual support and helps develop a feeling of interconnectedness and cohesiveness among the group members.

The development of interconnectedness and cohesiveness creates a climate of safety and acceptance in which members trust one another and therefore are likely to engage in productive interchanges (Corey & Corey, 1987). As a facilitator, the group leader helps the participants express their problems and provides support as members explore aspects of themselves. She or he essentially helps group members reach their individual goals as well as group goals through this mutually influencing process.

APPRAISING/EVALUATING   The group leader and members of the group should appraise the ongoing process and goals of the group. It is particularly helpful to do this during and after each group meeting. The leader can initiate a discussion on what is happening in the group, the direction it seems to be taking, how it helps certain participants and not others, and the kinds of issues that may be helpful in the next group session. Group members should be encouraged to become part of this appraisal process. Leaders sharing with the group their evaluations of what is happening in the group helps the members become more aware of how they influence each other. As a result of this process, constructive changes or new goals can be implemented to enable the group to fulfill more of each member's stated needs.

TERMINATING THE GROUP   Leaders need to know when and how to help the group end each session. Before the end of a session, they should help the members apply what they have learned in the group to their individual life situations or environments. After summarizing what happened during a session, or emphasizing some important point that emerged, they can help the session end by suggesting mini-goals for group members to work toward until the next meeting.

In some instances, the leader will determine that it is appropriate for a member to leave the group. This decision should be based on all available information that pertains to the client, such as the client's stated goals, his or her past and present ability to achieve stated goals, and whether the group is still useful for the client's present situation.

It is also the leader's responsibility to help the group determine whether it has completed its work and whether it is time to disband. If the group has previously highlighted a clear set of goals, developed constructive group guidelines, and consistently monitored its progress, the decision to terminate the group will be easy for leader and members alike.

THE WORKER IN THE COMMUNITY

As human services systems have developed to identify and meet human needs, new and diverse activities and functional roles have been created for workers. Workers are spending increasing time in community settings because of the need to locate services for clients, to enlist the aid of various organizations in developing new services, and to provide information that might help prevent problems. As any system gets larger, workers need additional skills and knowledge to understand and effectively use the resources available within the system.

The individual and group skills previously examined in this chapter are, of course, components of all human services activities. As the contemporary worker has become more involved in various aspects and activities of the community, the need for additional knowledge and skills has emerged. Additional skills useful for the community worker are the following:

- Advocating
- Negotiating
- Organizing
- Coordinating
- Educating
- Planning
- Consulting
- Gathering information
- Acting as liaison
- Lobbying
- Reaching out

By examining some of the functional roles and activities most often performed by workers in the community, you can begin to understand why these skills are needed and how they might be used.

ADVOCACY

Advocacy in the human services has become, if not a major function of human services workers, an essential one. In fact, both the National Organization for Human Services (NOHS)'s Ethical Standards of Human Services Professionals and the National Association for Social Workers (NASW)'s code of ethics makes it clear that workers, whenever and wherever needed, should advocate for their clients. This point of view is strongly supported.

While there are many definitions and many types of advocacy, Ezell's (2001, p. 8) definition is particularly clear and helpful: "Advocacy consists of those purposive efforts to change existing or proposed policies or practices on behalf of or with a client or groups of clients." Schneider and Lester (2001, p. 19) add that advocacy is "action oriented," and they assert that "action is a fundamental basis for advocacy." They go on to explain that "while actions may constitute very different activities, the essential elements of initiative, taking steps, participation, engagement, expending energy, and involvement must be present."

Some of the different types of advocacy practiced by social workers are identified by Schneider and Lester (2001) as client, class, legislative, and administrative. Ezell (2001) lists and defines 13 types of advocacy that human services workers practice, including case, class, internal (administrative), legal, legislative, and community advocacy.

Essentially, the role of the human services worker in advocacy is to represent the client and help her or him acquire whatever resources are needed. Together, the worker and client identify the needs of the client so that the appropriate resources can be obtained. For example, suppose a client has been denied social security or welfare benefits to which she is entitled. The worker discovers that the denial was based on an error on the part of the provider. The worker can literally act for the client, confronting and negotiating the bureaucratic mazes to ensure that the client receives the services and benefits she is entitled to receive. Often this work involves gathering and coordinating substantial amounts of information concerning the services sought. The information might include criteria and procedures necessary to qualify for the various programs. As the representative of the client, the worker may, in appropriate instances, actually plead the client's case to individuals, agencies, or government services within the larger system.

Knowledge of many advocacy activities and skills is essential here, since the process can be extremely frustrating. Ezell (2001) points out that "in each case, the practitioner is seeking change by arguing, provoking, negotiating, giving, lobbying, litigating, representing, or influencing." In order to be successful, these activities require certain characteristics of the worker as well as the use of the various skills. Schneider and Lester (2001) see the effective advocate as being action-oriented, patient, hopeful, and opposed to injustice. Ezell (2001, p. 22) cites the qualities of being persistent, tenacious, and patient as well as assertive and flexible. Advocates also need to be skilled in negotiating, resourceful, persuasive, and able to deal with conflict. Such characteristics and skills can make the difference between success or failure in obtaining the needed services or achieving change.

COMMUNITY ORGANIZING

Community organization is a method of practice taught in schools of social work as well as other educational institutions and disciplines. Practitioners are referred to as community organizers, change agents, and community workers, among other titles. The community organizer tries to help bring various sections of the community together to create, improve, or maintain programs, agencies, or organizations. Examples might include the development of job training programs within an agency or as an independent organization. Helping create a needed after-school program or family clinic could be other goals of the community and worker.

In order to be effective, the change agent must recognize that communities consist not only of individuals but of organizations, both formal and informal. Human services workers are generally educated to understand and work most often with individuals and small groups; however, knowledge and understanding of how organizations—private, public, formal, or informal—develop and function is essential for the community organizer. Michael, Daley, and Netting (1994, pp. 40–41) emphasize this clearly when they state, "Professionals need to understand the inner workings of organizations while at the same time see beyond formal organizations, recognizing and valuing the importance of natural support networks that are not organizationally based but that play essential roles in the everyday lives of people."

In order to accomplish tasks like those mentioned, the community organizer must know the community politics and financial resources as well as all other possible resources. Knowing who has influential power in the community is very important. It is also very helpful if the worker is a skilled and articulate speaker, for it is often necessary to persuade individuals, groups, or committees to see a particular point of view. The change agent must be able to work independently and under pressure while being aware that assistance and approval are needed from other quarters. Horman (1999, p. 99) points out, "A critical issue you will face as a change agent is that of obtaining sanction for your efforts." That sanction (or permission) must come from those whom the change agent is trying to affect, or represent, or from the worker's employer. Patience, sensitivity, and diplomacy are essential characteristics for the effective community organizer.

Community Outreach

Human services workers who perform outreach activities can generally be found working directly in the clients' environment. In many instances, a client may be unable or unwilling, owing to physical or emotional illness, to come to a specific human services center. In this case, the outreach worker actually visits the client's residence and helps with a variety of concerns related to all aspects of daily living. A typical service involving these types of activities is a homebound-elderly program. Senior individuals can become, through illness or other factors, unable to accomplish certain tasks for themselves. The worker's activities here might involve helping the client shop for groceries, teaching the client how to budget money more effectively, informing and educating the client about health and nutrition concerns, and helping the client learn or relearn many daily activities that other people take for granted.

Other outreach activities and services focus on the recently discharged psychiatric patient, who may require some form of help to make the transition back into community living. Here, the worker might be involved in teaching a client how to use forms of public transportation, linking clients to other services available in the community, and helping clients develop a range of personal interests that could enhance their quality of life. It is often the outreach worker who is the primary liaison between clients in the community and available community services.

Case Management

Consumers of human services frequently need more than one form of support to meet their needs. With so many types of services available within our human services delivery system, how do people know which services are appropriate for their specific needs? How do they know where to access those services or how to coordinate several available services? Who monitors the ongoing effectiveness of these services to ensure that the clients are reaching their desired goals?

A helping hand from a community outreach worker.

Case management is the answer to these questions. Through case management, human services workers help those in need negotiate the complicated systems designed to deliver legal, medical, and social services and to help them obtain services in an appropriate and timely manner (Rubin, 1992). If executed properly, case management assures a high quality of care to those in need. The tasks and roles usually labeled *case management* can also be referred to as *care coordinator*, *service coordinator*, or *service management* (Kane, 1990). Different human services organizations often use different terms to designate the same activity. Regardless of the term used, case management has become one of the cornerstones of service delivery in our contemporary human services system.

Although the terms *case management* and *case manager* are relatively new (in use over the past 25 years) in the human services field, the activities associated with these terms have their roots in the earlier human services movement of 40 to 50 years ago. With the widespread mandate of deinstitutionalization beginning in the 1960s, case-management activities became prominent as many thousands of mentally ill people who were formerly institutionalized were discharged into community settings. Most of these discharged patients continued to need a variety of services that were no longer located or provided within their former institutions. In a fragmented system of services, case management became a viable means to access and provide services for this population.

Today case managers are found in such areas as community mental health centers, children's services, public welfare agencies, programs for senior citizens, substance-abuse treatment programs, vocational rehabilitation services, programs for people with special needs, health care systems, legal systems, and many more (Mehr, 2001).

It is important to realize that case management is not a single event, performed by the case manager only at the time she or he first meets a client. Rather, it is an ongoing process providing services over a period of time. The amount of contact with the client will vary depending on the specific needs of the client. Case managers will arrange for, coordinate, develop, provide, and/or oversee services for the person or persons who might benefit from accessing resources (Poindexter et al., 1999). Woodside and McClam (2002) point out that the goal of case managers is to teach those who need assistance to manage their own lives but to support them when expertise is needed or a crisis occurs.

Human services workers who function as case managers have job responsibilities that focus on the "whole person." The case manager becomes the primary worker who understands the client's total life situation. A case manager has the responsibility for the comprehensive care of the client, often making sure there is a quality control so the client does not risk becoming lost in the system. Case-management duties are not limited to one area of human services training. Social workers, psychologists, counselors, nurses, and generalists may each have case-management responsibilities. Some of the diverse work activities and core functions include the following:

Assessment. Gathering all necessary information regarding the client. This can include family history, insurance data, housing information, and so on. Establishing and prioritizing client needs and goals. If needed, an interdisciplinary team may be established to represent the various needs of the client.

Treatment planning. Developing a comprehensive plan of action that will enable the client to reach his or her optimal level of functioning.

Service implementation. Linking and providing the client with access to the needed services. The case manager may contact the various agencies or personnel who will be serving the client to coordinate treatment goals.

Counseling. Often the case manager works directly with the client either in person or through consistent telephone communication. This ongoing contact allows the case manager to help the client with a variety of questions or concerns.

Advocating. Contacting appropriate agencies/programs or government services and representing the client in an effort to arrange for whatever services may become necessary, such as vocational training, housing, health services, or counseling.

Coordinating. Overseeing and monitoring the client's coordinated system of treatment to ensure that all services work together toward the desired goals.

Record keeping. All essential information regarding the client must be maintained, updated, and periodically reviewed.

Evaluating and monitoring. Periodically assessing the continued value of all services provided to the client. The treatment plan itself must be reviewed for its continued effectiveness. Contact must be maintained with all service providers to assure continued suitability of services.

The following example illustrates some of the various daily work activities of a case manager.

Kim is employed as a case manager with a large community mental health center. This center has a variety of programs and services, which include an outpatient clinic, day treatment program, prevocational training center, sheltered workshop, and social support system. Kim has a caseload of 20 clients. During the morning hours she conducts an intake interview with a new client and gathers all pertinent information regarding the client's personal history. She later attends a staff meeting where various program directors discuss the progress of several of Kim's clients. After the meeting, Kim spends a great deal of time on the telephone trying to arrange for the eligibility of several of her clients to receive public assistance funds and arrange for a group home placement for another client. After lunch, Kim goes across town to visit two different vocational training programs to assess the suitability of each program for three of her clients. The remainder of the day is spent back at the center, where Kim meets individually with two clients to discuss problems they are having with public assistance, health insurance, and a group-home living arrangement.

Providing Information

One of the major tasks confronting human services is to educate and inform the public. Often people can prevent small problems from becoming larger ones if they only know where to turn for help, what legal rights they possess, and what alternatives are available to them. Access to information can actually prevent some prevalent social problems.

To provide information to the community, human services workers are involved with many aspects of our daily lives. For example, workers can be found visiting local high schools to provide current information on topics such as drug abuse, birth control, and alcoholism. In other segments of the community, workers are likely to be involved with civic or church-related groups, providing information concerning social security benefits, welfare procedures, or family planning. Many community mental health centers have a specific consultation and education department with the designated task of providing these types of information to a particular community. A more in-depth examination of the role of prevention in the human services field is provided in Chapter 8.

Additional Reading

Aguilera, D. C. (1998). *Crisis intervention: Theory and methodology*. St. Louis: Mosby.

Austin, M. J., Brody, R. P., & Packard, T. (2009). *Managing the challenges in human service organizations*. Los Angeles: Sage Publications.

Barsky, A. E. (2000). *Conflict resolution for the helping professions*. Pacific Grove, CA: Brooks/Cole.

Brill, N. I., & Levine, J. (2005). *Working with people* (8th ed.). Boston, MA: Allyn & Bacon.

Dalton, J. H., Elias, M. J., & Wandersman, A. (2002). *Community psychology: Linking individuals and communities*. Belmont, CA: Wadsworth.

DeJong, P., & Berg, I. K. (2002). *Interviewing for solutions* (2nd ed.). Pacific Grove, CA: Brooks/Cole.

Ellis, A., & Yeager, R. J. (1989). *Why some therapies don't work*. Buffalo, NY: Prometheus.

Evans, D. R., Hearn, M. T., Uhlemann, M. R., & Ivey, A. E. (2008). *Essential interviewing* (7th ed.). Belmont, CA: Thompson/Brooks/Cole.

Green, J. W. (1995). *Cultural awareness in the human services* (2nd ed.). Boston: Allyn & Bacon.

Halley, A. A., Kopp, J., & Austin, M. J. (1998). *Delivering human services: A learning approach to practice* (4th ed.). New York: Longman.

James, R. K., & Galliland, B. E. (2001). *Crisis intervention strategies* (4th ed.). Pacific Grove, CA: Brooks/Cole.
Julia, M. C. (1996). *Multicultural awareness in the health care professions*. Boston: Allyn & Bacon.
Miller, W. R. (Ed.). (1999). *Integrating spirituality into treatment*. Washington, DC: American Psychiatric Association.
Murphy, B. C., & Dillon, C. (1998). *Interviewing in action*. Pacific Grove, CA: Brooks/Cole.
Okun, B. F. (1997). *Effective helping: Interviewing and counseling techniques* (5th ed.). Pacific Grove, CA: Brooks/Cole.
Patti, R. J. (2009). *The handbook of human services management*. Los Angeles: Sage Publications.
Welfel, E. R. (1998). *Ethics in counseling and psychotherapy*. Pacific Grove, CA: Brooks/Cole.
Woodside, M., & McClam, T. (2006). *An introduction to human services* (5th ed.). Pacific Grove, CA: Brooks/Cole Thomson.
Young, M. E. (1998). *Learning the art of helping*. Pacific Grove, CA: Brooks/Cole.

References

Avila, D. L., Combs, A. W., & Purkey, W. W. (1978). *The helping relationship sourcebook*. Boston: Allyn & Bacon.
Axelson, J. A. (1985). *Counseling and development in a multicultural society*. Pacific Grove, CA: Brooks/Cole.
Benjamin, A. (1978). *Behavior in small groups*. Boston: Houghton Mifflin.
Brammer, L. M. (1981). *The helping relationship—process and skills* (4th ed.). Upper Saddle River, NJ: Prentice Hall.
Brill, N. (1995). *Working with people: The helping process* (5th ed.). New York: Longman.
Brill, N. I. (1998). *Working with people* (6th ed.). New York: Longman.
Brill, N., & Levine, J. (2005). *Working with people: The helping process* (8th ed.). Boston: Pearson.
Brown, L. N. (1991). *Groups for growth and change*. White Plains, NY: Longman.
Caplan, G. (1964). *Principles of preventive psychology*. New York: Basic Books.
Carkhuff, R. R., & Berenson, B. G. (1967). *Beyond counseling and therapy*. New York: Holt, Rinehart & Winston.
Chang, J. (2005). Pressure points. *Sales and Marketing Management. 157*(4), 18.
Combs, A. W., Avila, D. L., & Purkey, W. W. (1978). *Helping relationships*. Boston: Allyn & Bacon.
Corey, G. (1991). *Theory and practice of counseling and psychotherapy* (4th ed.). Pacific Grove, CA: Brooks/Cole.
Corey, G., & Corey, M. S. (1987). *Groups: Process and practice* (3rd ed.). Pacific Grove, CA: Brooks/Cole.
Corey, G., Corey, M., & Callanan, P. (1993). *Issues and ethics in the helping professions* (2nd ed.). Pacific Grove, CA: Brooks/Cole.
Corey, G., Corey, M. C., & Callanan, P. (1998). *Issues and ethics in the helping professions* (5th ed.). Pacific Grove, CA: Brooks/Cole.
Cormier, W. H., & Cormier, L. S. (1985). *Interviewing strategies for helpers: Fundamental skills and cognitive behavioral interventions* (2nd ed.). Pacific Grove, CA: Brooks/Cole.
Cowen, E. L., Leibowitz, E., & Leibowitz, G. (1968). Utilization of retired people as mental health aides with children. *American Journal of Orthopsychiatry, 38*, 900–909.
Danish, S. J., & Haner, A. L. (1976). *Helping skills: A basic training program*. New York: Human Services Press.

Dillard, J. M. (1987). *Multicultural counseling*. Chicago: Nelson-Hall.

Erikson, E. H. (1963). The A-B-C method of crisis management. *Mental Hygiene, 52,* 87–89.

Ezell, M. (2001). *Advocacy in the human services*. Pacific Grove, CA: Brooks/Cole.

Galliland, B. E., & James, R. K. (1988). *Crisis intervention strategies*. Pacific Grove, CA: Brooks/Cole.

Garvin, C. D. (1981). *Contemporary group work*. Englewood, NJ: Prentice Hall.

Goroff, N. N. (1983). Social group work as a reflection of the affirmation of the human beings' dignity, worth, and integrity. In N. Goroff (Ed.), *Reaping from the field—From practice to principle*. Proceedings of Social Group Work through 1981 (Vol. 1). Hebron, CT: Practitioners Press.

Greenstone, J. L., & Leviton, S. C. (2002). *Elements of crisis intervention* (2nd ed.). Pacific Grove, CA: Brooks/Cole.

Hackney, H. L., & Cormier, S. (2009). *The professional counselor: A process guide to helping* (6th ed.). Upper Saddle River, New Jersey: Pearson.

Ho, D. Y. F. (1985). Cultural values and professional issues in clinical psychology: Implications from the Hong Kong experience. *American Psychologist, 40*(11), 1212–1218.

Hoff, L. A. (1995). *People in crisis: Understanding and helping*. San Francisco, CA: Jossey-Bass.

Horman, M. S. (1999). *Promoting community change: Making it happen in the real world.* (2nd ed.). Pacific Grove, CA: Brooks/Cole.

Ivey, A. E., Ivey, M. B., & Simek-Downing, L. (1987). *Counseling and psychotherapy: Integrating skills, theory, and practice* (2nd ed.). Upper Saddle River, NJ: Prentice Hall.

Johnson, D. W. (1986). *Reaching out—Interpersonal effectiveness and self-actualization* (3rd ed.). Upper Saddle River, NJ: Prentice Hall.

Kane, R. A. (1990). The relevance of case management. In B. S. Fogel, A. Furino, & E. F. Gottlieb (Eds.), *Mental health policy for older Americans* (pp. 201–220). Washington, DC: American Psychiatric Press.

Kanel, K. (1999). *A guide to crisis intervention*. Pacific Grove, CA: Brooks/Cole.

Kanel, K. (2008). *An overview of the human services*. Boston: Lahaska Press.

Kohut, H. (1984). *How does psychoanalysis cure?* Chicago: University of Chicago Press.

Kottler, J. A. (2008). *A brief primer of helping skills*. Los Angeles: Sage.

Lewis, M. H., Lynch, M. L., & Munger, P. F. (1977). The influence of ethnicity on the necessary and sufficient conditions of client-centered counseling. *Journal of Non-White Concerns, 5,* 134–142.

Lindemann, E. (1944). Symptomology and management of acute grief. *American Journal of Psychiatry, 101,* 141–148.

Mabe, A. R., & Rollin, S. A. (1986). The rate of a code of ethical standards in counseling. *Journal of Counseling and Development, 64*(5), 294–297.

May, R., & Yalom, I. (1989). Existential psychotherapy. In R. J. Corsini & D. Wedding (Eds.), *Current psychotherapies* (4th ed., pp. 363–402). Itasca, IL: Peacock.

Mehr, J. (1995). *Human services: Concepts and intervention strategies* (6th ed.). Boston: Allyn & Bacon.

Mehr, J. (2001). *Human services: Concepts and intervention strategies* (8th ed.). Boston: Allyn & Bacon.

Michael, J. D., Daley, S., & Netting, E. F. (1994). In M. J. Austin & J. I. Lowe (Eds.), *Controversial issues in communities and organizations* (p. 106). Boston: Allyn & Bacon.

National Association of Social Workers. (1982, September). Suit settlement favors confidentiality of records. *NASW News, 27*(7).

National Organization for Human Services. (2000). Ethical standards of human service professionals. *Human Service Education, 20*(1), 61–68.

230 Chapter 5

Neukrug, E. (2008). *Theory, practice and trends in human services* (4th ed.). Belmont, CA: Thompson/Brooks/Cole.

Pedersen, P. (1990). The constructs of complexity and balance in multicultural counseling theory and practice. *Journal of Counseling and Development, 68*(5), 550–554.

Pedersen, P. B., Draguns, J. G., Lonner, W. J., & Trimble, J. E. (Eds.). (2008). *Counseling across cultures* (6th ed.). Los Angeles: Sage.

Poindexter, C. C., Valentine, D., & Conway, P. (1999). *Essential skills for human services.* Belmont, CA: Thomson/Wadsworth.

Rogers, C. R. (1961). *On becoming a person.* Boston: Houghton Mifflin.

Rubin, A. (1992). Case management. In S. M. Rose (Ed.), *Case management and social work practice* (pp. 5–20). New York: Longman.

Saeki, C., & Borrow, H. (1985). Counseling and psychotherapy: East and West. In P. Pedersen (Ed.), *Handbook of cross-cultural counseling and therapy* (pp. 223–229). Westport, CT: Greenwood.

Samantrai, K. (2004). *Interviewing in health and human services.* Belmont, CA: Thomson/Wadsworth.

Schneider, R. L., & Lester, L. (2001). *Social work advocacy.* Pacific Grove, CA: Brooks/Cole.

Schulman, E. D. (1991). *Intervention in the human services* (4th ed.). St. Louis: Mosby.

Shebib, B. (2002). *Choices.* New York: Allyn & Bacon.

Slaikeu, K. A. (1990). *Crisis intervention: A handbook for practice and research* (2nd ed.). Boston: Allyn & Bacon.

Slovenko, R. (1973). *Psychiatry and the law.* Boston: Little, Brown.

Spiegler, M. D. (1983). *Contemporary behavioral theory.* Palo Alto, CA: Mayfield.

Sue, D. W. (1996). Ethical issues in multicultural counseling. In B. Herlihy & G. Corey (Eds.), *ACA ethical standards casebook* (5th ed., pp. 193–200). Alexandria, VA: American Counseling Association.

Tarasoff v. Regents of the University of California. (1976). *Pacific Reporter*, 2nd Series, 551, 340.

Truax, C. B., & Carkhuff, R. R. (1967). *Toward effective counseling and psychotherapy.* Chicago: Aldine.

Van Hoose, W., & Kottler, J. (1986). *Ethical and legal issues in counseling and psychotherapy* (2nd ed.). San Francisco: Jossey-Bass.

Wicks, R. J. (1979). *Helping others: Ways of listening, sharing, and counseling.* New York: Chilton.

Woodside, M., & McClam, T. (2002). *An introduction to human services* (4th ed.). Pacific Grove, CA: Brooks/Cole.

Zunker, V. (2008). *Career, work and mental health.* Los Angeles: Sage.

CAREERS IN HUMAN SERVICES

INTRODUCTION

All human services share the goal of helping people live healthier and more productive lives. The broad range of career fields within human services that share this goal includes mental health, education, health, social services, vocational rehabilitation, child care, and housing. A variety of specific job titles are used within each of these fields. Considering the wide range of career options, it is not surprising that the beginning worker often feels uncertain about which path to follow. This chapter is intended to provide basic career information to help you make an informed choice about your options in the field of human services.

Coverage of a representative cross-section of human services careers has been selected, as it is not possible to describe in the space of a chapter all the career options. The emphasis is on career fields that are attracting the large majority of individuals entering human services today. These fields include generalist human services work, physical therapy, creative arts therapy, occupational therapy, clinical psychology, counseling, alcohol and substance abuse counseling, social work, and psychiatry. Because psychiatry demands lengthy, difficult, and costly training, this career may not attract the same numbers of students as other career options in the human services field. It is examined in this chapter because the majority of human services workers are likely to come into contact with psychiatrists in their professional work. Some knowledge of the psychiatrist's background and training may therefore be helpful. Although alcohol and substance abuse counseling can be viewed as one of the specializations within the broad field of counseling, its expanding occupational demand warrants a more in-depth description. Therefore, a separate section is presented in this chapter examining more closely this growing career path.

You will notice that a great deal of overlap exists among careers in terms of work setting, duties, and levels of responsibility. To help you obtain additional information about each career field described, names and addresses of professional organizations associated with each field are provided at the end of this chapter. For more in-depth information regarding these and other human services careers, see our companion book titled *The Helping Professions: A Careers Sourcebook* (Burger & Youkeles, 2000).

GENERALIST HUMAN SERVICES WORK

Many educators feel that the term *paraprofessional*, widely accepted in the past, no longer accurately reflects the knowledge, abilities, skills, and training today's graduates of recognized undergraduate human services programs possess. They feel that graduates of such programs should be considered professional human services workers. Another group of educators believes that the professional label should be reserved for only those who have attained a graduate degree in one of the traditional human services fields, such as psychology or social work. Here, the term *generalist human services worker* will be used, and this controversy will be discussed further in Chapter 9.

FUNCTIONS

The work roles and functions of generalist human services workers vary greatly. Generalist workers represent the largest number of workers and usually have the most contact with those in need. In some instances the duties of generalist workers are similar to those of professionals.

The generalist human services worker may perform some of the same duties as the traditional professional, but the extent of decision making, the level of responsibility, and the range and depth of activity are not as great (Schmolling, Burger, & Youkeles, 1981). For example, as a staff member working within a social service agency, a generalist worker might perform preliminary interviews and client screening, make home visits, gather information, execute administrative functions—including preparing reports or setting fee schedules—and act as a member of a treatment team. The professional worker might also perform these functions and, in addition, might make diagnoses, provide short- and long-term psychotherapy, and plan specific courses of treatment or action. Although an overlap of duties may exist, the traditional professional most often acts in a supervisory capacity and is, therefore, given greater responsibility for all work performed.

During the 1960s, the worker shortage in human services greatly spurred the training and use of generalist human services workers. The new workers not only helped alleviate the shortage but also provided services in many ways (Sobey, 1969). However, the influx of generalist workers into the field caused tension and controversy to develop between them and the traditional professionals in many agencies. This tension was caused, in part, by the belief of generalist workers (and certain professionals as well) that advanced graduate or professional training was not always necessary to perform many functions in human services satisfactorily. Others believed that advanced education and/or traditional professional training was essential for many tasks. This controversy (discussed further in Chapter 9) continues to the present day.

There are many specific job titles within the broad category of generalist human services work. Different institutions, agencies, and programs use various titles to refer to generalist workers. For example, a state psychiatric hospital may use the job titles of psychiatric aide, mental health aide, mental health technician, or mental health trainee. A social services system might use the job titles of social work aide, social work associate, or community worker. Not only are there a variety of titles, but other designations are also used to refer to a specific level of work and responsibility within a given job title. For example, as a mental health aide, one might be at level I, II, III, IV, or V. Each higher level usually denotes a greater degree of responsibility and/or supervisory function and also carries with it a higher salary and greater prestige. These various levels indicate a career ladder approach in human services similar to that of the civil service system. The list below illustrates some of the many current job titles held by generalist human services workers:

Case associate

Residential counselor

Residential manager

Social work associate

Social work assistant

Patient tech

Case worker

Intake worker

Mental health worker

Crisis intervention counselor

Client advocate

Child advocate

Case coordinator

Psychology assistant

Community outreach worker

Gerontology aide

Mental health aide

Protective services worker

Group home worker

Life skills instructor

Assistant counselor

A Day in the Life of a Generalist Human Services Worker

Amy E. earned her A.S. degree in Human Services from a community college. She is presently employed as a milieu therapist in a halfway house serving ten deinstitutionalized mental patients. There are five female and five male residents served by seven staff members consisting of a director, an assistant director, and five generalist workers called milieu therapists.

A typical day for Amy might look like this:

9:00–9:30 A.M.: Amy reads the reports of what occurred with the residents during the previous evening and overnight. She notes that John had an intense argument with Dan during the evening and that the anger did not lessen before bedtime. She will keep an eye on both residents and try to help them deal with their anger without hurting each other.

9:30–10:00 A.M.: Amy meets with other staff members to discuss plans for the day. They discuss who will be liaison to job sites and sheltered workshops, who will supervise the making of meals, who will accompany residents to hospital or doctor appointments, and similar assignments.

10:00–11:00 A.M.: Amy meets with John and Dan, whose display of anger is of concern to other residents and the staff. She attempts to help them discuss their feelings toward each other and resolve their differences before they become a risk to themselves and others.

11:00 A.M.–12:00 P.M.: Amy attends a case management meeting with the assistant director. They discuss plans for Judy, a resident who is presently able to enter a sheltered workshop on a limited basis and who must also see her therapist regularly.

1:00–2:30 P.M.: Amy calls and/or visits the different job sites and sheltered workshops in which residents are placed. She meets with a supervisor to discuss the problems or progress of the residents. On this day there are no particular problems or signs of noticeable progress on the part of any of the residents.

2:30–4:30 P.M.: Amy meets with the residents assigned to the sheltered workshop to discuss the happenings of the day and any problems they may have encountered. Mary tells Amy that she is upset about how the workshop supervisor spoke to her. The group then discusses how Mary might respond to the supervisor.

4:30–5:00 P.M.: Amy writes up her notes on her work with the residents and her perceptions of the residents' progress or problems. These notes are shared with the entire staff to be used in making future plans to help the residents.

It is clear that Amy is very interested in and enjoys her work. It is a learning experience and could be even more so if there were more professional supervision.

The following examples illustrate more clearly some of the functions of generalist workers. It must be emphasized that these examples represent only a limited portrayal of generalist human services work drawn from a broad range of activities.

Example A: Social Work Assistant III

Ms. G. has a bachelor's degree in psychology and is a generalist human services worker under the job title Social Work Assistant III in a nursing home. She is a member of a treatment team, along with an M.S.W., certified social worker, a master's degree-level psychologist, and a psychiatrist. The team meets twice weekly, during which time Ms. G. shares information of social and emotional significance observed during daily interactions with specific clients. The goal of these meetings is to develop and monitor treatment plans that may be required for individual clients. Other aspects of her weekly work activities include a great deal of patient contact, such as leading a weekly discussion group with clients, transporting nonambulatory clients to meals and appointments, and assisting an art therapist who conducts weekly classes for the clients.

Example B: Mental Health Assistant II

Mr. F. is a generalist human services worker who has an associate of science degree in community mental health and works in a large psychiatric hospital under the job title Mental Health Assistant II. He already has basic academic and fieldwork experience in the mental health field, but he is required to participate in a year-long training program conducted by the hospital for all its generalist worker staff. These workshop training programs are designed to familiarize the generalist worker with hospital procedure and to teach specific treatment approaches, methods, and problem-solving techniques. Mr. F.'s primary duties involve working with a professional social worker to conduct daily therapeutic group discussions with the clients, implementing individual treatment programs with clients, attending treatment team meetings with other generalist workers and professional staff, and performing a variety of clerical duties such as ordering various supplies for the ward to which he is assigned. In addition, Mr. F. regularly conducts tours through his ward and provides information for visiting students who are currently enrolled in college mental health programs.

Example C: Psychiatric Aide III

Ms. C. is a generalist human services worker who has a high school diploma and one year of college coursework. She works in the day treatment program of a community mental health center under the job title Psychiatric Aide III. Ms. C. works with former long-term institutionalized patients who attend this program as part of their discharge treatment plan from the hospital. She leads various groups with clients on a daily basis. The group topics often include nutrition and health, current events, money management, and basic adult reading and writing. She often organizes and arranges trips with clients to various activities and events in the community. As a member of a treatment team, she works with social workers, psychologists, and psychiatrists to help develop treatment plans for the clients in her program. A great deal of her work involves helping clients with activities of daily living, which include shopping for groceries, getting help with housing problems or welfare problems, buying clothing, and using the public transportation system.

TRAINING AND EDUCATION

Training for a generalist human services worker career is usually accomplished by one of two routes. The first route involves formal completion of a two- or four-year college or university academic human services program. These degree-granting programs prepare the individual for an entry-level position in the human services field. In order to meet the demands for highly trained and educated human services workers, associate degree level programs began to spring up across the country. These programs conferred degrees in human services or mental health, and were soon followed by baccalaureate and more recently graduate degrees in human services. Today, there are more than 500 human services programs in colleges all across the United States (http://www.nationalhumanservices.org). In addition to training students in direct skills, these human services programs curricula include courses in the liberal arts, social sciences and psychology as well as courses specific to working with various human service populations, such as gerontology, substance abuse counseling and, domestic violence. Most programs also include field-based courses that provide students with an opportunity to apply what is learned in the classroom to clients in social service and community-based agencies. The two-year program is the primary route to a generalist worker career. Completion of a four-year college program is usually viewed as preparation for a more advanced professional career.

A four-year program might have class and fieldwork requirements similar to the two-year program but usually requires more extensive coursework in other areas as well. The four-year program places greater emphasis on liberal arts studies and offers more advanced coursework in specific types of therapy, plus additional skills training.

The second route to becoming a generalist human services worker is through training offered by specific institutions such as psychiatric hospitals, social service agencies, or community mental health centers. These institutions usually have on-the-job or in-service training programs for individuals who lack a formal college degree but desire a generalist worker career. Such programs usually provide basic courses focusing on administrative procedures, patient and staff issues, counseling or treatment methods, medical issues, and other selected topics pertaining to that specific institution. It should be mentioned that some agencies hire generalist workers but provide little or no training. This lack of generalist worker training has raised serious questions and concerns.

The National Organization for Human Services (NOHS) was founded in 1975 and has developed into the organization for human services professionals, educators, and students. Not only has NOHS encouraged the development of innovative models of service and education but by developing a code of ethics for human services, NOHS also has secured its place among other professional organizations, such as NASW (National Association of Social Workers) and APA (American Psychological Association). In addition, NOHS publishes a professional journal, holds an annual conference, and has established The Council for Standards in Human Services Education (CSHSE) in order to ensure consistency in human services education programs. As a result of their efforts, NOHS has elevated the level of the provision of human services, created high standards in education throughout the United States, and has contributed much towards elevating the level of professionalism in the human services field.

REAL LIFE HUMAN SERVICES WORK

I have been employed in the same Nonprofit Agency in Brooklyn, New York for over 20 years. This organization is dedicated to increasing individuality, independence, community inclusion and productivity for adults with developmental disabilities. My professional career began as a community college intern when I was hired as a substitute worker in a group room. Ultimately this led to my being hired as an Assistant Group Leader. I quickly rose to Group Leader, Case Coordinator, and presently, Program Supervisor. My current role as program supervisor is challenging on a daily basis. I am responsible for insuring consumer safety and that each group is provided with active programming. My administrative duties also include staff development regarding goals, review and implementation. In addition, I facilitate meetings to insure that all consumers' needs and concerns are being met.

Finally, I collaborate with parents, Medicaid service coordinators and managers on issues that warrant attention, as well as interview and screen potential consumers of our program. Some days I feel overwhelmed and other days I feel fabulous that I really do make a difference in people's lives. I am considering applying to graduate school to receive further training in the field of developmental disabilities.

Rosemary DeCarlo, A.A.B.A.

PHYSICAL THERAPY

Physical therapy involves the physical rehabilitation of people who have disabling conditions of the musculoskeletal and neuromuscular systems. These conditions may include sports injuries, fractures, chronic pain, strokes, cerebral palsy, spinal cord injuries, and degenerative joint diseases. Physical therapy uses physical agents such as light, sound, electricity, water, air, and exercise to treat and prevent these conditions.

Physical therapy clinicians include physical therapists and physical therapist assistants. Physical therapists evaluate patients and plan and carry out individualized treatment plans that best suit the patient's conditions. Physical therapists may also delegate all or part of the treatment of a patient to physical therapist assistants. Physical therapist assistants perform physical therapy treatments and regularly report to a supervising physical therapist.

FUNCTIONS

Physical therapy clinicians work in a wide variety of clinical settings. According to a 2002 American Physical Therapist Association survey, physical therapy clinicians practice in private and hospital-based outpatient facilities, acute-care hospitals, patients' homes, skilled-nursing facilities, primary and secondary schools, academic institutions, rehabilitation centers, health and wellness centers, industrial facilities, and research centers.

Physical therapy clinicians may develop an interest in working with a particular patient population. They then acquire expertise through on-the-job training, continuing education, and post-professional degree programs. The wide variety of employment settings and clinical opportunities make physical therapy a rewarding career.

Even though the clinical settings and opportunities are diverse, physical therapy clinicians participate in common experiences. Regardless of the setting, they are involved in one-on-one interaction with patients. This interaction is essential for effective rehabilitation. Physical therapy clinicians work closely with their patients to improve their ability to transfer from sitting to standing and ambulate, improve range of motion of joints and strength of muscles, decrease pain, and enhance functional abilities. These clinicians may spend many hours, over a period of several weeks, working directly with patients to facilitate rehabilitation.

TRAINING AND EDUCATION

Physical therapists are trained in post-baccalaureate degree programs. The majority of physical therapy education programs award the master's degree; however, several programs offer doctoral degrees. Preparation for either of these degree programs includes an undergraduate background in the basic sciences, psychology, and mathematics. Physical therapist assistants are trained at the associate degree level. Generally, these two-year programs include general and basic science education, as well as a series of technical courses and clinical experiences.

A Day in the Life of a Physical Therapist

Marcia is a staff physical therapist in a metropolitan acute care hospital. This facility has an inpatient rehabilitation unit, an outpatient unit, and an acute-care unit. Marcia splits her day between treating patients in the acute-care unit and in the inpatient rehabilitation unit.

A typical day for Marcia looks like this:

8:00–9:00 A.M.: Marcia checks her scheduling board for new patients. She assigns two or three of her patients to a physical therapist assistant and prepares to evaluate and treat new patients. She meets briefly with her supervisor to discuss clinical and administrative issues.

9:00–11:30 A.M.: Marcia evaluates and treats five or six patients. In between treating patients she consults with nursing staff, social workers, and physicians concerning the status of her patients related to discharge planning, transfer, and progress in physical therapy.

11:30 A.M.–12:00 P.M.: Marcia documents discharge summaries, interim notes, and returns phone calls to other members of the interdisciplinary team.

1:00–4:00 P.M.: Marcia works one-on-one with her four rehabilitation patients. One patient has a lower extremity amputation, another has had a stroke, the third patient has a fractured hip, and the final one has a spinal cord injury. Marcia performs mat, transfer, ambulation, strengthening, and movement facilitation activities with these patients.

4:00–4:30 P.M.: Marcia documents the progress of her rehabilitation patients.

5:00–6:30 P.M.: After leaving work, Marcia visits the homes of three recently discharged patients and provides therapy care. Her treatment sessions emphasize training in functional activities such as stair climbing, moving from sitting to standing, and activities of daily living. These patients were referred to Marcia from a local home health care agency.

7:30 P.M.: Marcia returns home after a long but rewarding day.

CREATIVE ARTS THERAPY

Dance, music, and art therapy constitute what are broadly referred to as **creative arts therapies,** or expressive therapies. Creative arts therapists use dance, music, or art in a therapeutic manner to facilitate an individual's insight, self-expression, and social awareness. Creative arts used in a therapeutic manner can provide a means of nonverbal communication in which an individual can express **psychological needs.** The fields of dance, music, and art therapy share many common characteristics, which will be discussed, but the fields differ regarding specific training and required skills.

FUNCTIONS

Creative arts therapists are employed in many settings, including public and private hospitals, nursing homes, mental health clinics, rehabilitation centers, senior citizen centers, public and private schools, and halfway houses. Many interesting and innovative programs using the creative arts have been established in prisons and facilities for the terminally ill. The creative arts have been shown to be a useful form of therapy for a wide range of populations, including the learning disabled, emotionally disturbed, mentally retarded, blind, deaf, and physically disabled.

Many creative arts therapists function as members of therapeutic treatment teams, particularly in agency or institutional settings. The creative arts therapist, as a member of this team, makes recommendations regarding a client's plan of treatment, evaluates a client's progress, and works directly with an individual client, group, or family. Consider the following example:

A creative arts specialist with expertise in art therapy is working with an emotionally troubled child in a residential treatment facility. The child is relatively nonverbal and feels somewhat threatened, unable to talk about her feelings and problems. Psychotherapy, which relies heavily on a person's verbal ability, has thus far been unable to uncover any specifically useful material with which to help the child understand and learn how to cope with her problems. The treatment team recommends art therapy as an appropriate means to facilitate more fruitful insights into this child. The creative arts therapist begins by having the child draw pictures of herself and her family and surroundings. This visual representation of the child's feelings and perceptions reveals a lot about the child's current problems. How the child works with the various art materials, such as oil paints, charcoals, and clay, also indicates and helps release high levels of tension and frustration. The creative arts therapist and the treatment team are now in a more advantageous position from which to evaluate the needs of the child and develop a more complete plan of treatment.

The creative arts therapist with expertise in dance or music can function in a manner similar to that of the art therapist. Dance therapy focuses on the nonverbal aspects of personality and behavior as represented by an individual's body movement. Music therapy can increase an individual's self-confidence, help develop a sense of accomplishment and personal satisfaction, improve eye-hand coordination, and increase an individual's attention span.

Children in creative arts therapy.

Whereas many creative arts therapists work in institutional settings, others work as consultants and/or maintain private practices in which they work with clients. Some therapists teach in training programs or college or university programs. The creative arts therapist may serve as an administrator in creative arts or expressive therapy departments in virtually all the settings previously described.

TRAINING AND EDUCATION

As mentioned earlier, training and educational requirements vary somewhat for the different types of creative arts therapists. The professional organization associated with each field develops criteria for professional recognition within the field.

ART At present, to be recognized as a creative arts therapist with expertise in art and to be professionally qualified to use the title of art therapist, one must obtain a master's degree in art therapy or complete a graduate-level training program in an institute or clinic that is accredited by the American Art Therapy Association.

DANCE In the field of dance therapy, the American Dance Therapy Association also considers a master's degree or equivalent graduate-level training to be the minimum for an entry-level position in the field. Successful completion of graduate training qualifies the creative arts therapist with specialization in the field of dance to use the title of dance therapist.

MUSIC The National Association for Music Therapy considers the completion of a four-year undergraduate degree with major emphasis in music therapy to be sufficient for professional recognition as a music therapist.

OCCUPATIONAL THERAPY

Occupational therapy is the selective and purposeful therapeutic use of activities to aid in the treatment of physical or mental disorders. Occupational therapy can serve as one part of an individual's overall treatment plan (along with other therapeutic approaches such as psychotherapy or physical therapy) or can be the sole therapeutic approach used to aid an individual. The range of uses of occupational therapy is enormous. It has proved a useful treatment for problems such as physical disabilities, emotional or developmental disorders, and injuries due to accidents. It is particularly useful in the teaching of daily living skills. All programs of treatment are designed for a client's specific needs and may consist of a single activity or a combination of activities. Activities may be educational, recreational, or social in nature and may include prevocational testing and training, personal care activities, and the use of creative arts.

FUNCTIONS

Occupational therapists are employed in a variety of settings, including but not limited to hospitals, mental health clinics, nursing homes, rehabilitation centers, day care centers, sheltered workshops, home health care agencies, and public and private schools. The majority of occupational therapists have positions in hospitals,

A visually impaired client engaged in occupational therapy.

and the greater part of clients served fall into the physically and emotionally disabled target populations. Of course, the everyday activities of an occupational therapist vary according to the setting and target population.

The occupational therapist very often functions as a member of a therapeutic treatment team. Other members of this team might include a psychologist, a psychiatrist, a social worker, or a nurse. As a member of this team, the occupational therapist is the specialist most often called upon to design and implement a program of activities to reduce specific disabilities and develop an atmosphere in which to promote restoration of ability. The treatment approach used most often to accomplish this involves three phases: assessment, treatment, and evaluation. Initially, assessment is needed to determine the individual's ability level. Based on the assessment, a treatment program is developed. At the final stages of treatment, the team performs an evaluation to judge the program's effectiveness.

Consider the example of an individual who is a stroke victim and has spent considerable time in the hospital. As a result of this illness, the individual must relearn basic skills such as feeding, dressing, walking, and speaking. The illness has also made his former employment difficult, if not impossible, and he must develop new interests and possibly a new career. Once the individual's level of abilities is assessed, a treatment program might include the following:

- Teaching the patient to use equipment (for example, a wheelchair, prosthetic device, crutches, or braces) to aid with eating, walking, speaking, and general mobility

- Working with creative materials (such as paints or clay) to improve coordination, build confidence, and provide a source of exercise
- Dealing with progressively more difficult materials (for instance, leatherwork, ceramics, or printmaking) to refine motor coordination, build strength, and increase work tolerance
- Prevocational testing to assess the individual's abilities and skills and to explore other talents
- Prevocational training to give the client practical experience in specific jobs

The individual's progress is consistently monitored throughout treatment, and an overall evaluation is done at the conclusion of the program. This determines whether additional treatment is needed or whether the individual is ready to resume activities of daily living. A patient may return to visit the occupational therapist periodically to discuss any problems that may arise. Treatment may be simple or complicated, depending on the client's needs. Highly experienced and talented occupational therapists actually design innovative therapeutic devices to meet the needs of a given situation.

Although most occupational therapists are involved in direct patient care, many perform a variety of other duties. A certain percentage of occupational therapists teach in college or university programs. Many perform administrative functions as directors of occupational therapy programs in hospitals or clinics. Still others maintain private practices and act as consultants to various programs and agencies.

TRAINING AND EDUCATION

The field of occupational therapy contains two forms of classification. One can be either a certified occupational therapy assistant (COTA) or a registered occupational therapist (OTR). Each requires a different form of preparation.

A certified occupational therapy assistant is one who completes an approved two-year associate degree program in occupational therapy from an accredited junior or community college. There are also various educational institutions that have one-year certificate-granting programs. Most programs require a combination of coursework and fieldwork training. A certified occupational therapy assistant most often works under the supervision of a registered occupational therapist.

The registered occupational therapist is required to complete a four-year course of study in an approved college or university program. The individual is then awarded a bachelor of arts or sciences degree in occupational therapy. A passing grade on a national certification exam administered by the American Occupational Therapy Association is required to be considered professionally competent for employment. Graduates of approved four-year programs are immediately eligible to take this certification examination. In certain situations, certified occupational therapy assistants can become eligible to take this exam through an accumulation of a minimum four years of job-related experience. Upon successful completion of the exam, the assistant can become a registered occupational therapist. A variety of master's degree programs in occupational therapy exist for those individuals who seek more advanced training in specific areas of the field.

TABLE 6.1 | HUMAN SERVICES JOB LISTINGS THROUGHOUT THE UNITED STATES

Agency	Position	Description	Location	Requirements	Salary
John F. Kennedy Elementary School	Social worker	Provide group and individual counseling, assist families with access to training and resources, and provide class lessons on social skills development	Milford, Connecticut	CT Certification	Based on contract
United States Navy	Social worker	Mental health inpatient and outpatient, diagnosing, evaluating and treatment, medical social work, case management and discharge planning, family violence, child developmental delays	National and worldwide	Master's or Ph.D. in social work	Highly competitive salary, loan repayment and relocation costs
Elderhealth Northwest	Homecase assistant	Provide personal care and household assistance to clients in their own environment	Seattle, Washington	High school diploma	Benefits available
NHS Human Services	Direct support professional	Interact with consumers with mental and intellectual disabilities in a variety of potential settings	Pittsburgh, Pennsylvania	High school diploma or G.E.D.	$13.00 hourly
Department of Correction	Social worker	Work under direction and be responsible for diagnosis and treatment of psycho-social problems of clients	Arkansas	Licensed social worker by the Arkansas Social Work Licensing Board	$28,745–$35,437 per year

Organization	Position	Job description	Location	Education	Salary
Arc Bridges	Direct support professional	Assist clients with daily living skills, meal planning, assistance with purchase and administration of medications, emergency response in case of serious illness, transportation, ability to keep current and accurate records related to job duties	Northwest Indiana	High school diploma	$8.44 per hour
Housing Families	Program manager (of homeless families)	Supervision of program case managers, provide coverage when needed, establish monthly coverage schedules, monitor and approve schedules for case managers	Malden, Massachusetts	High school diploma	$34,000–$38,000 per year
Timber Ridge Treatment Center	Camp counselor/youth worker/wilderness instructor	Supervising at-risk males between the ages of 12 and 17 in a wilderness setting	Gold Hill, North Carolina	High school diploma	$23,660 yearly with a $300 sign-on bonus
Good Shepherd Communities	Direct care professional	Assisting adults with disabilities in daily living skills/tasks	Fremont, California	High school diploma	$10.90 per hour
North American Family Institute (Riverside School)	Special education teacher	Teaching math to teen boys with behavior and psychiatric issues	Lowell, Massachusetts	B.A. and experience with emotionally disturbed youth	$35,000–$42,000 per year

CLINICAL PSYCHOLOGY

Clinical psychology is the specialization within the broad field of general psychology that focuses on the diagnosis and treatment of mental and emotional disorders. Of specific interest to clinical psychologists are the causes of abnormal behavior. Clinical psychologists use all applicable scientific methods in their investigation of behavior. These methods may include psychological testing, controlled experiments, and direct observation.

FUNCTIONS

Clinical psychologists engage in a wide variety of work activities, including research, testing, counseling, psychotherapy, teaching, supervising, and consulting. This range of work activities may be performed in psychiatric hospitals, mental health clinics, hospitals, training institutes, public and private schools, research centers, colleges and universities; and federal, state, and local government programs. The type of setting often defines the clinical psychologist's primary work activities and the range of his or her responsibilities. To illustrate this diversity of settings and work activities, consider the following examples of a psychiatric hospital, public or private school, and community mental health center.

SETTING A: PSYCHIATRIC HOSPITAL The clinical psychologist conducts individual and group psychotherapy sessions with patients. As a member of the ward treatment team, he or she helps develop and monitor the individual treatment plans for patients. A clinical psychologist often administers a battery of psychological tests to a patient in an effort to better determine the nature and scope of the client's problems. This specialist may conduct a group ward meeting with all the patients twice weekly to discuss problems or grievances, disseminate new information that may affect patients, and help patients adjust to the ward environment

A Day in the Life of a Clinical Psychologist

Sam G. is a clinical psychologist who was recently awarded a Ph.D. by the graduate school of a large university in the Midwest. He is employed by a state mental hospital located near the capital city of his home state as a staff psychologist on an acute admissions ward. The patients are all males who have recently suffered serious breakdowns involving some loss of contact with reality. Many of the patients on this ward are confused, agitated, and highly emotional.

What follows is a brief description of a typical day in Sam's professional life:

9:00–9:30 A.M.: As usual, Sam begins his day with a visit to the nursing station. He talks to the charge nurse about several incidents that took place during the night. One patient assaulted another during an argument about stolen money. No serious injury was involved. Because Sam is not treating either patient, no intervention on his part is needed.

9:35–10:25 A.M.: Sam attends the staff meeting with the team leader of the ward, who happens to be a senior psychologist. Also present is the psychiatrist who is primarily responsible for medication of patients on this and another ward, a social worker, a psychiatric nurse, and two mental health therapy aides. Discussion focuses on a 38-year-old male schizophrenic who feels strongly that he is ready for discharge. Various members of the team express doubts about the patient's readiness to go back to the community.

Sam is asked to administer a battery of psychological tests to judge the patient's degree of contact with reality.

10:30–11:20 A.M.: Sam conducts a psychotherapy session with a young, streetwise, male patient who has a history of multiple substance abuse. During this session, Sam focuses on the patient's hostile attitudes toward various members of his family. Unless there is some reduction in these negative feelings, it seems unlikely that the patient will be able to live at home again.

11:30 A.M.–1:00 P.M.: Sam supervises two psychology interns who are learning the rudiments of testing under his direction.

2:00–3:00 P.M.: After lunch, Sam administers an intelligence test to the patient discussed at the earlier meeting. He plans to administer personality tests including the Rorschach inkblot test on the following day.

3:00–4:10 P.M.: As usual, Sam reserves the later part of the afternoon for his written work. He puts the finishing touches on his report on a patient tested several days ago. Then he makes some notes on his therapy patients.

4:15–5:00 P.M.: Sam confers informally with the senior psychologist about a research project on which they will collaborate. Essentially, it is a continuation of Sam's thesis research on thinking processes of schizophrenic patients.

It goes without saying that Sam is involved in informal contacts with patients and staff at various times during the day and that he has occasional phone conversations with other professionals. Basically, Sam likes his position at the hospital; however, he believes that there is an overemphasis on medication there. He would like to see more in the way of group and individual therapy with increased time spent in therapeutic activities. In general, he feels the patients spend too much time sitting around watching inane daytime TV programs.

The clinical psychologist may be asked to conduct a staff workshop in his own particular area of expertise as part of the hospital's ongoing staff development program. As a member of the senior clinical staff, he can also supervise the work of various generalist human services workers and other staff members. As a representative of the hospital, the clinical psychologist often consults with other hospitals, agencies, programs, or the court system in reference to specific patients, program development, or treatment issues. The clinical psychologist may also maintain a private practice with individuals or groups, in addition to these primary work responsibilities.

SETTING B: PUBLIC OR PRIVATE SCHOOL   In a school setting, the clinical psychologist is most often involved with counseling children to help promote their social and intellectual development. Students who are most often in need of the services of a clinical psychologist might include those with learning disabilities or maladaptive behavior problems or those experiencing temporary crisis situations. The clinical psychologist often administers standardized psychological tests to help determine the nature of a student's present problems.

The clinical psychologist frequently consults with teachers concerning the specific needs of students. He may, in cooperation with teachers, develop special programs of instruction for students whose disabilities require such individualized programs.

SETTING C: COMMUNITY MENTAL HEALTH CENTER   The majority of clinical psychologists functioning in community mental health centers serve as clinical members of outpatient treatment programs. Other primary work activities vary according to the nature and scope of the clinic. For example, whereas some clinics may be organized solely for outpatient services, others may provide additional services such as day treatment programs, social programs, medical services, prevocational training, and residential services. The clinical psychologist may be involved in any or all such available services, depending on interest and expertise.

In the outpatient setting the clinical psychologist usually maintains a caseload of clients. The number of patients in a given caseload varies depending on the size of the clinic, number of other staff members, and number of clients being served. The average number of clients being treated by a single clinical psychologist per week might be 25. The methods of treatment used by clinical psychologists vary greatly. The treatment method often depends on which psychological theory or theories the particular clinical psychologist believes to be most effective. The treatment approaches most often practiced are derived from the psychoanalytic, humanistic, or behavioristic models, described in Chapter 4. The outpatient clinician conducts individual and/or group or family sessions with his or her clients to treat specific problems. The clinical psychologist works in a treatment team, with the help of other staff members, to design and monitor individual client treatment plans. As a supervisor, the clinical psychologist oversees the training and quality of work of generalist human services workers and other staff.

Community psychology is a relatively new specialization in the field of psychology. It has become clear to many psychologists that traditional therapeutic and counseling services could not reduce the increasing incidents of individuals manifesting maladapted behaviors. Prevention of community and individual psychological problems, as well as the promotion of wellness and social competence, is a major focus of community psychologists.

The efforts of psychologists have turned to working in the community. Using psychological principles and working together with other professionals as well as using available resources, the community psychologist helps plan programs that not only deal with existing problems and issues, but also help prevent problems from occurring in the first place. Such programs might include prevention of teenage pregnancy, family violence, effects of alcoholism, and employment loss, among others. Additional material on community psychology and examples of prevention programs will be described and discussed in Chapter 8.

Training and Education

Training for a career in the field of clinical psychology begins with the attainment of a bachelor's degree with a major emphasis in psychology. This degree alone does not qualify an individual to become a psychologist; further graduate-level preparation is required. Many individuals pursue a master's degree in psychology as their final degree, whereas others consider the master's-level training an intermediate step before entering a doctoral program in clinical psychology. Individuals can enter a Ph.D. program in clinical psychology directly after attaining the B.A. degree.

One can become a master's-level psychologist and function in the field. Job opportunities and salaries are, however, generally less than those available to the Ph.D.-level psychologist. The doctoral-level training most widely accepted is a Ph.D. program approved by the American Psychological Association. Most Ph.D. programs require five years of graduate study, during which time the student completes a range of coursework and clinical internship of approximately one year's duration. The student is placed in a setting such as a psychiatric hospital to fulfill his or her internship requirement. The student intern is supervised in performing a variety of tasks in which he could be involved after the completion of graduate study. Internships usually provide a good experience for the student to learn firsthand what it is actually like to perform the duties of a psychologist.

The last phase of graduate study, after all coursework and internship requirements have been met, involves writing a formal dissertation. The dissertation is an original piece of research conducted by the student under the supervision of a committee of selected faculty members. The student is awarded the Ph.D. upon successful completion of the dissertation.

A new type of doctoral program granting a doctor of psychology degree (Psy.D.) has been recently approved by the American Psychological Association. A number of graduate schools are offering this new degree. A doctoral dissertation is not required, as the major focus of the training is the development of clinical skills. This type of program is designed to appeal to those individuals more interested in clinical psychology than research or academics.

Most states have some form of licensing and/or certification requirements, including a written examination that must be fulfilled by clinical psychologists. In certain states, licensing law restricts the use of the title *psychologist* to those individuals who have met the requirements of that state. These laws are designed to stop unqualified individuals from practicing therapy.

COUNSELING

Counseling is a career designed to help people consider their choices and options in life, thereby preventing or overcoming specific crises, or problems. Counselors help clients develop goals and objectives that contribute to a healthy lifestyle. A primary goal of counselors is to encourage cognitive and behavioral change. Over the last 20 years, counseling has become an extremely diverse field of study. Counselors are trained to offer support and advice to individuals and groups who are seeking help in areas such as alcohol and drug addiction, child abuse, or reaching career and academic objectives. They also help clients seeking advice regarding marital, family, and spiritual issues.

Unlike psychologists, counselors place little, if any, emphasis on long-term analysis and psychodynamics. Counselors prefer to offer alternatives and possible solutions to specific problems of daily living. An addiction counselor, for example, may suggest a 12-step program to an alcoholic and offer support and advice during the recovery period. A marriage counselor may choose to see a couple and suggest ideas and skills that will enable them to achieve a happy and satisfying relationship. Since the ultimate goal of counseling is to encourage cognitive and behavioral change, it is the counselor's responsibility to help the client identify maladaptive behavior, learn healthy decision-making skills, and develop abilities that prevent problems from recurring.

This career offers the deep satisfaction that comes from helping others achieve a secure and satisfying lifestyle. In addition to personal satisfaction, counselors have a variety of academic degrees and employment opportunities to choose from.

Counselors, based on their individual strengths and level of interest, can pursue an A.A., a B.A., an M.A., or a Ph.D. degree in a number of different specialties. In addition to academic degree programs, many colleges and universities also offer certificate programs in specialized areas of counseling such as alcohol and substance abuse and marital and family counseling.

The need for increased alcohol and substance abuse prevention and expanded treatment strategies has received considerable national attention. A consequence of this awareness has been the demand for additional training programs and personnel. The work of the alcohol and substance abuse counselor will be examined more closely later in this chapter.

For students who prefer pursuing a degree, the field of counseling offers two general areas of study: rehabilitation counseling and school counseling. (Other areas of interest, such as geriatric counseling and marriage and family counseling, are also becoming popular.) Individuals who plan on focusing their efforts on treating people with physical, mental, or emotional disabilities will choose rehabilitation counseling, and those who choose to work with children in a public or private school setting will choose school counseling. (Individuals who are interested in working with school-age children with physical disabilities will want to focus on rehabilitation counseling.)

FUNCTIONS

The role that the counselor takes when working with a client obviously depends on the type of problem being addressed. The role of a rehabilitation counselor, for example, generally entails consulting with medical and psychological specialists to fully understand the nature of the disability. The role of the school counselor, on the other hand, is somewhat different in that she will meet with the student, various school personnel (teachers, social worker, school psychologist, and principal), parents, and sometimes community leaders. Clearly there are similarities and differences between rehabilitation and school counseling. The roles and responsibilities of a counselor are described next.

REHABILITATION COUNSELOR One of the main goals in rehabilitation counseling is to help the client make a realistic estimate of limits imposed by the disability. In many cases, the counselor is faced with the client's refusal to recognize the seriousness of the problem. For example, a construction worker may deny that his cardiac condition requires a change to a sedentary kind of work. Other clients may completely give up on life. An ex-psychiatric patient may feel too anxious to consider any type of employment. In each case, the counselor helps the client make a realistic appraisal of what she can and cannot do. A good relationship between the two helps attain this goal.

During initial contacts, the counselor generally reviews the client's school experience, job history, hobbies, and interests. The counselor listens attentively and tries to conduct the session so that the client will gain insight. If indicated, the counselor might arrange for psychological testing to supplement the information already available.

Testing provides information about the patient's intelligence, level of academic achievement, and personality traits. Aptitude tests give an idea of how well the client would do at clerical, mechanical, numerical, or other tasks. The client is observed during the testing. It is obviously important if the client shows extreme anxiety, irritation, or discouragement while working on a difficult task.

Some rehabilitation centers are equipped with shops where patients can try various activities such as carpentry, electronic assembly, drafting, clerical work, and sewing. By being able to actually accomplish a new task, the client gains the confidence that comes from success. These sample work programs also help the client build up tolerance for prolonged activity. Some disabled persons know how to do a job but can work only for an hour or two. The counselor encourages the client to build up enough tolerance to meet the requirements for at least part-time employment.

The counselor explains the rehabilitation program to the client's family, suggesting various ways they may help. The family members are sometimes just as unrealistic as the client in coming to grips with the disability. For example, in the case of disabled children, the parents usually have to be persuaded to let the children do more on their own. Sometimes, the parents of mentally challenged children have to overcome their shame about the child's limited capacity. If the family members are not happy with the rehabilitation plans, they may sabotage the entire process.

When the client is ready, the counselor begins the final phase of the rehabilitation process, which is placement in the community. To be successful at placement, the counselor keeps up good relationships with employers and community agencies. The experienced counselor knows the local job market and can find positions even for people with serious disabilities.

Clients unable to compete in the job market may be placed in a sheltered workshop. Here, limited workers can earn money for doing productive work, usually on a piecework basis. A sheltered workshop may do the job of assembling ballpoint pens for a local manufacturer. Although paid less than the minimum wage, these workers derive satisfaction from their earnings. Even a modest paycheck can mean a lot to someone who has never worked before.

If at all possible, the client is seen for follow-up interviews in order to discuss any problems that might have come up in the placement. Perhaps the client is not getting along with fellow workers or is having a problem with transportation to and from the job. Whether the problems are deeply psychological or practical in nature, the counselor tries to find solutions. The relationship between client and counselor may continue for months or years.

SCHOOL COUNSELOR Counselors who choose to work in a different type of environment with younger clients may choose a career in school counseling. The primary responsibility of the school counselor is to help students who may be experiencing educational, social, and/or personal problems. Traditionally, the main responsibility of the school counselor was limited to educational and behavioral problems. If, for example, a student was not meeting certain academic standards in class, a teacher would ask the school counselor to assess the student's strengths and weaknesses and make some recommendations regarding how that student could improve his or her academic performance in class. In other cases, if a student was exhibiting inappropriate behavior in class, the school counselor would be asked to interview the child and determine what was causing the inappropriate behavior. In this type of case the counselor could make some helpful suggestions to the child's teacher and/or parents and may decide to see the child for regular counseling sessions.

© Jeff Greenberg/Alamy

School counselor and student.

Today, the school counselor has taken on some new dimensions. It is not uncommon for the school counselor, in addition to her traditional responsibilities, to be asked to counsel a high school student taking drugs, or a junior high student having difficulty adjusting to his parents' recent divorce, or the elementary student coming to school with a black eye. Issues such as these are becoming more commonplace in our schools, and school counselors are taking a leadership role when dealing with these problems.

School counseling has become an extremely broad field of study. School counseling is no longer limited to working with teachers and parents. Today's counselor must not only have experience working with a host of diverse problems; she must also be able to work with a team of specialists. School counselors often consult with psychologists, social workers, physicians, and community leaders in their attempt to facilitate the academic and emotional development of their students.

In today's world it is essential for the school counselor to have the knowledge and expertise it takes to help a 15-year-old who is failing her courses, having difficulty adjusting to changes at home, and taking drugs as a way of dealing with her feelings. In this, and in other typical situations, the school counselor must know how to assess and evaluate the problem, have the skills to counsel the child, know how to use outside agencies, and, finally, have the ability to offer suggestions to other staff members and parents.

As we move closer to an interdisciplinary approach to mental health, it is essential that school counselors understand that they will be an important member of a team. And as a member of that team, they have a responsibility to help their clients reach their full potential in life. In addition to choosing what roles they will play in a client's life, counselors also have the opportunity to choose the type of setting in which they would like to work.

Work Settings for Counselors

Although some rehabilitation counselors are employed in hospitals, Veterans Administration counseling centers, sheltered workshops, prisons, and private practice, the majority work in state or local rehabilitation agencies. The Rehabilitation Service Administration, a federal agency in partnership with state vocational rehabilitation agencies, constitutes the major funding source for services to the disabled.

Some rehabilitation agencies have a large staff and extensive facilities and offer a wide variety of services. In some large cities the state rehabilitation agency may even have separate units for mentally challenged persons, former psychiatric patients, cardiac cases, and other specific disabilities. In rural areas, however, the agency may consist of little more than a counselor, a small office, and a car.

School counselors primarily work in public or private schools with children in grades K–12. School counselors are also found in colleges, prisons, alternative school programs, the military, private industry, and sometimes community outreach centers.

The population and type of problems the beginning counselor chooses to work with will decide where he works. For example, the counselor who wants to work with young children who have emotional and learning disabilities will want to consider working in a private or public elementary school. The counselor who wants to work with teenagers who are victims of substance abuse or domestic violence will want to look toward working in a high school or community outreach center. Opportunities in the high school environment also include career and vocational counseling, as well as designing and participating in various prevention and intervention programs.

Again, note that only some of the specialized areas within the counseling field have been chosen for discussion. Other specializations such as marriage and family counseling, gerontological counseling, career counseling, or pastoral counseling are also available career paths. More information regarding these specializations can be obtained by contacting the various professional organizations. A listing of these organizations appears at the end of this chapter.

TRAINING AND EDUCATION

Although not mandatory, it is strongly recommended that the student attend a two-year graduate program in rehabilitation or school counseling. (Recent statistics show that 6 of 10 counselors have a master's degree.) A few colleges offer introductory courses in rehabilitation and school counseling at the undergraduate level, but these courses are not intended to equip a student to become a rehabilitation or school counselor. With a B.A., a student might be able to get a job as a counselor trainee or employment interviewer. It is becoming more difficult to work up to full-fledged rehabilitation or school counseling jobs because more employers are requiring graduate training for these positions. Therefore, beginning counselors are often encouraged to look at other specialties such as employment counseling, career counseling, geriatric counseling, and marriage and family counseling.

Students should plan to attend a four-year college with a major in behavioral sciences, including courses such as abnormal psychology and sociology. Any course that provides some basic medical background and deals with various counseling issues will be particularly useful for students specializing in rehabilitation counseling. Some command of a second language, such as Spanish, is considered very useful in this field. At least a year before graduation, the student should write to the Office of Human Development Services for a recent list of schools receiving training grants from the federal government. Also, the student should request catalogs from all of the schools she might possibly be interested in attending. If financial help is needed to pursue training, the program director has information about student aid. Most graduate schools can arrange aid for students who meet certain requirements.

Before choosing one of the many programs available, students who are interested in counseling should contact the Council of Rehabilitation Education or the National Board of Certified Counselors for a list of approved programs of study.

GRADUATE TRAINING The two-year graduate programs include study of behavioral sciences and the cultural and psychological aspects of a variety of disabilities. There is also an emphasis on clinical skills such as interviewing and group leadership. The theories and techniques of counseling are taught in the classroom and then applied in supervised practice. During this internship, the student works with real clients and learns how to be supportive while at the same time encouraging the client to move toward greater self-reliance and self-fulfillment. The program is rounded out with practical information about community resources, and, in the case of rehabilitation counseling, some knowledge of physical and occupational therapy.

Once training is complete, the student should contact city, state, and federal agencies for information on various counseling positions and entry requirements.

LICENSES AND CERTIFICATION Rehabilitation counseling, once a field with little professional status, has greatly developed. As the profession matures, there will be increasing pressure for rigid requirements for employment, training, and certification. The Commission on Rehabilitation Counselor Certification has recommended a set of standards for certification. The certified rehabilitation counselor (CRC) must meet minimum standards of training and experience. Those with CRC status take part in a program of continuing education to ensure consistent competence. At present, certification is not generally required for employment in many states. One may assume that holding CRC status will help in both advancement and obtaining new positions. The history of new certification levels in any field shows that once they are established, the more motivated people in the field seek to qualify for them.

Licensing and certification for school counseling are up to the individual state and cities in which the school counselor plans to work. Most schools, however, do look favorably on those counselors who have been certified by the National Board of Certified Counselors (NBCC) as national certified school counselors (NCSCs). School counselors are also encouraged to apply for certification as a certified alcohol counselor (CAC), certified drug counselor (CDC), or certified alcohol and drug counselor (CADC). Counselors can also obtain certification in specialties such as geriatric counseling and marriage and family counseling.

ALCOHOL AND SUBSTANCE ABUSE COUNSELING

Alcohol and substance abuse is a part of our society. Problems associated with alcohol and substance abuse cut across all socioeconomic levels, gender, religion, professional status, and age. It has become so prevalent and commonplace that almost everyone in their lifetime will be touched by its consequences.

Alcohol and substance abuse is directly related to and contributes to a majority of other problems such as automobile accidents, domestic abuse, suicide, health issues, legal issues, and homicides, among others. Counselors in any setting can expect to see a number of their clients involved in one way or another with alcohol or substance abuse issues.

FUNCTIONS

Central to the role of counselor in this specialization are diagnostic interviews, accurate assessment, and treatment planning. Improper assessment and faulty diagnosis can lead counselors to ineffective treatment plans and inappropriate expectations for therapy; however, assessment and diagnosis of substance abuse is not an exact science. At present, there is no single medical or psychological test that can determine with absolute certainty that an individual is drug or alcohol dependent (Stevens & Smith, 2001). Therefore, it is essential that counselors become familiar with the various psychometric instruments most often used in the diagnosis and assessment of substance abuses. Several examples include the Michigan Alcoholism

Screening Test (MAST), the Drug Abuse Screening Test (DAST-20), and the CAGE Questionnaire. Each of these instruments is commonly administered to various populations in a variety of settings.

The primary function of the counselor is to provide help and develop specific treatment plans to meet the needs of the client. Each client's goals and treatment outcome are unique, although cessation of the substance abuse behavior is the central goal. Alcohol or substance abuse is only one part of an individual's life and must be viewed in the context of other life problems or events. Treatment cannot be solely focused on ending alcohol or substance use, but must also include rehabilitation in such areas as occupational functioning, psychological well-being, and social involvement (Lewis, Dana, & Blevens, 2002). The counselor will work with clients to establish short- and long-term goals. Goals will likely include the following:

- Attaining greater stability in personal and family relationships
- Developing coping mechanisms
- Improving problem-solving skills
- Learning to recognize feelings and express them appropriately
- Acquiring stress-reduction techniques
- Setting career goals
- Improving financial stability
- Cultivating social skills

The counselor will assess the client's needs and potential for further treatment and, if necessary, link the client to appropriate community and agency resources.

TREATMENT SETTINGS

Alcohol and substance abuse counselors are employed in a variety of treatment settings. A setting is an environment in which alcohol or substance abuse treatment services are provided. Treatment settings range from least restrictive to most restrictive. In this sense, restrictive settings refer to the type of social structure and physical environment provided for the client. For example, a locked-in patient ward or a hospital would be considered restrictive, whereas an outpatient substance abuse program located in the community would be considered less restrictive.

Clients need to be placed in the types of settings that match their diagnosis and the degree of severity of their illness for their treatment to be effective. The goal is to provide the least restrictive environment that offers the optimal type of services matching the needs of the client (Stevens & Smith, 2001). Detoxification centers, residential rehabilitation programs, day treatment programs, and therapeutic communities are some examples of treatment settings.

DETOXIFICATION CENTERS **Detoxification** refers to the complete withdrawal of addictive substances such as alcohol, **hallucinogens**, barbiturates, or heroin. Detoxification centers may be located within a hospital setting, or they may be freestanding clinics. The length of stay for the client is usually 1 to 2 weeks.

While detoxification is primarily a physiological and medical process, it also has various psychological and social implications for the client. Within the setting, counselors, as well as medical personnel, provide necessary services to stabilize the individual through the withdrawal process. Detoxification is usually considered the beginning of treatment with follow-up treatment in another setting such as individual therapy, counseling in an outpatient program, or a residential program.

RESIDENTIAL REHABILITATION PROGRAMS Residential rehabilitation programs were historically utilized for the treatment of alcoholism, but today these programs provide treatment for a full range of substance abuse behaviors. These programs may be found in hospitals, but the great majorities are in nonmedical settings. These programs emphasize the psychological and social issues related to addiction rather than the physiological or medical factor. Average client stays can range from four months to a year (Jaffe, 1995).

The purpose of these programs is to help clients gain a better understanding of their problems and help them to develop long-term recovery goals. These programs are often viewed as intermediate care facilities where clients reside within a structured environment and receive continuous treatment. Treatment most often includes individual, group, and family therapy. The goals of the program seek to provide clients with skills for maintaining abstinence, relapse management, and a greater understanding of personal issues underlying their addictions.

DAY TREATMENT PROGRAMS Day treatment programs offer a full range of substance abuse treatment services where clients may live at home or in another setting and attend these structured programs during the day. Programs such as these may be located in hospitals or freestanding settings. Services may include individual, group, or family therapy, as well as discussions focused on specific topics, self-help skills training, and family education groups. Normally, these types of programs offer services 5 days a week. An average length of stay for the client is 3 to 4 weeks (Frances, Wilson, & Wiegand, 1997).

THERAPEUTIC COMMUNITIES Therapeutic community programs are most commonly associated with drug addiction, particularly opiates. They are residential programs usually found in freestanding, nonmedical environments. The therapeutic community is often located in a somewhat isolated environment away from the stresses of the mainstream community. Average length of stay can be a year or longer (Lewis et al., 2002). Mutual help between and among clients, commitment to the treatment community, and a collective effort represent the core values within this type of environment.

Approaches to treatment may include individual and group therapy as well as an emphasis on peer counseling. Cohen (1985) states that therapeutic communities share the following common characteristics:

- An emphasis on personal responsibility
- Mutual assistance
- A system of rewards and punishments
- A structured and disciplined environment
- Self-examination and confession
- Separation from society
- Emphasis on work

OUTPATIENT COUNSELING PROGRAMS   Outpatient counseling services can be found in a variety of community settings. Many community mental health professionals, functioning in outpatient programs as well as in private practice, specialize in addictions counseling. Often, various types of social service agencies provide counseling services for the recovering individual. Outpatient services can be individualized to suit the schedule and the needs of the client. Treatment goals can be short- or long-term. The frequency of visits and participation in either individual or group counseling or both is based upon the client's individual treatment plan. Outpatient settings usually treat only those clients who can function independently, are motivated for treatment, and have a proven record of abstinence.

EMPLOYEE ASSISTANCE PROGRAMS   Many human resource departments within business or corporate settings offer various counseling programs within the workplace. The focus here is to provide a range of mental health services to aid in the job performance of its employees. Counselors in this setting focus primarily on assessment and referral of alcohol or substance abuse behavior rather than long-term treatment goals. Counselors will often link the client to appropriate treatment alternatives outside of the workplace, because they are not expected to provide long-term therapy within this setting. When they counsel employees, the goal is to provide temporary support and assistance so that the client can gain or regain self-responsibility and manage his or her problem situation (Lewis & Lewis, 1986).

TRAINING AND EDUCATION

The field of alcohol and substance abuse counseling has experienced an increased awareness of the need to more vigorously advance the professional development of its workforce. Counselors are being called on to deliver services that require an ever-increasing base of knowledge and skills. Many states have responded by establishing education credentialing standards needed to become a certified addictions counselor. This movement has sought to insure a minimum level of competency for those who meet the credentialing standards. Each state varies in its standards but most require specialized coursework and documented supervised field experience (an average of 300 clock hours) prior to passing a written exam.

Examples of the type of knowledge and skill areas most often required for credentialing purposes will likely include the following:

- Knowledge of the variety of theories and models of addiction
- Knowledge of the behavioral, psychological, physical, and social effects of chemical abuse
- Skill in recognizing an individual's potential for chemical abuse or dependence
- Skill in using the established diagnostic criteria for chemical abuse, among others
- Knowledge of medical and pharmaceutical resources in the treatment of chemical dependence
- Knowledge of prevention and treatment techniques
- Knowledge of ethical standards of practice

Individuals who wish to qualify for credentialing can obtain the necessary knowledge and supervised experience in several ways. Across the country there are many independent, for profit, state-approved training programs available that offer the necessary specialized coursework and will arrange for the required supervised fieldwork experience. Upon completion of this program one will be eligible to take the state credentialing exam for certification in the field. Another career path is to enroll in a college or university that offers a state-approved program containing the necessary coursework and supervised field experience. In this manner, individuals can receive college credit at the same time they are meeting eligibility requirements for credentialing.

An increasing number of colleges and universities are offering academic degrees at the baccalaureate and master's levels in substance abuse counseling. It is important to note that individuals can receive certification in this field with different levels of academic preparation. In addition there are private state-approved programs that provide necessary training. Many states simply require the minimum of a high school diploma as the educational level required to pursue certification. On the other hand, many established professionals in various allied health fields such as psychology, social work, and nursing may seek to become additionally certified in this specialization. Formal educational requirements and training requirements for certification vary from state to state. The individual seeking specific information should contact their state office of Alcoholism and Substance Abuse Services.

MENTAL HEALTH COUNSELING

Mental health counseling is a new and distinct profession within human services. Mental health counselors provide a full range of services to individuals, couples, families, adolescents, and children. They practice in a wide variety of settings including independent practice, hospitals, social service agencies, substance abuse treatment centers, and many more. They assess and diagnose mental illness, provide psychotherapy, perform treatment planning, provide substance abuse counseling, and crisis management.

TRAINING AND EDUCATION

In order to become a licensed mental health counselor, one needs to have earned a master's degree in counseling, or a closely related mental health discipline, such as psychology or social work. In addition, they need to have completed at least two years of post–master's level supervised clinical work and passed a state or national licensing exam. At the time of writing, 49 states and the District of Columbia license or certify mental health counselors for practice. Only California does not. The American Mental Health Counselors Association is the professional membership organization that represents the mental health counseling profession and has developed its own rigorous code of ethics.

SOCIAL WORK

Social work focuses on helping individuals realize their potential to live as fully and successfully as possible. The practice of social work addresses itself to the full range of human problems that confront individuals in almost all areas of life. Social workers help individuals, families, and groups cope with personal problems and also try to help shape society to be more sensitive and responsive to human needs. Social work emphasizes three basic methods in the helping process: casework, work with groups, and community organization. Further descriptions of these methods are given in Chapter 5.

Because human problems frequently overlap professional boundaries, social workers often function within the many allied human services fields such as health, criminal justice, community service, or education.

FUNCTIONS

As previously described, social workers function in a variety of settings with a variety of duties and responsibilities. Some examples of social work settings are mental health clinics, public and private hospitals, nursing homes, rehabilitation centers, health care agencies, public and private schools, social service agencies, correctional institutions, senior citizen centers, and colleges and universities. When referring to different kinds of social workers, one is usually referring to the setting in which the social worker is employed rather than to basic differences in training or social work practice (Schmolling et al., 1981).

Although individual functions and activities vary among social workers, there are common work activities. One such activity involves face-to-face contact with clients, or those receiving services; this personal contact is referred to as direct practice. Direct practice can be performed in most settings. For example, the social worker employed by a psychiatric facility (psychiatric social worker) might work with individuals or groups to help them solve their specific emotional problems. The social worker employed by a school system (school social worker) might counsel individual students concerning specific school or social problems. The social worker might work with families and different groups in a variety of settings. A series of therapeutic sessions might be used to help the family improve communication and solve specific family problems. The social worker employed by a community agency might function as a community organizer and have direct contact with many elements of the community. The social worker in this role usually helps individuals, groups, and organizations improve conditions and services in their community. Many social workers also maintain private practices in which they offer a range of psychotherapeutic services to individuals, families, or groups.

Many social workers provide supervision to other professional and nonprofessional staff. A more experienced social worker might supervise the work of others by providing advice about developing individual client treatment programs and alternative treatment approaches or by offering suggestions concerning how workers can improve their professional competence.

Administration, research, education, and consultation are also areas of concentration for social work practice. The amount and extent of administrative responsibility vary according to the experience and training of the individual as well as with the type of employment setting. For example, the duties of a senior administrator of an agency or facility might include designing specific programs of service, developing and monitoring budgets, supervising personnel, and evaluating the effectiveness of programs. In general, a senior administrator is responsible for making sure the various programs fulfill their stated missions or purposes.

A social worker in a rape crisis center.

A Day in the Life of a Social Worker

Gary is a licensed certified social worker with an M.S.W. degree. He works in a settlement house located in a poor neighborhood of a large city. Gary was promoted to the position of supervisor of the teenage division, serving boys and girls between the ages of 13 and 17. He supervises two licensed and certified social workers, a dozen generalist human services worker club and activity leaders, and three graduate students of social work. Gary and his staff work in the afternoons and evenings.

A typical day for Gary might look like this:

1:00–2:00 P.M.: Gary meets with his supervisor, the program director of the agency, to discuss the plans of the teenage division, problems and progress of the staff, teenagers and their groups, and budget issues. For example, Gary is concerned about one of his professional staff members who is having personal problems, affecting the quality of his work.

2:00–3:00 P.M.: Gary chairs the teen division staff meeting. The staff and Gary bring up problems they are having in their work with the teenagers. They explore ways of dealing with the problems and how they might improve the entire program. One of the things they talk about is the importance of sharing information on individuals and groups that are having behavior problems so that all the staff can pool their knowledge and be more effective in helping those with problems.

3:00–4:00 P.M.: Gary has a supervisory conference with one of the graduate social work students to discuss the student's efforts in helping his group members limit their aggressive behavior in the agency and on the street.

4:15–5:45 P.M.: Gary meets with a coed group of older teenagers who are dating and are concerned about intimacy, sexuality, and parenting.

7:00–8:00 P.M.: After dinner, Gary meets with a group of parents concerned about the possibility of their teenage children becoming drug users.

8:00–9:30 P.M.: Gary meets with the teenage council, made up of representatives of the teenage clubs in the agency, to listen to their plans, problems, and feelings about the teenage programs. Gary tries to help the council resolve its problems as well as develop and carry out its plans.

9:30–10:00 P.M.: Gary makes notes on the meetings of the groups he led directly. Gary is kept busy as supervisor of a large program. He enjoys working with teenagers, even though at times they are prone to impulsive behavior and resist any authority.

The social worker may work closely with various agencies, facilities, or branches of government as a consultant. For example, he may be requested by the court system to give a professional opinion or provide specific information regarding a client who is accused or convicted of a crime. Consultants may also help an agency develop or reorganize a particular department or program.

Many social workers engage in research or education activities. Experienced social workers can function as teachers or professors in social work training programs at colleges and universities. Social workers involved in research may investigate programs, develop theories, or gather data concerning who needs help, where and what type of help is needed, or how a service may be improved.

TRAINING AND EDUCATION

The National Association of Social Work, the governing body in this field, determines the criteria for the professional social worker. Currently, the minimum requirement set forth for acceptance as a professional social worker is satisfactory completion of a bachelor's degree program in social work and acceptance for membership status in the NASW. The college program must be accredited by the Council on Social Work Education.

Bachelor's degree programs in social work (B.S.W.) prepare individuals for entry-level positions in the field. Coursework stresses different aspects of the field, which might include the history of social work and the practice of social work in different settings. In addition to coursework emphasizing social work, the student is exposed to a broad liberal arts background. All accredited programs require the student to complete 300 hours of supervised fieldwork. The student is placed in a selected social work field site and, under the supervision of a professional social worker, gains experience working directly with clients.

Traditionally, the only route available to becoming a professional social worker has been to attain a master's degree in social work (M.S.W.). This requires completion of a graduate program (usually two years of full-time study). The recent development of B.S.W. programs means the M.S.W. is not the only route to social work; however, the master's degree is often necessary for advancement in the field. In fact, many professional social work agencies, institutions, and facilities set the M.S.W. as a requirement for supervisory positions.

One does not necessarily have to possess a B.S.W. degree to gain acceptance into an M.S.W. degree program. Individuals possessing undergraduate degrees in other fields, such as psychology or sociology, may be accepted for graduate study, provided they meet other criteria established by individual schools.

M.S.W. training requires two years of supervised fieldwork. The coursework, for the most part, pertains exclusively to the profession of social work, with many schools emphasizing the common elements of direct practice and increasing the student's knowledge of the field. M.S.W.-degree-granting programs, like all B.S.W. programs, must be accredited by the Council on Social Work Education.

In recent years, doctor of social work (D.S.W.) programs have been established in various colleges and universities. This doctoral-level program seems to attract social workers whose primary interests are in pursuing advanced level training in the areas of teaching, administration, and social policy. A D.S.W. program, like many other doctoral programs, usually takes an average of four years to complete and includes a program of required coursework and the successful completion of a doctoral dissertation.

PSYCHIATRY

Psychiatry is the medical specialty that investigates, diagnoses, and treats mental, emotional, or behavioral disorders. Psychiatrists are initially trained as medical doctors. As such, they are the only category of human services professionals legally authorized to prescribe medicine.

FUNCTIONS

Psychiatrists, because of their extensive training and preparation, generally occupy positions of elevated status within the human services field. This is reflected by their high salaries and the scope and depth of their responsibilities. For example, within a therapeutic team composed of other human services workers, the psychiatrist often functions in a leadership or supervisory capacity. The majority of psychiatrists maintain some type of private practice, but few contribute all their professional time to treating patients in a private setting. The psychiatrist may also work in a clinic or hospital setting, perform consultations, conduct research, teach, or occupy an administrative position. A psychiatrist's specific function varies according to the setting in which she is working, but all licensed psychiatrists can prescribe medication.

The psychiatrist who works in a psychiatric hospital is involved in many activities. For example, he normally carries a specified caseload of patients. As mentioned earlier, the psychiatrist is most likely also a member of a hospital team in which patient treatment plans are developed and monitored, and the possible discharge of improved patients is discussed. The psychiatrist is often called on to consult with other workers in the hospital concerning specific cases in which a psychiatric opinion is requested. Psychiatrists also act as expert consultants to courts, prisons, and other public and private institutions.

Many psychiatrists engage in work that is primarily administrative, such as directing a psychiatric hospital staff or program, directing a mental health clinic, or overseeing a governmental program such as the National Institute of Mental Health. The psychiatrist serving in this capacity is largely involved in the development of programs, budget preparation and monitoring, and staff management. As an administrator, the psychiatrist establishes the framework within which other professionals work.

Research and training are other possible career areas for the psychiatrist. Research opportunities and interests are varied, and the range of possible research subjects is enormous. For example, the psychiatrist might study the effect of a certain drug on a specific disorder, the impact that maternal stress has on a newborn child, or the effects of a new treatment approach. As a teacher, the psychiatrist may be found in medical schools, institutes, and colleges and universities.

An additional area of specialization now emerging for the psychiatrist is that of community psychiatry. Community psychiatry is based on the belief that the community should play a more vital role in preventing and treating mental illness. Prevention and treatment are accomplished by means of a variety of community programs. The psychiatrist involved in this field is most likely employed by a community mental health center. In this context, she might be involved with designing community programs such as residential centers for formerly institutionalized patients, working with schools to establish programs for troubled youth, or designing social programs for senior citizens.

TRAINING AND EDUCATION

The training of a psychiatrist is lengthy and demanding. Many individuals do not realize that preparation for such a career actually begins as early as high school with attainment of excellent grades. A solid aptitude for science and mathematics is necessary because a great deal of required coursework is in these areas. The aspiring psychiatrist usually majors in a premedical course of study in undergraduate school. A premed program frequently includes courses in inorganic and organic chemistry, physics, biology, and advanced mathematics.

Application to medical school is made after the student has been granted a bachelor's degree. Medical school is a highly demanding four-year course of study. During these four years, the student learns the practice of medicine and is considered a full-fledged physician upon graduation from medical school. Following medical school, the new physician must enroll in another course of study called the residency. It is during this four-year program that the physician specializes in the field of psychiatry. The training may take place in one of several settings, including university medical centers, accredited psychiatric hospitals, and psychiatric divisions of general hospitals. The coursework and practice are devoted exclusively to psychiatry, and it is within this framework that the physician sharpens his or her clinical skills.

The psychiatrist is able to take an examination certifying competence in the field upon satisfactory completion of his or her residency training. He is now awarded a certificate in the specialty of psychiatry until passing the national exam administered by the American Board of Psychiatry and Neurology. This certification is not a legal requirement for a physician to practice psychiatry, but the board-certified psychiatrist normally has more career opportunities and enjoys greater acceptance in the medical community.

LIFE COACHING

FUNCTIONS

Among some of the newer related human services occupations is the job of life coach. Although around since the 1970s, the field of life coaching has grown considerably over the past five years. Life coaches help people define their goals and remain motivated to reach their goals in careers, relationships, health, and personal growth. They help people to explore their options in life and support and affirm the positive and creative in each of their clients. Contrary to psychotherapy, coaching focuses on the future instead of the past and is strengths-based. Life coaching is highly pragmatic, utilizing weekly homework assignments and exercises in enabling a client to reach his or her goals.

The International Coaching Federation (ICF) states that it has more than 12,000 members worldwide (http://www.lifecoachinformationforum.com). Most life coaches are employed in a private practice setting, similar to that of a psychotherapist. Although some coach clients face to face, many life coaches work by telephone, allowing them the freedom and flexibility to work at home and to draw from a broad geographical client base. Other coaches work within a business consultation model, similar to that of an organizational psychologist and coach clients "on site" at the work place. Life coaching specialties include personal, health, relationship, spiritual, career, financial, business, and many others. Some life coaches specialize even further, identifying a niche population, such as "women experiencing career issues in mid-life" and marketing their services to such a specific group.

TRAINING AND EDUCATION

At this time, there are no formal educational requirements for life coaches. However, many life coaches come from related fields such as psychotherapy, while others are from such varied backgrounds as business, education, and the arts. For many, life coaching is a second career where they utilize their education and years of experience to enhance their ability to coach others.

Most life coaches do attend coach training. There are a number of coaching institutes throughout the United States and the world, including Coach University, Coaches Training Institute, Life Purpose Institute, and Life Coach Training. Some life coaches complete the requirements of their training programs and receive certification from their programs. Others do not.

The International Coaching Federation is the closest organization that coaching has for accreditation, although at present, there are no universally accepted credentials for coaches and no licensing requirements as well. Other accreditation organizations include The International Coach Federation, the International Association of Coaching, and the European Coaching Institute. The credentialing process is a rigorous one, which includes both written and oral examinations and many hours of supervised coaching. It is likely that over time the relatively young field of life coaching will develop a credentialing process that is uniform and universally accepted.

PROFESSIONAL ORGANIZATIONS

For more information about the career areas discussed in this chapter, you can write to any of the organizations listed on the following pages.

GENERALIST HUMAN SERVICES WORK

National Organization for Human Services
6240 Old Highway 5
Ste. B-5, #214
Woodstock, GA 30188
http://www.nationalhumanservices.org

Council for Standards in Human Services Education
Northern Essex Community College
Elliott Way
Haverhill, MA 01830-2399

National Association of Human Service Technologists
1127 Eleventh St., Main Floor
Sacramento, CA 95814

PHYSICAL THERAPY

American Physical Therapy Association
1111 North Fairfax Street
Alexandria, VA 22314-1488

CREATIVE ARTS THERAPY

American Art Therapy Association
427 E. Preston St.
Baltimore, MD 21202

American Dance Therapy Association
2000 Century Plaza, Suite 230
Columbia, MD 21044

American Music Therapy Association, Inc.
8455 Colesville Road, Suite 1000
Silver Spring, MD 20910

MARRIAGE AND FAMILY THERAPY

American Association for Marriage and Family Therapy
112 South Alfred St.
Alexandria, VA 22314

International Association of Marriage and the Family
c/o American Counseling Association
5999 Stevenson Ave.
Alexandria, VA 22311

MENTAL HEALTH

National Mental Health Association
2001 North Beauregard St., 12th Floor
Alexandria, VA 22311

OCCUPATIONAL THERAPY

American Occupational Therapy Association
6000 Executive Blvd.
Rockville, MD 20852

CLINICAL PSYCHOLOGY

American Psychological Association
P.O. Box 2710
Hyattsville, MD 20784-0710

COUNSELING

American Counseling Association
5999 Stevenson Ave.
Alexandria, VA 22304

American Mental Health Counselors Association
810 N. Fairfax Street Suite 304
Alexandria, VA 22314
800-326-2642

Council for Accreditation of Counseling
and Related Educational Programs
5999 Stevenson Ave.
Alexandria, VA 22304

ALCOHOL AND SUBSTANCE ABUSE COUNSELING

National Association of Alcohol and Drug Abuse Counselors
901 North Washington Street, Suite 600
Alexandria, VA 22314

SOCIAL WORK

Council on Social Work Education
1600 Duke St.
Alexandria, VA 22314-3421

National Association of Social Workers
750 First St. NE, Suite 700
Washington, DC 20002-4241

PSYCHIATRY

American Medical Association
51 N. State St.
Chicago, IL 60610

American Psychiatric Association
1700 Eighteenth St. NW
Washington, DC 20009

PSYCHOANALYSIS

American Psychoanalytic Association, Inc.
309 East 49th St.
New York, NY 10017

Additional Reading

Barton, W. E., & Sanborn, C. J. (Eds.). (1978). *Law and the mental health professions: Friction at the interface.* New York: International Universities Press.

Doweiko, H. E. (2002). *Concepts of chemical dependency* (5th ed.). Pacific Grove, CA: Brooks/Cole.

Duignan, P., & Rabushka, A. (Eds.). (1980). *The United States in the 1980s.* Stanford, CA: Hoover Institution.

Howatt, W. A. (2000). *The human services counseling toolbox.* Pacific Grove, CA: Brooks/Cole.

Human Resources Development Center. (1980). *Paraprofessionals in deinstitutionalized settings: A systematic study of effective use and potential.* New York: National Child Labor Committee.

Lewis, J. A., & Durant, A. (1995). *Addictions counseling: A multicultural perspective.* Teleclass Study Guide. University Park, IL: Governor's State University.

Meyers, R. J., & Smith, J. E. (1995). *Clinical guide to alcohol treatment: The community reinforcement approach.* New York: Guilford.

Monohan, J. (Ed.). (1976). *Community mental health and the criminal justice system.* Elmsford, NY: Pergamon.

Muchinsky, P. M. (1997). *Psychology applied to work* (5th ed.). Pacific Grove, CA: Brooks/Cole.

Posthuma, B. W. (1996). *Small groups in counseling and theory: Process and leadership* (2nd ed.). Boston: Allyn & Bacon.

Santrock, J. W. (1991). *The science of mind and behavior.* New York: Brown.

Sharf, R. S. (2000). *Theories of psychotherapy and counseling* (2nd ed.). Pacific Grove, CA: Brooks/Cole.

Van Wormer, K. (1995). *Alcoholism treatment: A social work perspective.* Chicago: Nelson Hall.

Van Wormer, K. (1997). *Social welfare: A world review.* Chicago: Nelson Hall.

Whitworth, L., Kimsey-House, K. and Sandahl, P. (2008). *Co-active coaching.* Mountainview, CA: Davies-Black.

References

American Physical Therapist Association. (2002). Membership survey. Retrieved July 28, 2002, from: www.apta.org/research/surveystat/pt_demo

Burger, W., & Youkeles, M. (2000). *The helping professions: A careers sourcebook.* Belmont, CA: Wadsworth.

Cohen, S. (1985). *The substance abuse problems: Vol. 2. New issues for the 1980s.* New York: Haworth Press.

Frances, R. J., Wilson, E., & Weigand, J. H. (1997). Hospital-based alcohol and drug treatment. In R. K. Schreter, S. S. Sharfstein, & C. A. Schreter (Eds.), *Managing care not dollars* (pp. 91–108). Washington, DC: American Psychiatric Press.

Jaffe, J. (Ed.). (1995). *Encyclopedia of drugs and alcohol* (1st ed., Vols. 1–4). London: Macmillan.

Lewis, J. A., Dana, R. Q., & Blevins, G. A. (2002). *Substance abuse counseling* (3rd ed.). Pacific Grove, CA: Brooks/Cole.

Lewis, J. A., & Lewis, M. D. (1986). *Counseling programs for employees in the workplace.* Pacific Grove, CA: Brooks/Cole.

Schmolling, P., Burger, W., & Youkeles, M. (1981). *Helping people: A guide to careers in mental health*. Upper Saddle River, NJ: Prentice Hall.

Sobey, F. (1969, November). Nonprofessional personnel in mental health programs: A summary report based on a study of projected support by the National Institute under contract #PL4366-967 (No. 5028). Washington, DC: National Clearinghouse for Mental Health Information.

Stevens, P., & Smith, R. L. (2001). *Substance abuse counseling: Theory and practice* (2nd ed.). Upper Saddle River, NJ: Prentice Hall.

CHAPTER CONTENTS

270

Critical-Thinking Activities

• Recognizing Deceptive Arguments

• Defining Poverty

• Evaluating Sources of Information

• Recognizing Stereotypes

Additional Reading

References

INTRODUCTION

Social policy, a topic usually discussed in advanced courses, is considered too complex by many to be included in introductory courses. However, social policy is a most appropriate topic for introductory courses in human services. Without an understanding of social policy, the human services worker cannot appreciate the significant impact it has on the design and delivery of services. This chapter will show some ways, direct and indirect, in which social policies affect the human services worker, as well as the consumer of human services. The first section of this chapter provides a general description of social policies with regard to what they do and whom they affect. The remaining sections focus on making and implementing social policies.

Throughout the chapter, examples show the relevance of social policy to the individual human services worker. In one section the role of the human services worker in introducing or initiating policy proposals is discussed. This is followed by a discussion of when and how the worker might influence the formulation or the final form of social policy. Finally, examples are given of how the human services worker affects existing policy and how policy affects the worker. The general focus is on the connections between social policy, the human services worker, and the delivery of human services. For you to understand these connections, a discussion of definitions, development, and implementation of social policies is required. Definitions of social policy are discussed first.

WHAT IS SOCIAL POLICY?

A policy, according to the *Random House Dictionary* (1978), is "a guiding principle or course of action adopted toward an objective or objectives." The word *social*, according to the same dictionary, refers to "the life, welfare, and relations of human beings in a community." Gil (1981) summed it up very well when he wrote that "social policies are a special type of policies, namely, policies which deliberately pertain to the quality of life and to the circumstances of living in society, and to intra-societal relationships among individuals, groups, and society as a whole" (p. 13).

Titmus (1974) makes it clear that the study of social policy includes an understanding of the political, social, and economic forces in society. Although such an understanding is beyond the scope of this text, it is certainly worth mentioning.

Titmus claims that "social policy can be seen as a positive instrument for change; as part of the whole political process" (p. 26). Another definition is that of Huttman (1981), who sees social policies as "plans of action and strategies for providing services" (p. 2). She adds that social policies have the goal of sound human relations. Another definition, dealing with a particular kind of social policy and one of more than passing interest to human services workers, namely social welfare policy, is the one given by Prigmore and Atherton (1979): "Social welfare policy is a generic term for the guidelines used for decision making on social welfare programs and issues" (p. 8).

Although there are many definitions of social policy, nearly all are characterized by certain aspects:

1. Social policy is problem oriented, that is, it seeks to improve an existing or anticipated condition.
2. Social policy is action oriented, that is, it outlines or describes programs that seek to effect change.
3. Social policy is focused on individuals or groups, such as the target populations described in Chapter 2.
4. Making social policy involves making choices regarding the kind and/or the extent of changes to be made.

Although there are many other aspects of social policy, for the purpose of this discussion, these four will be highlighted.

What impels a society, or a group or individuals for that matter, to expend hard-earned and limited resources to help those in need? Is such behavior a demonstration of democratic values or religious beliefs, or is it a matter of survival for society? There appears to be no single answer. In the past, all of these factors have played a significant part in the efforts to help those in need. Now let us take a brief look at past social policies.

SOCIAL POLICY IN THE PAST

Social policies in **preliterate societies** were not perceived as such. They were plans for survival that assured food, shelter, and protection against predators, hostile groups, and hostile environments. Physical survival was the goal. The success of the plans depended on the mutual efforts of the family or tribe. Without these efforts, individual survival was jeopardized.

As families or tribes settled in one place and developed villages of relative permanence, and as populations increased, more of the support necessary for survival was provided by the extended family. In these different circumstances, those without a family were still able to survive, if only marginally.

When communities grew even larger and more complex, organized religion began to provide aid to those who had no family or whose family did not have the resources or ability to provide the needed support. Caring for homeless children, the mentally ill, the physically disabled, and the hungry became a major concern of organized religion. These humanitarian efforts seemed to prevent the turmoil and conflict that often result from threats to survival. Keep in mind the important fact that efforts and plans designed to improve the lives of those in need also eliminated a threat to the existing **power structure**. Large numbers of hungry, desperate people were frequently candidates for riot and rebellion.

SOCIAL POLICY IN MODERN TIMES

The rapid and significant changes that typify modern industrial society caused organized religion, private organizations, and individuals to escalate their efforts to help those in need. The loosening of family bonds, the rise in crime, and the increase in the numbers of mentally ill, elderly poor, disabled, and those living in poverty made it impossible for existing institutions to provide the necessary support for the needy. Their values, plans, and policies did not undergo basic changes; they just did not have the resources in the form of funds, workers, or material to provide the needed help. It is important to note and remember that morality is supposedly a basis for social (welfare) policies, but this value is always in competition with other political and economic values (Beverly & McSweeney, 1987). An example of this competition is what occurred during the 1995–1996 struggle between conservatives and liberals while trying to agree on a bill to balance the U.S. budget by the year 2002. This issue is addressed later in more detail.

As problems grew in size, number, and complexity, governments had to step in to develop and implement programs to prevent starvation and to provide opportunities for individuals to gain resources for an adequate life. An underlying purpose was to reduce dissatisfaction with the existing political or power structure. Looking at the bottom line, it is obvious that social policies do not stem from humanitarian values alone but also derive from the desire of those in power to remain in control of society's wealth and resources. This is why governments focus on social policies that deal with basic needs such as food, shelter, clothing, and medical care.

Private human services agencies also deal with these kinds of problems, but on a much smaller scale. In addition, they focus on providing help in meeting higher-level needs, such as belonging and self-actualization (described in Chapter 1).

Some human services workers believe that the best way to help is through working for social and economic policies that provide for a more equitable distribution of economic resources and power among the haves and the have-nots. Two basic types of effort have been the mainstay of this approach to date. The first type is the government subsidy (that is, welfare), which attempts to provide decent food, shelter, clothing, and other necessities of life to families and individuals who, for one legitimate reason or another, cannot obtain or accept employment. The second type of effort is the attempt to provide training and jobs for those who are able to work so that they can pay for decent food, shelter, clothing, and the other necessities of life. So far, and for a variety of economic and social reasons, these efforts seem to satisfy few. Here, too, competition of social, economic, and political values takes place. For instance, unofficial, or unstated, economic policy required that a minimum of 5% remain unemployed to prevent inflation. That changed when the unemployment rate dropped to 4% in 2000 without causing inflation. Baker (1995) called these people "those vital paupers." Yet the struggle to develop policies aimed at creating jobs, job training, low-cost housing, and comprehensive welfare reform that are acceptable to policymakers and the public is still in progress. A substantial

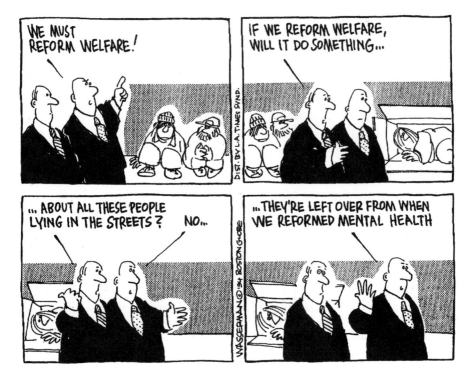

part of this struggle is based on the ambivalent feelings of much of the population as depicted in the comic strip.

Meanwhile, human services agencies, for the most part, try to help people adjust to the existing social and economic situation. Agencies, in effect, seek to maintain the **status quo**. Regardless of the basic motives behind social policy, it seems clear that unless and until more successful or satisfying programs are devised to provide for the basic needs of people who are unable to provide for themselves, much suffering, turmoil, and conflict will result.

PURPOSE AND TYPES OF SOCIAL POLICY

The purpose of social policy today, put simply, is to improve the lives of people. Most often, policy is designed to meet the needs of selected populations, such as those mentioned in Chapter 2. Accordingly, there are many different types of social policies. The most familiar type is social welfare policy, mentioned earlier. Other types of social policies include housing policy, mental health policy, child welfare policy, and unemployment policy.

Within each of these general categories are more specific plans or policies. For example, in the case of housing policy, the focus might be on housing for senior citizens or perhaps housing for the poor or for migrants. Mental health policy could include policies dealing with aftercare services, outpatient clinics, or prevention programs. So, although the common purpose of social policy is to meet needs, it is important to recognize that there are many kinds of policies that concern almost all human needs.

THE SCOPE OF SOCIAL POLICY

Social policy affects most, if not all, people in society, from the cradle to the grave. For instance, there are social policies that deal with abortion, birth control, child care, child abuse, teenage drinking, young adult drug abuse, marriage, and divorce, as well as policies relating to older adults and, yes, even death. The number and kinds of policies and programs implemented and/or proposed by federal, state, local, and private agencies are indeed impressive. It should be noted that because of the sheer number of programs implemented, one can find inconsistencies in purposes and goals.

Not only do social policies affect us throughout our life span, but they also affect us in almost every aspect of our daily existence. Most certainly, they influence us in regard to Maslow's hierarchy of needs described in Chapter 1. For example, policies dealing with basic physiological or survival needs, such as hunger and thirst, try to prevent malnutrition and eliminate starvation in our society. The food stamp program is one example of such a policy. Safety needs are met through housing and law enforcement policies, to name just a few. An example of a met safety need is a program to provide shelter for the homeless population in New York City. Other kinds of safety needs are met by programs focusing on automobile safety, food and drug monitoring, and public transportation. Programs dealing with these and other needs are often influenced by other kinds of government policies.

Other kinds of government policies include foreign policies, economic policies, educational policies, transportation policies, and defense policies. It is important to recognize that social policies are not the only policies focused on improving society in one way or another. For instance, economic policy also attempts to improve society. One might define economic policy as the decisions of those in power concerning money matters. The tax policy described in the first chapter provides a clear picture of how an economic policy might help improve society by creating new jobs. Miller (1985) believes that the goals of economic policies and social policies should be the same—essentially a pro-employment, pro-poor policy. He further claims that, although it might not be apparent, in actual practice "economic policy is about children and families, as much [as], if not more so than, is social policy" (p. 62).

This focus on improving conditions for children and families became very clear in the struggle over the effort to balance the budget by the year 2002. The attempt to achieve this goal centered on the size of the reduction in the rate of expenditures for helping children, poor families, senior citizens, and the disabled, among others; and methods for achieving that reduction. The claim of both conservative and liberal lawmakers and others was that the goal must be reached so that our children would not be burdened by having to pay off our debt if the budget were not balanced. The goal of balancing the budget by the year 2002 was not only reached but also surpassed: Significant surpluses in the billions of dollars were achieved with larger surpluses anticipated. Tax policies put into place by conservatives since then have virtually eliminated those surpluses. These funds—according to liberals as well as others—could be used for social programs, or at least not cut from social programs to pay for tax breaks for corporations and the wealthy.

When one considers all the different types of policies, at least two things become quite clear. First, there are a tremendous number of policies and programs dealing with issues in every aspect of our lives. Second, a need to decide the relative importance of different policies is obvious. Clearly, a hierarchy of importance in the various social policies exists. Some people claim that providing funds for the food stamp program is more important than providing outpatient services in the community for released mental health patients. Regardless of how one determines which policy is more important than the others, it is inevitable that policies are in competition with one another.

This competition is resolved sometimes through compromise and very often through the exercise of raw power. It is rare for everyone to agree on which social policies to promote or on which policies are more important. Gilbert and Specht (1974) state clearly that "different choice preferences will be registered by different policy planners, depending upon the values, theories, and assumptions given the most worth and credence" (p. 49). It's important for human services workers to know who these policy planners are. The concept that compromise and power provide the means for resolving the competition between social policies is discussed in the following sections.

MAKING SOCIAL POLICY

As indicated earlier, one aspect of social policy is that it is problem oriented; that is, it attempts to improve the lives of people who need help in meeting certain needs. If people were able to meet their needs through their own efforts, society would not need to develop programs to help them. It is when the needs cannot be met by the individual that social policies and programs are brought to bear.

As noted earlier, often very serious differences and controversies emerge regarding the kind and extent of help required, how the help should be provided, and who deserves or needs the help. How, then, is social policy made? Because it is problem oriented, it begins by focusing on unmet needs.

IDENTIFYING UNMET NEEDS

The first step in social policy formulation is to identify unmet needs. On the surface, this seems to be a very simple task. However, there are some problems even here. In this tremendously complex society of ours, there are so many unmet needs that it is difficult to select those that demand a social policy and program. Could there be, should there be, policies and programs that meet all the unmet needs of all the people all the time? If not, whose needs and which needs should we attempt to meet? Shall we be concerned about the unmet needs of the wealthy or concentrate on the needs of the poor? If, as most people might agree, we should focus primarily on survival, or **life-sustaining needs** such as adequate food, what direction shall we go from there? What about other unmet needs? Should we be concerned only about the unmet needs that are beyond the control of the individual, or should we also help people who contribute to their own difficulties because of ignorance, poor judgment, or foolishness? Other questions also need to be asked. Should social policies be based on the number of people affected? If so, how many people constitute the required number to merit the introduction of a policy and a program?

Another major problem in regard to policy formulation is that society is in a constant state of change. And not only is society changing, but individuals, workers, planners, and organizers are changing with society. Alinsky (1971) made the point that for an organizer "truth to him is relative and changing; everything to him is relative and changing" (p. 11). The same holds true for the social planner. Change is not an easy or comfortable process to undergo. It is a process that often, if not always, brings on conflict with oneself or with others, for people change at different rates and in different directions.

Another question comes to mind: In a changing society, don't social problems change without intervention? For example, not long ago, living together without marriage was not only frowned upon but actively discouraged and prohibited. Today, in an ever increasing number of states and jurisdictions, it is permissible and recognized legally in many ways for unmarried couples to live together. A changing society, in effect, has eliminated a problem and the affected social policies. After all, aren't some problems in society only temporary?

A final question remains—who answers all the questions just posed, and how?

WHO IDENTIFIES SOCIAL PROBLEMS?

Who has the power to determine which issue should be identified as a social problem requiring the formulation of a social policy for its resolution? Power in this context refers to the ability to influence, sway, and somehow persuade a significant number of individuals to recognize and declare that an unmet need is a social problem. According to Alinsky (1971), it is this kind of power that begets even greater power. In other words, the more people one influences, the more influence one can exert. Such power, however, is not easily come by. In fact, many professionals in the human services field, such as Meyer (1983), feel that "politicians control the power to define who is to be defined as poor, sick, unemployed, homeless, or uncared for" (p. 99). She goes on to state unequivocally that "the criteria used to define these conditions are political and economic." Setting poverty levels and acceptable unemployment rates is a political decision based mainly on economic factors. For instance, as indicated previously, prior to the year 2000, the minimally acceptable unemployment rate of 5% was generally recognized as the point at which a lower rate would lead to inflation.

Private citizens, regardless of their economic status, can also be instrumental in identifying social problems. A layperson may not identify the problem as Maslow or other professionals might, but that does not mean that the identification is any less accurate. In fact, problems are often more clearly and accurately identified by laypeople. For example, one of the largest and most powerful advocacy groups that focuses on the problems and needs of the mentally ill is the National Alliance for the Mentally Ill. It was started by two mothers. This is an excellent example of how a social problem was identified by private citizens. Usually, however, an individual's problem does not become identified as a social problem just because it is known by the individual. As indicated earlier, numbers are essential when trying to identify a problem as a social problem. In most instances, private individuals need the help of human services experts and others to have a problem recognized and established as a social problem.

The human services worker, when working with a population to meet certain needs, often becomes aware of other unmet needs. The objective of the worker is to try to obtain the appropriate services for those in need. Human services workers can be, and often are, instrumental in determining unmet needs and in influencing policy. To accomplish this task, the worker must assess the number of individuals involved and the kind and degree of disadvantage involved. Furthermore, the reasons for the lack of services must also be established, for they will have a direct bearing on decisions the worker must make in an attempt to rectify the problem.

The pressing need for human services workers to actively participate in the formulation of solving policy decisions was established many years ago. Harold McPheeters, one of the pioneers in the field of human services, affirms this need in his 1992 address to members of The National Organization for Human Services Education: "Thus, for self interest alone, human service educators must be involved in public policy and politics related to human services. In addition, human service educators, with their depth of understanding of human service needs and programs, should be involved in helping key government officials make better policy decisions for human services" (McPheeters, 2004, p. 259).

Among the many reasons for a lack of needed services in a community, four seem to be prevalent. First, there might not be any resources in the community (or anywhere else, for that matter) to provide the needed service. Second, the resources might be available in the community, but the individuals in need might not be aware of their existence. Third, even if the resources are known, those in need might not know how to use such resources. Fourth, those in need might not be eligible for the services; that is, they might not meet age, sex, racial, income-level, neighborhood, or other criteria determined by the providers of the services.

In the instances where a lack of knowledge about existing resources, or how to use such resources, is the major stumbling block, the worker's main role might be supplying needed information to those seeking the services. Where there are no resources, or where eligibility requirements are not met, the worker may be required to enter the realm of social policy to meet clients' needs.

Austin, Skelding, and Smith (1977) point out that risk is involved when fighting for the rights of those in need and when attempting to affect policy. Advocating, they rightly claim, often means speaking out, confronting agencies, and sometimes risking one's job. This raises the question that all human services workers ask themselves at one time or another: should you try to defend the consumer's right to service, or should you keep quiet and accept things as they are? Increasingly, human services workers and agencies are standing up and being counted when the need arises. Unfortunately, this does not occur as often as one might wish. Azarnoff and Seliger (1982) indicate clearly that "advocacy has risks which impede action for many staff people. Dismissal or loss of advancement must be considered as a realistic threat" (p. 209). Whether one is successful in obtaining the needed services is often a function of how one goes about the attempt. The worker must exercise tact, skill, and a judicious use of power to win support for new programs.

INITIATING SOCIAL POLICY

Once a problem has been identified as a social problem, the next step might be to inform others about the situation. Informing and educating other workers and clients are some of the necessary steps in the process. The human services worker, usually a member of an agency staff, might inform his or her coworkers and/or supervisor of an unmet need. The worker might then try to enlist their aid in an attempt to meet the need. By informing other clients, the worker makes others aware of the problem and thus may arouse additional interest and support. The hope and intent are to mobilize as much strength as possible in the effort to obtain the needed service.

This kind of approach often leads to contacts with individuals and groups who have the influence and resources to help resolve the problem. These influential people include politicians, professionals and their organizations, and government officials who might initiate an investigation in order to determine the breadth and depth of a particular problem. The results of the investigation are then examined and presented to those who make the decisions regarding programs and policies.

Policy advocacy is a form of advocacy that deals with social policy. Sherraden, Slosar, and Sherraden (2002) describe collaborative policy advocacy as a unique opportunity to develop a significant voice in constructing state social welfare policy. For a more detailed description of advocacy see Chapter 5. Here are some additional ways to influence policy decisions:

1. Learn about political candidates' positions on human services issues.
2. Actively work for political candidates whose positions you support.
3. Network with other human services providers to support/lobby for specific reform.
4. Participate in public hearings/discussions.
5. Learn your local legislative process.

Who Are the Decision Makers?

The decision makers include board members and/or executive directors of voluntary agencies; and local, county, state, or federal legislators. The majority of the local, county, and state legislators are, according to Lynn (1980), only "political amateurs." Even today, for the most part, they are part-time legislators. The board members of voluntary agencies are generally part-time volunteers. How these part-time "political amateurs" affect the human services and the making of social policies will be discussed in the section on pressure and lobbying.

Sometimes it is the client population together with human services workers who initiate the move toward the introduction of new programs and policies. Years ago on the Lower East Side of New York City, the director of a sectarian agency's summer sleep-away camp was approached by community residents of various faiths and races to discuss providing camping services for their children. The community members pointed out the desperate need for these services that could not be met by other agencies in the community. They also pointed out that many children attending the director's camp did not live in the community. The director agreed to accept some of the children in question. Within a relatively short time, the agency served all those who desired service, with the understanding that the agency would maintain its sectarian nature and goals. Community members in this example used their power to influence the policy of a community agency. Basically, agencies determine their policies, and the recipients of services have limited power to significantly change them.

Baker and Northman (1981) suggest that citizen involvement in policy determination is really a form of **redistribution of power** that previously did not allow for such sharing. Dobelstein (1980), on the other hand, asserts that "even in the present consumer-oriented society, those who are the principal recipients of welfare policies are rarely involved in making welfare decisions" (p. 30). Unfortunately, this too often holds true today. Although one might agree with the latter point of view, it may be a mistake to underestimate the power of the consumer and/or the human services worker to affect policy. It is sometimes impossible to tell in advance whether one will be able to shape programs and policies, and to what extent. Actually, one may be able to influence such decisions more than one might imagine. As far as the individual worker is concerned, opportunities for initiating programs occur more frequently on the local than on the state or federal levels. As an ancient Chinese philosopher was reported to have said, "A journey of a thousand miles starts with a single step."

FACTORS IN ESTABLISHING SOCIAL POLICY

Azarnoff and Seliger (1982) affirm that the president and Congress pass the laws and formulate policies based on their perceptions of what the public wants and needs. What is the basis of their perceptions? Often it is the result of research or the pressure of groups and individuals lobbying for or against a certain policy. These factors are looked at in this section.

An example of how laypeople affect social policy.

RESEARCH

The basic sources of information used in deciding policy are studies, surveys, experiments, reports, and records. Data gathered from these sources are examined, interpreted, discussed, and presented to the president and Congress for their consideration. This process also takes place on the state and local levels and involves the legislatures and executives of each **jurisdiction**. Voluntary agencies formulate their policies and programs in essentially the same manner. Data are gathered, examined, interpreted, discussed, and presented to the executive and board of directors for their decisions.

It is rare indeed that agencies, governmental or voluntary, devise policies or programs without going through this process. Sound research and its application, although not guarantees of perfect policies or programs, are extremely useful tools in developing sound social policies and programs.

The Community Mental Health Centers Act of 1963 is an excellent example of how research can be used to develop policies and programs to help the mentally ill. In this instance, it was a presidential commission that gathered data on the increasing numbers of people in need of mental health services. The lack of trained personnel, facilities, and resources was highlighted in the report of the commission. Congress adopted legislation that provided funds to set up community mental health centers throughout the country. In addition, funds for training more personnel were made available. The intent was to reduce the number of people needing long-term hospitalization. Much was accomplished, but, as with almost any complex problem, solutions were only partially achieved and other problems were created.

Unfortunately, the research in this instance did not provide enough data to avoid some of the problems that developed. Some problems are not the fault of the research. In too many instances, the information asked for is limited to specific and existing problems rather than also focusing on predicting and preventing future problems.

Research, surveys, and studies have been devised to prove a point rather than to gather data and let the chips fall where they may. Other situations have occurred in which the individuals conducting the research (often human services workers themselves) have had little knowledge of acceptable methods of gathering and interpreting valid and reliable data. **Anecdotal records** and similarly limited types of studies have all too frequently been the basis for program policy changes. These approaches are, at best, questionable.

There have also been instances when agencies have ignored or discarded data that did not enhance the image or viability of the agency. Capoccia and Googins (1982) suggest that in an environment of limited choice of policy decisions or limited funding, mobilization of interested groups and the exercise of power become more important than research in assessing needs. They add that the more limited the choices, the less the chances are for determining need through an objective, or rational, process. Social policy decisions may be determined, not by objective analysis of the issues, but rather by emotional and general descriptions, all too frequently provided by the media (Miringoff & Opdyke, 1986). The media's effect on social policy will be examined shortly.

The results of biased or inadequate research have sometimes led to poorly planned policies and programs. Such policies might be considered politically practical, but they might also be useless and destructive to those they are intended to serve. Witness the deinstitutionalization policy and program for the mentally disabled. Mechanic (1980) states that "large numbers of mental patients were released from hospitals into the community without adequate preparation, appropriate services, or consideration of the social costs" (p. 83). He adds, significantly, that whereas the thrust for such programs came from many sources, a major one was the economic pressures on state governments. He points out that the programs were generally supported by mental health professionals who held overly optimistic views of anticipated results. What did result in many instances was patient "dumping," leading to community fears and resistance, along with victimization of patients by the unscrupulous as a result of the lack of support services. More adequate research regarding the needed criteria for facilities for patients, the number of patients involved, and the level of support services might have led to more successful programs.

PRESSURE AND LOBBYING

When studying the development of social policies on the federal level, one becomes awed by the pressure brought to bear on Congress and the president to influence the development and purposes of social policies and programs before a final decision is made. Clymer (1995) describes the growth in the number of **lobbyists**. He tells us that "about 6,000 lobbyists are currently registered; perhaps three to ten times as many will now have to [register]" (p. 36). He also points out that the definition of lobbyists has been expanded from its current narrow range of those who spend the majority of their time with members of Congress to include those part-timers who also work with the staff of Congress or executive branch agencies. When one adds the countless individuals and groups, including many human services worker organizations, that march, testify, send letters, make calls, and otherwise attempt to influence the lawmakers, it becomes clear that there are awesome pressures on Congress and the president.

The question, then, is how does all this constant pressure affect our policymakers' perceptions and decisions regarding policies and programs? The issue is no longer the number of lobbyists, but rather who the lobbyists are, who and what they are lobbying for, and the amount of funds needed to influence legislators and thus legislation. Birnbaum (2000) claims that almost anyone who works in Washington sooner or later becomes aware that money plays too large a role in politics. A member of the U.S. House of Representatives emphasized the point when she exclaimed that money is absolutely essential to what happens (Lewis, 1998). An indirect yet extremely effective form of lobbying is the use of campaign funds or finances. It is apparent that since the 1990s the great increase in election campaign contributions by corporations and very wealthy individuals to political parties and politicians has had the most significant influence on legislation.

Corporate welfare, a term referring to the billions of dollars given to corporations through legislation such as tax abatement, subsidies of all kinds, and tax loopholes, has a definite effect on legislation. An example is the farm subsidy legislation passed in the year 2000 that gave $190 billion, primarily to corporate farmers. It makes little or no difference whether it is on state or local levels; the general outcome is that the decision makers give those with the most clout (money) and political

Antiwar demonstration.

contacts the majority of what they want. Clearly, regardless of what decisions are made, not everyone will be happy.

One of the problems in trying to change policy on the state and local levels is that most state and local lawmakers are generally overworked and underpaid. Most state and local legislative bodies are in session on a part-time basis. Some meet only once every two years and have a small part-time staff. Because much social-policy legislation may be new and unfamiliar to them, they generally listen to those who can have the greatest influence on their political lives. Consequently, they are very responsive to the power groups in their local and state communities. These groups include local corporations, business people, developers, unions, religious groups, homeowners, and the media, among other interest groups. According to Dye (1987), public opinion has a limited effect on the decision makers. It is even truer today. Most ordinary people do not write or talk to their legislators. Unfortunately, most eligible voters do not even vote, thus allowing powerful lobbyists of large corporations and those with huge sums of money to become much more effective.

Human services agencies and their constituents, usually the poor and minority groups who do not vote in large numbers, most often do not compete effectively with the power of the groups mentioned earlier. Human services agencies have the best chance of being heard when an issue raises a great deal of compassion and costs very little to resolve. In difficult economic times, such as recessions, human services agencies are among the first to feel the economic pinch. Fund-raising efforts of human services agencies and foundation gifts cannot make up for cuts. It is important to note that government money is the major source of income for nonprofit human services agencies. However, there have been times—as in 1995—when the economy was quite strong and still funds for social programs and agencies were significantly cut.

The boards of directors of nonprofit human services agencies consist primarily of affluent, well-meaning, dedicated, and frequently knowledgeable part-time volunteers whose major functions are to raise money and determine policies for their own organizations. Their familiarity with and knowledge of how best to serve their **constituents** are secondhand and quite limited, coming most often from the administrators they hire and from the media. Their major concern is raising funds, for it is money that significantly affects the policies they develop and the programs they provide.

THE MEDIA

Few can question that "Americans perceive the media as quite powerful" (Davis, 2001, p. 3). When we read newspapers and magazines, watch TV, or listen to the radio, we may not always be fully aware of attempts to influence our views of all types of issues and policies, including social policies. Many critics and members of the general public "believe that the press, meaning reporters, editors and others connected with journalism, express some of their ideologies and biases in their work" (Davis). This may be done by selecting which stories to highlight and by "slanting" them in either a liberal or a conservative direction. When politicians or lobbyists discuss the details of policy matters in the media, we frequently do not take sides or think that the issues are important enough to affect us. However, when the media cover issues that obviously affect a large portion of a population directly (regarding their health and pocketbook), people listen and policies are often changed. An example of this phenomenon was the coverage of the 1993–1994 struggle over the health care issue.

A more recent example of how media influences policy is the struggle to "end welfare as we know it," which was discussed in Chapter 1. With regard to the ending of welfare as we know it, however, other questions come to mind. Who, for example, are the "we"? How much do we know about all, or any, welfare programs and what they do, whom they serve, and what criteria are used? Do we know the strengths as well as the weaknesses of specific programs? One wonders how many among politicians and human services workers, much less the general population, really know the welfare system well enough to ethically support, much less vote to change, something so complex.

Politicians know how important it is to use the media to achieve their goals. The media, with its own interests in governmental policies and legislation, knows how important the support of politicians is in achieving its goals. "While direct causal relationships between these media and political change cannot yet be demonstrated ... it is difficult to avoid the strong inference that this is probably the case" (Kahan, 1999, ix). Lobbyists, all types of organizations, and all types of groups and individuals know how important it is to use the media to achieve their goals. Remember, it is only through the media that the general population becomes aware and/or somewhat knowledgeable of issues and makes its opinions known. Polls run by or reported by the media are also used to sway the opinions and

"Welcome to 'All About the Media,' where members of the media discuss the role of the media in media coverage of the media."

votes of people. It is important to know who took the surveys, what questions were asked, who interpreted the raw data, and so on before accepting the polls as gospel.

One must also be careful, however, when listening to or reading about issues. Awareness of the sources of information, the accuracy of the material, and the pros and cons of the issues should be kept in mind. Politicians, for instance, will frequently make general statements that are, at best, exaggerated and, at worst, false to sway opinions. Almost every day in the battles over the budget, welfare, and medical coverage, politicians use such phrases as "the American people want" or "the American people believe." One must remember that in 2000 a little over one-third of eligible voters voted. Of that group, a little over one-half decided who was to represent them. Yet on the national level, politicians claim "the American people want" this, that, and so forth. These kinds of statements, often used by politicians, their supporters, and lobbyists, are examples of techniques described in the critical-thinking activity "Recognizing Deceptive Arguments," at the end of this chapter.

Human services workers need to learn how to use the media to help gain support for their work and point of view. The amount and kind of support they obtain will be in large measure dependent on their ability and skill in the use of the media.

Furthermore, to be effective advocates and helpers, human services workers must be able to distinguish fact from opinion and provable statements from unprovable statements and recognize deceptive arguments. They must also be able to recognize stereotypes, evaluate sources of information, and distinguish between bias and reason if they are to be effective workers and professionals. To help develop these skills, critical-thinking activities taken from those used and described in detail in the Opposing Viewpoints and Current Controversies series of Greenhaven Press (San Diego, CA) can be very useful. Examples of these activities are at the end of this chapter.

OPPOSITION

Opposition refers to efforts to defeat proposed policies or to changes in existing policies or programs. These efforts play an important role in determining the final form of accepted policies and programs. Sometimes there is little change in the original proposal as a result of opposition; other times, one might have some trouble recognizing the original idea. The degree of transformation is related to the strength of the opposition and the nature of the compromise reached by the opposing groups. Compromises might be in philosophy, funding, resources, politics, or a combination of these factors. For example, the struggle by conservatives and some fiscally conservative liberals to end welfare as we know it has engendered a great deal of opposition by most liberals. Although welfare reform legislation has finally been enacted, it required significant compromises on the part of Congress and the Clinton administration. It did not, however, fully satisfy conservatives or liberals.

Opposition is frequently based not on moral, political, or philosophical issues but rather on self-serving economic factors. The survival of an agency or program has been known to be a major obstacle to new policies or policy changes. Jobs of human services workers are often at stake, and this factor, as difficult as it might be to acknowledge, has been known to be a major obstacle to eliminating or changing an obsolete or ineffective agency or program.

IMPLEMENTATION OF SOCIAL POLICY

Once a policy has been decided on, regardless of its purpose or limits, a program must be devised and carried out if the policy is to have any impact. Remember, a policy is a plan or guide: it tells us what to do, not how to do it. One could approach the policy in many ways. Some agencies might focus on providing information and education through the media. Yet another approach would be to attempt to discover the causes of a problem through research and then develop a program to deal with those causes. In an actual program, any one or a combination of these and many other approaches is considered an effort to implement a policy.

The discussion that follows provides some idea of what is involved in developing programs to implement social policy. It includes additional insights regarding opportunities for human services workers to affect programs and policies. The purpose is to introduce you to some of the factors at work in the **implementation** of social policy.

One of the many nonprofessional groups that affect social policy through their representatives and by testifying before legislative bodies.

FUNDING

"Money makes the world go 'round!" "Money talks!" "Money isn't everything!" There seems to be some truth in all those comments. With regard to social policies, it is almost certain that the availability of funds determines whether a policy is established, or implemented. Money also determines the degree to which a policy is implemented. For instance, the policy of most states is to provide adequate treatment and living facilities for patients in mental hospitals. In practice, however, there are too many institutions that provide little or no treatment along with minimal custodial care. Unfortunately, the same holds true with regard to many institutions serving the aged, the mentally challenged, and juvenile offenders. In most situations, the excuse given for these conditions is lack of funds. This is very frequently the case. What is also true, however, is that how available funds are used is a factor in determining the degree to which a policy is implemented and the degree of success of a program. On the other hand, it should be understood that although ample funds do not guarantee the effective implementation of policies, insufficient funds do guarantee ineffective implementation of policies.

Another problem of funding social policies occurs when a policy is decided on and no funds are appropriated to carry out the policy. In some cases, monies are appropriated but are not permitted to be spent (Fill, 1974). Federal, state, and local governments have often mandated programs without providing sufficient funds to implement them efficiently. Obviously, funds are vital to the process of implementing policy.

It is clear that funding influences policies and policies influence funding. It is also clear that human services workers are seriously affected in their efforts to carry out policies depending on the level of funding available to them.

INTERPRETATION OF POLICY

A second factor that has a significant impact on policy implementation is the way policy is interpreted. Interpreting policy means more than just explaining policy. According to the *Random House Dictionary* (1978), interpretation is "construing or understanding in a particular way." It involves an understanding or conception of another's words or deeds. The question here, of course, is how social policies are interpreted. It is useful, at this point, to make a distinction between general policy and operational policy. For example, the elimination of poverty is a general policy. How one goes about eliminating poverty—for instance, through welfare programs or government work programs—involves operational policy (Huttman, 1981). In other words, a general policy states a broad objective, whereas operational policy is concerned with the methods and procedures used to meet the objective.

The interpretation of general policies is generally without controversy. Few would argue with the policy of trying to eliminate poverty. Problems arise, however, on the operational level when it becomes necessary to determine the income at which a person or family is considered to be living in poverty. Further questions then arise. To what extent should people be helped, under what conditions, and for how long? Different states, jurisdictions, and agencies have different criteria for resolving such questions.

It is apparent that policies can be significantly affected when interpreted differently by those who determine policy and those who implement policy. To complicate matters, both the target population and the general public also become involved in interpreting policy. When conflicts arise around the interpretation of policy that cannot be resolved by the parties involved, the courts are sometimes called on to settle the issues.

WHO IMPLEMENTS POLICY?

A third significant factor in implementing policies is the question of who implements them. Human services workers are usually the ones who actually deliver or provide the services to those in need. These workers include those described in Chapter 6 and others, such as vocational counselors, community developers, and the police. Human services workers are instrumental in the successful implementation of policies and programs.

The degree of success of these policies and programs is determined by the amount and kind of training the worker has received. Some time ago, a conference of human services workers and researchers concerned with providing psychotherapeutic services to minority groups was offered. It became very clear, in the papers presented and the discussions that followed, that the training of those providing services to minority populations was not adequate to assure the success of such programs. A lack of sensitivity and a lack of knowledge regarding the needs of minority group members were major obstacles to successful interventions.

It is clear that training of human services workers, regardless of the type or level of service, is critical to the successful implementation of programs and policies. The increasing trend toward registration, licensing, and testing of human services workers attests to the importance of training and competence in the view of consumers of human services and employers of human services workers. Improved competency and training not only increase the chances of successful implementation of programs but also increase the abilities and credibility of workers in their efforts to identify people's needs and to develop new social policies or improve old ones.

CRITICAL-THINKING ACTIVITIES[1]

RECOGNIZING DECEPTIVE ARGUMENTS

People who feel strongly about an issue use many techniques to persuade others to agree with them. Some of these techniques appeal to the intellect, some to the emotions. Many of them distract the reader or listener from the real issues.

A few common examples of argumentation tactics are listed below. Most of them can be used either to advance an argument in an honest, reasonable way or to deceive or distract from the real issues. It is important for a critical reader to recognize these tactics in order to rationally evaluate an author's ideas.

1. *Bandwagon*—the idea that "everybody" does this or believes this.
2. *Categorical statements*—stating something in a way that implies there can be no argument or disagreement on the issue.
3. *Personal attack*—criticizing an opponent personally instead of rationally debating his or her ideas.
4. *Testimonial*—quoting or paraphrasing an authority or celebrity to support one's own viewpoint.

The following activity helps you sharpen your skills in recognizing deceptive reasoning. The statements below are derived from the viewpoints in this chapter. *Beside each one, mark the letter of the type of deceptive appeal being used. More than one type of tactic may be applicable. If you believe the statement is not any of the listed appeals, write N.*

1. The Supreme Court has a greater obligation to protect the rights of victims than those of criminals.
2. It is clear to every intelligent person that the Eighth Amendment to the U.S. Constitution, protection against cruel and unusual punishment, does not bar the use of victim impact statements.
3. Victim reforms will destroy the constitutional rights of the accused.
4. The conservative, prejudiced Supreme Court judges are too stupid to recognize the rights of the accused.
5. Every decent lawyer believes the harm a victim suffered because of a defendant should be considered when determining punishment.
6. Victims have absolutely no rights at all.

---

[1]These critical-thinking activities are taken from the Opposing Viewpoints Series, copyright © Greenhaven Press Inc; reprinted with permission.

7. Everyone agrees that victim reforms are false promises made by legislators seeking to please voters worried about crime.

8. The victims' rights movement developed because victims of crime felt they had no rights in the criminal justice system.

9. Thurgood Marshall, a pro-criminal, bleeding-heart liberal, considers the harm a victim suffered irrelevant in a criminal trial.

10. As Justice John Paul Stevens correctly points out, the defendant should have more rights than the state in a criminal trial.

11. Victim impact statements force juries to base their decisions on emotion rather than on objective facts.

12. As Deborah Kelly, chair of the American Bar Association's Victims' Committee, accurately concludes, victims' satisfaction with the criminal justice system depends more on how they were treated than how severely their assailants were punished.

13. Everyone knows that judges let criminals off too easily.

14. Intelligent people agree that victims' rights deny the accused the right to a fair and impartial trial.

15. As the Chief Justice of the U.S. Supreme Court, William H. Rehnquist, states, there is no constitutional rule that excludes victim impact statements.

DEFINING POVERTY

Much of the debate over how serious poverty is in America revolves around how poverty is defined. There are two general methods of defining poverty. One is to use a relative definition—measuring the wealth and income of a certain population, and finding out who has the least relative to the others. This process does have limitations. For instance, most people would argue that the men in the foreground of the cartoon are still poor, even if there are people worse off than they are. Conversely, in a country populated by millionaires, a person with only a half-million dollars would be considered poor.

Another method of defining and measuring poverty is to use an absolute definition. This method sets a minimum standard of income and/or wealth, regardless of how many people are above or below the standard. A major drawback to absolute definitions is that they don't consider other factors, like differences in cost of living. The couple making $7,132 a year will live more comfortably in rural Iowa than in New York City.

In this exercise you will create your own definition of poverty. Consider again the men in the cartoon on the following page. Most people would consider poor a person who does not live in some sort of home or shelter. By this definition the men in the cartoon are poor.

But most people would not consider poor a person who couldn't afford a cabin cruiser. Most people view cabin cruisers as luxuries, not one of life's essentials. What does it mean to be poor?

STEP 1

Working in small groups, discuss the items listed below. Mark E for essential items—things you believe people must have. Mark N for nonessential items—items that are luxuries a person could live without.

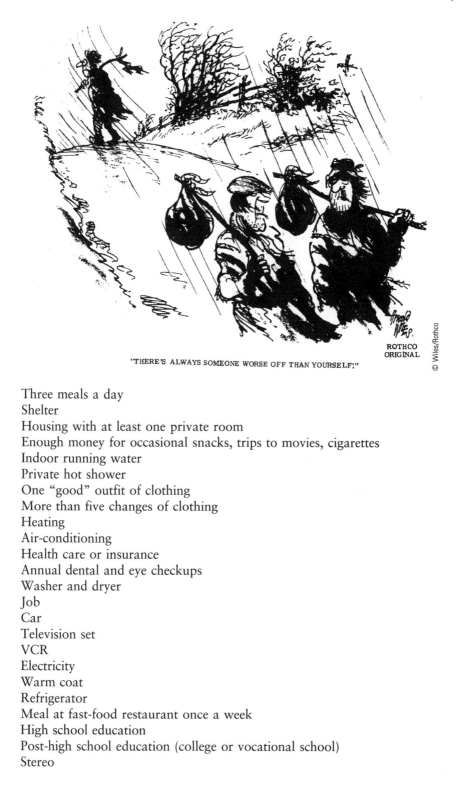

"THERE'S ALWAYS SOMEONE WORSE OFF THAN YOURSELF!"

ROTHCO
ORIGINAL

© Wiles/Rothco

Three meals a day
Shelter
Housing with at least one private room
Enough money for occasional snacks, trips to movies, cigarettes
Indoor running water
Private hot shower
One "good" outfit of clothing
More than five changes of clothing
Heating
Air-conditioning
Health care or insurance
Annual dental and eye checkups
Washer and dryer
Job
Car
Television set
VCR
Electricity
Warm coat
Refrigerator
Meal at fast-food restaurant once a week
High school education
Post-high school education (college or vocational school)
Stereo

Radio
Telephone
Personal computer

If necessary, add other items you believe are essential.

STEP 2

Discuss the following questions with your class or group.

1. Examine your list of essential items. Which ones are actually essential to survival, and which are essential to a "humane" existence—a level above bare survival?
2. Write an item-based definition of poverty: "A person suffers from poverty if he or she lacks these items: _____, _____, _____, ..."
3. How absolute is your group's definition? If a person lacked only one of your essentials, is he or she still poor? If a person has several nonessentials but lacks some essentials, is he or she still poor?
4. Do you think your definition of poverty is better or worse than the two described in the introduction of this activity? Why? What drawbacks does your definition have?

EVALUATING SOURCES OF INFORMATION

A critical thinker must always question sources of information. Historians, for example, distinguish between primary sources ("firsthand" or eyewitness account from personal letters, documents, or speeches, etc.) and secondary sources (a "secondhand" account usually based upon a firsthand account and possibly appearing in a newspaper or encyclopedia). A published diary of a welfare mother is an example of a primary source. A book review of the mother's diary is an example of a secondary source.

Interpretation and/or point of view also play a role when dealing with primary and secondary sources. For example, the welfare mother might strongly believe that any form of welfare is degrading. Her personal experience affects her view of the welfare system. The secondary source, too, should be questioned as to interpretation or underlying motive. The book reviewer might have strong feelings regarding the necessity of welfare and criticize the diary because of his personal bias. It is up to the researcher to keep in mind the potential biases of his/her sources.

This activity is designed to test your skill in evaluating sources of information. Imagine you are writing a report to the governor on how to reform the state welfare system. You decide to include an equal number of primary and secondary sources. Listed below are a number of sources that may be useful for your report. Carefully evaluate each of them. Then, place a "P" next to those descriptions you believe are primary sources. Second, rank the primary sources assigning the number "(1)" to what appears to be the most accurate primary source, the number "(2)" to the next most accurate, and so on until the ranking is finished. Repeat the entire procedure, this time placing an "S" next to the descriptions you feel would serve as secondary sources and then ranking them.

If you are doing this activity as a member of a class or group, compare your answers with those of other class or group members. Be able to defend your answers. You may discover that others will come to different conclusions than you. Listening to the reasons others present for their answers may give you valuable insights in evaluating sources of information.

P OR S   RANK IN
                                                                      IMPORTANCE

_____ 1.   copies of the forms people fill out to
              receive welfare   _____

_____ 2.   interviews with children growing up on
              welfare   _____

_____ 3.   a book on poor Americans and welfare
              programs from 1900 to 1950   _____

_____ 4.   an article by a social scientist who
              compares state-by-state welfare
              benefits and poverty statistics   _____

_____ 5.   a local television news feature about a
              pastor who works with poor families in
              her neighborhood   _____

_____ 6.   a statewide poll on how people feel
              about welfare   _____

_____ 7.   a novel based on the author's
              childhood growing up under welfare   _____

_____ 8.   a magazine article about a company
              that hires people on welfare   _____

_____ 9.   a speech by a U.S. senator on welfare
              cheats   _____

_____ 10.   a pamphlet published by a conservative
              organization titled "How Welfare
              Exploits the Poor"   _____

_____ 11.   a pamphlet published by a leftist
              organization titled "How Welfare
              Exploits the Poor"   _____

_____ 12.   welfare mothers speaking as guests on
              the Oprah Winfrey show   _____

RECOGNIZING STEREOTYPES

A **stereotype** is an oversimplified or exaggerated description of people or things. Stereotyping can be favorable. However, most stereotyping tends to be highly uncomplimentary, and, at times, degrading.

Stereotyping grows out of our prejudices. When we stereotype someone, we are prejudging him or her. Consider the following example: Mr. Smith believes all poor people are lazy. Whenever he sees a homeless person on the street or on television, he asks himself, "Why won't that person look for a job?" He disregards any other possible reason why that person is homeless. Why? He has prejudged all poor people and will keep his stereotype consistent with his prejudice.

... Consider [the following statements] carefully. Mark S for any statement that is an example of stereotyping. Mark N for any statement that is not an example of stereotyping. Mark U if you are undecided about any statement.

If you are doing this activity as a member of a class or group, compare your answers with those of other class or group members. Be able to defend your answers. You may discover that others will come to different conclusions than you. Listening to the reasons others present for their answers may give you valuable insights in recognizing stereotypes.

S = stereotype; N = not a stereotype; U = undecided

1. Many Jews have succeeded economically despite anti-Semitism.
2. Jews have a way with money.
3. Two out of three poor adults are women.
4. Most people on welfare are lazy.
5. Many black youths do not have jobs.
6. Many black youths don't want to work.
7. Divorced men are chauvinists who refuse to pay child support.
8. Mothers do not make good workers.
9. Many poor people live in single-parent households.
10. Most Hispanics are illegal immigrants.
11. Women are more likely than men to quit work to raise their children.
12. All white businessmen discriminate against women and minorities.
13. In cities across the country, millions of blacks live in poverty.
14. Many women have babies in order to go on welfare.
15. All people who want to cut welfare are racists.
16. The poor are different from the rest of us.
17. Most feminists are social radicals.
18. The median income of Japanese Americans is higher than that of Anglo-Saxons.

ADDITIONAL READING

Borjesson, K. (Ed.). (2002). *Into the buzzsaw: Leading journalists expose the myth of a free press*. Amherst, NY: Prometheus Books.
Davis, R. (1994). *Politics and the media*. Englewood Cliffs, NJ: Prentice Hall.
Jansson, B. S. (1994). *Social policy: From theory to policy practice*. Pacific Grove, CA: Brooks/Cole.
Nader, R. (2002). *Crashing the party: Taking on the corporate government in an age of surrender*. New York: Thomas Dunne Books.

REFERENCES

Alinsky, S. D. (1971). *Rules for radicals*. New York: Vintage.
Austin, M. J., Skelding, A. H., & Smith, P. L. (1977). *Delivering human services: An introductory programmed text*. New York: Harper & Row.

Azarnoff, R. S., & Seliger, J. S. (1982). *Delivering human services*. Upper Saddle River, NJ: Prentice Hall.

Baker, F., & Northman, J. E. (1981). *Helping: Human services for the 80s*. St. Louis: Mosby.

Baker, R. (1995, January 17). Those vital paupers. *New York Times*, p. A19.

Beverly, D. P., & McSweeney, E. A. (1987). *Social welfare and social justice*. Upper Saddle River, NJ: Prentice Hall.

Birnbaum, J. H. (2000). *The money men: The real story of fund-raisings' influence on political power in America*. New York: Crown.

Capoccia, V. A., & Googins, B. (1982). Social planning in an environment of limited choice. *New England Journal of Human Services*, 2, 31–36.

Clymer, A. (1995, December 16). Congress sends lobbying overhaul to Clinton. *New York Times*, p. 26.

Davis, R. (2001). *The press and American politics: The new mediator* (3rd ed.). Upper Saddle River, NJ: Prentice Hall.

Dobelstein, A. W. (1980). *Politics, economics, and public welfare*. Upper Saddle River, NJ: Prentice Hall.

Dye, T. R. (1987). *Understanding public policy* (6th ed.). Upper Saddle River, NJ: Prentice Hall.

Fill, H. J. (1974). *The mental breakdown of a nation*. New York: New Viewpoints.

Gil, D. G. (1981). *Unravelling social policy: Theory, analysis, and political action towards social equality* (3rd ed.). Cambridge, MA: Schenkman.

Gilbert, N., & Specht, H. (1974). *Dimensions of social welfare policy*. Upper Saddle River, NJ: Prentice Hall.

Huttman, E. D. (1981). *Introduction to social policy*. New York: McGraw-Hill.

Kahan, M. (1999). *Media as politics: Theory, behavior, and change in America*. Upper Saddle River, NJ: Prentice Hall.

Lewis, C. (1998). *The buying of the Congress: How special interests have stolen your right to life, liberty, and the pursuit of happiness*. New York: Avon Books.

Lynn, L. E. (1980). *The state and human services: Organizational change in a political context*. Cambridge, MA: MIT Press.

McPheeters, H. L. (2004). Policy, politics, and human services: An address given to members of the National Organization for Human Service Education, on October 9, 1992. In H. S. Harris, D. C. Maloney, & F. M. Rother (Eds.), *Human services: Contemporary issues and trends* (3rd ed., p. 259). Boston: Allyn & Bacon.

Mechanic, D. (1980). *Mental health and social policy* (2nd ed.). Upper Saddle River, NJ: Prentice Hall.

Meyer, C. H. (1983). The power to define problems. *Social Work*, 28, 99.

Miller, S. M. (1985, Winter). Reforming the welfare state. *New York Social Policy*, 15(3), 62–64.

Miringoff, M. L., & Opdyke, S. (1986). *American social welfare policy: Reassessment and reform*. Upper Saddle River, NJ: Prentice Hall.

Prigmore, C. S., & Atherton, C. R. (1979). *Social welfare policy: Analysis and formulation*. Lexington, MA: Heath.

Random House Dictionary. (1978). New York: Random House.

Sherraden, M. S., Slosar, B., & Sherraden, M. (2002). Innovation in social policy: Collaborative policy advocacy. *Social Work*, 47(3), 209–221.

Titmus, R. M. (1974). *Social policy: An introduction*. New York: Pantheon.

White, T. H. (1982). *America in search of itself: The making of the president 1956–1980*. New York: Harper & Row.

CHAPTER X

PREVENTION IN HUMAN SERVICES

INTRODUCTION

"No major disorder in a population has ever been eliminated by providing one-to-one treatment," stated the report of the Task Panel on Prevention (1978, p. 214) of the President's Commission on Mental Health. Does this mean that treatment of major disorders is of no use? Not at all! Treatment and rehabilitation are essential methods of working with patients. They are, however, not the only effective tools of human services. One must remember that prevention is a future-oriented process whereas treatment is a more immediate procedure. What this statement by the Task Panel does mean is that other approaches are needed if society hopes to successfully cope with the increasing number of individuals who are dysfunctional. One such approach is preventing disorders from developing in the first place.

Although prevention is not a new idea in the human services field, it is rarely addressed in introductory human services texts. When it is discussed in such texts, it is most often covered only briefly. However, applause is given to the recent growth of prevention programs in the human services, and many are convinced of the great potential of these programs. Therefore, why not introduce the subject of prevention to those planning to enter human services? Human services need not be limited to the repairing, or patching up, of dysfunctional persons through treatment and rehabilitation. Prevention is an area that deserves equal time. By introducing the concept of prevention in an introductory text, perhaps human services training programs will be encouraged to begin covering prevention with the same thoroughness now given to treatment and rehabilitation. Adequate information on prevention programs also offers the human services student another option regarding career choice.

The first part of this chapter focuses on what is targeted in prevention efforts. A brief history of such efforts follows. The remainder of the chapter includes a discussion of the different levels of prevention and the rationale for the importance of prevention efforts. The chapter ends with an examination of current prevention programs and obstacles to the development of prevention programs.

DEFINING PREVENTION AND ITS TARGETS

To *prevent* means to keep something from happening. In the field of medicine, it is quite clear what one attempts to prevent. Illness, injury, and premature or unnecessary death are the three major targets of prevention programs in medicine. In the human services—not including medicine—the major targets are not so clearly defined or identified. The Task Panel on Prevention (1978) of the President's Commission on Mental Health felt strongly that efforts should focus on the prevention of "persistent, destructive, maladaptive behaviors" (p. 219). These behaviors include child abuse, drug abuse, criminal activities, and desertion of family, among many others.

The panel also stated that psychological and social disorders should be the target of prevention programs. Obviously, many stressful situations, such as puberty, illness, and death, cannot be kept from occurring. The goal, then, is to prevent the situation from causing the kind of psychological and social disorders that have been mentioned. Situations such as the recession that occurred during the early part of George H. W. Bush's administration—with the resultant loss of jobs, along with medical benefits, investments, pensions, retirement funds, and often homes as well—create a great deal of uncertainty and stress. How to keep these losses from becoming overwhelming and causing disorders such as alcoholism, family disintegration, and depression, as well as other maladaptive behaviors, is the focus of prevention efforts of the human services.

President George W. Bush formed the President's New Freedom Commission on Mental Health on April 29, 2002, because of his desire to help people deal with the stresses and fears brought about via the kinds of problems mentioned above. The commission's focus is on how to reform the mental health delivery service system, which includes treatment and prevention programs, so that it is more efficient and effective. More details about the work of the commission are given later in the chapter.

PREVENTION IN THE PAST

In this section, our focus is on the history of prevention efforts in the human services. Because it is impossible to separate the history of prevention programs from the history of human services, some of the material discussed here will necessarily overlap with material in Chapter 3.

ANCIENT PRELITERATE AND LITERATE CIVILIZATIONS

People have always tried to find ways to prevent hunger, injury, illness, and death. In preliterate civilizations, rituals, prayer, and sacrifices were used in the hope of preventing such catastrophes. These preventive rituals focused not only on hostile animals, environments, and people, but also on the weather and other natural phenomena that influenced the supply of food and shelter.

Ancient literate civilizations also used many of the "preventive" methods of preliterate groups, such as prayer and ritual. However, a movement away from the priest, shaman, or religious healer slowly developed. There was an increasing awareness that in many cases illness and death were due to natural rather than supernatural phenomena. Interestingly, some early efforts at prevention were successful even though the actual causes of the diseases were not known. In ancient Greece, for example, Hippocrates noted that a particular disease, now thought to be malaria, developed and spread near swamps. When people avoided these areas or when the swamps were filled in, the disease abated (Bloom, 1981). Thus, malaria was prevented even though people did not know that it was carried by mosquitoes. In Ancient Rome, sewers and aqueducts were built to overcome unpleasant living conditions created by the smell of waste products and the taste of polluted water. As a result, illness caused by poor sanitation and contaminated water was unknowingly prevented.

FIGURE 8.1 | THE VICTIM, 1868. ILLUSTRATION BY AB HOUGHTON FOR TENNYSON'S POEM. AN ARCH-DRUID IS ABOUT TO SACRIFICE THE KING'S SON TO SAVE THE PEOPLE FROM THE PLAGUE. AT THE LAST MOMENT THE QUEEN TAKES THE BLOW AND BECOMES THE SACRIFICE.

THE DARK AGES AND THE RENAISSANCE

With the coming of the Dark Ages, medical practices reverted to an emphasis on prayer and rituals. According to Catalano (1979), medicine in Europe at that time became essentially a combination of pagan myth and Christian prayer, then considered the best protection against illnesses of any kind. (This change is described in more detail in Chapter 3.) Prevention efforts related to illness, hunger, and poverty made little headway during the Middle Ages. The Church did, however, provide care and food to many in need, which prevented hunger and the accompanying stress-related problems.

The Renaissance and the Age of Reason saw a return to acceptance of more scientific medical practices. **Quarantines** were used to prevent the spread of disease. Inoculation against smallpox was developed. New drugs were found to be useful in treating and preventing diseases. During the seventeenth and eighteenth centuries, other practices and discoveries prevented some diseases. For example, improvement of sanitation projects, promotion of general cleanliness, and a beginning understanding of contagion all helped in prevention of disease.

As in Hippocrates' time and Ancient Rome, the lack of knowledge of causes of specific illnesses was not always an obstacle. Scurvy, for example, was practically eliminated without an understanding of vitamin deficiency, simply by a naturally occurring change in diet toward more fresh fruits and vegetables. Unlike physical illness, though, mental illness continued to be treated largely according to religious beliefs. Many medical doctors as well as the public at large perceived the prevention of mental illness as something that required prayer, religious ritual, and living a life free of sin.

THE NINETEENTH AND TWENTIETH CENTURIES

The nineteenth and twentieth centuries saw greater advances in medicine. Pasteur introduced the germ theory of disease. Ehrlich introduced the idea of a chemical "magic bullet" against specific diseases, the idea that a single medication could cure or prevent a particular disease. Clinical laboratory diagnosis and specialization became the trend. In the field of mental illness, advances were also being made, though at a slower rate. Haindorf, in the early nineteenth century, introduced the concept that emotional conflicts that disturb the normal functioning of the body result in mental illness. Groos, before Freud, believed that humans are affected by physical forces they are not aware of and that these forces determine their behavior (Alexander & Selesnick, 1966).

Some significant, though rudimentary, efforts to prevent mental illness were made in the latter part of the nineteenth century and the early twentieth century. For example, the settlement house movement represented a major attempt to help people deal with the perils and pressures of poverty, hunger, crime, poor education, sweatshops, and filthy living conditions. Actually, the primary focus was not on the prevention of mental illness but rather on helping the millions of immigrants coming to America establish themselves in their new homeland. Exploitation of these people, many of whom did not even know the language, was the rule. Human services workers of that era were convinced that this exploitation and its attendant hardships contributed to high rates of juvenile delinquency, crime, alcoholism, and poor health. Efforts to improve the condition of the immigrants had a secondary, happy result of preventing some mental health problems.

Settlement house workers believed that education was the key to helping the exploited immigrants out of poverty. Some progressive politicians also tried to alleviate the plight of the poor, and their attempts continued over many years. Although the settlement house movement and cooperating politicians did not have the political power to make significant changes in the distribution of resources, they did help sensitize the general public to the plight of poor immigrants.

The movement that probably attained the greatest success in preventing the exploitation of the poor was the **union movement**. Unions were formed and supported by exploited workers. Their efforts were supported by the settlement houses, other institutions, and liberal political leaders. The unions not only prevented exploitation of their members through the **collective bargaining** process but also actively promoted legislation that increased opportunities for the poor to break the cycle of poverty and its accompanying disorders. **Minimum wage laws** and unemployment insurance are examples of such legislation.

The unions, in effect, brought about a significant increase in resources for their members and millions of others entering or already in the workforce. Although the workers did not suddenly become rich, they were much better off financially than before the advent of unions. Economic pressures, one of the avowed causes of emotional stress, were significantly reduced for many. Ironically, unions today are very often seen as the cause of economic problems such as high prices and inflation that lead to emotional stress. Whether or not such a view is accurate or justified, there is no question that the union movement was—and still is, according to some—a powerful force in enhancing the lives of union members and working people in general.

The latter part of the nineteenth century and early part of the twentieth century also saw movement in determining the relationship between some physical and behavioral problems. There was a recognition that syphilis in its later stages caused many behavioral problems such as impulsive and bizarre actions. During the first 20 years of the twentieth century, the **mental hygiene movement**, one of the most significant reform movements, was initiated by Clifford Beers and his associates. The main impetus for this movement was the autobiography of Beers, a former institutionalized mental patient. His book, *A Mind That Found Itself*, helped establish the National Committee for Mental Hygiene, which had the stated aim of preventing mental disorders.

An article in the first issue of the committee's journal, *Mental Hygiene*, stated that "a healthy life-style could save people from insanity, hence the importance of educating the public as a means of preventing mental illness" (Dain, 1980, p. 103).

THE 1960s THROUGH THE EARLY 2000s

Most prevention programs in this country prior to the 1960s were aimed at physical diseases and were carried out largely by the Public Health Service. It was not until the 1960s that prevention efforts related to disabling behaviors were again seriously considered. Federal laws were passed that had an impact on prevention efforts in mental health and behavioral disorders. Some of the more familiar pieces of legislation were the following:

- Mental Health Centers Act of 1963
- Economic Opportunities Act of 1964—The War on Poverty
- Comprehensive Alcohol Abuse and Alcoholism Prevention, Treatment, and Rehabilitation Act of 1970
- Child Abuse Prevention and Treatment Act of 1974
- Juvenile Justice and Delinquency Prevention Act of 1974
- Establishment of an Office of Prevention within the National Institute of Mental Health in 1982

It should be noted that four of the acts listed specifically include the word *prevention* in their titles. The other two, although not specifying prevention in their titles, most certainly had prevention efforts as an integral part of their programs. In addition, Congress began to earmark funds for research in prevention activities.

The development and growth of community psychology since its conceptualization in 1965 was most significant to the field of prevention. Many psychologists maintained that traditional forms of helping people (such as therapy in the office) were not very effective in the struggle to eliminate, or even stem, the tide of problems that are frequently the cause of maladaptive behaviors. Community psychologists attempted to connect the individual to the forces in the community that affected that individual's quality of life.

Community research to determine the needs of the individual and community is an essential tool of community psychologists. The research also helps identify current as well as possible or anticipated problems in the community. According to Dalton, Elias, and Wandersman (2001), there are four current trends in the field of community psychology:

- Prevention and competence promotion
- Community building, citizen participation, and empowerment
- Understanding human and cultural diversity
- Developing "adventuresome" research methods to match the complexity of [the] community phenomenon

Another important development in the field of prevention was the convening of the first national colloquium on Professional Education in Prevention in 1988. The focus of the conference was on training prevention professionals. There was also discussion of credentialing, evaluating, and testing various prevention models and programs. Sponsors of the conference included the National Prevention Network, the Illinois Department of Alcoholism and Drug Abuse, the Illinois Certification Boards, Inc., and the National College of Education. Although the sponsors were for the most part involved with alcohol and drug abuse causes and programs, the concept of prevention professionals applied to other fields as well, and was regarded as a concept most welcome and long overdue.

A program developed in the 1990s appears to be a major primary prevention effort, although it does not use the word *prevention* in its descriptive material. It is called the *Family Development and Credentialing Program* (FDC) and was initiated by the New York State Department of State, Division of Community Services. The response, in part, to the question raised in its material—why is the FDC necessary—is as follows: For too long, services have been available only when a family is in crisis or about to disintegrate. Public interventions have focused on "rescuing and fixing" families rather than helping families develop their capacity to solve problems and achieve long-lasting self-reliance. Now on both the state and national levels, families, service providers, and policymakers are joining together to reorient the way services are delivered toward a more family-focused and strengths-based approach (New York State Family Development Training and Credentialing Program, 1995). It is hoped that other institutions and jurisdictions become involved in similar projects.

REAL LIFE HUMAN SERVICES WORK

As the Executive Director of a small non-profit agency in the Greater New Orleans area, I oversee the day to day operations to provide shelter and counseling to victims of domestic violence, sexual assault, stalking, and human trafficking. "Metro" serves both males and females of all ages and strives to create an atmosphere which is welcoming to persons from very diverse backgrounds and cultures.

Metro serves persons needing to hide from their abusers by providing safe and hidden housing at one of three shelters at scattered sites in the city and surrounding suburbs. Approximately 250 women and children are housed each year. Men requiring safe haven are placed in motels. Other victims who do not need shelter come to one of Metro's seven outreach offices for counseling, advocacy, legal services, and support.

Working in a shelter system is both challenging and rewarding. No two days ever seem the same as we try to provide community education, train law enforcement personnel, grocery shop for persons from vastly different cultures, and provide educational and recreational activities for the children and the adults. The idea is to support and strengthen the victims seeking our services in any way that will empower them to become independent and able to be self-sufficient. Over the years, I have seen victims return as volunteers. I have seen terrified women reclaim their lives and then speak out in the community against the violence. I have seen children literally blossom in an abuse-free environment.

All the services are both free and confidential. Another aspect of my job is to find the financial resources to sustain the program. This is accomplished through fundraising, grant writing, and soliciting donations. The support that the community provides is truly amazing. Here are just a few examples: Churches cook meals for the shelter residents, high school students come to read to the children, service organizations build play equipment, local veterinarians offer to house pets that the fleeing victims bring with them.

Dale Standifer, MSW, LCSW
Metroplitan Center For Women and Children
Jefferson, Louisiana

LEVELS OF PREVENTION

The various state and federal prevention programs that have been mentioned focus their efforts on different levels of prevention: primary, secondary, and tertiary. The concept of *levels* originated with the Public Health Service and has generated some controversy within the field of human services regarding the definition of each level. These differences will be described after a definition and example of each of the three levels of prevention.

PRIMARY PREVENTION

Primary prevention in the human services is designed to prevent a disorder, disability, or dysfunction from occurring in the first place. An example of primary prevention might be a program to help the unemployed learn new skills and use support networks and thus prevent depression, alcoholism, and other psychological disorders resulting from unemployment. In the medical field, the shots given to prevent polio, the flu, or tetanus are examples of primary prevention at work.

Primary prevention is seen by Price, Bader, and Ketterer (1980), Cowen (1980), and the Task Panel on Prevention (1978) as being principally concerned with the reduction of new cases of disorders in a community. If, for example, families with severely mentally retarded children are helped to learn new ways of dealing with their children and how to use all the resources provided for such problems, it might well prevent the onset of family strife or other emotional problems that would keep the mentally retarded individual or other family members from functioning at their potential. Stemming the ever increasing number of disorders that develop among

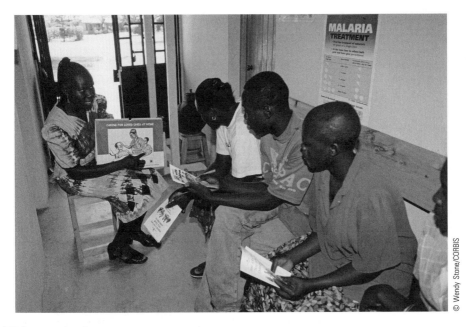

AIDS prevention for teenagers.

families facing difficult and different problems is one of the goals of primary prevention.

Another example involves child abuse. Studies have indicated that people who were abused as children are more likely to become child abusers, delinquents, and prone to various kinds of societal violence. If such individuals are identified, they can be helped to learn other ways of dealing with their children prior to becoming parents. This approach might well prevent that type of destructive and maladaptive behavior from occurring at all.

The Task Panel on Prevention (1978) claims that "primary prevention involves building the strengths, resources, and competence in individuals, families, and communities that can reduce the flow of a variety of unfortunate outcomes—each characterized by enormous human and societal costs" (p. 213). When one looks at the "flow of unfortunate outcomes," such as divorce, desertion, delinquency, and depression, brought on by these or other problems, one can clearly imagine "the enormous human and societal costs" and thus the need for primary prevention programs. Such programs involve providing education and training to help individuals and families to cope successfully with difficult problems.

An additional but critical aspect of primary prevention, according to Cowen (1982), is that it must be group-oriented, or mass-oriented. This does not mean that such programs should not deal with individuals, but rather that the major focus should be on large and/or specific populations. These populations are referred to as *target populations, high-risk groups,* or the *general population.* Although these groups may not be demonstrating any disorders, their circumstances, as described earlier, are such that many of them are probably vulnerable or open to such disorders.

SECONDARY PREVENTION

Secondary prevention can be defined as the early detection and treatment of dysfunction. If, for example, parents noticed that their teenage child was beginning to use alcohol and do poorly in school, and if they sought and obtained help for their child, that would be secondary prevention. In such an instance, the aim would be to help the youngster refrain from using alcohol and improve in schoolwork—in other words, to stop the progression of the problem and solve it. Secondary prevention in medicine is similar. Treatment is focused on eliminating symptoms of an illness and helping the patient get well.

According to Goodstein and Calhoun (1982), secondary prevention "involves early diagnosis and treatment of a disorder at a stage when problems may be nipped in the bud" (p. 499). Price et al. (1980) see the goal of secondary prevention somewhat differently, as an attempt "to shorten the duration of the disorder by early and prompt treatment" (p. 10). If, for example, a young child of an alcoholic parent began to show signs of withdrawal, and the nonalcoholic parent took the youngster for help, many would consider this to be secondary prevention. It would include diagnosis and treatment in an attempt to "nip the problem in the bud," or at least to shorten the duration of the problem.

There are those, however, who would claim that this is treatment of an existing disorder. The maladaptive behavior (that is, withdrawal) has already begun; it has not been prevented or kept from occurring. What, then, if anything, has been prevented? Those who claim that early and prompt treatment is secondary prevention assert that if the intervention or treatment is successful, the signs of withdrawal are reduced or eliminated. In effect, intervention has prevented increased or continued withdrawal and therefore should be considered to be a significant prevention effort. One could argue either way as to whether one should call this example treatment or prevention.

In our view, the very existence of a disorder takes the effort out of the realm of prevention and places it in the category of treatment. Although it is true that prevention efforts could focus on an individual, the major thrust of prevention is toward reaching groups at risk, target populations, or the general population. This may be a technical point, but it does have significance as an obstacle to the development of primary prevention programs. This point is discussed more fully later in the chapter.

TERTIARY PREVENTION

Tertiary prevention is generally defined in terms of efforts to rehabilitate and return to the community those afflicted with severe mental disorders. For example, some mental patients suffer from delusions; that is, they believe they are someone else, such as Napoleon, God, or Superman, and they try to behave as if they were such figures. It is this behavior that keeps them from functioning successfully in society. Patients with certain types of physical problems likewise cannot function successfully in society. The solution in both cases is to place the patient in an institution where she or he can be rehabilitated and, it is hoped, eventually return to the community.

A medical example might be an individual who lost a leg, was fitted with an artificial one, and was taught to walk with the new leg. Tertiary prevention, according to Price et al. (1980), is an attempt "to reduce the severity and disability associated with a particular disorder" (p. 10). Goodstein and Calhoun (1982) describe tertiary prevention in more detail. From their point of view, "tertiary prevention includes efforts to reduce the overall damaging effect of a disorder, to shorten its duration, and to rehabilitate those afflicted for reentry into the community" (p. 499).

If those delusional individuals referred to earlier were treated in an institution and were again able to live and function in the community, they would be considered examples of tertiary prevention by many in the human services. Here again, one might ask what is being prevented. From one point of view, permanent disability or continued institutionalization is the prevention target. Another point of view states that the tertiary prevention is actually rehabilitation. That is, it restores the individual to better health. It should be noted that most tertiary prevention programs are focused not on a mass of people or on large groups of people but rather on individuals and/or small groups.

WHY AN EMPHASIS ON PRIMARY PREVENTION IS CRUCIAL

Community psychology is one of the few but growing number of human services professions that recognize and believe in the critical importance and **efficacy** of primary prevention, as well as the promotion of wellness and social competence. What is so important about the idea of primary prevention in the human services? Four major reasons have been put forward to support primary prevention as a top priority. One reason was provided at the very beginning of this chapter: According to the Task Panel on Prevention (1978) and others in the Public Health Service and in private practice, there has never been a major disease or disorder eliminated through treatment alone. If this is so, it becomes clear that treatment and rehabilitation efforts cannot hope to completely eliminate serious disorders.

The second reason to emphasize primary prevention is that there are not enough human services personnel to treat or rehabilitate all those in need. Although it is true that more people are entering the human services field, educators agree that the training of personnel cannot keep up with the increasing numbers of clients. The primary focus of training has been, and still is, on treatment and rehabilitation. A shift to emphasize prevention might be the only solution to the shortage of personnel.

To make things more difficult, the economic policies of the early 1990s caused a reduction in support of the human services in general. This decrease in support occurred alongside an increase in the number of people needing help due to problems of unemployment, people living longer and becoming more dependent, more families breaking up, and child abuse.

Other problems, such as battering of women—the leading cause of injury to women (Faludi, 1991)—suicides, school dropouts, crime, and AIDS, are not getting the attention they need.

As if that were not enough, the 2001 National Household Survey on Drug Abuse finds that an estimated 109 million people over 12 years of age drink alcohol. Over 20% (about 21 million) participated in binge drinking. Almost 13 million were considered heavy drinkers. Underage drinkers, 12 to 20 years of age, totaled about 10 million youngsters (Substance Abuse and Mental Health Services Administration, 2001). Still another problem is indicated in a news release by the National Institute on Alcohol Abuse and Alcoholism (NIAAA). It reports that about 19 million children from birth to 17 years of age are exposed to family alcoholism, alcohol abuse, or both (National Institute on Alcohol Abuse and Alcoholism, 1999).

This situation reminds one of the story of a man fishing off the bank of a wide and fast-flowing stream. While fishing, he sees a person being swept along with the current. He quickly throws the person a line and pulls him to safety. Before he can do anything more, he spots another person being swept downstream, and he pulls him out also. Just as he does this, he sees a few more people struggling in the current. He calls for help as he pulls someone else out of the surging water. Others come to help as still more people are caught in the current. However, it soon becomes impossible to pull everyone out of danger. There are too many victims and not enough helpers. As more and more people float downstream, more and more are lost. It finally dawns on someone to head upstream and try to keep people from falling into the stream in the first place. Many feel that human services workers had best head upstream before they too become less and less effective.

The third reason that primary prevention should be a priority is that society pays a huge financial cost for disorders that are not prevented. According to the Seventh Special Report to the U.S. Congress on Alcohol and Health, the estimated cost of alcoholism and alcohol abuse was more than $136 billion in 1990 and about $150 billion in 1995 (Secretary of Health and Human Services, 1990).

A police officer teaches young students the dangers of substance abuse—an example of active primary prevention.

The fourth reason for the promotion of primary prevention is that emotional and behavioral disorders exact an enormous "human cost," referred to in the preceding quote from the Task Panel on Prevention. Human costs have to do with personal pain and suffering. Perhaps the only way to truly realize these costs is for us to try to personalize them. Everyone has had to face, at some time or another, a painful or terrible experience. Some remember the fear of being left behind when parents separated. Some remember the shame of having a "drunkard" in the family. Others who have had a mentally ill person living in the same house can still feel the anxiety, fear, and frustration in that situation. The guilt, shame, and apprehension of having a mentally retarded child still affect many others. The anger and fear of living with a drug addict are still with many. The terror after being abused, mugged, or raped may not ever leave victims or their loved ones.

How many can recall the gut-wrenching pain and sense of helplessness of watching a loved one suffer and die due to illness? How many remember the rage and bitterness they felt when their disabled child or they themselves were made fun of or denied an opportunity to go to school? There is also the feeling of desperation, frustration, and rage known by African Americans, Latinos, and other minority group members when they or their children are abused and denied the opportunity to grow and prosper. These enormous human costs are the assaults on the emotions and strength of those affected directly and indirectly. Some of the effects radically change the lives of those who, without help, cannot cope successfully with such traumas and too often become alcoholics, abusers, addicts, or mentally ill or develop some other disorder, thus increasing the number of people needing treatment and rehabilitation.

A brief description of what happens when the type of stress just described leads, for example, to alcoholism will bring the issue into sharp focus.

- Alcohol contributes to 100,000 deaths yearly (McGinnis & Foege, 1993).
- Approximately 10,000 murders a year are alcohol-related.
- Victims report each year 183,000 rapes and sexual assaults involving alcohol, as well as 197,000 robberies, 661,000 aggravated assaults, and nearly 1.7 million simple assaults (U.S. Department of Justice, 1998).
- A third of all suicides each year involve alcohol.
- A third of all arrests each year are alcohol-related.

On the college level alone, 1,400 students between 18 and 24 years of age die each year from alcohol-related injuries, 500,000 are injured while under the influence of alcohol each year, 600,000 are assaulted by another student who was drinking, and 70,000 were victims of alcohol-related sexual assault or date rape. In addition, many thousands are involved in unsafe sex, have academic and health problems, and have attempted suicide (National Institute on Alcohol Abuse and Alcoholism, 2002).

Remember, this listing is only a sample of the data on the effects of alcoholism. It does not include data on preteen and teenage alcohol abuse described earlier, death and injuries in the house or workplace, or injuries in auto accidents. Left out are the data on physical and mental illness and disabilities, forcible rape, family disintegration, and many other problems related to alcoholism and alcohol abuse. Still, a significant, sustained federal program to prevent alcohol abuse is not in place. Such a program might include approaches such as these:

- Mandating the listing of health hazards of alcohol on all alcohol containers. (The government has mandated a very limited warning regarding the health hazards of alcohol to be placed on all forms of liquor containers.)
- Mandating a very clear presentation of health hazards of alcohol in advertising in the print, television, and radio media.
- Considering a ban on advertising alcohol altogether. Nations banning the advertising of alcohol have approximately 16% less consumption, and those that prohibit beer and wine ads have 11% lower use. Fatality rates are lower by 10% and 23%, respectively (National Institute for Alcohol Abuse, 1993).
- Raising the federal excise tax on alcohol and particularly on beer, as was done with cigarettes.
- Increasing prices on alcoholic beverages, which may be especially effective at reducing addictive consumption by younger, poorer, and less educated consumers (National Institute for Alcohol Abuse, 1993).
- Enforcing the 21-year-old drinking age on college campuses, where three-quarters of the students are under the legal drinking age and the massive marketing of alcohol still continues (Sessel, 1988).

Many state and local alcohol prevention programs are in progress. They include, among others, raising the drinking age to 21, significantly raising the tax on liquor products, limiting the availability of alcohol purchases to specific outlets, strict enforcement of DWI (driving while intoxicated) and similar laws, and initiating education programs in schools and communities.

The February 8, 2003 interim report of the President's New Freedom Commission on Mental Health provides other reasons and impetus for the development of primary prevention programs. As indicated in Chapter 2, the prevalence figures translate into millions of adults and children disabled by mental illness. Furthermore, the report points out that about half of those who need treatment do not get it. The quality of care for those who get treatment may be less than adequate. For racial minorities the rate of treatment and the quality of care is poorer than that for the general population. The report emphasizes that the system needs "dramatic reform," although it also depicts model prevention and treatment programs that are ongoing. An effective prevention program included in the report is described later in this chapter.

Primary prevention programs are geared to help people learn how to deal successfully with their problems and stress so that they are less likely to develop the disorders that have been described. A greater number of prevention programs could make possible a greater reduction in both human and societal costs.

The acknowledged inability of treatment and rehabilitation programs alone to stem the tide of people in need of human services makes increased primary prevention efforts almost mandatory. A brief look at the two types of strategies used in primary prevention programs will provide a clearer picture of how these programs are developed and how they work.

PRIMARY PREVENTION STRATEGIES

Both active and passive prevention strategies are used in the development of prevention programs (Gilchrist & Schinke, 1985). *Passive strategies* refer to broad informational-type approaches, such as warnings on cigarette packages or television programs discussing and describing ways to prevent AIDS. *Active strategies* involve working directly with the target populations in developing skills that enable individuals to deal successfully with pressures and problems that might lead to dysfunction. For example, the *life skills model* is an active strategy that includes problem solving, making thoughtful and helpful decisions, and recognizing consequences of behavior (Gilchrist & Schinke). Other skills include identifying behavior options, examining the advantages and disadvantages of the various options, and communication and listening skills (Snow, 1985).

The various skills of active strategies are best described by Briar (1985), when he points out that they essentially contain "cognitive and behavioral elements that are aimed not only to help people prevent social and health problems but also to help people promote personal competence and adaptive functioning" (p. 8). A brief look at a sample of primary prevention programs and a listing of major areas in desperate need of primary prevention programs will be helpful at this point to give you a sense of the scope of such efforts and a clear idea of their goals.

A SAMPLE OF PRIMARY PREVENTION PROGRAMS

Primary prevention programs have been growing in number since the mid-1970s. Many of them have been short-term, research, experimental, or demonstration programs limited in terms of time and funding. Much of the data derived from these programs indicates positive results in improving individuals' abilities to cope with stress. These data and results can be and have been used to develop additional theories and programs focused on long-term results. There are long-term programs—although too few from the point of view of proponents of primary prevention—that are ongoing. In any case, it should be noted that the final results of these long-term programs are not yet available, for it is impossible to tell whether the targeted disorders have been prevented for the entire life spans of those in the various programs.

One program aimed at reducing teenage pregnancies, Girls Inc., included 750 girls 12 to 17 years of age (Brody, 1991). They were all at high risk of becoming pregnant. The program consisted of a mother-daughter workshop, an assertiveness training workshop, an educational and career planning workshop, and sessions on sexuality that also provided contraceptive services. It was reported that the number of pregnancies was reduced by 50% among the girls 15 to 17 years of age in this program. The number of girls aged 12 to 14 years who subsequently began having sexual intercourse was also reduced by 50%.

The results of the Girls Inc. program showed that high-risk characteristics for teenage pregnancy (being welfare-dependent; from a single-parent, female-headed household; living in an urban environment; having peers and relatives who were pregnant teenagers) were not insurmountable obstacles to a well-planned prevention program. The director of the program pointed out that the cost of the program per year per girl was $116. The director estimated that delaying a single pregnancy until after teenage years could save society $8,500 (Brody, 1991); one assumes these savings would be made in a range of welfare benefits.

Tableman, Marceniak, Johnson, and Rodgers (1982) describe a pilot program of stress management training involving women on public assistance who were generally isolated and subjected to more than average stress in their lives. None of the women were in crisis, nor did they display maladaptive behaviors that required treatment. The women took part in 10 sessions, during which they learned skills and methods of reducing stress that helped them change their perceptions of their situations. The program resulted in significant change in the participants' lives. They were no longer isolated and were able to function more effectively with less stress, thus preventing the kinds of behavioral disorders discussed earlier. The program has been further tested and used with different populations living under stressful conditions.

Another primary prevention program was developed by the Roman Catholic Church because of the increase in the number of divorces. Couples wishing to be married in the Church now go through a series of group meetings, led by a member of the clergy, to discuss the responsibilities, joys, and strains of marriage. Childbirth, child rearing, sex, and other aspects of marriage are among the many topics discussed. The goal is to prevent many of the problems occurring in marriages from becoming serious enough to cause behavioral disorders, family disintegration, and divorce.

The last primary prevention program to be described here centers on promoting mental health in rural areas through informal helping (D'Augelli & Vallance, 1981). Provision of human services in rural areas is more difficult than in urban areas. For example, because of the smaller populations in rural areas, isolation is usually greater and transportation is not readily available. Many rural residents have close family and community ties, and asking for help from "outsiders" is not looked upon with much favor.

Some rural communities have an informal system of helpers. The project under discussion was designed not only to encourage such a system but also to teach members of the community to train those residents who make up this informal system. The focus was to build on the existing strengths of the community by training the local helpers to become more efficient in helping residents deal with personal problems, job loss, sudden illness or injury, and other problems in living. This approach permits local residents to teach other local residents skills in the helping process, and thus they do not have to share problems with or ask for help from outsiders. This method also increases the number of helpers and provides additional sources of support to those who are faced with problems in living before maladaptive behaviors are developed. This particular prevention program is an ongoing one staffed by local volunteers.

The President's New Freedom Commission on Mental Health is an example of an early intervention to prevent mental health problems. This program has been considered so successful it is now being used in 230 cities in 23 states. Following is a description:

Program. Nurse-family partnership.

Goal. To improve pregnancy outcomes by helping mothers to adopt healthy behavior, to improve child health and development, to reduce child abuse and neglect, and to improve families' economic self-sufficiency.

Method. A trained nurse is sent to the home of a high-risk woman during her first pregnancy and extending through the first year of her child's life. The nurse helps young, typically unmarried women learn how to parent and to avoid risky behavior. The nurse follows a visit-by-visit approach to help women adopt healthy behaviors and responsibly care for their children.

Results. For mothers: 80% reduction in abuse of their children, 25% reduction in maternal substance abuse, and 83% increase in employment. For children (15 years later): 54–69% reduction in arrests and convictions, less risky behavior, and fewer school suspensions and destructive behaviors.

Areas in which primary prevention programs can make a significant difference are

- Mental illness
- Crime
- Alcoholism
- Child abuse
- Teenage pregnancies
- Rising juvenile crime
- Violence
- Battered women
- AIDS
- Increased teenage drug abuse
- Physical illness
- Immunization of children
- Lack of pre- and postnatal care for poor women

Community mental health centers develop prevention programs as well as provide treatment services. One such center, the Center for Preventive Psychiatry in White Plains, New York, states that its mission is "to promote positive mental health attitudes and prevent the onset of mental illness, or reduce its impact, through programs of early identification and treatment, community education, professional training, consultation and research." Unfortunately, there are not sufficient community mental health centers to provide the needed services described.

OBSTACLES TO DEVELOPMENT OF PRIMARY PREVENTION PROGRAMS

Although a growing number of primary prevention programs are operating throughout the country, funding for such programs is quite limited in comparison to the funds available for treatment and/or rehabilitation programs. What is frightening is that this is true even in life-and-death situations such as the AIDS epidemic. That no one would object to the elimination or significant reduction of the disorders described earlier seems certain. Why, then, the persistent reluctance to fund and develop primary prevention programs in the human services field? As indicated in Chapter 5, the community psychologists' focus is on both prevention and wellness promotion. It should be noted that even among community psychologists there is a "continuing debate about where the emphasis of time and resources for prevention efforts is best placed" (Dalton et al., 2001). Should efforts emphasize prevention of disorders or the promotion of wellness and social competence?

The choice is not to enter the debate but rather describe the greater difficulty in overcoming the obstacles to developing prevention programs and obtaining resources for them. There seem to be three major categories of obstacles to funding and development: professional, political, and economic. An examination of just a sampling of these obstacles will give you a greater understanding of the problems surrounding the introduction of primary prevention programs. Note that these problems are very closely interrelated.

PROFESSIONAL ISSUES

Professional issues that create problems regarding the growth of primary prevention programs include the training, practice, philosophy, and ethics of human services workers and human services professions. Very few two- or four-year training programs for human services workers discuss, much less focus on, primary prevention theory or skills. Few, if any at all, train workers for careers in the field of primary prevention. Graduate school training is equally limited in terms of primary prevention. For the most part, the training of human services workers is focused on treatment and/or rehabilitation theories and skills. This training leads, naturally, to practice concentrated on treatment and rehabilitation. These services are, in addition, the major services of most agencies in which human services workers are employed.

From a theoretical or philosophical perspective, the fact that primary prevention is not seen the same way by all human services workers creates an additional obstacle to the growth of primary prevention programs. No *one* definition of primary prevention is accepted by all human services workers. Furthermore, a group of mental health professionals in a report to the New York State Commission of Mental Health (Prevost, 1982) states that "the distinctions among primary, secondary, and tertiary prevention do not provide meaningful guidance for the formulation of programs and policies" (p. 3). The group adds that the concepts have triggered more arguments than action. For example, when a particular disorder, such as drug abuse, is treated successfully, some might claim that the successful treatment actually prevented a potential crime and thus is really primary prevention. This perception does not include the element of intent, considered to be an essential aspect of primary prevention in mental health (Cowen, 1980). The intent in the example is to stop the drug abuse, not to stop a crime.

Another issue that causes confusion centers around whether primary prevention efforts should concentrate on the causes of disorders or the "trigger," or "spark," that sets off a disorder. To add to the dilemma, the question of whether to approach disorders with a biological, psychological, or sociological emphasis is raised. In a *biological approach*, disorders are thought to be caused by physical problems such as brain damage, chemical imbalances, pollution, physical disability, or other similar difficulties. In a *psychological approach*, disorders are thought to be caused by a lack of knowledge or an inability to cope with emotional stress. In a *sociological approach*, disorders are thought to be caused by institutions or systems that do little to eliminate racism, unemployment, crime, poverty, hunger, poor housing, and similar societal ills.

Ethical questions regarding primary prevention programs also arise from the point of view of some human services workers. Some workers claim that if primary prevention programs were aimed at high-risk groups, unforeseen and unfortunate consequences could occur. An example of a high-risk group would be children from broken homes or children with alcoholic parents. The children would have to be identified as such, which could lead to additional problems and violations of privacy. Moreover, the children would have little or no voice in this matter even though they might be adversely affected.

Another ethical issue raised by some is that if primary prevention programs are aimed at entire communities or populations, what responsibility do providers have to those in the community who feel no need or want no part of the programs?

Still another issue, as Califano (1994) describes it, is that "[d]octors are not trained or paid to seek or counsel patients about disease prevention or health prevention, and among those that do, instruction comes to only a few hours" (p. 145). Sadly, this is also true in the training of most human services workers.

For all these reasons, many professionals are reluctant to expend their resources and efforts on primary prevention to the same degree as for treatment and rehabilitation programs.

POLITICAL ISSUES

Certain political issues are also obstacles to the development of primary prevention programs. For example, ours is a crisis-oriented society. That is, our society does not usually react to problems unless they become great enough to affect large numbers of people. It requires a storm of protest or concern to move legislators to initiate attempts to deal with the problem.

The early outcry regarding the AIDS epidemic is a clear example of how a crisis affects the political system. Initially, there was a great deal of resistance to doing much about the issue because AIDS was considered a "gay" problem, one limited to a minority population. The political reversal was abrupt and powerful when politicians realized that the epidemic was spreading to the heterosexual community. The lack of a sense of crisis in the view of the public and many human services workers in addition to the lack of unanimity among politicians and professionals regarding the efficacy of primary prevention programs provides little impetus for the political system to press for the development and funding of such programs. Furthermore, how can one justify the use of limited resources to prevent disorders that only *might* occur?

Califano (1994) points out, "As long as big bucks are in treatment and the projects are in sick care, that's where members of Congress and influential lobbyists will center their efforts; there are precious few political contributions to be found in health promotion and disease prevention" (p. 245). Unfortunately, here, too, the same holds true for the human services field.

ECONOMIC OBSTACLES

Economic obstacles to primary prevention efforts pointed out by the Task Panel on Prevention (1978) include limited resources and funding practices. Limited funding of human services also limits the development of new and uncertain or unproven programs. To take increasingly scarce resources away from treatment and rehabilitation programs and from people who are in immediate need of assistance to fund new and, in the eyes of many, questionable primary prevention programs is not acceptable to many in the human services field. Yet, according to Califano (1994), "perhaps the biggest deterrent to health promotion and disease prevention efforts is the fact that the big bucks are in promoting unhealthy habits and treating poor health" (p. 145). He points out that prevention costs money up front and saves money later, which is an obstacle that lawmakers seem unable to overcome. Once again, these factors hold true in the human services field as well as in the medical professions.

Furthermore, the cost of primary prevention programs serving large populations is very high, even though the cost per person is much less than the cost of treatment and rehabilitation of one person. In addition, most hospitals and other human services institutions are not prepared for primary prevention programs and are certainly dependent on the income derived from their treatment and rehabilitation services. Primary prevention programs might well affect that income adversely. The same threat to income faces those human services workers in private practice. Recipients of **third-party payments** through their clients' medical insurance could also be affected financially.

SUMMARY OF PRIMARY PREVENTION PROGRAMS

The obstacles to primary prevention programs that have been discussed here can all be overcome, and must be overcome if we are to see improvement in the delivery of human services. A strong bias in favor of primary prevention programs has been made obvious in this chapter on purpose. The human services profession does not need to, nor can it afford to, stand still regarding the development of primary prevention programs until critics are satisfied and all questions are answered. Sufficient research has been done to warrant significant increases in funding of primary prevention programs and continued research in this area. The old cliché that an ounce of prevention is worth a pound of cure is particularly appropriate here. From an economic, social, professional, and moral perspective, it is clear to us that the human services must become more than a "repair shop" for individuals and society.

It is heartening that human services educators and professionals have an awareness of the vital importance of prevention. This is evidenced by the inclusion of prevention courses in schools of social work and by the existence of programs of preventive psychology designed to train psychologists in prevention practices (Price, 1983). Primary prevention programs are essential in the fight against dysfunctions, disorders, and disabilities.

ADDITIONAL READING

Albee, G. W., & Gullota, T. (Eds.). (1997). *Primary prevention works*. Thousand Oaks, CA: Sage.
Elias, M. J., & Tobias, S. E. (1996). *Social problem solving: Interventions in the schools*. New York: Guilford.
Jason, L. A., Hess, R. E., Felner, R. D., & Moritsugu, J. N. (Eds.). (1987). *Prevention: Toward a multidisciplinary approach*. New York: The Horworth Press.
Swift, M., & Weirich, T. (1987). Prevention planning as social and organizational change. In J. Hermalin & J. A. Morell (Eds.), *Prevention planning in mental health*. Sage Studies in Community Mental Health (Vol. 9). Newbury Park, CA: Sage.

REFERENCES

Alexander, F. G., & Selesnick, S. T. (1966). *The history of psychiatry: An evaluation of psychiatric practice from prehistoric time to the present*. New York: Harper & Row.
Bloom, M. (1981). *Primary prevention: The possible science*. Upper Saddle River, NJ: Prentice Hall.
Briar, S. (1985). Foreword. In L. D. Gilchrist & S. P. Schinke (Eds.), *Preventing social and health problems through life skills training*. Seattle: University of Washington School of Social Work.
Brody, J. E. (1991, October 8). Helping teenagers avoid pregnancy. *New York Times*, p. A14.
Califano, J. A. (1994). *Radical surgery: What's next for American health care?* New York: Times/Random House.
Catalano, R. (1979). *Health, behavior and the community: An ecological perspective*. New York: Pergamon.
Cowen, E. L. (1980). The wooing of primary prevention. *American Journal of Community Psychology, 8*, 258–284.
Cowen, E. L. (1982, Spring). Primary prevention research: Barriers, needs and opportunities. *Journal of Primary Prevention*, 131–137.
Dain, N. (1980). *Clifford W. Beers: Advocate for the insane*. Pittsburgh: University of Pittsburgh Press.

Dalton, J. H., Elias, M. J., & Wandersman, A. (2001). *Community psychology: Linking individuals and communities.* Belmont, CA: Wadsworth.

D'Augelli, A. R., & Vallance, T. R. (1981). The helping community: Promoting mental health in rural areas through informal helping. *Journal of Rural Community Psychology, 2,* 1.

Faludi, S. (1991, September/October). Blame it on feminism: What's wrong with women today? Too much equality. *Mother Jones,* 24–29.

Gilchrist, L. D., & Schinke, S. P. (1985). Prevention of social and health problems. In L. D. Gilchrist & S. P. Schinke (Eds.), *Preventing social and health problems through life skills training.* Seattle: University of Washington School of Social Work.

Goodstein, L. D., & Calhoun, J. F. (1982). *Understanding abnormal behavior: Description, explanation, management.* Reading, MA: Addison-Wesley.

McGinnis, J., & Foege, W. (1993, November 10). Actual causes of death in the U.S.A. *Journal of the American Medical Association, 270*(18), 2208.

National Institute for Alcohol Abuse. (1993). *AHRW, 17,* 140, 262.

National Institute on Alcohol Abuse and Alcoholism. (1999, December 30). News release. One in four children exposed to family alcohol abuse or alcoholism.

National Institute on Alcohol Abuse and Alcoholism. (2002). A snapshot of annual high-risk college drinking consequences.

National Institute of Mental Health. (2001). The numbers count: Mental disorders in America.

New York State Family Development Training and Credentialing Program (FDC). (1995). Some questions and answers [brochure].

Prevost, J. A. (1982, March). *Policy framework for preventive services.* New York: New York State Office of Mental Health.

Price, R. H. (1983). The education of a preventive psychologist. In R. D. Felner, L. A. Jason, J. N. Moritsugu, & S. S. Farber (Eds.), *Preventive psychology: Theory, research and practice.* New York: Pergamon.

Price, R. H., Bader, B. C., & Ketterer, R. F. (1980). Prevention in community mental health—The state of the art. In R. H. Price, F. Ketterer, B. C. Bader, & J. Monahan (Eds.), *Prevention in mental health: Research, policy, and practice* (Vol. 1). Newbury Park, CA: Sage.

Secretary of Health and Human Services. (1990). *Seventh special report to the U.S. Congress on alcohol and health.* Rockville, MD: U.S. Department of Health and Human Services.

Sessel, T. V. (1988, January 1). Two ways to reduce underage drinking. *New York Times,* p. 30.

Snow, W. H. (1985). Skills training for coping with life changes. In L. D. Gilchrist & S. P. Schinke (Eds.), *Preventing social and health problems through life skills training.* Seattle: University of Washington School of Social Work.

Substance Abuse and Mental Health Services Administration. (2001). Alcohol use. *2001 National Household Survey on Drug Abuse.*

Tableman, B., Marceniak, D., Johnson, D., & Rodgers, R. (1982). Stress management training for women on public assistance. *American Journal of Community Psychology, 10,* 357–367.

U.S. Department of Justice. (1998). Alcohol and crime: An analysis of national data on the prevalence of alcohol involvement in crime. Washington, DC: U.S. Government Printing Office.

CHAPTER 9

CURRENT CONTROVERSIES AND ISSUES

CHAPTER CONTENTS

INTRODUCTION

You may have gathered by now that the human services field is quite complex. Complete agreement regarding philosophies, methods, goals, services, funding, or anything else just does not exist nor, from our point of view, should it. At times controversies and differences are stimulating, healthy, and valid and lead to creative solutions. At other times, these disparities are repetitious, meaningless, and destructive. Too frequently they consume time, energy, and resources that might be better used providing needed services. To this end, it is highly recommended that students become familiar with the books in the Opposing Viewpoints series, published by the Greenhaven Press, that deal with issues of concern to human services workers.

The purpose of this chapter is to present a sampling of basic controversies and issues in the field of human services that have not yet been resolved and may never be resolved to everyone's satisfaction. The questions raised in this chapter influence all human services workers. The human services worker is more directly affected by some issues than others, but they all impact the worker and the services provided. Prior knowledge of these and other controversies helps workers know what they might expect from colleagues, politicians, consumers of human services, and the general public. This knowledge can be instrumental in helping workers provide more effective services.

No attempt is made to resolve these issues here. Views are often implied by the way issues are presented. Furthermore, there are no expectations that the reader come to any specific conclusions or agree with any particular point of view. Whereas issues, conditions, and people change, many old issues reemerge that give the appearance of new issues. These so-called new issues have, in all probability, been with us in one way or another, to one degree or another, for as long as the human services profession has existed. Some examples are discussed in this chapter. The idea is to examine them and understand their significance to human services workers and to the provision of human services, for they very frequently raise questions regarding one's personal and professional values and ethics.

CLASH OF VALUES IN SOCIAL POLICIES

At the outset, it is worth repeating that complete agreement about social policies in the human services rarely occurs. Social policies are supposedly based on morals and values; however, no consensus exists about what is morally right. Jansson (1988) identifies five moral issues involved with social welfare policies. In discussing them, it will become quite clear that they are all closely related and overlap each other in many ways. Following are the issues and some of the questions they raise.

1. *Morality of social services.* Who shall receive services, and on what terms? (p. 5)
Questions: Shall services be given to only those who are unable to work? What about (a) those who cannot find work or (b) those who cannot earn enough to stay above the poverty line? Should those who receive benefits be required to work in the community? Should those on welfare not receive increased benefits for additional children?

2. *Nature of social obligations.* For what needs and problems is society responsible, and which shall receive priority? (p. 5)

Questions: Are we our brothers' keepers? Is society responsible for providing for all who cannot care for themselves? Should society provide for only food, shelter, clothing, and medical care? What about education, cultural enrichment, and economic needs?

3. *Preferred interventions.* What kind of policy remedies should be chosen to address specific social problems? (p. 5)

Questions: Should drug abusers be jailed, or should drugs be legalized? Should society emphasize treatment and prevention of drug abuse, or should the focus primarily be on keeping drugs from entering the country and on enforcement of antidrug laws? Should society prohibit abortions, or continue to allow them, and on what terms? Should there be gun control, and on what terms? Should society force the homeless into shelters or hospitals, or jail them if they refuse to go to either?

4. *Compensatory strategies.* Should society give preferential assistance or treatment to members of specific groups that lag behind the rest of the population in economic and other conditions? (p. 5)

Questions: Does not society do this through welfare and other programs?

The real question is, to what extent and when does society provide assistance and treatment? Should society guarantee basic health care for those who cannot afford such care? Should affirmative action programs, which seek to guarantee jobs, education placements, and contract work to members of minorities, take precedence over equal opportunity programs?

5. *Magnitude of federal policy roles.* What policy powers should federal authorities possess, and what should be the magnitude of federal social spending? (p. 5)

Questions: Is the federal government too large? Are state and local governments better able to know and understand the needs of their people? Should the federal government step in to meet the needs of its citizens if state and local governments cannot? Does the federal government, through its policies and funding power, wield too much influence on state and local policies and practices? Should federal social spending be limited to maintaining a balanced budget or until additional taxes are needed?

The various interest groups continue to disagree in their answers to these and many other questions. A brief look, however, at just a few specific issues dealing with welfare, life, and death will further exemplify the problem.

WELFARE

The proposals being considered for several years by states to deny benefits to single mothers on welfare who then have additional children raise many moral issues. Conservatives felt that such benefits reward welfare mothers for having more children, thereby providing an incentive for them to become welfare dependent. Conservative opinion was that it is basically irresponsible to bring children into the world if one cannot adequately provide for them. Should society support this perceived irresponsible behavior? Liberals argued that society has an obligation to take care of those in need and that children should not be punished for the behavior of their parents. They also question the assertion that denial of benefits for additional children is an effective way to help the mothers become more independent. They question whether the proposed cuts would really discourage these women from having additional children. Could not society find better ways of helping welfare mothers become independent of the welfare system?

Better yet, can society not find a way to end poverty?

EUTHANASIA

The issue of euthanasia was revived suddenly and sharply when a doctor helped a woman suffering with Alzheimer's disease commit suicide. The doctor was charged with murder, but the case was dismissed because there was no state law that prohibited assisted suicides. The same doctor, through the use of devices he developed, assisted two other women to commit suicide (Two doctor-assisted suicides, 1991). In both instances, the doctor provided the means, and the women committed the act. There was no doubt that the women wanted to die; however, several disturbing ethical questions remain. Should assisted suicides be allowed? If so, other questions need answering. Who is to assist, and under what circumstances? Should these decisions be made by the patient, family, doctor, community, all, or a combination of some of these?

What criteria should be used to justify active (assisted) or even passive (unassisted) euthanasia? Should the criteria be age, finances, quality of life, life expectancy, health, or any other condition? Should euthanasia be legalized? Should the federal government attempt to override the decision of the voters of a state to legalize euthanasia? The Hemlock Society, a group that supports suicide and assisted suicide for the dying, strongly endorses the right to die and the legalization of euthanasia (Humphry, 1991).

Let us take a closer look at how the clash of values creates problems that directly affect human services workers, consumers, and people in general. In presidential campaigns and budget or legislative battles, one constantly hears contestants speak of American values, or what is right. Are the American values of conservatives more valid than those of liberals? Who decides what values are American values? Do liberals know more about what is right than do conservatives? What about individuals, schools, churches and synagogues, or any other institutional perceptions of American values, or of what is right or moral? How one resolves these questions is essential, for it is their attempted resolution that allows us to struggle somewhat successfully as a democratic society. Some issues that highlight this struggle, which were touched upon in previous chapters, follow.

For example, is it an American value or morally right both to perpetuate corporate welfare and significantly limit welfare to the poor? Some claim that each is an American value and morally right because it helps the poor get off welfare and helps the economy and the effort to balance the budget. Others claim that corporate welfare should be cut because it is too costly and helps corporations and businesses rather than the individuals in need.

Is it an American value or morally right to maintain a minimum wage that does not provide enough income to raise individuals and families above the poverty level? Some still claim that raising the minimum wage any higher will create inflation and cause the loss of jobs; therefore, it is better not to increase it. Completing the exercise "Ranking American Values" at the end of this chapter might help clarify the many differences and issues regarding the use, and frequent overuse—most often by political candidates and their supporters—of the concept of American values.

Aside from these being significant moral issues and sources of controversy in our society, they are perfect examples of how social policies are influenced through the interpretation of policies and laws (discussed in Chapter 7).

REPRODUCTIVE CHOICES

When does life begin? This is a question that has been fiercely debated for many years. For some it is a philosophical or scientific question, while others view it as a religious one. The issue of abortion and whether women should have the right to choose whether or not to have a child is a deeply personal belief as well as a national political issue. The Supreme Court in its 1973 *Roe v. Wade* decision affirmed that women should have the right to choose. Since that time antiabortion and pro-choice groups have continued to battle on many fronts.

Various Supreme Court decisions since the 1973 landmark case have weakened the original *Roe v. Wade* decision. In 1992 the Supreme Court upheld a Pennsylvania law requiring physicians to give counseling to women seeking abortions and mandated a 24-hour waiting period before receiving an abortion. Several other states have passed laws restricting abortions in various ways. Additional restrictions include informed consent, parental notification, and allowing abortion only in cases of rape, incest, and risk to the woman's health. Many of these restrictions are now being contested in the courts (Mandell & Schram, 2006).

Advances in medical science have created additional reproductive choices as well as further ethical and moral questions. Couples unable to conceive children are increasingly turning to in vitro fertilization (IVF) and/or intrauterine insemination (IUI). The national odds for twins are 1 pair per 90 live births. However, over the past two decades, primarily as a result of IVF and IUI treatments, the twinning rate has doubled nationally. Another contributing factor to the increase in twin births is the rising average age of pregnant women; the older the woman, the more eggs released. For women who undergo successful fertility treatments, the rate of multiple births is about one in three. Even though triplets are still somewhat rare, the rate has gone up 300% in twenty years (Bernard & Lindren, 2006). Some couples who have undergone fertility treatment in the hope of having a single child are now faced with the increased possibility of multiple births. Many such couples have elected to have a "reduction" of the pregnancy to a single fetus, that is, reducing the multiple pregnancy of two or three to one.

Often considerations to have a reduction include the increased health risks to the mother and child associated with multiple births, increased financial strains on the family, and increased potential for marital stress and strain on the couple. Decisions to conceive artificially as well as to reduce the pregnancy are often fraught with a complex mix of legal, moral, religious, and political issues.

As discussed more fully in Chapter 5, a human services worker's personal values are always present when working with clients. Should you attempt to hide your own views so your bias does not subtly influence the choices of your client? Will your values and beliefs interfere with your work with a client when a referral to another worker might be appropriate? These and other ethical questions continue to be debated today. Some within the field, such as Tjeltveit (1986), suggest that referrals are appropriate when moral, religious, or political values are centrally involved in a client's presenting problems. This may cause the worker to be unable to maintain objectivity. However, as Corey, Corey, and Callahan (1998) point out, merely having a conflict of values does not necessarily require a referral; it is possible to work through such a conflict to a successful resolution. When dealing with individuals for whom issues such as these are of central importance, it is essential for workers to be aware and clear about their own beliefs and values. Workers must convey their views, and make their positions known to the client so that their biases do not interfere with the client's decision-making process.

GOVERNMENT: HOW MUCH SUPPORT FOR THE NEEDY?

In the 1980s and 1990s, the struggle over the federal budget highlighted a major controversy affecting human services workers and programs. The Reagan and Bush administrations and Congress significantly reduced funding for some programs that provided a safety net to help the truly needy. Even in the 1960s, at the height of President Johnson's Great Society when the Democrats were in the majority in both houses, there was tremendous pressure to reduce domestic spending (Califano, 1994). The pressure was focused primarily on programs serving those in need. According to many liberals, whenever pressure is on to reduce spending, there seems to be a pattern of primarily reducing domestic spending for the needy over reducing spending for defense or other needs. One needs only to look at the proposed and actual cuts in budgets over the years to see how direct support and indirect support for those most in need are targeted for reduced aid.

The proposed cuts and reduced rate in spending for social programs starting in 1995 in an effort to achieve a balanced budget in 2002 were successful. That there will be reductions in the rate of domestic spending is a certainty; however, what specifically will be cut and by how much are examples of a clash of values between conservatives and liberals. The question raised in the title of this section (that is, how much support for the needy?) provokes further discord regarding values and morality. One might say there is never enough support as long as over 39 million people live in poverty, over 40 million have no health insurance, and so on. Other conservatives and liberals point out that we cannot afford to help everyone. Although agreement is found in this regard, little agreement can be found on how much we can afford, who should be helped, and by what means. We do know, however, that too many need health care, jobs, nutrition, shelter, vaccines, treatment for mental illness, and welfare, among many other necessities.

The changes in the budgets of social programs raise key questions regarding the role of government in providing services. Who has the ultimate responsibility for the welfare of those in need? Is it the local, state, or federal government? Does government have responsibility for the welfare of only those who are poor? These and other questions will always be raised as long as there are people in need, funds are limited, and those in power make decisions that reflect their values and philosophies. A look at some of those who seek support and the issues they face will help identify the problems one must deal with as a human services worker.

TARGET POPULATIONS: THE STRUGGLE FOR SUPPORT

The struggle for support takes place on two major fronts. One is the struggle to gain the moral support of the public, the media, and professionals. That generally involves convincing others that your goals are just and good. The second front, closely related to the first, is the struggle to gain financial support.

Throughout the late 1990s, three populations frequently made the headlines: welfare **recipients**, AIDS patients, and the homeless. The reason they were so often in the news was that society was desperately trying to provide additional and more effective programs to help and to cope with these people.

One major problem in trying to develop more successful programs for these groups is how they are perceived by others. Much of the public, much of the media, and many politicians, legislators, officials, and, yes, human services workers have a negative attitude toward these people (Dye, 1987; Marin, 1987). Richardson (1998) reports that frustration and fear of AIDS have given rise to the passage of a series of laws intended to protect the public from people infected with HIV. For the homeless and welfare recipients, the myths about these populations contribute to the public's negative attitudes. (These issues will be discussed further later in the chapter.) Although many others have very positive attitudes and do whatever they can to help these groups, effective programs are difficult to develop without significant public, media, and professional support.

A second major problem that makes the development of more successful programs very difficult is the diversity of values and points of view regarding the most effective ways of dealing with these groups. These two factors lead to the third problem, namely, that of funding programs for these and other needy populations. The variety of possible solutions given by the professionals involved with developing programs, as well as those offered by the public and the media, reflects the different and often conflicting philosophies and values that create problems in shaping effective policies and programs. The first group to be considered here will be people with AIDS.

The AIDS Epidemic

The question of priorities in the funding of treatment and research programs of various social and medical problems has become quite controversial. Because a limited amount of funds is provided for these programs, if funds are increased for one program, must they be reduced in another program? Such a conflict over delegation of funds has now become quite heated in the fight against AIDS. The powerful AIDS lobby has been fighting for and demanding significant increases in funding for treatment and research for their constituents. However, significant controversy persists about the level of funding that should be supplied for various diseases. According to Califano (1994), the federal government reported that fewer than 800,000 deaths were due to heart disease and over 500,000 were due to cancer in 1993, but 25,000 people died of AIDS.

Over the years, funding of approximately $1–1.5 billion or more was provided for the fight against each of these diseases. In spite of the difference in the number of fatalities, which has been fairly consistent in recent years, Edmondson (1990) urges that the fight against AIDS should be funded at a much higher level than before for two reasons. First, two-thirds of those who die of cancer are over 65 years of age, and over half of those who die of heart disease are over 75 years of age. By comparison, most people who die of AIDS are under 40 years old. Therefore, the lives of AIDS patients were cut short, often before their real contributions to society could be made. Those who died at later ages had made their contribution and had lived fuller lives. The second reason given by Edmondson for increased funding for the fight against AIDS was that AIDS is infectious. What would you decide if it were in your power and you had to make such a decision?

There are two additional controversial practices regarding the AIDS issue, both aimed at reducing the spread of the virus: (a) exchanging dirty needles for clean ones for drug users, and (b) distributing condoms to high school students. There was no guarantee, according to the critics, that the exchanged needles would not be shared among users. The feeling was that such a program also encouraged drug use. Meanwhile, the New Haven program of exchange, authorized by the Connecticut state legislature, provided evidence that such programs could be successful.

The distribution of condoms in high schools under specific conditions has been approved in Philadelphia, San Francisco, Los Angeles, and New York City, among other jurisdictions. The approval in each case was attained not without controversy and struggle. In New York City, for example, it was approved only after a long— and still continuing—struggle against the program by many parents, religious organizations, and others. Opponents of the program claim that none of the demonstration programs was actually proven effective, and there was no guarantee that the condoms provided would actually be used. Such programs, it was felt, encouraged young people to engage in sexual intercourse.

These issues regarding funding and how best to develop programs to prevent the spread of AIDS have led to a great deal of frustration and struggle. The attempt by some infected individuals to purposely infect others has created additional fears. These problems have given rise to a series of laws to protect the public. Some of them overrule previous privacy protection. Some require notification of partners of an infected individual. Others demand testing of segments of the population, and many states make it a crime to purposely and knowingly infect someone (Richardson, 1998).

What else can one, should one, do to help prevent the spread of AIDS?

- Isolate victims from the uninfected population?
- Prohibit children infected with the AIDS virus from attending regular school or day-care centers?
- Distribute free hypodermic needles to drug addicts to prevent the sharing of needles and thus the spread of the virus?
- Teach contraceptive methods in elementary and secondary schools as a form of prevention of the spread of AIDS?
- Mandate testing for the virus and specify who shall be tested?
- Make the names of those who test positive available to the public?

THE HOMELESS

When one looks at the problems of the homeless, one finds many different attitudes and approaches to solving them. A conservative candidate in the 1992 presidential race recommended that the homeless be forcibly taken to shelters or jailed if they resisted and tried to sleep on the streets. Other candidates did not appear to feel that homelessness was an election-year issue, even though the problem seemed to be increasing. Advocates for the homeless, however, strongly urge an increase in low-income subsidized housing.

Others believe that deinstitutionalization is a major cause of homelessness and that mental patients make up the majority of the homeless. Mental illness, however, is not a major cause of homelessness. According to the National Law Center on Homelessness and Poverty, about 25% of the homeless are mentally ill. Truly major causes of homelessness are unemployment, **underemployment**, and the lack of affordable rental housing. A survey by the U.S. Conference of Mayors, 1998, found that about 27% of the homeless population work and are still without a home.

Nevertheless, in some jurisdictions the mentally ill become a political football. If, for example, most of the homeless are considered mentally ill, they become a state problem; if they are not, they are a local problem. Kozol (1988) and Johnson (1990) both make the point that poverty, not mental illness, is the major cause of homelessness, even though some homeless people do need psychological treatment. Income and subsidized housing, they believe, would resolve the issue.

For the homeless, should we and can we:

- Allow them to sleep in public places and on the streets?
- Allow them to use and sleep in abandoned buildings?
- Allow them in any business or residential neighborhood they choose?
- Allow them to forage in garbage for food or anything else of value to them?
- Force them off the streets and into shelters or hospitals against their will?
- Provide subsidized housing?

WELFARE RECIPIENTS

The third group, welfare recipients, is also of major concern to society. Many taxpayers resent paying taxes to support welfare recipients who are all too frequently stigmatized and stereotyped as being lazy, cheats, and welfare-dependent. However, few of these very same taxpayers and others realize how many people receive government benefits in one way or another (Abramovitz, 1983). For example, tobacco, sugar, and dairy farmers, among others, are paid billions of tax dollars each year to limit production and to maintain price levels that assure profits. Are they the truly needy? What about all those who are able to take deductions on income taxes for health costs, interest on mortgages, entertainment for business, and other items? Although the government does not actually pay cash to these more affluent people, it is, in effect, telling them that they can keep the money they would have to pay were the deductions not allowed. These deductions total billions each year. Actually, it turns out that the more money one makes, the more benefits one may get through increased deductions (Abramovitz, 1991). What about community and state college students who obtain federal and state aid? Tax monies are supporting them in obtaining an education even if they are paying the full tuition. Do they and all the others mentioned see themselves as "welfare recipients"? Clearly, we taxpayers have fewer problems with government aid dispensed to "us" rather than to "them," especially when the "others" are poor and in need of food, clothing, and shelter. The question really is, why are these kinds of benefits acceptable and those for the truly needy less so?

Should it be mandated that welfare recipients

- Take whatever jobs are available, including dead-end jobs?
- Accept jobs, even if the wages would be less than their welfare benefits?
- Participate in job-training programs?
- Perform community work, if jobs are not available, in exchange for some of their benefits?
- Have their extra benefits reduced for additional children?
- Pay the actual cost of their education in community and state colleges (they are all subsidized by state and local tax monies)?

The many questions raised with each group are controversial enough in their own right. Additional questions arise that may be of particular concern to human services workers. One question has to do with the problem of individual rights versus rights of the public. Another question has to do with the apparent effort to control these **target populations** in some fashion. Are we not really attempting to devise behavioral and social controls for people who, for the most part, are victims of situations beyond their control, and who, for the most part, have not broken any laws? Other controversies in the human services center around the effects of a conservative government and/or a recession on social programs. The basic question is, whose benefits shall be cut?

Regardless of who has control of the purse strings, be they liberals or conservatives, there will always be a limited amount of funds made available for social programs. This is clearly a political decision. The general trend has been that in times of prosperity and/or when liberals are in power, social programs are funded more generously. When conservatives are in power, support for social programs is usually significantly reduced. The major questions then become, which programs shall be reduced or eliminated? Shall it be programs serving senior citizens, or school lunch programs, or programs for people with disabilities? What about programs for the homeless, the mentally ill and retarded, or the poor? Who shall make the decisions?

What criteria would you use in making these choices? These kinds of questions and their answers create all kinds of tensions in the human services field. Peirce (1982) perhaps answers some of these questions when discussing budget cuts made by the local, state, and federal government. He points out that "the stark fact is that the budget cuts it makes are far deeper in subsidized housing, in job training, in welfare and education programs of primary benefit to poor people than to programs the middle class utilizes most—social security, Medicare, civil service, and military pension levels" (p. 14).

Although it is generally acknowledged that all of the groups receiving support have a legitimate claim to that support, it becomes clear that some programs will lose funding when cuts have to be made. Several things happen in situations like this. First, the agencies serving the different target populations, and the members of those populations, start competing strenuously with one another for available funds. The most articulate and organized of the various target populations, the ones with the most political influence, generally are more successful in gaining support and funds. As an example, the outcry some time ago by the recipients of social security about the threat of reduced benefits tempered efforts in benefit reduction.

When funds are cut and staff reductions occur, caseloads tend to increase. This then requires a screening process that assures those in most need get service, while others are turned away. The increased caseload puts additional pressure on the workers, and services to the needy often suffer. Competition and struggle for existence shift the focus, energies, and resources away from a unified effort by target populations and the human services field to increase overall funding for social programs. This kind of competition seems to demand that the strong shall survive and the weak shall perish.

SEXUAL EXPRESSION AMONG OLDER ADULTS

In the past, the subject of sexuality among older adults was a topic that received little or no attention. Human services and health care professionals, for the most part, discouraged any type of sexual activity for this group. The prevailing opinion was that older people should gradually disengage from active pursuits, and that this disengagement should include withdrawal from sexual interest and expression. Many professionals even believed that sexual needs and desires simply ceased to exist among older adults.

Today, however, as we continue to live longer and healthier lives, human services and health care professionals are beginning to reexamine their beliefs about

Active senior couple taking a break from cycling to kiss each other.

sexuality in late life. Advances in medicine, pharmacology, and medical technology have given all of us the opportunity to pursue an active lifestyle well into late life, including the expression of sexual intimacy. Because of these changes, part of the new role of professionals, especially those working in residential facilities, is to understand the role of sexuality in late life and to promote conditions that allow sexual expression among older adults. As McInnis-Dittrich states in her book *Social Work with Older Adults* (2009), "sexual interest [among older adults] is an expression of a continuing need for love and intimacy."

Unfortunately, many professionals have been slow to respond to this need to reexamine attitudes about sexual expression in late life. Some find it difficult to change because of traditional attitudes or because the mere thought of a parent or grandparent engaging in any type of sexual activity is distasteful. Others still view sexual activity among older adults as a health risk, while some others view it as immoral. Clearly, these attitudes can influence how human services and other professionals interact with their older clients, and whether or not they are supportive of their clients' desires for sexual intimacy.

It is crucial that professionals reexamine their attitudes toward sexual intimacy needs in late life, because the number of older adults is rapidly growing. The U.S. Census Bureau (2008) estimates that by 2030, one out of five of our population will be age 65 or older. If current trends continue, a significant proportion of these individuals will decide to live in some type of residential facility such as senior housing, assisted living, or adult homes. Many of these seniors will wish to continue to experience sexual intimacy. The human services professionals who serve them will therefore need to develop constructive attitudes toward late life sexual expression in order to ensure quality of life for their clients.

Clearly there is a need for educational workshops to inform professionals about the sexual needs of older adults (Edwards, 2003). These workshops should also help professionals examine their own personal feelings in this area. Over the past ten to fifteen years, some workshops have been developed to address this need for professional training; however, most of these have been too brief and were often received with amusement or lack of interest by the professionals attending them.

Recent research (Low, Lui, Lee, Thompson, & Chau, 2005) suggests that workshops about late life sexuality should include several main components.

> *Phase 1: Sensitivity training.* In order for professionals to develop new strategies for helping older adults meet their sexual needs, the professionals themselves must be open to a new way of thinking about late life sexuality. This phase of training should focus on helping professionals to change their negative or outdated attitudes toward sexual intimacy among older adults.
>
> *Phase 2: Information and education.* This phase of training involves providing professionals with information about late life sexuality. For example, professionals need to know that the number one preferred sexual activity for older adults is kissing and hugging, while sexual intercourse is third. It is also important for professionals to understand the potential benefits of sexual expression among older adults. For instance, in a 2004 AARP survey, older adults reported that sexual activity improved the quality of their lives.
>
> *Phase 3: Assessment and evaluation.* The third, and for some professionals the most important phase, should be assessment and evaluation. Our ultimate objective as

professionals is to help older adults make healthy, self-directed decisions about their lives. However, we also need to ensure that older adults who suffer from dementia are protected against sexual exploitation. Therefore, professionals need training in how to assess decision-making capacity in older adults so they can determine whether the older adult truly understands the potential benefits and consequences of sexual activity. How to adequately address the sexual intimacy needs of older adults with dementia is a challenging, controversial, and difficult question.

An alternative approach is to include older adults along with professionals in educational groups focused on late life sexuality. Some facilities in New York City, for example, are developing groups that include both staff and residents. Under the guidance of a trained group leader, staff and residents express their needs and concerns regarding sexual expression among residents. Many facilities are also trying to find ways to provide the necessary privacy for sexual expression within the context of a residential living situation.

- What are your personal feelings about sexual intimacy among older adults?
- Should nursing home residents who are not married be allowed privacy for sexual intimacy?
- How do you balance the need to protect people with dementia from sexual exploitation versus their need for sexual expression?
- How do we best help older adults protect themselves against sexually transmitted diseases?
- To what extent does a staff member assist an older adult in sexual expression? For example, do they go as far as to purchase sexual aids for them?

PROFESSIONALISM IN THE HUMAN SERVICES

Two major and muted struggles have developed among human services workers over the years. Both struggles involve money, status, and levels of responsibility. One conflict occurs between generalist human services workers and traditional professional human services workers. The other conflict occurs among traditional professional human services workers. Fortunately, these quarrels have not had significant ill effects on the direct services provided by the human services workers themselves. It is nonetheless important to know and understand the different points of view of the various contestants, as well as to recognize that all is not sweetness and light in the helping professions. A brief description of the issues follows.

Since the introduction of indigenous community leaders as paraprofessionals in the War on Poverty of the 1960s, the number of workers in the human services has grown steadily and rapidly. In addition, the responsibilities, knowledge, training, and competence of generalist human services workers have, from their point of view, increased to a level comparable to that of traditional professional human services workers. Furthermore, large numbers of generalist human services workers, and some traditional professional human services workers, believe strongly that many generalists outperform traditional professional workers. These convictions on the part of generalist human services workers are the basis for strong feelings about the differences in pay, status, responsibilities, and opportunities for advancement between generalists and traditional professional human services workers.

Many educators believe that graduates of recognized undergraduate human services programs should be considered professionals. Generalist human services workers assert that, although they do not have graduate degrees, the combination of their life experiences and limited formal education are "credentials" equal to those obtained through advanced formal education.

Many human services educators are convinced that human services is a profession and that graduates of recognized college human services programs should be considered professionals. In addition, some feel that human services is an evolving profession. These and other human services educators assert that most criteria needed for the establishment of the traditional human services professions have been met in regard to the human services. These criteria include, among others, a professional membership organization, regional and nationwide annual professional conferences, journals, standards for approval of college human services curricula, and an organization to approve college programs (for example, the Council for Standards in Human Services Education). Furthermore, according to other human services workers and educators, the growth of graduate degree programs in human services is further proof of professionalism in the human services.

On the other hand, human services workers with advanced degrees feel that their advanced intensive training provides them with greater knowledge and skill in providing specific services and enables them to function at a significantly higher level than can generalist human services workers. Professionalism, they assert, is based on the attainment of a specific body of knowledge unique to that field and gained only through traditional professional schools. Much of the knowledge and skill referred to by traditional professionals deals with clinical functions in addition to supervisory and educational responsibilities directly related to their specific profession. These professions might include psychology, occupational therapy, social work, and others described in Chapter 6.

In addition, these professionals feel strongly that until college human services programs are accredited by an organization sanctioned by the Council on Post-Secondary Accreditation, the human services is not yet a profession. The council is the only organization sanctioned by the U.S. Department of Education to allow specific groups to provide recognized accreditation. These people also believe that until human services is recognized and incorporated into the Civil Service Systems as a profession, it is not to be considered a profession. The struggle goes on, and you will be faced with this issue in one way or another, to one degree or another, as a human services worker.

The efforts of generalist human services workers to gain recognition and parity with traditional professionals are duplicated among the traditional professionals themselves. The main issue is which traditional professionals shall be eligible for third-party payment without the need to be supervised by those with higher standing or credentials. Third-party payment is payment to the traditional professional by an insurance company, such as Blue Cross or Medicare, for services provided to the client. Third-party payment permits many more individuals to obtain help that they otherwise could not afford. Third-party payment also significantly increases the amount of income for agencies and traditional professionals who provide services to the needy.

Who, then, among the traditional professionals is eligible to receive these third-party payments? Most traditional human services professionals, particularly those in private practice, are eager to be included in these programs. Medical doctors and psychiatrists are included in all such programs. In most jurisdictions psychologists are included, and in others they are not. Social workers and other traditional human services professionals are also not included everywhere. In certain situations, some traditional professionals are included in these programs only if they are supervised by a traditional professional of another discipline.

Professionals in one discipline object strenuously to being supervised by those in other disciplines. A more recent issue centers on the armed forces' permitting psychologists to prescribe psychotropic medication. Should this practice be permitted for all trained psychologists? Will other professions seek the same or other privileges? Is the practice helpful to clients? These and other questions arise as competition between and among human services workers exists.

Another complication is that competition for jobs has increased in recent years as a result of the growing number of professionals and cuts in programs and services. Unfortunately, few if any positive changes have occurred regarding these professional issues to date.

Acceptance into these insurance programs is achieved, for the most part, through legislative action at local, state, or national levels. Therefore, the professional organizations representing the different disciplines lobby to have their members included in these programs. Professional groups already included in the plans often oppose the inclusion of new groups, claiming that they are only trying to protect the public. Some think there is enough to go around for everyone and that the constant competition for high status, recognition, and control does little for the image and dignity of human services workers.

Another professional issue that is being raised among many social workers involves whom social workers serve. Specht and Courtney (1994) state the issue clearly:

> Today, a significant proportion of social workers are practicing psychotherapy, and doing so privately, with a primarily middle-class, professional, Caucasian clientele in the 20- to 40-year age group. The poor have not gone away; there are more of them now than at any time in recent memory. Certainly many professional social workers are still committed to the public social services, to helping poor people and dealing with social problems, but a large part of the profession is "adrift in the psychiatric seas." (p. x)

They further claim that it is the former kinds of students and practitioners "that the profession needs if it is to realize its original mission" (p. x). Jacobson (2001) supports this view asserting that what has been destructive to this mission "has been the encroachment of therapeutic practice on the field as a whole" (pp. 51–61). Few can doubt that we are in desperate need of such human services workers. Huff and Johnson (1993) recognized this issue when they wrote the following:

> Since its birth, social work has been in the vanguard of many national reforms, often speaking on behalf of populations who are too beleaguered to forcefully represent themselves. Of late, too many social workers have abandoned the traditional mission as advocates for social justice. Social workers must rededicate themselves to leading a new reform movement dedicated to a more equitable redistribution of America's wealth. (p. 315)

The same might be said regarding many other human services workers.

THE ROLE OF HUMAN SERVICES WORKERS

Is the role of the human services worker to help individuals solve their interpersonal problems? Is it to help them cope with the stress brought on by financial difficulties, physical disabilities, or other outside pressures? Or is it to try to help change those conditions that create the problems in the first place?

During the War on Poverty in the latter part of the 1960s, agencies were formed to fight poverty, racism, and crime, among other problems. Federal, state, and local governments, as well as some private foundations, funded these agencies. The workers in an agency located in a high poverty and crime area helped local residents learn their rights in the courts. The workers went to court with their clients to protest against police brutality when it occurred. They taught them how to organize and conduct rent strikes when the tenants were not getting service. They also defended people who were on welfare whenever they needed help (Krozney, 1966). The focus of human services workers during those years was mainly on helping people cope with injustice (Morales & Sheafor, 1980). The main concept was gaining and using power, and people did protest and fight against injustice. However, in one case, the protests and struggles aroused those who were threatened by these actions and who in turn brought pressure on those in power to curtail the funding for such projects. This, in effect, changed the nature of the role of the workers. No longer able to use government funds to fight "the Establishment"—government agencies and supporters—human services workers shifted their focus to helping clients adjust to their situation.

There are still many human services workers who feel that helping people adjust to their problems is not a very useful activity. To adjust to poverty, racism, crime, mental illness, and similar problems rather than to make every effort to combat or prevent these problems is seen by many as a losing battle.

Poverty still exists, and the gap between the wealthy and the poor continues to grow. The number of people in need of mental health services has increased, even though mental hospitals have released large numbers of patients. Child abuse and partner abuse have increased. Treatment and living conditions of senior citizens leave much to be desired. All this has occurred in spite of the efforts of human services programs to date.

What else, then, can a human services worker do? "Become more of an activist," urge the activists. "But activists are seen as radicals by the public, government officials, and other human services workers," is often the reply. It is true that activists in the human services do not often win a lot of friends. The activist role usually stirs controversy and involves some risk. A worker some years ago prevented clients from entering an unlicensed nursing home and was reprimanded by his agency. The worker, with the help of his union, not only had the reprimand withdrawn but initiated action on a state level to change the rules regarding placing people in unlicensed nursing homes. The worker was successful in that instance. Activists, unfortunately, are not always successful; but if there is to be any chance for success in eliminating injustice, there must be activists. Today, however, the practice of advocacy is growing and accepted in the human services professions. (See Chapter 6 for details.)

WHOM DO HUMAN SERVICES WORKERS SERVE?

The answer to this question seems obvious and simple. In theory, it might be. However, in practice, significant issues arise. For example, suppose you are a human services worker in a mental hospital. The policy is to discharge patients as quickly as possible. One of your patients has been selected for discharge, and you are asked to follow through, but you are convinced that the patient is not able to function outside the institution. He is generally stabilized in the institution, however, and has been there for over six months without creating trouble, so "get him out" is the word. What do you do? You are working for the hospital, and it is under pressure to discharge as many patients as possible in the shortest time possible. You are also responsible for the patient's well-being. What happens if you do not discharge the patient? What happens if you do discharge the patient? This situation has actually occurred, not once but many times, in state institutions.

There are several possible answers to the question, "Whom do human services workers serve?" They include the client, the agencies for which they work, the government, society in general, and themselves. Some workers would claim that it is possible to serve all of these but not at the same time or to the same degree. In any case, human services workers might soon be required to make difficult choices regarding whom they serve.

An even more complicated situation arises if and when workers who are paid by third parties, such as insurance companies or Medicare, must give detailed reports of service to the companies. These reports identify not only the individuals but also the nature of the problem and the course of treatment. In effect, this is a break of confidentiality and a way of influencing the treatment provided. The insurance companies and managed care organizations often may attempt to limit or control the course of treatment. Do you as a human services worker go along with this kind of program, thus serving yourself with regard to payment and future patients? Do you refuse such a program and patients enrolled in those programs? Do you work with the patient anyway, even though payment might be reduced? Whom do you really serve—yourself, the insurance company, the client, or all three?

What about the situation in which you might be serving the taxpayer? Such a situation came up when eligibility criteria for disability payments were revised, and thousands of disabled persons were denied payments. The object here was to save the taxpayers' money and to cut costs to help reduce the federal deficit. What do you do when asked to administer such a program? Where do your human services responsibilities lie? Do they override your fiscal or administrative responsibilities?

The last example involves a much broader issue. It raises the questions not only of whom we serve, but also of when we serve them and at what cost. As stated previously, all the present efforts of human services have not been able to provide services for all those in need. Choices must be made. How do you, the human services worker, make them? Furthermore, if one chooses to become an activist or to work in prevention programs, those in need of specific help are denied your services. These kinds of choices affect those in need, other human services workers, professional organizations, legislators, and the public in general.

Without further description or comment, many other controversial issues in the following list and those already described should provide you with more than enough material to ponder at this point.

Large-scale rally for immigrant rights.

- Illegal immigration
- Legal immigration
- Poverty
- Violence in the media
- Unemployment
- Alcoholism
- Gambling
- Sexual harassment
- Criminal justice
- Hunger
- Mental illness
- Health crisis

All this may be confusing, but it can also be stimulating and exciting to struggle with these issues and discover your own way as a competent human services worker.

A BASIC READING AND THINKING SKILL[1]

RANKING AMERICAN VALUES

This activity will give you an opportunity to discuss with classmates the values you and your classmates consider important and the values you believe are considered most important by the majority of Americans.

PART 1

Step 1.   Working in groups of four to six students, each group should rank the values listed in what the group considers the order of importance to the majority of Americans. Assign the number 1 to the value the group believes is most important to the majority of Americans, the number 2 to the second most important value, and so on until all the values have been ranked.

Step 2.   Each group should compare its ranking with others in an all-class discussion.

Step 3.   The entire class should discuss the following questions.

1.   What noticeable differences do you see between the personal rankings in part 1 and the perceived rankings of the majority of Americans in part 2?
2.   How would you explain these differences?
3.   What conclusions would you draw about America's future in light of your rankings in parts 1 and 2?

ADDITIONAL READING

Mandell, B. R., & Schram, B. (2006). *An introduction to human services: Policy and practice* (6th ed.). Boston, MA: Allyn & Bacon.

REFERENCES

Abramovitz, M. (1983). Everyone is on welfare: "The role of redistribution in social policy" revisited. In I. Colby (Ed.), *Social welfare policy: Perspectives, patterns, insights.* Belmont, CA: Wadsworth.

Abramovitz, M. (1991). Putting an end to doublespeak about race, gender, and poverty: An annotated glossary for social workers. *Social Work, 36,* 380–384.

Bernard, S., & Lindren, H. (2006, June 12). Gangs of New York. *New York Magazine,* pp. 22–23.

Califano, J. A. (1994). *Radical surgery: What's next for America's health care?* New York: Times Books/Random House.

Corey, G., Corey, M. S., & Callahan, D. (1998). *Issues and ethics in the helping professions* (5th ed.). Pacific Grove, CA: Brooks/Cole.

Dye, T. R. (1987). *Understanding public policy* (6th ed.). Upper Saddle River, NJ: Prentice Hall.

Edmondson, B. (1990, March). Why AIDS deserves what it gets. *American Demographics,* p. 28.

---

[1]The following is from Opposing Viewpoints Series. Copyright © Greenhaven Press Inc. Reprinted with permission.

Edwards, D. J. (2003, February). Sex & intimacy in the nursing home: among many issues, resident privacy is key. *Nursing Homes*, pp. 13–19.

Huff, D. D., & Johnson, D. A. (1993, May). Phantom welfare: Public relief for corporate America. *Social Work, 38*(3), 311–315.

Humphry, D. (1991). *Final exit: Practicalities of self-deliverance and assisted suicides for the dying.* Eugene, OR: Hemlock Society.

Jacobson, W. B. (2001). Beyond therapy: Bringing social work back to human service reform. *Social Work, 46*(1), 51–61.

Jansson, B. S. (1988). *The reluctant welfare state: A history of American social welfare policies.* Belmont, CA: Wadsworth.

Johnson, A. B. (1990). *Out of bedlam: The truth about deinstitutionalization.* New York: Basic Books.

Kozol, J. (1988). Mental illness does not cause homelessness. In L. Orr (Ed.), *The homeless: Opposing viewpoints* (pp. 109–111). San Diego: Greenhaven.

Krozney, H. (1966). *Beyond welfare: Poverty in the super city.* New York: Holt, Rinehart & Winston.

Low, L. P. L., Lui, M. H. L., Lee, D. T. F., Thompson, D. R., & Chau, J. P. C. (2005, August). Mandell, B. R., & Schram, B. (2006). *An introduction to human services: Policy and practice.* Boston: Allyn & Bacon.

Marin, P. (1987, January). Helping and hating the homeless: The struggle at the margins of America. *Harper's Magazine*, pp. 39–49.

McInnis-Dittrich, K. (2009). *Social work with older adults* (3rd ed.). Boston, MA: Allyn & Bacon.

Montenegro, X. P., & Fisher, L. (2005, May). Sexuality at midlife and beyond: 2004 update of attitudes & behaviors. *AARP The Magazine*, pp. 18–21.

Morales, A., & Sheafor, B. W. (1980). *Social work: A profession of many faces* (2nd ed.). Boston: Allyn & Bacon.

Peirce, N. R. (1982, Summer). New federalism and the social services: Friends or foes? *New England Journal of Human Services, 2*, 13–19.

Richardson, L. (1998, September 25). Wave of laws aimed at people with H.I.V. *New York Times*, pp. A1, B4.

Specht, H., & Courtney, M. (1994). *Unfaithful angels.* New York: Free Press.

Tjeltveit, A. C. (1986). The ethics of value conversion in psychotherapy: Appropriate and inappropriate therapist influence on client values. *Clinical Psychology Review, 6,* 515–537.

Two doctor-assisted suicides ruled homicides. (1991, December 19). *New York Times*, p.A29.

U.S. Census Bureau. (2008), from http://www.census.gov

GLOSSARY

acceptance Viewing another's thoughts, feelings, and attitudes as worthy, even if one doesn't agree with them.

acupuncture A traditional Chinese medicine in which needles are placed at key points along energy pathways of the body in order to restore energy balance.

advocacy Representing a client to obtain needed services.

advocate One who supports clients in obtaining services.

AFDC Aid to Families with Dependent Children: public assistance to families with children who have little or no income.

affective disorder A type of psychological disorder characterized by recurrent episodes of mania, depression, or both.

almshouse (poor house) A type of shelter created by the Government of England during the 1600s to house the disadvantaged.

alternative medicine Various approaches to diagnosis and treatment that fall outside of conventional medical treatments.

Alzheimer's disease A chronic and progressive brain disorder characterized by loss of cognitive functions, such as short-term memory.

amphetamines Stimulant drugs that initially produce an energizing or euphoric effect, sometimes followed by sudden "crashes" and depression.

anecdotal records Information or events recorded but unsupported by hard evidence.

animism The belief first held by primitive peoples that spirits inhabit inanimate objects such as rivers, volcanoes, or rocks, as well as living things.

Antabuse Trade name for disulfiram: a drug used in the treatment of alcoholism, causing an unpleasant reaction when alcohol is consumed.

antidepressant A type of drug used to elevate mood in depressed persons.

assessment Determining the scope of someone's problem, disability, or disorder.

asylum A place of refuge that provides food, shelter, and protection. The term came to be applied to a place of refuge for the unsound of mind.

attending The ability of the helper to be free from distraction and fully focused on the client. To "be there" for and with someone.

authenticity The act of being oneself or being real and not a phony.

338

aversive therapies Treatment methods employing punishment or noxious stimulation to reduce the frequency or strength of an undesirable behavior, for example, the use of Antabuse to control alcoholism.

barbituates A class of sedative-hypnotic compounds, sometimes used to treat insomnia, epilepsy, and anxiety.

behavior therapy The application of the principles of learning and conditioning theory to treatment of psychological and behavioral problems.

belongingness and love needs Needs for a feeling of closeness to others; third level of human needs on Abraham Maslow's hierarchy of needs.

benzodiazepine A class of chemically related compounds used to reduce tension and anxiety; diazepam (Valium) is an example.

biofeedback A technique used to help people gain voluntary control over a physiological function, such as blood pressure, by means of a device that provides a visual or auditory signal reflecting the strength of the response.

block grant Federal funds given to states to provide programs for a wide range of service needs.

budget An estimate of the income and expenses needed to carry out programs for a fiscal year.

burnout Job-related anxiety that adversely affects one's job satisfaction and personal life.

central nervous system (CNS) The part of the body containing the brain and spinal cord.

child abuse Actions involving physical or emotional injury to a child, as well as neglect of the child's basic needs.

classical conditioning The kind of learning that takes place when a neutral stimulus is paired with a stimulus that automatically produces a reflex response; the neutral stimulus comes to elicit the response.

clinical psychology The branch of psychology specializing in the diagnosis and treatment of mental and emotional disorders.

cocaine A drug derived from the coca plant that generally acts as a behavioral stimulant and may also produce anxiety and addictive cravings.

code of ethics A set of beliefs and standards of behavior/practice that serves to clarify and unify a particular field.

cognitive behavioral therapy (CBT) A type of therapy based upon the cognitive or thinking model that stresses how the way in which we perceive the world affects our emotions.

collective bargaining Negotiating union contracts on an industry-wide basis.

community mental health The provision of a coordinated program of mental health care to a specified population in a community setting, usually contrasted with provision of service in a large institution removed from the community.

community organizing The process of working toward the provision of a new or improved program for an underserved population in the community.

compensation The process of attempting to overcome real or imagined defects and weaknesses.

compulsion A strong desire to perform a senseless, ritualized form of behavior.

confrontation The process of presenting various information/feedback to the client for his or her personal benefit; often viewed as a challenge.

congruence A characteristic of genuineness referring to behavior in which a person's words and behavior seem to match.

conservative position A philosophy emphasizing traditional American values including self-reliance, personal liberty, and respect for private property, often accompanied by a distrust of government's efforts to help the needy.

constituents People who select, or elect, others to represent, or serve, them in some manner.

counseling A process that helps people to consider their choices and options in life.

crack A street name for a smokable form of concentrated cocaine that may be highly addictive.

creative arts therapy The use of creative activities such as music, art, and dance to facilitate personal insight, self-expression, and social awareness.

crime An act committed in violation of a law.

crisis intervention A type of help designed to meet the needs of a person faced with an unusually difficult life situation.

criteria Standards.

daily hassles Everyday, minor annoyances or mishaps.

data Collected information or facts, usually for purposes of analysis.

defense mechanisms Tactics and strategies, such as denial and rationalization, that an individual may use to reduce awareness of guilt, anxiety, or other unpleasant feeling states.

deinstitutionalization The practice of discharging inmates from large institutional settings to the community, particularly of those chronically mentally ill patients who would otherwise be kept in a hospital for extended periods of time.

demonology A system of beliefs first practiced by prehistoric people in which behavior was thought to be influenced by evil spirits (demons).

detoxification The process of eliminating accumulations of alcohol or other drugs from the body, often under medical supervision and as a first step in treatment of addiction.

developmentally disabled Individuals with a significant delay in one or more of the following areas of development: cognitive, language, and psychosocial skills.

diagnosis The act of identifying a disease on the basis of its signs and symptoms.

discrimination Unfair treatment against certain groups of persons in matters of employment, housing, and education based on prejudicial attitudes.

dissociative disorder A disorder, such as multiple personality, in which one part of the personality seems separated, or screened, from another.

due process A constitutional right guaranteeing a hearing process in a case of grievance.

dysfunction A state of abnormal functioning during which one is unable to fulfill the expectations of society.

efficacy Effectiveness, efficiency.

ego In psychoanalytic theory, the rational part of the personality that mediates between the demands of instinctual urges, conscience, and reality.

electroconvulsive therapy (ECT) A therapy, used primarily to treat severe depression, in which an electrical current is passed through the brain for a brief period.

Elizabethan Poor Laws An official policy, created under the rule of Henry VIII of England in 1601, establishing a system of shelter and care for the poor.

empathy The ability to see things from another's point of view.

esteem needs The desire to be a respected, competent, or even superior person. Included in the second level of Maslow's hierarchy of needs.

euthanasia A way of causing a painless death, usually to end the suffering of people dying of an incurable disease.

extended family A family including not only parents and children, but also grandparents and other relations.

eye movement desensitization and reprocessing (EMDR) A type of mind-body therapy.

feedback The process of conveying information between client and helper.

food stamps A government program designed to offset some of the food expenses of poor people who qualify.

free association A technique used in psychoanalytic therapy in which the client is asked to speak freely, saying whatever comes to mind without concern about the effect on the listener.

generalist human services worker A human services worker concerned with a wide range of individual problems rather than a specific or specialized area of concern.

genuineness The ability to express true and honest feelings.

geographic decentralization A psychiatric hospital procedure in which patients are placed in hospital wards based on their last place of residence in the community prior to admission.

ghetto An inner-city area inhabited by poor people.

hallucinogen A psychedelic drug, such as mescaline, that produces marked distortions in perceptual experience.

heroin An opiate, used for its sedative effects, that is produced by a chemical modification of morphine.

holistic perspective The viewpoint that assumes the whole is greater than the sum of its parts or that the whole has properties that cannot be inferred from the parts.

human services Organized activities that help people in the areas of health, mental health, criminal justice, recreation, education, and related spheres.

human services model The theoretical view that emphasizes unfulfilled needs as major causes of human disorders. It employs a treatment approach based on satisfaction of human needs as a means of preventing and ameliorating dysfunction.

humanistic perspective A school of psychology that emphasizes subjective experience and the desire of each person to realize his or her full human potential.

id In psychoanalytic theory, the part of the personality containing the basic instincts, urges, and desires.

immune system The body's first line of defense against disease, consisting of complex mechanisms that detect and destroy foreign invaders such as bacteria and viruses.

implementation Putting a plan or program to work.

incidence The number of new cases of a condition reported during a given period of time, such as the previous year.

indigenous worker One who lives in the community in which he or she works.

industrialization The widespread utilization of factory and machine-based methods of production, as opposed to earlier reliance on hand tools.

inpatient One who lives in an institution 24 hours a day, where treatment is provided.

Inquisition A religious tribunal (court), established in the 13th century under Pope Innocent III, given the primary responsibility of seeking out and punishing all crimes associated with witchcraft and heresy.

intelligence The ability to learn, to think logically, and to behave adaptively.

intelligence quotient (IQ) A score or value given to intelligence based on test performance, with a score of 100 indicating average ability.

interest group An organization focusing on a single area of concern and attempting to influence others to take steps favorable to its agenda.

intervening The act of stepping in and attempting to change or modify a person's behavior or situation.

interviewing Specialized pattern of communication with specific goals.

involuntary service A decision that a service is necessary for an individual made by another individual, an agency, or court.

jurisdiction Usually a geographical area in which legal power is exerted.

La Bicetre A mental institution in France in the late 1790s in which the director, Phillipe Pinel, expressed the notion that some of the insane could be cured and that forcible restraint in the management of the mentally ill was not always useful or necessary.

laissez-faire economy A doctrine first introduced by Adam Smith in 1776 in his book, *The Wealth of Nations*, holding that an economic system functions best when there is no interference by government.

learning The process by which experience brings about a relatively permanent change in behavior.

least restrictive alternative A client's right to treatment in settings that interfere the least with his or her personal freedoms.

less eligibility A concept established by the government of England in 1830 creating guidelines for assistance to the disadvantaged; any assistance given to these people must be lower than the lowest wage given to any working person.

liberal position A philosophy emphasizing the role of government in providing services to those who are unable to be self-supporting.

life-sustaining needs Needs such as food, clothing, and shelter.

lithium carbonate A metallic element used in the treatment of mania and depression.

living system In systems theory, cells, organisms, and human organizations are defined as living systems; that is, they are open to the environment, act as if motivated to achieve goals, and have some degree of self-control.

lobbyist One who is paid to represent the interests of an organization, usually regarding some form of legislation.

lobotomy (prefrontal lobotomy) A surgical procedure used to treat severely disturbed mental patients in which the frontal lobes of the brain are severed from the deeper centers; now rarely performed.

major tranquilizer A type of medication used in the treatment of schizophrenia and other psychotic states.

managed care Health care insurance systems that contract with a network of hospitals, clinics, and doctors who agree to accept set fees or flat payments per patient.

mandated program A program ordered by a court or legislative body to be carried out.

mania A mood disorder characterized by elation, extreme talkativeness, and generally increased behavioral activity.

MAO inhibitors Drugs that act to allow the neurotransmitter, norepinephrine, to build up and thereby alleviate depression. These drugs require that the patient follow a special diet, and may have undesired effects.

marijuana The crushed leaves, flowers, and small buds of the hemp plant (*Cannabis sativa*) that contain a mild hallucinogen and may produce feelings of euphoria.

medicaid A government insurance program that pays some medical expenses for low-income people who qualify.

medical model The view that behavioral and emotional problems are analogous to physical diseases.

medicare A public health insurance program designed to help pay some medical and hospital expenses of the elderly.

mental hygiene movement (MHM) A reform movement of the early 20th century that aimed at establishing a relationship between physical and behavioral problems.

mental illness Psychological, emotional, or behavioral disorders and the view that these disorders are diseases of the mind.

mental retardation A state of intellectual impairment shown in delayed maturation, a less-than-average capacity to learn from experiences, and a lowered ability to maintain oneself independently.

methadone Dolophine: a synthetically produced opiate narcotic used to treat heroin addiction, but is itself addictive.

methamphetamine A highly addictive stimulant that affects the central nervous system.

minimum wage laws Wage and hour standards for workers established by law.

minor tranquilizer A type of drug used primarily to reduce tension and anxiety.

morphine A pain-relieving drug derived from opium.

motive A specific need or desire, such as hunger or achievement, that energizes and directs behavior.

multicultural perspective To see, hear, or understand information from another's culture, free of judgment or cultural comparisons; the ability to see things from another person's racial or ethnic background.

narcotic antagonist A relatively new type of drug that blocks the euphoric effects produced by heroin or other opiates.

narcotics Potentially addicting drugs derived from opium, including heroin, morphine, and codeine.

natural disaster An event in which forces of nature, including earthquakes and hurricanes, have a destructive effect on a human population.

New Deal A system of social and economic legislation government aid programs designed to benefit the mass of working people; established by President Franklin Delano Roosevelt in the 1930s.

nonjudgmental attitude Behavior that does not impose one's own personal values and standards on others.

objectivity The process/quality of noting the verifiable facts of an event.

obsession A disturbing, unwanted repetitive thought.

occupational therapy The selective and purposeful therapeutic use of activities to aid in the treatment of physical or mental disorders.

operant conditioning A type of learning in which the likelihood of a voluntary behavior is increased or decreased by reinforcement or punishment.

opiates A class of addictive drugs—including opium, heroin, and morphine—that dulls the senses, reduces pain, and induces feelings of well-being.

opium The crude resinous substance taken from the opium poppy.

outpatient A person who receives treatment for a mental or physical disorder outside the hospital setting, usually in an office or clinic setting.

paraphrase To reword a message using one's own words rather than the words of others.

paraprofessional One who works alongside a professional but does not possess an advanced (graduate) academic degree.

parole Release of an inmate from prison after part of the sentence has been served. The person is then supervised by a parole officer for the remainder of the sentence.

partial hospitalization A program, usually for mental patients, in which part of the day is spent in an institution and the remainder is spent in a community setting.

phobia An exaggerated or extreme fear of a stimulus or situation.

physical dependence A state in which a person needs a certain drug to function normally; the state becomes apparent when withdrawal of the drug leads to distressing symptoms.

physical therapy Involves the physical rehabilitation of people who have disabling conditions of the musculoskeletal and neuromuscular systems.

physiological needs Basic needs for physical survival; the lowest level on Abraham Maslow's hierarchy of needs.

poverty line The level of income the federal government considers sufficient to meet basic requirements for food, shelter, and clothing.

power structure Those who control the sources of power—usually economic and political power.

prejudice Negative feelings or attitudes toward certain racial, religious, or ethnic groups based on overgeneralizations about these groups.

preliterate societies Societies that existed prior to the introduction of writing or written records.

prevalence The total number of existing cases of a particular disorder or condition.

primary prevention Programs and activities designed to prevent people from developing a physical or psychological disorder.

primary social supports The network of social relationships, including friends and family, that provides gratification of a person's needs.

privatization Arranging for private companies to take on certain jobs and functions formerly done by government.

probation Suspending the sentence of a convicted offender and placing him or her under the supervision of a probation officer.

prognosis The expected outcome of an illness or disorder.

Protestant work ethic A social philosophy that supports the accumulation of wealth as a reward for hard work and condemns idleness as almost sinful.

psychiatry The medical specialty that investigates, diagnoses, and treats mental, emotional, or behavioral disorders.

psychoactive drug Any compound that alters mood, feeling state, or behavior.

psychoanalysis A school of psychology originated by Sigmund Freud and the treatment method derived from his theories.

psychological needs Basic needs such as love, self-esteem, and self-actualization.

psychopharmacology The development and use of drugs to treat mental illness.

psychosurgery Brain surgery, such as prefrontal lobotomy, used to modify severely disturbed behavior.

psychotherapy The treatment of personal, emotional, and behavior problems by psychological means.

quarantine Isolating people to prevent the spread of disease.

recidivism Repetition of a crime by someone who was previously incarcerated, and their possible re-arrest and return to prison.

recipients In the human services field, those who receive benefits from a human services agency.

redistribution of power In the human services field, the political empowerment of those with no power.

rehabilitation A helping process designed to assist people with disabilities to achieve the highest possible level of productive functioning.

reinforcement An event that increases the probability that a given response will recur.

reliable data Data that consistently give the same results when used in the same way.

safety needs Human needs for a stable, predictable, and secure environment.

St. Mary's of Bethlehem One of the earliest public asylums, incorporated in 1547 in London; this first English "lunatic asylum" became popularly known as "Bedlam," a term later synonymous with states of frenzy and excitement.

secondary prevention Early detection and intervention to keep beginning problems from becoming more severe.

self-actualization In Abraham Maslow's hierarchy of needs, the desire to fully express one's inner nature and talents.

self-awareness The quality of knowing oneself.

self-concept The set of positive and negative attitudes one uses to evaluate oneself.

self-help groups Individuals who meet without professional help to provide mutual support for shared problems.

settlement house movement Begun in the period of the late 1800s to early 1900s, a reflection of early human services philosophy. Each settlement house offered a variety of human services to the disadvantaged. Newly arrived immigrants were the initial population served.

sexism Discrimination against a person on the basis of gender.

side effect Any drug-induced effect, often undesirable, that accompanies the primary effect for which the drug was intended.

Social Darwinism A group of ideas first expressed by Herbert Spencer as an interpretation of Charles Darwin's writings on evolution. Spencer applied Darwin's theory of natural selection to human beings and supported the premise that disadvantaged people who are unfit for society should not be helped.

social policies Plans dealing with the quality of life and of society in general.

social support A group of individuals who may share common expenses and provide emotional and/or physical support.

social welfare A series of programs and/or services aimed at helping people who need help in supporting themselves.

social work The field focusing on helping individuals realize their potential to live as fully and successfully as possible.

somatic experiencing (SE) A type of therapy focused upon the discharging of trauma energy from the body.

status quo The existing conditions or situations.

stereotype A set of beliefs or perceptions about groups of people, or ideas shared by a number of people, often not based on fact.

stigmatize To characterize or identify as disgraceful, negative, or harmful.

stress The condition that comes about when the demands of a situation place a strain on a person's resources.

subjectivity The process/quality of experiencing a personal, private, possibly biased view of an event.

summarize To use the skill or technique of restating what the client has expressed during a series of counseling/therapy sessions.

superego In psychoanalytic theory, the part of personality containing the moral standards of society as interpreted by the parents to the child.

Supplemental Security Income (SSI) A public program that provides a minimum income for blind, disabled, and elderly persons who have little or no financial resources.

systematic desensitization A therapy designed to gradually reduce fear about a particular stimulus by substituting a relaxed response for the fear response.

systems theory A holistic approach that assumes the human being is made up of smaller subsystems, such as cells and organs, but that the human being is in turn part of larger systems, such as family and society.

target population A group of people, such as the poor or the elderly, selected for help by human services.

terrorism The use or threat of violence to convey a political message to a group, usually a government.

tertiary prevention Efforts to rehabilitate those affected with severe mental disorders and return them to the community.

theory A concept that attempts to explain the relationships between events and that may be used to predict or control those events.

third-party payment Payment to a professional from a client/patient's insurance coverage.

token economy A procedure in which tokens are used to reward members of a group or community for performing certain desirable behaviors; the method may be used in schools, prisons, and mental hospitals.

transference In psychoanalytic therapy, the tendency of the client to displace feelings, attitudes, and defenses originating in a previous relationship onto the therapist.

trephining A primitive medical treatment first practiced by certain prehistoric people in which a hole is bored into the skull to allow evil spirits a route to leave the body.

tricyclics A class of medications that may reduce depressive symptoms by blocking neurotransmitter reuptake mechanics, thereby increasing the activity of norepinephrine and serotonin. They are considered to have higher success rates than the MAO inhibitors.

underemployment The condition in which people are working at jobs below their level of skill and/or are working part-time because they cannot get full-time jobs.

undocumented worker An individual from a foreign country coming illegally into this country in search of employment.

unemployment insurance A government program that provides an unemployed worker with a weekly cash benefit for a limited time, usually 26 weeks.

union movement Organized efforts to improve working conditions and wages started by groups of workers who banded together in the latter half of the 19th century.

voluntary agencies Agencies that are private and profit making; nongovernmental institutions.

voluntary service A client's decision that some form of help is needed, followed by a contract for such service.

withdrawal symptoms The often-distressing symptoms that occur when a heavy user stops ingesting alcohol or other drugs.

welfare A system of governmental assistance to the poor. Often used as the term associated with Aid to Families with Dependent Children (AFDC).

workfare A system of governmental assistance to the poor requiring the recipient to perform work activities as a criterion for assistance.

Name Index

A

Abramovitz, M., 326, 336
Adamy, J., 24, 51
Addams, Jane, 135
Albee, G. W., 144, 150
Alexander, F. G., 300, 316
Alinsky, S. D., 277, 294
Alle-Corliss, L. & Alle-Corliss, R., 7, 51
Alley, S., 145, 150
Altman, K. A., 117, 120
Anderson, B. S. & Zinsser, J. P., 37, 38, 51
Andriola, J., 137, 150
Anglin, D. M., 102, 120
Archibold, R. C., 96, 120
Arkin, R., 5, 52
Arthur, R. J., 43, 54
Asch, A., 84, 120
Asclepiades, 129
Ashford, J. B., 14, 53
Atherton, C. R., 60, 121, 272, 295
Austin, M. J., 278, 294
Avila, D. L., 193, 196, 228
Axelson, J. A., 212, 228
Ayllon, T., 180, 185
Azarnoff, R. S., 278, 280, 293
Azrin, N. H., 180, 185

B

Baker, F., 280, 295
Baker, R., 273, 295
Barefoot, J., 43, 55
Barringer, F., 28, 52
Baruth, L. G., 184, 185, 186

Bassuk, E. L., 89, 111, 113, 120
Bazell, R. J., 96, 120
Beatty, W., 5, 52
Beck, A. T., 181, 186
Beers, Clifford, 301
Beirne-Smith, M., 110, 123
Bell, C. J., 67, 121
Benjamin, A., 219, 228
Berenson, B. G., 194, 228
Bernard, S., 322, 336
Berry, D. B., 71, 73, 120
Berube, A. & Katz, B., 28, 52
Beverly, D. P., 273, 295
Birnbaum, J. H., 282, 295
Black, S. & Goodwin, J., 43, 54
Blankley, T., 24, 52
Blevins, G. A., 256, 268
Bloch, S., Croch, E., & Reibstein, J., 6, 52
Bloom, B. L., 43, 52, 138, 139, 150
Bloom, M., 298, 316
Blumstein, A., 103, 120
Bonner, E., 12, 52
Borich, G. D., 108, 120
Borrow, H., 212, 230
Bowean, L., 29, 53
Braga, A. A., 106, 107, 121
Braginsky, B. M., 64, 120
Braginsky, D. D., 64, 120
Brammer, L. M., 193, 194, 228
Breakey, W. R., 112, 120
Breuer, Josef, 169
Briar, S., 310, 316
Bridwell, L., 5, 55
Brieland, D., Costin, L. B., Atherton, C. R., 60, 121
Brill, N., 193, 196, 205, 212, 228
Broder, 24

Subject Index